EQUALITY,
DECADENCE,
and MODERNITY

EQUALITY, DECADENCE, and MODERNITY

THE COLLECTED ESSAYS OF
STEPHEN J. TONSOR

Edited with an Introduction by
Gregory L. Schneider

WILMINGTON, DELAWARE

The editor dedicates this book to the members of the Philadelphia Society, past and present, and to the memory of Henry Regnery.

Library of Congress Cataloging-in-Publication Data:

Tonsor, Stephen J. (Stephen John), 1923–

    Equality, decadence, and modernity : the collected essays of Stephen J. Tonsor / edited with an introduction by Gregory L. Schneider. — 1st ed. — Wilmington, Del. : ISI Books, c2005.

        p. ; cm.
        Includes bibliographical references and index.
        ISBN: 1932236627
        1932236635 (pbk.)

        1. Culture. 2. Sociology. 3. Civilization, Modern—1950– I. Title.

HM626 .T66 2005   2005921727
306—dc22   0506

Published by: ISI Books
                Intercollegiate Studies Institute
                P.O. Box 4431
                Wilmington, DE 19807-0431
                www.isibooks.org

Book design by Kara Beer
Manufactured in the United States of America

Table of Contents

Acknowledgments

An edited book typically does not involve as many people in its production as a monograph. But there are still a few people to thank. I would like to thank Jeff Nelson and Jeremy Beer at ISI Books for their interest in and support of this project. ISI Books has been faithful in its objective of publishing high-quality works on subjects of tremendous value to the defense of Western civilization. It has been a privilege working with ISI and I look forward to doing it again. I would also like to thank Stephen and Caroline Tonsor. Their graciousness and helpfulness to a historian they had not even met when the book was originally proposed will be something I will always remember. The archival staff of the Hoover Institution at Stanford University provided professional assistance and warm hospitality during my two visits there in the completion of this project. I would also like to acknowledge my colleagues at Emporia State University, especially John Sacher and Clay Arnold, who have heard enough about conservatism to last a lifetime. Don Critchlow of Saint Louis University also provided a sounding board for ideas and continued friendship. My wife Petra provides a comfortable place for me to work and allows me the time to complete my research and writing. Our children, Bailey and Balin, are not always as cooperative, but their distractions are welcome.

Finally, I would like to thank the Earhart Foundation for granting me several research grants that allowed me to take the necessary time to conduct research at the Hoover Institution. Without their beneficial and most welcome support, I would not have discovered the Tonsor-Regnery correspondence and would have been the poorer for not having done so. I also thank the Emporia State University Faculty Research and Recognition committee for supplying funds that allowed me to complete the project.

The dedication pays tribute to an organization of conservative intellectuals whose pursuit of truth and spirit of fellowship provides me with con-

tinuing intellectual stimulation. In recognizing Henry Regnery, I am pay-
ing tribute to a remarkable man of letters whose long friendship with
Stephen Tonsor was of signal importance for the culture and community
of American conservatism.

Gregory L. Schneider
Topeka, Kansas
August 2004

Editor's Introduction

Culture and civilization is never held in place by men acting out of rea-
soned purposefulness but rather out of the sum of blind human needs, the
quest of mankind . . . for order, security, love, beauty, and the truth. . . .
Society is preserved by the common need rather than the individual
desire.[1]

—Stephen J. Tonsor

One of the joys of writing contemporary history is that one may get a
chance to meet the people one writes about. Certainly this has as
many pitfalls as attractions; what if something you write offends your subject? What if they think you got it all wrong? Unlike the subjects of Henry
Adams, George Bancroft, Francis Parkman, or most other historians who
choose to write about the deceased, the subjects of the contemporary historian linger on, perhaps ill served by the attention they receive. But writing contemporary history serves an important purpose, for "all history begins as contemporary history," as the French historian Marc Bloch argued.
Some contemporary historians are fit to be cultural and political critics
shaping the first interpretations of historical events. They help craft the
zeitgeist through their writings and the best among them are long cited no
matter how many historical revisions of their arguments are produced.

Among conservative historians few shaped the zeitgeist with the grace,
wit, and learning that Stephen J. Tonsor displayed in his long career. A
European intellectual historian by training with an undergraduate degree
in philosophy, Tonsor taught his entire academic career at the University
of Michigan in Ann Arbor. He received his PhD in history from the University of Illinois after doing graduate work at the Universities of Munich
and Zurich following World War II. A native of Jerseyville, Illinois, who
was born on a farm on November 26, 1923, Tonsor served in the Army
Signal Corps during World War II and saw combat in the Pacific theater.

He was a man in love with the past, but one who also saw his role as a man of ideas fighting the culture wars and defending traditionalism from contemporary challengers in the academy and society. In this way he served as an astute conservative cultural critic. Often he fought a rearguard action, especially on campus. Yet he stayed the course and without doubt positively impacted thousands of undergraduate and graduate students at the university who would have been ill served without his steadfast convictions, which were beautifully expressed in erudite lectures.[2]

Tonsor is not a well-known conservative intellectual. For one thing, he has been eclipsed by the political trajectory of the conservative movement, and while he was a contemporary of Russell Kirk, Richard Weaver, and William F. Buckley Jr., men rightly credited for their influence on the development of conservatism, Tonsor never gained the recognition within the movement he truly deserved, at least not outside of a small circle of intellectuals at places like Liberty Fund, the Intercollegiate Studies Institute, or the Philadelphia Society. Just as importantly, he published only a couple of books and never wrote a philosophical or historical work equal to Weaver's *Ideas Have Consequences* or Kirk's *Conservative Mind*, though he did produce an unappreciated body of work that in its historical and philosophical sagacity and its sophisticated and witty treatment of topics such as education, history, and conservatism compares favorably with that of these far better-known, and more widely read, conservative authors.

I was never a Stephen Tonsor student; thus, the following collection is not a festschrift owed to a scholarly mentor. My attraction to Tonsor's work occurred as part of my own education in conservatism. While always an anticommunist, sometimes a Catholic—and usually a skeptical one—I was not always a conservative. I had backed Ronald Reagan and accepted most of what political conservatives fought for on campus in the 1980s. But I only discovered the principles of tradition and order by reading conservative authors in graduate school, reading that gave my youthful fancies a philosophical base that had been lacking up to that time. Many people recognized the danger of communism during the Cold War, but very few became truly conservative; that is, very few accepted the idea that the heritage of the West was genuinely threatened by communism (or multiculturalism or various other ideologies of our postmodern age). A member of the Philadelphia Society, I had heard Tonsor speak many times but had never met him. I had read his essays in *Modern Age*, many of which appear in this book, but never did it occur to me just how vitally important was his work in the defense of order and tradition. Tonsor once wrote that he was "proud that most of my views are reactionary."[3] It was clear to me that he could have easily chosen the term counterrevolutionary to describe himself. And I felt like I was becoming a counterrevolutionary as well.

My revelation concerning Tonsor's importance came while I was doing research in the Henry Regnery papers at the Hoover Institution. I had written a book on the conservative organization Young Americans for Freedom, had finished an anthology of conservative thought, and was embarking on a wider history of conservatism in the twentieth century. Looking through the Regnery papers, I encountered "the letters." Like Saul on the road to Damascus, I experienced a transformation, though I stretch the analogy too far if I describe it as a religious experience. What I found were examples of a cultural conservatism absent from the regnant political doctrines emanating from Washington and missing from my research on political conservatism. I was enamored, and if I had a horse to fall off of, I would have fallen.

The correspondence between Henry Regnery and Stephen Tonsor, close to thirty years of letters, sat before me. I read about German culture, American literature, history, academics, politics, religion, music, gardening, wine, family life, publishing, and, especially, ideas. From Regnery I gained a fuller appreciation of the culture of my native Chicago and his role in shaping it. From Tonsor I gained an education in intellectual history and in the culture of Catholic Germans in the upper Midwest. Both men were Germanophiles; Tonsor's family, I found, heralded from the same region of Germany as mine and, as I later discovered, had similar migration patterns, coming to America through the port of New Orleans and disembarking upriver, Tonsor's family in Missouri and Wisconsin, mine in Iowa. In their rich and wonderful correspondence, I found what I had lacked in my conservative education thus far—a cultural framework. This was the non-material, nonpolitical conservatism from whence the movement in America had been shaped, but from which it had moved as it took the path to power.

Tonsor wrote beautiful prose and had the uncanny ability to say what he wanted to say in one draft, writing it out longhand with ink pen in a self-assured script. Most of his published works began as lectures for his courses; it is still hard to determine, seeing the handwritten essays in his papers at the Hoover Institution, which essays were meant for the classroom and which were meant for publication. But it is clear that the lectures became the basis of his published work. He never published a historical monograph, instead concentrating on projecting through his courses the shape of his historical writing, typically driven by a pointed argument. A drafted manuscript on the history of equality remained unpublished (two of the projected chapters were published in *Modern Age*).[4] A history of decadence also remained unpublished. It is clear that the history of decadence began as lectures; significant portions of both manuscripts are included herein for the first time.

Despite his obvious eloquence and wide learning, Tonsor chose to publish relatively little, at least in book form. An edited collection of Tonsor's writings on education, *Tradition and Reform in Education*, was published in 1974. The majority of the essays in that book were speeches Tonsor had given to a wide variety of institutions over the course of a particularly active phase of his career from 1969 to 1972. Some of the essays were published in *Modern Age* and *National Review*. I have chosen not to include essays from this volume since the book itself is widely available in many university libraries. He also published, in 1959, a pamphlet titled *National Socialism: Conservative Reaction or Nihilistic Revolt?* A long-planned manuscript on the German youth movement went uncompleted, and there is no evidence from Tonsor's files, save for a few lectures on the topic, that he began to draft a manuscript on the subject, for which he had completed the research.

As befits an intellectual historian, Tonsor's interests were eclectic. He was an expert on many topics, including Lord Acton, Edmund Burke, German youth, myth, and architecture. But one of his most important functions as a critic came in his commentary on educational matters. It was in this capacity that he attracted some prominent national attention. In April 1969 he spoke before the National Association of Manufacturers on "Alienation and Relevance in Higher Education." The article was reprinted in the *Chronicle of Higher Education* and Tonsor received hundreds of letters asking for copies of the speech. The article also attracted the interest of President Nixon, who had the article circulated among the White House staff after Health, Education and Welfare Secretary Arthur Fleming brought it to Nixon's attention. Nixon praised Tonsor and endorsed the traditional views expressed in the speech, saying "it is the most significant and perceptive analysis of what is wrong with our approach to higher education."[5] Gratified by the attention, Tonsor delivered dozens of speeches per year in various forums on the topic of education and even received invitations to apply as president of various universities (he was considered for several such appointments, including the presidency of the University of Dallas). He turned down the offers, telling *National Review* editor Frank Meyer, "The pressures of the past year are slowly melting away. In many respects it was a bad year because the degree of psychological dislocation nearly overwhelmed me. It became increasingly difficult for me to decide just who I was and what I wanted to do with my life; (too many half opportunities). For the most part I have put that behind me. In the Fall I shall return to the academy where I suspect I belong and should stay."[6]

From 1969 to 1971 Tonsor also served as secretary for the Earhart Foundation. Located in Ann Arbor, the foundation was established in the 1950s as the Relm-Earhart Foundation and was funded by Harry Earhart, the founder of the White Star Refining Company, a prominent motor oil refinery. Tonsor benefited throughout his career from the foundation's generosity, as did many of his graduate students, who often received Earhart grants that provided them with travel funds for research and grants to complete dissertations. Tonsor served as secretary of the foundation without quitting his job at Michigan and worked for three years—mainly in the evening and on weekends—to streamline the foundation's procedures for awarding grants. Earhart's president, Richard Ware, later credited Tonsor's diligence with saving the foundation from fiscal ruin. Tonsor briefly considered an opportunity to become the permanent secretary of the Earhart Foundation, writing out the pros and cons of teaching versus foundation work; but, though tempted, he once again chose to stay at Michigan.[8]

Tonsor constantly worried about the state of the humanities in American universities. Such concerns certainly were intensified by the general anarchy prevalent on many campuses during the 1960s. In an op-ed piece in the *Detroit News* published on May 31, 1970, on the heels of a tumultuous spring at many colleges and universities, including Michigan, Tonsor wrote:

> Today we are being overwhelmed by a tidal wave of filth. Every tarnished and disreputable motive, every despicable and ignoble action, every degraded and perverted sentiment, every vulgar and ugly view is paraded and praised in the press and from the pulpit, in the halls of the legislature and from the endowed chairs of the university. . . . The University of Michigan has lost its credibility in this state and is on its way to losing its intellectual stature in the nation because it is managed by craven administrative hacks who possess neither courage nor conviction.[9]

Speaking the truth to power was a Tonsor trademark. He was unafraid to bite the hands that fed him in his pursuit of campus stability and an educational system that emphasized excellence. It was a concern that grew as he aged. A few years before his retirement from teaching, Tonsor would tell Henry Regnery, "It must be apparent to everyone that our Universities are sick—that is, apparent to everyone but university presidents. At one point in our history University presidents were great men; names widely known to make them touchstones of culture and cultivated dignity. Now they appear in the evening newspapers as potential felons little better than the shady junk bond and stock market sharks such as Michael Millken. What has gone wrong?"[10] A few months later he would add: "I am very fearful of a collapse of the Humanities on a national scale. It is as though there was some intellectual equivalent of the AIDS virus which got inside the minds of administrators and faculty under fifty. I don't know what the answer to this problem is. These people are all in place and will control the universities and colleges for at least another twenty years. It is rather like the takeover of the German universities by the Nazis."[11]

The purpose of education, Tonsor thought, was to uphold truth and community, order and beauty. The university was no longer serving that purpose, a particularly dispiriting fact for a traditional conservative who had dedicated himself to defending those principles and inculcating them in the minds of his students.

Tonsor also wrote many essays on conservatism in America, a major concern in his scholarship and in his active life as a conservative intellectual. I have included many of these essays within this collection. One of his first essays on this topic, "The Conservative Search for Identity," published in Frank Meyer's splendid anthology *What Is Conservatism?* (1964), depicts Tonsor's identification with the so-called fusionist conservatism then being established. He wrote, "[I]f conservatives are finally to achieve the common agreement necessary to the establishment of both principle and party, they must reconcile themselves to the dialectic of freedom and authority and must capitalize on the values of their divided heritage."[12] Tonsor would remain loyal to the fusionist doctrine, at least in a political sense. He was a Republican and supported presidents Richard Nixon, Ronald Reagan, and George W. Bush, even though he was discomfited by their more politicized conservatism. He understood the necessity to balance an intellectual conservatism with the reach for political influence. He often did not like how conservatives governed in Washington, but he refused to enter into sectarianism when it came to politics—a bit of a conundrum, given the emerging paleoconservatism evident in his views by the 1990s. When Paul Gottfried charged that Tonsor was not a "real conservative," Tonsor wrote, "I don't subscribe to a conservative credo—a kind of 39 articles of the Right. I never have abdicated my moral autonomy and my rationality and I don't intend to do so now that I am becoming an old man."[13] Tonsor's conservatism, emanating as it did from the Midwestern prairie and from his Catholicism, combined elements of democratic authenticity with intellectual vanity. He could be dismissive of those conservatives who were not literate and intellectual, while at the same time supportive of the democratic ethos of politicians like Reagan or George W. Bush. He was suspicious of power in its most crass political sense. He was especially critical, therefore, of how conservatives flocked to Washington to embrace power during the 1980s and after, disliking the turn towards public policy and think-tank conservatism that made his status as an academic conservative rather tenuous in the new conservative order.

Tonsor rejected sectarian tendencies on the Right but could be caustic in criticizing those whom he believed placed their interest in power above the principles of conservatism. When a new, more populist-oriented "new Right" began to emerge in the early 1970s, he argued that an alignment with individuals such as George Wallace was not possible:

> A number of conservatives have argued for an alliance with populism—have argued that there is room for the hardhats and rednecks under the big tent of a broadly defined conservatism. I understand the temptation, for these groups are of great political importance. I do not believe ... that such an alliance can be formed. And the fact of its impossibility will save conservatism from the temptation of a politics that is reactionary rather than progressive. The conservative intellectual is not going to spend his time constructing defenses for decadent forms.[14]

He was critical of conservatives who abused the trust of their peers while engaging in a quest for political power. He told the Philadelphia Society in 1999 that "there have ... been those men who saw conservatism as a way to personal status and power, men devoid of any purpose other than, as one of my students observed, 'an ego-splat.' I knew well one of these dark men from the gutter. He lied to himself. He lied to his friends. He created a fictitious past for himself. He even lied in creating objects for his inordinate hatreds. He lied as to his purpose and beliefs and he harmed the movement and those in any way connected with him."[15]

"There is no greater enemy of community than the lie," Tonsor wrote. Community was the ultimate value in Tonsor's conservatism. Speaking of his friend Henry Regnery's contributions to conservatism, he wrote that "the key to this conservatism was communal and cultural rather than abstractly political or economic. Randian Libertarianism and liberal economic determinism were never a serious part of the conservative movement."[16]

Thus, as a number of pieces gathered here further demonstrate, while Tonsor was always interested in preserving some sort of fusionist consensus among conservatives, he never wavered from a fight if he believed that such a consensus was threatened. In "The Second Spring of American Conservatism," Tonsor praised the neoconservatives, placing them in a continuum of conservatism which recognized their contributions to "the restoration of liberty, order, community, and value in American society." He noted that "a new generation of intellectuals ... are forging a new body of conservative social theory and practical application." The neoconservatives were interested in realms of politics and policy which the first generation of conservatives, "wrestl[ing] with the intellectual problems of their time," had neglected.[17] This was indeed a warm welcome for the predominantly Jewish ex-liberals and ex-socialists who formed the first generation of neoconservatives in the late 1970s.

But when he believed the neoconservatives had moved too far away from conservative principles, Tonsor was not above delivering pointed criticism. Indeed, his most famous speech was the one he delivered at a particularly tense meeting of the Philadelphia Society in April 1986. Society president M. E. Bradford had put together a program on conservative identity. Bradford, a professor of English at the University of Dallas and a southern conservative, had been chosen by Ronald Reagan in 1981 to be chairman of the National Endowment for the Humanities. But a political firestorm ensued when columnist George Will criticized Bradford for having published unfavorable assessments of Abraham Lincoln. Reagan eventually settled on University of Texas professor William Bennett, who had published extensively in neoconservative journals, as his nominee for chairman of the NEH. Traditional conservatives were furious. Many of them believed that Bennett's hiring signified a hijacking of the conservative movement by neoconservatives. Although such neocons were not "true conservatives," it was charged, they nevertheless now controlled the institutions, think tanks, and major journals of the conservative movement. Bradford provocatively sought an open forum to discuss what had happened to conservatism.[18]

Tonsor's paper, "Why I Too Am Not a Neoconservative" would be the most provocative piece he ever delivered or published. A brilliant polemic, elegantly written and witty, the essay is often mistaken as an attack on neoconservatives only, when in many respects he excoriated all conservatives, period. Still, the most famous lines, delivered, as Jeffrey Hart has written, with "a pit-bull fury," targeted neoconservative intellectuals specifically: "It has always struck me as odd," said Tonsor,

> even perverse, that former Marxists have been permitted, yes invited, to play such a leading role in the conservative movement of the twentieth century. It is splendid when the town whore gets religion and joins the church. Now and then she makes a good choir director, but when she begins to tell the minister what he ought to say in his Sunday sermons, matters have been carried too far. I once remarked to Glenn Campbell of the Hoover Institution that had Stalin spared Leon Trotsky and not had him murdered in Mexico, he would no doubt have spent his declining days in an office in Hoover Library writing his memoirs and contributing articles of a faintly neoconservative flavor to *Encounter* and *Commentary*.[19]

And Tonsor did not stop there. "Politics has always been inseparable from culture, and both ultimately derive from religion," Tonsor said, and the conservative religious worldview "is Roman or Anglo-Catholic; its political philosophy, Aristotelian and Thomist; its concerns, moral and ethical; its culture, that of Christian humanism." "If neoconservatives wish us to take their conservatism seriously, they must return to the religious roots, beliefs, and values of our common heritage. They cannot dither in the halfway house of modernity and offer us technical solutions that touch the symptoms but never deal with the causes of contemporary disorder."[20] When he was asked by Arnold Beichman whether he would reject as conservatives James Burnham, Whittaker Chambers, Frank Meyer, George Orwell, Paul Johnson, and Arthur Koestler because they were once Communists, Tonsor replied, "Would you accept an ex-Nazi?"[21] This impertinent reply seemed to more accurately reflect the tensions in the room than Tonsor's true feelings, for he had accepted as friends and colleagues many of the ex-Communists who had become movement conservatives, especially Frank Meyer. But Tonsor's argument that conservatism had its roots in Roman and Anglo-Catholic sources seemed to leave little room for Jewish neoconservatives within the movement and was (unfairly) interpreted as anti-Semitic.

Tonsor's views on neoconservatives hardened as he grew older. In a 2004 speech delivered at the Philadelphia Society's fortieth anniversary meeting, Tonsor declared,

> to be "neo" is to live in danger. Mutant types in culture and in biology are, as any sophomore student of biology knows, nearly always fatally flawed and prone to an early and ugly demise. . . . Henry [Regnery's] long and generous life should remind conservatives of who they are and where they have been. It should return them to their common roots, their paleo-selves, and to the unassailable achievements of community and culture that characterized this movement. We owe Henry a great debt which I fear may be lost in the klaxon-din of those who call themselves neoconservatives.[22]

Indeed, as he aged Tonsor began to drift away from the fusionist conservatism that had defined his earlier public career. He came to the defense of those he knew in the movement, the community of friends and values which had been the focal point for his life of the mind. "As one grows older," he wrote, "one becomes more and more the self given by time and history. One becomes, in short, increasingly paleo. At twenty we are still in rebellion against our heritage. At eighty we often ask ourselves whether or not we have been true to that heritage."[23] Stephen Tonsor was clearly true to his heritage—his Catholic faith, Western culture, and conservative community. By serving as a mentor to thousands of students, he helped to preserve—in one small corner of academia—the heritage and values of the conservative mind. Men of greater power and influence within the conservative movement achieved far less.

Before meeting him I had corresponded with Tonsor for several years. I had waited once to meet him after a Philadelphia Society speech, but the wait was too long (a virtual fan club milled around him). So I was excited as I made the turn onto Morton Avenue in Ann Arbor and parked in front of his modest wood-frame two-story home. Stephen and Caroline Tonsor had raised four children in that house and now, at age eighty-one, lived there alone, the same house they had moved into after he secured a tenure-track position in the University of Michigan history department in the mid-1950s. Like the other houses on Morton Avenue, most of which were inhabited by people who worked or taught at the nearby university, this one dated from the 1920s. Oak trees, some elms, and many maples lined the streets, providing welcome shade on this relatively warm midsummer day. There were many "John Kerry for President" and "Peace Now" signs in the front yards on Morton Avenue, but as I walked up the steps to the Tonsor home there was only an American flag.

I was greeted with warmth from the Tonsors. Stephen, his white hair closely cut, was wearing a short-sleeve green shirt and black frame glasses. He looked like a Midwestern farmer. Caroline was dressed in a flower-patterned house dress, her hair gray and back in a bun, looking the part of the grandmother or old-fashioned schoolteacher. There were two chairs in front of a fireplace and next to both a stack of papers, journals, books, and letters. A glass of sherry, a splendid meal, and warm conversation followed. For the next two days I was treated to a hospitality that hundreds of students, friends, colleagues, and family have received over the years, a magnanimity and graciousness that defied all expectations. When I departed I told him that with good fortune I would soon finish the collection of essays and turn over the manuscript to ISI Books. He simply replied, "I am a historian, I can wait." He has waited long enough.

As I made my goodbyes I was reminded of something Tonsor once wrote. "The early conservative movement was a community. . . . One could come into a strange town and find immediate hospitality and companionship. . . . There was a bond of hospitality and friendship. . . . A room full of five hundred people eating rubber chicken is no substitute for a night at Mecosta, Woodstock, or Three Oaks."[24] As I drove off, I thought that Morton Avenue should be added to his list.

Hope and History

For certain men history is a contagion. At a distance of five hundred miles some ideological typhoid Mary will infect them with an intellectual fever. In the first century they became Christians, in the fourth century they became Arians, in the thirteenth they became Catharists, in the sixteenth century they became Lutherans and Baptists, in the eighteenth century they became Freemasons, and in the twentieth century they become existentialists and Communists. Such a man was Whittaker Chambers.

The world is filled with enthusiasts caught up in their God-filled trances, vomiting the poetry of their ecstasy at every street corner. The tribe of failed prophets and bankrupt dreamers is a numerous one and the commonplace of disillusion and the anguish of disappointed love have become the stereotypes of our century. Failed Gods and failed men dot the intellectual landscape as thickly as the exhausted mechanisms of Detroit decorate the desolate edges of cities. Once Gods endured through the millennia and the heroes who served them gave their names to generations of children for a thousand years. There must be many "Adolfs" in Germany now grown to manhood and many men in the Soviet Union named for Stalin whose names in so short a time have once more slipped back into the realm of the unnoticed and the unreverenced. Why then one more book of recollections by a former Communist? What can remain to be said which has not previously been said?

The truth is that Whittaker Chambers was no ordinary Communist; indeed he was no ordinary man. His recollections would be interesting and his observation of life important had he in his teens become simply a Christian Scientist (which was a possibility), or had he taken his avocation for a vocation and become simply a farmer. The intensity of his perceptions and the broad humanity of his commitments lifted him out of the ordinary. He thought of himself as a prophetic figure and his books are the product of deep religious conviction. The title *Witness* bears a prophetic connotation that reaches beyond the liberal and historic implication of Chambers's testimony before a congressional committee and the bar of justice. The short piece "Jonah" in *Cold Friday*, surely one of the best modern retellings of an Old Testament story, reveals a good deal about the role Whittaker Chambers chose for himself. The tone of his writing is monotonously oracular, at times flatulently prophetic. But even in the role of prophet Chambers was disarmingly unconventional, claiming for his utterance no more validity than is characteristic of an informed guess. There is a modesty, an honesty, and a humility in spite of the portentous note and the exalted tone.

Prophecy was the office to which Chambers felt God called him. Left to his own devices he would have chosen to be a poet. And poet he was though his muse was never adequate to his need. His vision was essentially poetic, his topic dismayingly prosaic. The reader too often finds the translator of *Bambi* writing self-consciously in the style of Henry Adams. Chambers as poet was at his worst talking to other people. He felt he must puff himself up and say something important. But the greater part of *Cold Friday* is a dialogue with himself, and here his poet's poise is certain, his vocabulary telling, his intonation lyric. No one has written more deftly and more surely of the predicament of modern man in the first half of the twentieth century. The test of the poet, the test of the historian, is his ability to evoke our innermost experience, to recount our past with such accuracy that we say "yes, that's the way it was." He gives a voice to the mute emotion and a life to the dead event.

Few poets write well about nature. There is too strong a temptation to recast it in terms of one's own wishes, to read into it man's values and his order. Only the unflinching realist writes adequately of the mysteries of nature. It is difficult to give the wolf and the serpent their due. In this regard Thoreau and Chambers share the same temper.

A great deal of Chambers's fascination with history was fascination with change, process, revolutionary transformation, growth. He was the sort of farmer who could hear the corn growing on a hot July day. He had the most acute sense of any shift in the climate of opinion, of any change, as he put it, "in the angle of vision." It was the very acuteness of this biological vision which filled him one moment with such dismay and pessimism and the next with surprise and reluctant hope. Would it be too wide of the mark to suggest that in part this awareness of growth and change was a manifestation of his own protean nature? Few men have lived by so many faiths, and I suspect none has done it and maintained the continuity and inner wholeness which Whittaker Chambers possessed. Most men, at some tragic point, are trapped like tadpoles on a mud flat by the receding waters of some mature opinion: Chambers was a creative, growing, learning person throughout his lifetime. There was an annual metamorphosis and in a number of essays he remarks on the psychological moment, the environment when those changes came. Most of us have had the same experience of renewal and new beginnings. Few of us have felt it so sharply or so persistently.

If these elements make Whittaker Chambers a prophet out of the ordinary he is nonetheless a prophet and principally a prophet. History and the meaning of history is a pivotal problem in Chambers's thought. But in this Chambers is the quintessential man of the twentieth century. Every man of his and our generation feels history not simply as the passage of time but as a lesion opened in his very soul. History has become the fundamental question for mankind. In it all the questions which have haunted men's minds have been subsumed. Revolutions are made and resistance offered in the name of history. The Christian metaphysic that lived for more than a thousand years estranged from history has once more returned to a faith rooted in the mystique of history, and God as primal cause has been displaced by "the Lord of History." Philosophy no less has felt the shift and reason has given way to process. Stability has been pulled down from its high place in man's esteem and innovation, flux and change command a loyalty once paid to that with which there was no change or shadow of alteration. The acuteness of the problem of history is testimony to the revolutionary nature of the historical process in our time. Yet it is well to recognize that the revolution through which modern man is passing is not of recent origin and is not simply the work of nasty Communists and liberals. It reaches back to the very beginnings of modernity, and indeed, was implicit in the earliest expressions of Western intellectuality. For this reason conservatism must, short of absolute and unremitting reaction, fail as Chambers realized, for it is always simply the defense of achieved revolution and the rejection of futuristic aspiration. Rationality, technology, science, and capitalism are all opposed to a conservatism rooted, as it necessarily is, in the status quo. The cause of conservatism is not well served if conservatives are little more than tired revolutionaries. And having rejected revolution at the deepest levels of his personality Chambers had the courage of his convictions and styled himself honestly as a reactionary and a "man of the Right" rather than a conservative. This distinction which Chambers makes with such force and clarity is an important one, for it goes to the heart both of the problem of modern man and of contemporary conservatism.

The stance of Chambers is a curious and instructive one. It was a historical accident that Chambers ever became a Communist. He was anticapitalist, to be sure, but he is equally antirationalistic and antitechnological. His Russian affinities seem rather to be with the Slavophiles than with the exponents of a radical modernity. There is a hunger for organic social structures, and indeed "organic" is one of the most approved and most used words in *Cold Friday.* In March 1953 (*Cold Friday,* 26–27) he is writing. "More and more, I incline to a view, not at all original with me, that the whole technological development of civilization was a wrong turning; that we are harvesting its inevitable consequences; that we are at the end of a historical phase for which the only possible solutions are presently to be made by the Bombs." There is then at the root of much of Chambers's thought a deep hostility to the technological and urban revolutions. Writing in the essay "Morningside" in *Cold Friday,* Chambers tells us of his instinctive distrust of cities. "With them [Jewish classmates at Columbia] I first entered the deep slums. I entered them with a shudder that I could not repress but which I was careful to conceal. I was brought up on the land, and ingrained in me is a countryman's, even a peasant's, distrust of cities, even those like Baltimore and Washington which I have come to love. New York City I loathe with an unabatable loathing" (129).

These attitudes Chambers shared with many exponents of the romantic Right and the Left of the nineteenth and twentieth centuries. Utopian and communitarian experiments with an emphasis upon an organic life close to the soil are hallmarks of the past two centuries. The revolt against capitalism and the effort to restructure society so as to eliminate exploitation, the cash nexus, and interest-taking was common to both the Right and the Left. Here as elsewhere the extremes converged. In a thinker like Henry George, agrarian romanticism is united with anticapitalism. Beneath and behind agrarianism, progressivism, monetary reform, and romantic utopianism lies an attempt to deal with the revolution in thought and techniques which had by the opening years of the nineteenth century engulfed the whole of Western society. It is well to emphasize, however, that the rejection of the emergent capitalistic, technological, scientific, and rationalistic order (or perhaps "chaos" would be a better word), was the stance of Right and Left alike. Those intellectuals in reaction were what C. P. Snow has very perceptively described as "intellectual Luddites." They demanded that we return to the age before the wheel. They sought a radical reorientation of society; a reconstruction of the social order which would eliminate money and make the spade once more the chief tool of cultivation. Nor were these "intellectual Luddites" ever very sympathetic to rationality or the critical spirit. The "narod" has always found "rural idiocy" particularly attractive. "The only kind of culture I know about is agriculture," asserted an American professor of history who stood in this tradition.

But these embattled artisans and peasants, anxious to restore a barter economy, introduce a vegetarian cuisine, give themselves over to free love and non-competition, or more modestly perhaps, simply desirous of destroying the "Gold bugs," were doomed to frustration. There has never been, short of an all-encompassing disaster, a voluntary return to a primitive technology once that technology has been replaced by one more sophisticated; one which gives man a better command of his environment. From the neolithic revolution to the hydrogen bomb, ideas and technology have steadily revolutionized society and mankind has welcomed each change, each social transformation no matter how disrupting its social consequences, enthusiastically. And they have done so because each change has brought with it the promise of a more abundant and a more satisfying life. The quantitative and qualitative quest for life is the story of every religion, every political system, every social order. It is, quite simply, what history is all about.

This quest is a quest intrinsic to men and most especially to Western civilization. We are all revolutionaries. We could not, even though we wanted to, renounce the course upon which, not ourselves alone, but the whole of humankind has determined. Conservatism, then, as an antirevolutionary movement is not a possibility. And it was the recognition of the overwhelming power of revolution that made Whittaker Chambers a Communist. Chambers, rejecting the degradation and compulsion that follows from the Marxian world view after a decade of intimate experience had no alternative but reaction. His postulates were simple: the West is thoroughly and completely revolutionary; all revolutions lead to communism; the West is doomed. As a consequence there were for him no alternatives; either reaction or revolution.

But was it after all historical accident alone that made Chambers a Communist? Why did he not simply subscribe to one of the romantic philosophies of reaction, or why did he not in the '20s, as he did later, subscribe to the historical pessimism of Oswald Spengler? The mood of the '20s, the mood which produced Spengler and accounted for the great vogue which Spengler enjoyed even in America is set down clearly by Chambers in his description of Columbia University: "It was the sense of historical sundown, the sense that man had reached one of the great jumping-off places— or what was worse, a place where it was impossible to jump because it was the end" (138). The truth, I suspect, is that Chambers was too young, still too inveterately hopeful, too American for a pessimism that offered no plan of action except the stoic advice to stand fast and suffer heroically. The commitment to communism, then, was a commitment to hope: A commitment to hope rooted in history at a time when hope, dependent upon the existence of a transcendent reality, upon a providential God, upon a Loving Father, was perishing in disbelief and forgetfulness. In effect Chambers tells us that he became a Communist because he was a religious man forced to live out his life amid the despair of the twentieth century. Dialectical materialism, a hope resident in history itself, would fill the metaphysical need and save as surely and as personally as had the Christian Christ and the Hebrew Jehovah. It was as though Chambers and his generation sought healing from the very source of its wound; as though history had it in its power to order what it had disordered; as though revolution could restore the social stability which it had dissolved. In a world of flux, history had become the only absolute.

And inevitably history failed. The failure was the failure that confronts all utopian expectations. Judgment day is postponed and the white-robed votaries of eschatology at long last abandon their hilltop watching places. Had Chambers lived only a little longer he might have witnessed Red Square filled with the market-day booths of happy and cunning peasant merchants rather than the massive military displays he knew so well. His Spenglerian vision superimposed upon the Marxian faith in the inevitable triumph of pre-ordained historical process did not permit him to see into and behind the phenomenological surface of that historical process. Not was it easy to do so, for everywhere in 1960 the West seemed to be in retreat before the forces of dialectical materialism, and this, as Chambers realized, not because of Communist strength but because of Western indecision and irresoluteness. Chambers quotes with approval the frequently encountered words of a visitor to the Soviet Union who said, "We have seen the future and we know it works." Had Chambers lived longer he might have found profit in quoting a more recent visitor who said. "We have seen the past and we know it has failed." For both the strength of communism and the weakness of the West were illusions.

It goes without saying that Chambers's dark view of the future was rooted in his dark view of human nature. He failed again to recognize that in the realm of politics we are literally saved by our sins. Communism will work in a sinless world, and only in a sinless world. This is perhaps the reason communism must assume as a basic postulate that sin does not exist. This accounts in part for the success of communal religious groups. The poor, wretched, human raw material with all its faults is not suitable building material for the classless society and it cannot, alas, be transformed by some magical process into "the new Soviet man." It would seem that while the Soviet system finds itself incapable of making men better, it has succeeded in making the moral and material lot of man infinitely worse. Our Western democratic societies, with all their imperfections and failures, have succeeded in a measurable degree in mitigating the impact of private failure upon the body politic and even, in many cases, harnessing the base motives of private interest and personal passion to the commonweal. On the contrary, in Soviet society every private failure is immediately registered as a public crime. In the very measure that men and societies are imperfect these imperfections are dramatically reflected in totalitarian societies. Failure, indeed, is the only way in which an oppressive political system can be rejected. Failure becomes a political action, a social protest, a silent negative vote. Political realists who value freedom must always be grateful for sin; it is the ultimate nemesis of tyranny.

Chambers's pessimism ultimately rests upon two basic propositions: that man without God has no recourse but to become a Communist, and that the Western world is without belief and lives in despair. Both of these propositions, it seems to me, are false. In the very last pages of *Cold Friday*, Chambers seems to have fought through to a serenity and a hope that strike one almost as a repudiation of the remainder of the book. The new mood was in part personal and in part due to historical experience. The Hungarian Revolution and Pasternak's *Doctor Zhivago* seem to have exerted a powerful influence upon him. He came to believe, as he quotes Ilya Ehrenburg saying, "If the whole world were to be covered with asphalt, one day a crack would appear in the asphalt, and in that crack grass would grow." Chambers felt that the satellite revolutions were events which possessed an importance equal to that of the original 1917 revolution. In short, the forces of human hope, human despair, human goodness and evil, mixed inextricably as they always are, finally overthrew a system which began by attempting to make men better than they are and ended by making men less than they might be. In short, Chambers rejected his own theory. That was as it should have been, for he was so much larger as a man than the diverse ideas in which he clothed his thought. He was so gloriously mistaken, so bravely wrong, so heroically in error.

There is a peculiar quality to the hope of Chambers and to the hope of modern man generally. It is largely negative. It is the product of a failed revolution. It is neither religious, nor emphatically social. It is a quiet and heroic assertion of the human desire for an ordered decency. It is a hope which is at bottom religious, though this religion falls far short of orthodoxy. Even the nihilism which so frequently grows in this post-revolutionary soil is an assertion of man's freedom. The world into which we are moving will be a pluralistic one. It will not be specifically Western in the conservative sense of that word. It will be a world largely indifferent to the religious and cultural values which we think of as specifically Western, but one which, having been revolutionized by the West, will have developed a free, industrial, urban society: democratic, secure, and individualistic. It will provide the possibility for the development of a new, unitary, and essentially religious culture.

All of this, however, remains a dream, a hope. What we know with some certainty now is that, barring some colossal accident, the fears Chambers expressed in his work, the fears of Western man in this tragic century, will go unrealized. They were not a part of some inevitable historical destiny as multitudes had hoped and many had feared. History revealed itself as the mistaken and the occasionally creative actions of men and groups of men. The greatness of Chambers's book does not lie in its insight into history but rather in its insight into a man who made history.

Part One: Decadence

Many of Tonsor's lectures on the problem of decadence in Western intellectual history had remained unpublished until now; the three included in this section appear in print for the first time. These lectures date from the 1970s and 1980s and reflect Tonsor's intense concern with the decline of traditional ideas and culture and its characterization. Planned as a book, Tonsor's papers at the Hoover Institution contain his completed series of lectures on decadence in Western culture.

1

Decadence Past and Present

Most bums and alcoholics living in cardboard boxes and sleeping atop air-conditioning grates know that something has gone wrong in their lives. One often encounters these lost souls, even in Ann Arbor. If questioned most of them will insist that their plight is not of their own making; that their lives are the fruits of circumstance; that life has given them less than was their due; that they are more sinned against than sinning, and that were the world different they would be different. In their more candid and saner moments they admit their guilt and confess the personal inadequacies that have brought them to their low estate. They are, in fact, decadents who have lost a sense of form, who are unable to make demands of themselves, who are unable to live up to commitments, whose lives are dominated by a sense of drift and worthlessness, seeking in intoxication the sense of well-being that ordinary lives in ordinary circumstances so rarely produce.

Not many of these lost souls would argue that they are decadent and living in a decadent era. And yet in microcosm their problems are the same as those of cultures in macrocosm—cultures that have lost their form and raison d'etre. It is well to remember this parallel between the personal and the social, the microcosm and the macrocosm. There is a close connection, though any discussion of decadence is far more complicated than this simple analysis would indicate.

We must remember in the first place that historical pessimism is quite different from decadence. The notion of decadence is a recent one, contemporaneous in origin with the notion of progress. Both decadence and progress are typical manifestations of "de-sacralized time." That is to say, in general, up to the eighteenth century historical pessimism rather than the notion of historical decadence was the commonplace conception. The cycle of the life of man was an analogue of the historical cycle. It was one of birth, growth, maturity, old age and decay, and finally death. As with the vegetative cycle, life could be renewed and growth restored. In history, the restoration of time, the abolition of time's erosion, was achieved by a repetition of the cosmogonic act; the repetition of the myth of creation. The remedy for historical decay was essentially religious and mythical. This conception of the periodic restoration of time lies behind pagan, non-Christian notions of historical restoration.

The demythologized Hebrew and Christian conception of history turned away from the repetition of the cosmogonic act to the idea of apocalypse and eschatology. According to this theory, the present order of history is abolished and a new creation is substituted for it. The effects of man's fall in the Garden of Eden and all the cosmic consequences that flow from it are finally overcome and abolished, and a new heaven and a new earth are substituted at the end of time for the present one, which has been disordered and decayed by sin. Both pagan and Judeo-Christian conceptions of historical pessimism are thus based on the notion of the progressive, spontaneous erosion of time. The solution, in both cases, is an essentially religious one. Thus, the healing and salvation of the individual is the consequence of an act of conversion; the appropriation of something that happens outside the self and the turning of the self to a source of strength and power that resides elsewhere. Personal soteriologies, theories of salvation, are not in fact very different from historical soteriologies, which call for a transformation of history.

In the eighteenth century, with the general demystification and secularization of thought, these religious solutions to the problem of the restoration of time and history seemed to the European intellectual elite no longer valid. Time's decay came to be thought of as irremediable and determined, just as the notion of progressive development seemed, on the other hand, inevitable. Both appeared as processes internal to or immanent in history and time and not external to them. The gods (or God) were able to restore the sacral time of the premodern world. The only restoration of time possible in the decadent history of the modern age is, at best, a turn of the cycle, endlessly and meaninglessly repeated.

Thus, the history of desacralized time is beyond any human act aimed at restoration. It is a determined declension about which nothing can be done. The heroic man, as in Spengler's theory, can only stand in place and watch the world crumble about him. Without modernity and desacralized time there could be no conception of decadence.

The second major element in the development of theories of decadence is the classical Greco-Roman paradigm. Few theories of decadence advanced in the last three centuries do not argue analogically from classical Greco-Roman experience to the contemporary experience of Western civilization. Indeed, most theories of decadence assume an exact parallel between the breakdown of classical civilization and the supposed decadence of the West. This parallel is most clear in the decay of republican political institutions, the coming of the Caesars, and the appearance of world empire. These events in the political sphere, it is usually argued, are accompanied by the decay of religion, the appearance of luxury, the growth of immorality, and the loss of form. Creativity slackens and art and literature decline. It is important to assert here that without the classical model there could and would be no clearly argued and articulated theory of decadence. It is the classical pattern of decay as applied to contemporary events which provides the model for decadence, and this classical model is in turn attached to the idea of desacralized time and a disbelief in the possibility of regeneration.

We should note that the theorists of decadence were reading time both backward and forward; moving from the present moment into the past and from the past into the present moment. The preoccupation with decadence from the second half of the eighteenth century to the present time was possible only because the experience of the classical world threw some doubt on the idea of progress that became so marked in the eighteenth century. The great debate as to the reality of progress could take place only in terms of the experience of classical history, and this in turn was possible only because of the intense study of classical history that characterized modern times. By the end of the eighteenth century there were more or less complete and coherent accounts of the histories of classical Greece and Rome, and these accounts had become the basis for eighteenth- and nineteenth-century political theory and statecraft.

One of the most characteristic aspects of all decadence theory is the presence of large amounts of historical guilt. Societies do not think of themselves as decadent until they first feel that they have in some sense fallen short either of the virtues of their ancestors or the demands of the present time. This guilt is not metaphysical—societies that feel themselves decadent rarely say that they have sinned against God; rather, they say that they have succumbed to the spirit of the times. While confession, forgiveness, and salvation is the remedy for sin against God, in a world in which God is dead, or at least religion is dead, there is no remedy. Only irremediable guilt remains.

This guilt often derives from what Mary Douglas in her book *Purity and Danger* calls "boundary transgression." Crossing a behavioral line from licit to taboo and forbidden behavior, crossing the line dividing consumption based upon need to consumption that is excessive, transgressions against racial or class boundaries—all are forms of boundary transgression that result in guilt and feelings of decadence. Thus, the concept of "form" is especially important to nearly all decadence theory. By "form" is most often meant lifestyle. In many instances the decay of aristocratic form and style is seen as a sign of decadence. Those who seek their pleasures among the deracinated denizens of bohemia—those classless members of the demi-monde—are viewed as decadent. When a whole society goes slumming it is viewed as being decadent. Just so, when intellectual and artistic standards are set not by an intellectual elite, conscious of its duty and dedicated to high culture, but by the riff-raff, the rock musicians, the jugglers and clowns, the thieves and murderers, men say something is wrong. The elite has abandoned its role of leadership. It is of this phenomenon that Arnold Toynbee speaks when he writes of "the abdication of the creative minority." It is this confusion of the orders, society seen not as an ordered structure but as a perennial saturnalia, a feast of fools, that is the ultimate boundary transgression and the ultimate loss of form.

Closely associated with the idea of "boundary transgression" in decadence theory is the idea that luxury dissolves, enervates, and makes a society effeminate. The military virtues decay. Men retreat from the public realm of civic obligation and service into a private realm of pleasure and enjoyment. The development of widespread luxury in a society is thought to parallel the development of tyrannical political forms. Tyrants encourage the development of luxury because they know that luxury leads to the decay of civic virtue. Luxury, it is thought, makes possible the excesses characteristic of the decadent society.

While boundary transgression in all its forms provides some of the most characteristic symptoms of decadence, the decline of religious belief and practice is seen as one of its chief causes. In ancient society the gods lost their compelling power in the affairs of human society. Philosophy, unbelief, and the appearance of new and exotic sects replaced the old religion. In eighteenth- and nineteenth-century society the belief in and practice of Christianity was abandoned by the intellectual elite. As Dostoyevsky observed, "If God is dead, everything is permitted." The only sources of human motivation now became the will to power and the will to pleasure. From de Sade to Nietzsche the message remains the same. However, when society is dissolved into a mass of competing egos and any principle of transcendent order disappears, there is no basis for an ordered civic life. Consensus as to the desired goals of society disappear, and a dictator or authoritarian government must impose an order from the outside. In creative, purposeful societies the order of political life derives from a consensus in values and an agreement on order arrived at internally in the society. Thus, a breakdown of the social order is the consequence of an inordinate individualism motivated by the quest for power and pleasure.

You will note something about decadence theories. Societies do not decay and fall into ruin because of what happens to them from the outside, but rather as the result of an internal process. It is not foreign invasions which cause decadence but rather decadence which makes foreign invasion possible. France in 1870 first becomes decadent and then is defeated by the Germans. Internal revolution and external threat are both viewed as the consequence of decadence. The fact is that most decadence theorists see barbarian invaders as a source of rejuvenation for a tired and decadent society. Consequently, the theory explained the rejuvenation of Western society and the creativity of the Middle Ages as a consequence of the barbarian invasions, and in the nineteenth century the Slavs, particularly the Russians, were supposed to perform the same service for the Western Europeans. For Spengler and Toynbee, the absence of a barbarian people capable of rejuvenating and restoring Western Europe is a problem. The theory is that fresh blood, a fresh infusion of creative vigor, will freshen the tired old society.

One of the most important evidences of social decadence is the breakdown of traditional political forms, either aristocracy or republicanism, and the appearance of Caesarism. This political revolution, which culminates in tyranny and imperialism, is the final stage in the cycle of constitutions and is the consequence of the decay of aristocratic forms and republican virtue. It transforms the army from a citizen body to a professional army of paid mercenaries. The state radiates its power outward to world conquest and domination and internal peace is purchased at the price of tyranny. In the nineteenth century decadence theorists associated the French Revolution with the onset of decadence. The arrival of Napoleon I and Napoleon III on the scene completed the picture of the evolution from a natural political order to tyranny.

The breakdown of the family, the dissolution of conventional sexual morality, and the increase in crime and suicide were all viewed as symptoms of increasing social decadence. Birth control and declining birthrates were seen as evidence of loss of the will to live. France viewed itself as decadent because of the decay of family life, an increase in perverted sexuality, a decline in the birthrate and an increased use of addictive drugs and alcohol.

Thus, the picture we get of nineteenth- and twentieth-century society when viewed through the eyes of the decadence theorist is of a society increasingly anxious and characterized by a loss of self-confidence. More importantly, it is a society filled with social guilt, a society that objectifies and externalizes this guilt in the form of decadence.

Since there was, according to most decadence theorists, no way of remedying the condition, decadence theory was not simply historical pessimism—it was historical despair. Science, with its emphasis on external causes, seemed to support the idea that the process was inevitable and hence to deepen the despair—thus racial and evolutionary theory. The second law of thermodynamics and notions about the impact and influence of the machine all left little room for human choice and human action.

When we examine the causes offered by the theorists of decadence we see immediately that the supposed causes are explanations after the fact. The theory of cycles, so prominent in the ancient world and so important in the nineteenth century, surely has little in the way of scientific value to recommend it. Even if we enlarge the total number of civilizations to nineteen or twenty, as does Toynbee, we still do not have a sufficiently large population upon which to base an empirical induction. In short, the notion of the historical cycle as an inevitable development is entirely without scientific validity.

The concomitant notion that the lifespan of a culture or civilization is a one-thousand-year period is equally without any scientific basis. The conception of the millennial cycle is, consequently, mythic rather than scientific in origin. We can trace its origin to the ancient Near East, and we know it was a commonplace idea in the Mediterranean world. It seems preposterous to me that twentieth-century man should interpret historical experience in terms of an idea that antedates both the Old and New Testament views of history.

In the third place, the notion of historical inevitability is a modern superstition. Men make history and history does not determine men. In part because of the use of the model of the natural sciences in humanistic study we have tended to seek inevitable scientific causes in order to explain human behavior and identify the dynamic forces in the processes of history. But to seek for natural scientific causes is an inappropriate analytic tool in the study of history. It is true, of course, that much of human behavior is causally determined. The facts of nature, geography, climate, population, the quest for food, and the location of resources all act as determining factors. It is equally true that economics and sheer accident—chance—act as powerful historical determinants. However, man in his free will and with his powers of invention and improvisation transforms the limiting conditions of the causally given. These conditioning factors are like a chess board. The board does not determine the moves but rather presents a set of possible alternatives that rise to astronomical numbers. Thus, man is not fated but rather makes or chooses his own fate. It is precisely the failure to make a choice that increases the determinative power of natural scientific causes. Man's power of invention, man's power of choice, again and again defeats nature and opens to mankind a new realm of freedom. Thus, the determined causal theories of decadence as a historical explanation offer us a mythical rather than a satisfactory historical explanation.

Racial theories of creativity have, as Gobineau knew, little explanatory power. Cultures create races; races do not create cultures. Spengler shared this theory with Gobineau, and it is a correct reading of what we know about the sources of human creativity. Evolutionary development is far too slow to account for civilizational change and development. The notion that some civilizations decline because their vitality runs out, or because the higher types in the culture gradually disappear, flies in the face of all that we know about the complicated nature of the gene pool.

The economy of Rome was very different from any modern Western economy. One can hardly argue from the economy of Rome to the economy of present-day West Germany. Even when the argument is made in more general terms, such as those employed by Brooks Adams, the schema seems radically faulty. After all, greed and the hunger for power are not exactly new as human motivations, and even when societies indulge these motivations to an unusual degree, as does ours, these motives seem hardly to qualify as a source of decadence.

Henry Adams's belief that the second law of thermodynamics accounted for a kind of cosmic decadence surely must be one of the most preposterous historical explanations ever offered. That it was an improper use of natural scientific explanation goes without saying. As with most decadence theorists, Adams first felt his society was decadent and then looked about for what he considered a plausible explanation.

The fact is that we do not have a plausible theory either of the origin of civilization or of its decline and dissolution. But perhaps dissolution is too strong a word. Remember that what we call the decline of Rome was only the way in which Rome turned into medieval culture. That process was one of creation as much as decline. In the East the Roman empire remained in place and was not overthrown until 1453 and the fall of Constantinople to the Turks. In this instance Rome became Byzantium, but we could hardly describe this process as "the fall of Rome." In terms of historical development, theories of decline and fall are not very useful. Of course, some cultures are simply destroyed from the outside, as was the Aztec and the Andean civilization of South America. While some historians argue that these two cultures were both decadent before they were destroyed, one might well argue that had the Spaniards not delivered the knockout blow these two cultures might have solved their problems and proceeded to the production of a civilization with as much permanence as that of India or China.

The causes of the dissolution of a civilization may be various and may differ one from another. It does not follow that all civilizations die of the same causes nor does it follow that the steps in their dissolution follow in the same sequential order. The evidence can be skewed to make the case that the pattern is the same but empirical study will usually find fault with the explanation.

If all of what I have just said is even nearly the case, we must ask whether or not there is any truth at all in the notion of decadence. It seems to me apparent that the symptoms of decadence which nineteenth- and twentieth-century theorists of decadence saw in their societies were harmful and dangerous. For instance, the loss of form and purpose in society is obviously undesirable. Sexual promiscuity and the employment of intoxicants is in the experience of all societies undesirable. Indeed, if such practices become very widespread they must eventually endanger a society's existence. Consequently, the danger of the symptoms that the theorists of decadence perceived was real enough. It goes without saying that Western society in the nineteenth and twentieth centuries was in crisis.

One of the problems of that crisis, however, was the fact that the very process of rationalization, the growth of natural science and the power that science gave man through technological application—recognized by almost all men as progress—only deepened the crisis. Thus, the ability to improve the production of food, our health, and our mastery over the environment has often led to the transformation of our civilization in ways we may not feel desirable. In other words, to remove the goad of scarcity from the population at large may produce behavior in the culture that will, in the long run, endanger society. Is it possible that we can have too much plenty and too much security? What we view as decadence may in some odd way be the penalty we pay for continued progress. Thus, the revolution in communications permits the rapid spread of harmful and destructive notions and values as well as those which are socially valuable. This is not a new problem. It is at least as old as the invention of printing.

If societies and civilizations do not become decadent we still may not entirely dismiss decadence as a problem. In other words, it may be that the central problem in the decline of societies is the decadence of elites and creative minorities. It is these creative minorities who impose their values on society and give form and style to a civilization. As Arnold Toynbee points out, these creative minorities secure their position of leadership through *mimesis* or imitation by the uncreative majority. We know that the number of creative individuals in any society is relatively small. If we were to admit that all those persons listed in *Who's Who in America* belong to this creative minority, the number would still be very small—and this would be to make a gross overestimate. Those ideas which transform society in science, invention, the arts, literature, religion, and politics are very few in number. If the leading two thousand creative people in America were to die tomorrow, our civilization would probably be fatally impaired.

It seems to me that the problem with this very special group is threefold. In the first instance the creative minority loses the power to attract and influence the uncreative majority. There are moments in the history of every civilization when the creative minority presents ideas or notions that are so esoteric, so far removed from the goals and hopes of ordinary men, that they are simply rejected. When this happens, governments change or fall, styles in literature and the arts change, scientific theories are transformed, and new religions appear. This is not an unusual circumstance; indeed we have seen it going on around us at the present time. The cultural values that we call "modernism" and have dominated Western society for the past hundred years are now under attack and are being rejected by many. We can see this happening in the sixteenth century in a much more dramatic fashion in the Protestant Reformation. In that instance a new creative minority appeared after a period of loss of belief and waning imitation by the uncreative majority. The general process of loss of faith in the old religion might easily be described as decadence. When the new creative minority and their ideas appeared they seemed to sweep all before them. The old dominant minority of monks, priests, bishops, and nuns did not simply disappear. Some of them became Lutherans or Calvinists or Sectarians. But many of them simply lost all faith in their society. Often they retreated still further into the meaningless and unreligious life that had helped to produce the Reformation in the first place. It is very easy to speak of the "decadence" of Catholicism, though no one at the time did because the concept had not yet been invented.

Something of the same sort happened to the feudal nobility at the advent of the modern state. The Burgundian nobility depicted by Johan Huizinga in *The Waning of the Middle Ages* is a good example of the process I am discussing. This nobility simply lost its function in society as better and more effective governing groups took their place. They did not simply go away or disappear. They held on, living a magnificently self-indulgent life that was essentially without meaning or purpose. They were, in fact, decadent. Their decadence is the consequence of their displacement, and that displacement is the result of their loss of a social role. The ideas they represented and created no longer possessed any compelling power. A new and more powerful creative minority had come to the fore.

In the second instance the creative minority for one reason or another—perhaps because of what Arnold Toynbee calls "Schism in the Soul"—no longer provides leadership but behaves irresponsibly. They say, as did Leo X, the Medici pope at the time of Martin Luther's publication of the Ninety-Five Theses, "God has given us the papacy; now let us enjoy it." They abdicate their role of leadership for private pleasures and self-indulgence. Remember that the leadership of the creative minority is bought at a fearful price. Its cost is discipline, self-denial, and work of the most difficult sort. It is very tempting, having achieved a position of greatness, to sit back and enjoy life. Values and beliefs are often only formal acknowledgments, while the once-creative elite lapse into a round of pleasure-seeking activity. When this happens we describe the elite as decadent, and we know that they are on the road to the dustbin of history.

Finally, there are moments in history when the costs of leadership are so great and the acquisition of skills and understanding so difficult that large numbers of people simply refuse to make the effort necessary for mastery. The craftsman loses his skill or fails to transmit it to the next generation, and the intellectual fails to transmit his knowledge from one generation to another. The consequence is a society that is barbarized.

All of these signs of decadence are not developments implicit in the historical givens; they are not the result of a cycle or the natural developmental pattern of societies but rather the consequences of the behavior of elites, the consequences of choices made by creative minorities. The society, the gene pool, remains the same. It may, if circumstances favor it, give rise to an Einstein, or it may, under other conditions (or even the same conditions) produce a common criminal. To understand this is to be more aware than ever before of the possibilities for good and for evil in human history.

2

Decadence and the Machine

Theories of decadence in the nineteenth and twentieth centuries are closely associated with the political, religious, social, and economic problems that achieved a new prominence and force in the eighteenth and nineteenth centuries. And these problems were perceived as inevitable developments beyond the reach of human choice to modify or to change.

Moreover, these problems appeared as the reflexes, the Janus-face, the dark underside of the doctrine of progress. Just as progress was viewed as an inevitable development imminent in the dynamic processes of history, so decadence was its other side. What is even more astonishing is the fact that the same set of factors were seen from one perspective as the very essence of progressive development, while viewed from another perspective they appeared as the cause and source of human decadence. In no other area is this trick of perspective so important as in attitudes toward the machine.

From the eighteenth century onward the machine came into its own. To be sure, Renaissance dreamers and artist-inventors had earlier seen the machine as a method of magnifying man's powers and increasing his command over nature. But with these earlier inventions, however, the machine was an extension of human power, an amplification of the specifically human.

By the eighteenth century the nature and the use of the machine had changed and it had come to replace man. The machine was no longer an amplification of man's power so much as it was a replacement for man. Moreover, the machine had begun to escape the control of man—it and machine techniques were becoming autonomous. Along with this escape of the machine from man's control there was a parallel development by which men fell under the control of the machine. Mankind became less and less human and more and more machine-like. No doubt this shift was due not to the fact that the character of machines was changing, but rather that machines were becoming more and more commonplace and many human actions were now replaced by mechanical performance.

At first the machine was viewed as a marvel of human ingenuity and the effects of the machine as wholly beneficent. The machine became the symbol of progress. It was widely argued that the high cultures of ancient Greece and Rome had been possible only because slaves had freed large numbers of human beings from servile work, permitting them to engage in the creative activity of high culture. The machine was to replace the slave, freeing mankind from the labor that had been his lot since mankind's expulsion from the Garden of Eden. The machine was the great hope of mankind because it was "labor-saving." Equally important was the fact that the machine would create the plenty which mankind as a whole had never previously known. Human existence would be transformed from a saga of scarcity to a tale of superfluity: "two chickens in every pot, two cars in every garage." In the eighteenth century the mechanization of the manufacturing of textiles made the machine's impact on the abolition of scarcity apparent. The time-consuming processes of carding, spinning, and weaving were replaced by mechanical operations that multiplied the availability of fabrics a thousand-fold. It seemed to many that mankind had entered an era of labor-free plenty. There could hardly be a more certain demonstration of progress. The curse imposed upon man because of his sin in the Garden of Eden had been lifted not through religious dispensation but through human ingenuity. The machine became central to all hopes for human progress in the nineteenth century, the keystone of the progressive theories of economic and political liberalism and Marxism alike. For Marx the machine was the ultimate tool by which "man made himself"; it provided the freedom from labor and freedom from want through which man could realize all of his God-like potentialities.

There was, however, a fly in the ointment, a crack in the cosmic picture window. In 1776, the most brilliant student of developing capitalism and the industrial process noted in *The Wealth of Nations,* "The man whose whole life is spent in performing a few simple operations . . . has no occasion to exert his understanding, . . . He naturally loses, therefore, the habit of such exertion, and generally becomes as stupid and ignorant as it is possible for a human creature to become. . . . His dexterity at his own particular trade seems, in this manner, to be acquired at the expense of his intellectual, social, and martial virtues."[1] The deleterious effect of the machine upon human nature remarked on here by Adam Smith is different from Rousseau's attack on the division of labor, which Rousseau makes in his essay on "The Origin of Inequality Among Men." Rousseau is worried by the relationship of the division of labor to the formation of classes and the exploitation of the labor of one man by another. Smith was concerned with the effects of the division of labor on the human personality.

Smith's friend and close associate, Adam Ferguson, in his book *An Essay on the History of Civil Society*—which, incidentally, antedated *The Wealth of Nations*—also perceived the stultifying effects of mechanical operations on human beings. He wrote:

> It may even be doubted, whether the measure of national capacity increases with the advancement of arts. Many mechanical arts, indeed, require no capacity; they succeed best under a total suppression of sentiment and reason; and ignorance is the mother of industry as well as of superstition. Reflection and fancy are subject to err; but a habit of moving the hand, or the foot, is independent of either. Manufactures, accordingly, prosper most, where the mind is least consulted, and where the workshop may, without any great effort of imagination, be considered an engine, the parts of which are men.

Note in this passage that Ferguson no longer views the machine as an extension and amplification of man but rather sees man as a part of the machine. However, Ferguson recognizes that the impact of the "separation of the professions" (the division of labor) is differential. Its effects are various.

> But if many parts in the practice of every art, and the detail of every department, require no abilities, or actually tend to contract and to limit the views of the mind, there are others which lead to general reflections, and to enlargement of thought. Even in manufacture, the genius of the master, perhaps, is cultivated, while that of the inferior work man lies waste. The statesman may have a wide comprehension of human affairs, while the tools he employs are ignorant of the system in which they are themselves combined. The general officer may be a great proficient in the knowledge of war, while the soldier is confined to a few motions of the hand and the foot. The former may have gained, what the latter has lost; and being occupied in the conduct of disciplined armies, may practice on a larger scale, all the arts of preservation, of deception, and of stratagem, which the savage exerts in leading a small party, or merely in defending himself.

Thus, Adam Ferguson points to the social consequences of this separation of the professions. The effect is not egalitarian.

In every commercial state, notwithstanding any pretension to equal rights, the exaltation of a few must depress the many. In this arrangement, we think that the extreme meanness of some classes must arise chiefly from the defect of knowledge, and of liberal education; and we refer to such classes, as to an image of what our species must have been in its rude and uncultivated state. But we forget how many circumstances, especially in populous cities, tend to corrupt the lowest orders of men. Ignorance is the least of their failings. An admiration of wealth unpossessed, becoming a principle of envy, or of servility; a habit of acting perpetually with a view to profit, and under a sense of subjection; the crimes to which they are allured, in order to feed their debauch, or to gratify their avarice, are examples, not of ignorance, but of corruption and baseness. If the savage has not received our instructions, he is likewise unacquainted with our vices. He knows no superior, and cannot be servile; he knows no distinctions of fortune, and cannot be envious; he acts from his talents in the highest station human society can offer, that of the counsellor, and the soldier of his country. Toward forming his sentiments, he knows all that the heart requires to be known; he can distinguish the friend whom he loves, and the public interest which awakens his zeal.

Ferguson points earlier in his essay to a most important development in modern Western society, one that was to play an enormous role in the debate concerning the government of modern societies: namely, the growth of a bureaucracy. He writes:

The advantage gained in the inferior branches of manufacture by the separation of their parts, seems to be equalled by those which arise from a similar device in the higher departments of policy and war. The soldier is relieved from every care but that of his service; statesmen divide the business of civil government into shares; and the servants of the public, in every office, without being skillful in the affairs of state, may succeed, by observing forms which are already established on the experience of others. They are made, like the parts of an engine, to concur to a purpose, without any concert of their own: and, equally blind with the trader to any general combination, they unite with him, in furthering to the state its resources.

Ferguson's argument is that the separation of the professions leads to the dehumanization and degradation of the individual, who loses his vitality, inventiveness, and martial spirit. The invention of bureaucracy removes men from the arena of political participation, and the development of class feeling deepens the degradation of urban populations. These developments are in the nature of the trade-off, and Ferguson is quick to point to the advantages in the division of labor. He poses the problem as an unsolved difficulty of commercial society, one for which a remedy may eventually be found.

The difficulties Ferguson discussed did not disappear and, indeed, became the subject of a major debate in the nineteenth century concerning the impact of the machine on human nature and political institutions. That the machine might lead to a transformation of political institutions became increasingly apparent as the nineteenth century moved on. There are, for example, intimations in Tocqueville's *Democracy in America* that some relationship exists between the development of what Tocqueville calls "the manufacturing classes" and the growth of authoritarianism. Tocqueville notes:

> There exists among the modern nations of Europe one great cause, independent of all those which have already been pointed out, which perpetually contributes to extend the agency or to strengthen the prerogative of the supreme power though it has not been sufficiently attended to: I mean the growth of manufactures, which is fostered by the progress of social equality. Manufacturers generally collect a multitude of men on the same spot, among whom new and complex relations spring up. These men are exposed by their calling to great and sudden alternations of plenty and want, during which public tranquility is endangered. It may also happen that these employments sacrifice the health and even the life of those who gain by them or those who live by them. Thus the manufacturing classes require more regulation, superintendence, and restraint than the other classes of society, and it is natural that the powers of government should increase in the same proportion as those classes.

These fears did not abate in the course of the nineteenth century; indeed, they were intensified as the century wore on and the full implications of the industrial revolution became apparent.

It should be pointed out that humanistic intellectuals, then and now, are largely antitechnological and antiscientific. Their view of the world remains preindustrial, one is tempted to say arcadian. Few of them understand technological processes, most of them are antimechanistic and anti-capitalistic, and nearly all yearn for the life of leisure that typified the preindustrial aristocratic classes. Little wonder then that so many of them in America and Europe viewed the machine with horror. Thoreau, Emerson, and Melville in America, Carlyle and Ruskin in England, formulated a social philosophy based upon the rejection of the machine and the substitution of a handicraft culture. It was necessary to check the growth of machine civilization before men were transformed into machines.[2]

In the first half of the nineteenth century the dialectic is that of autonomy/automation. There was hope that the machine would be brought under control, that man might exert a continued autonomy. Many, of course, saw no conflict and viewed the machine as the promise of progress. Marxists, socialists, social Darwinists, capitalists, and political liberals all praised the freedom, plenty, and extension of man's power that they believed the machine promised them. These feelings were especially strong in North America, Africa, South America, and Australia, where the machine was the one great force that could be applied to the conquest of the wilderness. For many nineteenth-century Americans it was the machine that made man's triumph over space, weather, hostile savages, and unfriendly environments possible. It was the iron horse, the Colt revolver, the barbed-wire fence, the windmill, the balloon-frame house, and "the plow that broke the plains" that made the rapid settlement of North America possible.

By the end of the century, however, the public mood was shifting both in Europe and America. It was no longer clear that man could dominate his technology, that he could remain master of his machines. He had created a civilization in which the machine and the industrial process had become indispensable, in which men had become dependent upon the machine, in which millions were forced at great psychological and physiological cost to serve the machine, in which the laboring millions all too often took on the characteristics of the machine.

Friedrich Georg Jünger, author of *The Perfection of Technology*, tells us in his autobiography that as a child he was made uncomfortable by the revolving turnstiles which permitted entry and exit to the zoo.[3] He disliked them precisely because the mechanism prescribed his actions. Once one was committed to the mechanism, choice and freedom had been lost. This was a child's perception, to be sure, but it had implications of great importance. The surrender to mechanism always involves the loss of freedom. Increasingly, it appeared to many in the late nineteenth century that once mankind had embarked upon the creation of a mechanical industrial civilization there was no possibility of turning back. Man was doomed to destruction at the hands of the machine.

The opposing views of the machine as the promise of unending progress and the machine as a dehumanizing monster that would eventually enslave and degrade mankind were nowhere more vividly presented than in the utopian and science-fiction literature of the late nineteenth and the twentieth centuries. Utopian and science-fiction novels presented the case for technology. The antiutopian novel, the dystopian novel, and a new, antitechnological science fiction carried on the debate that had began more than a century before.[4]

The shift from the notion of the machine as servant, the machine as a nonhuman slave, to the conception of the machine as master and the human being as servant and slave was not completed until the last two decades of the nineteenth century. Until then there seems to have been hope that the process could be mastered and that the machine could be employed in such a fashion as to lead to man's liberation.

In no thinker is the new view of the machine more interesting than in the thoughts of Herbert George (H. G.) Wells (1866–1946).

Wells was a man who wanted to believe in the power of the machine to ameliorate the lot of mankind. He was a poor boy and a poor young man who climbed into a position of cultural and political importance through the power of his mind and his driving ambition. He was the first major English-speaking writer who had been trained as a scientist and who was able to make some fair assessment of technology. His novels and short stories are landmarks in the development of science-fiction as a genre. He was a socialist by temperamental inclination as well as intellectual conviction. One might suppose Wells to have been a wholehearted supporter of the machine.[5]

That assumption would be incorrect, for Wells, like his contemporaries, was fearful of the machine. Herbert Sussman notes:

> When he finally turned from teaching to the more lucrative career of writing, Wells sought to convey the excitement of scientific speculation that he had himself experienced in his own short career as a biologist. But even in his role as spokesman for the new scientific elite, he could not escape the nineteenth-century fear of the machine. He had heard Morris speak at Hammersmith; he had discussed news from nowhere in the dissecting room. His earliest imaginative works, the scientific romances, are symbolic tales in which for Wells, as for writers throughout the nineteenth century, the machine is the emblem of modern civilization. And just as Wells was able to deliver to his son a sermon "in which he made a great point of monogamy and fi-

delity," so too he was able to argue both sides of the question of progress. In describing technology, Wells often resembles the narrator of the *War of the Worlds* who, hidden in the Martian camp and in imminent danger of a particularly unpleasant death, is still fascinated by the Martian machinery. Even Wells's explicitly anti-utopian writing describes in detail the advanced technology brutalizing the proletariat. But to the conventional symbolic use of the machine as metonymy for industrialized society, Wells, the first scientifically trained writer of the machine age, adds a further meaning. The machine becomes the symbol of the specifically scientific mind, and the scientific romances fables illustrating the inadequacy of pure science divorced from intuitive morality. And in continuing the Victorian literary criticism of pure reason, Wells also continues the ambivalence toward science itself. For every selfless investigator of nature's secrets, there is a mad scientist. The well-intentioned time-explorer is matched by Griffen, the homicidal scientist of the *Invisible Man.*

Wells, who is often identified with the idea of scientific utopia—a utopia made possible by the machine—was anything but an assured and reassuring prophet. To be sure, Wells's essay *A Modern Utopia* breaks with the tradition of utopia as a pastoral idyll. In *A Modern Utopia* it is the machine that makes self-fulfillment possible. Indeed this book is an attack upon the world projected by John Ruskin, and were we to read no farther we might suppose that Wells was wholeheartedly in favor of a totally mechanized society. However Wells knew well that scientists and technologists could not be trusted—that the machine gave them great power—a power that might eventuate in madness and the destruction of human values and human life.

> … Wells also accepted the Victorian commonplace that machine-tending is both physically and morally degrading, but instead of using the convention of contemporary realism, like Dickens or Ruskin, he finds a new form for the old argument in the Butlerian mode of evolutionary fantasy. With an air of scientific credibility, the biological and psychological effects of mechanization are projected into the future in concrete, physical form. The first fictional example of this evolutionary mode is the Morlocks.
>
> And yet this new genre is combined with older conventions of machine literature. Lest the reader miss the connection between the factory and Hell, the Morlocks are placed under-

ground, from where, in true diabolical fashion, they emerge
during the night to carry off the inhabitants of the upper world.
This conventional association of the machine with Hell runs
throughout the scientific romances. In *When the Sleeper Wakes,*
the entire proletariat is confined to labyrinthine "under ways"
through which the Victorian visitor is guided like a modern
Dante; in *The First Men in the Moon,* the Selenite workers also
tend their machines in dark tunnels.[6]

Moreover, Wells explores a new fear that arises out of a combination of
Darwinism and the machine. Suppose that the machine produces modifi-
cations in the physiology and psychology of the machine-tender so that a
new race of subhuman machine-tenders is produced. Here it is not an "under class" but an "under race" that is produced. Indeed this "under race" is
just the opposite of Nietzsche's Übermenschen.

Wells's application of Darwin to the literature of the machine
created new figures adequate to the depth of late nineteenth-
century pessimism about technological progress. The mental
history of the time-traveler, from his elation as he stands at the
beginning of a seemingly limitless progress to his final disen-
chantment, recapitulates the response of the nineteenth century to the machine.
     ... *The War of the Worlds* (1898) continues to criticize mecha-
nization through the literary use of evolutionary figures. The
physical grotesqueness of the Martians, like the animality of
the Morlocks and the effeminacy of the Eloi, is an evolutionary
extrapolation of the present effects of the machine.[7]

In an 1893 magazine article, "Man in the Year Million," Wells predicts that
the physical, muscular man will be largely modified and his brain will be
tremendously enlarged; all brain and no muscles. "Only the hand, the teacher
and interpreter of the brain, will become constantly more powerful and
subtle as the rest of the musculature dwindles"; the men of the future will
have "expanding brains . . . great sensitive hands and diminishing bodies."
From these facetious musings, he created the Martians, the emblem of effete mechanized man; observing these flaccid brain cases with gaping months
and waving tentacles, the narrator comments:

The perfection of mechanical appliances must ultimately su-
persede limbs. . . . [T]he tendency of natural selection would lie
in the direction of their steady diminution through the coming

ages.... We men, without bicycles and road-skates, our Lilenthal
soaring-machines, our guns and sticks and so forth, are just in
the beginning of the evolution that the Martians have worked
out. They have became practically mere brains, wearing different bodies according to their needs just as men wear suits of
clothes and take a bicycle in a hurry or an umbrella in the wet!

Had Wells been the only one to have entertained these fears of the
withering away of the physical prowess of mankind we would find him an
entertaining fabulist rather than a prophetic novelist. The fact is that Wells's
fears were widely shared. Not only did the machine transform man, it transformed the environment. The machine and the structures associated with
it overwhelmed the imagination and transformed the world into a mechanical, nonliving landscape. It dominated the mind of man and transformed
man's thought processes.

In *The First Men in the Moon* we see clearly where a machine civilization
may lead. Cavor, the inventor of an anti-gravity propellent, is accidentally
left behind on the moon and makes a series of broadcasts to earth describing what he has found there. The "Selenites" are the lunar machine-
tenders.

The bulk of these insects, however, who go to and fro upon the
spiral ways . . . are, I gather, of the operative class. "Machine
hands," indeed some of these are in actual fact—it is no figure
of speech; the single tentacle of the moon-calf hind is replaced
by huge single or paired bunches of three, or five, or seven dig-
its for clawing, lifting, guiding, the rest of them no more than
subordinate appendages to these important parts. . . .

The making of these various sorts of operatives must be a
very curious and interesting process. . . . Quite recently I came
upon a number of young Selenites, confined in jars from which
only the fore limbs protruded, who were being compressed to
become machine minders of a special sort. The extended "hand"
in this highly developed system of technical education is stimulated by irritants and nourished by injection while the rest of
the body is starved. . . . [T]hat wretched-looking hand sticking
out of its jar seemed to appeal for lost possibilities; it haunts me
still, although, of course, it is really in the end a far more humane proceeding than our earthly method of leaving children
to grow into human beings, and then making machines of them.

At the very end of his life, after writing for fifty years, Wells produced a final summing up, *Mind at the End of Its Tether*. It is a book filled with despair at the human predicament and hardly the apologia one would expect from the great apostle of progress, if that, indeed, was what he had been.

E. M. Forster, having read many pieces by Wells, which seemed to Forster a glorification of the machine, set out to write a long short story that would refute what Forster believed to be Wells's unexamined optimism and progressivism. The story was entitled "The Machine Stops," but rather than contradicting Wells it underlined themes that Wells had earlier developed. In this account of human civilization in the future,

> the human population resides underground, living singly in compartments where, at the pressing of buttons, mechanical devices supply water, food, air, beds, medicine, music, and communicating devices.

Travel outside the compartments, although provided for, becomes rare, with a resultant deterioration in skin and musculature: Vashti, the central character, is described as a "swaddled lump of flesh" with "a face as white as a fungus." Originally the interlocking, supportive mechanism that sustained life in the compartments had been directly superintended by its designers; as their dependence became habitual, however, the human agents seemed to lose control over the functioning of the apparatus, which had been supplied with self-repairing mechanical aids. Soon they began to pray to it. That was the beginning of the end: "But Humanity in its desire for comfort had overreached itself. It had exploited the riches of nature too far. Quietly and complacently, it was sinking into decadence, and progress had come to mean the progress of the Machine."[8]

Eventually the mechanism collapses, taking with it in its demise the compartmentalized inhabitants. But they were already dead in all but name, the living dead. Kuno, Vashti's son, had tried to explain this to her before the end:

> Cannot you see . . . that it is we who are dying, and that down here the only thing that lives is the Machine? We created Machine to do our will, but we cannot make it do our will now. It has robbed us of the sense of space and the sense of touch, it has blurred every human relation and narrowed down love to a carnal act, it has paralyzed our bodies and our wills, and now it compels us to worship it. The Machine develops—but not on our lines. The Machine proceeds—but not to our goal. We only

exist as the blood corpuscles that course through its arteries, and if it could work without us it would let us die!

Hope for regeneration lies only in the rude bands of escapees or natives who exist outside the orbit of mechanized society completely. . . .[9]

By the 1920s this view of man's relation to the machine had became a common one. The revolution in the division of labor produced by the assembly line and time-motion studies no doubt had important consequences in the increasing pessimism with which the machine was viewed. Equally a source of pessimism was the pervasive materialism and consumerism that machine production engendered.

Yevgeny Zamyatin's *We* is a criticism of the machine and the materialism associated with the machine.[10] Zamyatin's novel is a protest against the implications of the Soviet system—the system not as it was but as it hoped to be. In the early days of the Soviet Union the great dream was that the machine would transform man and society. Lenin had defined communism as "socialism plus electrification." Zamyatin attempts to make explicit what the impact of mechanization on Russian society would be. He saw the end result as decadence.

Better known and perhaps more important is Aldous Huxley's *Brave New World,* the most original of the early antiutopian novels. Clearly it was an attack on what Huxley thought was the utopian model proposed by H. G. Wells. In May 1931, Huxley commented in a letter: "I am writing a novel about the future—on the horror of the Wellsian Utopia and a revolt against it. Very difficult. I have hardly enough imagination to deal with such a subject. But it is nonetheless interesting work." In August of that year he wrote to his father:

I have been harried with work—in which I have at last, thank heaven, got rid of a comic, or at least satirical, novel about the future, showing the appallingness (or at any rate by our standards) of Utopia and adumbrating the effects upon thought and feeling of such possible biological inventions as the production of children in bottles (with consequent abolition of the family and all the Freudian "complexes" for which family relationships are responsible), the prolongation of youth, the devising of some harmless but effective substitute for alcohol, cocaine, opium, etc.—and also the effects of such sociological reforms as Pavlovian conditioning of all children from birth and before birth, universal peace, security and stability. It has been a job writing the book and I'm glad it's done.

The book was published in 1932 and in 1946 Huxley wrote a new Foreword for the book in which he argued that

> [t]he theme of *Brave New World* is not the advancement of science as such; it is the advancement of science as it affects individuals. The triumphs of physics, chemistry and engineering are tacitly taken for granted. The only scientific advances to be specifically described are those involving the application to human beings of the results of future research in biology, physiology and psychology. It is only by means of the sciences of life that the quality of life can be radically changed. The sciences of matter can be applied in such a way that they will destroy life or make the living of it impossibly complex and uncomfortable; but, unless used as instruments by the biologists and psychologists, they can do nothing to modify the natural forms and expressions of life itself. The release of atomic energy marks a great revolution in human history, but not (unless we blow ourselves to bits and so put an end to history) the final and most searching revolution.

What we see in Huxley's novel is a shift in ground of the argument. Of course the machine is important in Huxley's novel. History is dated before and after Ford and the denizens of Huxley's utopian world cross themselves with an F. However, unlike Wells and other writers on the problem of science, technology, and the machine, the machine cannot produce evolutionary change in human individuals; cannot alter their ability to judge and evaluate. That can be done only through actual biological tinkering and the restructuring of mankind through psychological modification. These, it appears to Huxley, are the terrible possibilities of the twentieth century. Biological modification, psychological conditioning, indoctrination—it was indeed a preview of the world of totalitarianism, of Big Brother. It is also the world in which we live: a world of biological manipulation, mind-altering drugs, and subtle media conditioning. Huxley was certain that decadence would be the end of this development. Thus, the terms of the argument about the effect of science and technical rationalism changed, but the result, human degradation and decadence, remained the same.

Mustapha Mond, the "Controller" of Huxley's Brave New World, says in a passage describing the advantages of this utopian society:

> "Awful? They don't find it so, on the contrary, they like it [that is, one of the tasks they do]: It's light, it's childishly simple. No strain on the mind or the muscles. Seven and a half hours of

mild, unexhausting labour, and then the soma ration and games and unrestricted copulation and the feelies. What more can they ask for? True," he added, "they might ask for shorter hours. And of course we could give them shorter hours. Technically, it would be perfectly simple to reduce all lower-caste working hours to three or four a day. But would they be any the happier for that? No, they wouldn't. The experiment was tried, more than a century and a half ago. The whole of Ireland was put on a four hour day. What was the result? Unrest and a large increase in the consumption of soma; that was all. . . ."

Huxley's fears, it seems to me, are far more real and the danger more pressing than the fears of nineteenth-century moralists who believed that when men were engaged in machine production they would, in fact, became like machines.

However, the fear of decadence through the mechanization of life did not disappear. Think of Charlie Chaplin's *Modern Times.* In this film Chaplin is caught up in the terrors of machine production and assembly-line labor. That these terrors are laughable does not make them any the less real. In short, the fact that Huxley envisioned new terrors did not abolish the old ones.

In 1925–26, Fritz Lang, the greatest of the Weimar German film producers and directors, produced the film *Metropolis*.[11] H. G. Wells wrote of it: "The other day I saw the most foolish film. I cannot believe it would be possible to make a more foolish one."

In the stylized world of the workers, everything is of an equally intense visual force. The working class is portrayed powerfully—slaves dressed in black, heads bent, anonymous creatures of labor walking through vaulted corridors, rhythmically keeping time like the Expressionist revolutionary choirs, sharply outlined ranks in which the individual no longer counts as a human being. In the machine center, they turn into hands on enormous dials jerkily executing their mysterious work to keep the gigantic wheels moving. They are more machines than human beings—more machine even than the robot that struts towards the camera.

There is a transformation which echoes Giovanni Pastrone's *Cabiria*: in Freder's eyes the machine center is transformed into the image of the God Moloch, with gaping mouth and gleaming eyes. A new shift of workers marches into the threatening maw on their way to the machines, in the same serried ranks.[12]

There is an accident, viewed through a screen of smoke and the horrified eyes of Freder (all elegant in white silk), who is frozen into an Expressionist diagonal as dark figures bearing the casualties file past, shot against the light. The scene immediately preceding this, with dark figures glimpsed as merely silhouettes in the dusty air and hazy light of the machine room, is again of great visual impact. The scene is presented without symbolism, with just that documentary approach which is Lang's great strength and which succeeds in counteracting the pomposity of much of the film."[13]

These films and novels point to the popularization of the idea that decadence was implicit in machine civilization. That this in fact was the case was illustrated in World War II and the Holocaust, in which men who were slaves were in fact forcibly molded to the machine and in which science and technology were successfully employed in such vastly antihumanitarian pursuits as to call into question the legitimacy of technical rationalism.

3

The Perception of Decadence

On September 21, 1902, the German poet Rainer Maria Rilke, in Paris ostensibly to write a monograph on Rodin, translated his anxieties and the elegiac, autumnal mood in which he found himself into the poem "Autumn Day."[1] The poet addresses God briskly, after the fashion of an officer who is unaccustomed to giving orders. "Now God," he says, "is the time. It's been a big summer / Let your shadows fall upon the Sundials and turn the winds loose on the fields / Order the last fruits to be perfect; give them still two intensely southern days and press in on them completion driving the last sweetness into the heavy wine." Then the poet reflects upon his own and the world's condition: "He who does not have a house has no time to build one now. He who is alone will long remain so; waking, reading, writing long letters and, as the leaves are driven, tramping here and there in the streets disconsolately."

Rilke's poem has fused the events of the season and the mood and incidents of the poet's life with a common European perception of the historical moment. To be sure the autumnal was Rilke's favorite landscape, and the poet's year seems to be filled with an unusual number of Septembers, Octobers, and Novembers. Nor is this poem, or the other poems by Rilke that deal with autumn, a poem of sensuous satisfaction in the sense of Keats's "To Autumn." Rilke's landscapes are not filled with the externalities of nature as are Keats's but rather are reflections of the seasons of the soul. Shortly before *Herbsttag* was written, Rilke and his young bride had abandoned housekeeping at Westerwede, and no doubt the poet felt acutely his failure to build and maintain a house. Moreover, Rilke imagined himself to be the descendent of Carinthian nobility; dispossessed, landless, and houseless, and houselessness typified what he felt to be the unjust fate of his family.[2] The poet's immediate experience provided the symbols, but the homelessness and loneliness of the poem is historic and even cosmic in its dimensions, rather than narrowly seasonal or personal. The great year draws to its close, the cycle of the seasons ends. Purposes and passions are dissolved in the triumph of time.

Rilke's great themes of death and regeneration, of alienation and loneliness, of the fall into time and the decay of the year, of sexuality and creative potency, are the themes of decadence, of a world grown weary and mistrustful of the ability of man and particularly the poet to act creatively.

That Rilke's poems dealing with autumn were eschatological-cosmological in intention is made clear by the poem "Autumn," written in Paris on the 11th of September 1902, only a few days before the composition of "Autumn Day."

> The leaves are falling, falling as from way off,
> as though far gardens withered in the skies;
> they are falling with denying gestures.
> And in the nights the heavy earth is falling
> from all the stars down into loneliness.
> We are all falling. This hand falls.
> And look at others: it is in them all.
> And yet there is one who holds this falling
> endlessly gently in his hands.[3]

These themes of love and death, of sexual vitality and potency lamed, of alienation and cosmological disaster, of a time corrupted and sentenced to death are, of course, the commonplaces of the European *fin de siècle* literary world. Rilke too suffered from that no longer mysterious *mal du siècle*, indeed its symbols and ideas formed the ideological substance of his work.

However, the validity of art resides, at least in part, in the universal resonance that it evokes. Decadence, which with Wilde or Rilke or George or Baudelaire or Huysmans might be (often was) discounted as a literary pose must be taken seriously when it becomes the substance of culture and politics. Recently, Oron J. Hale has suggested that the autumnal mood at the turn of the century is a kind of afterthought, a trick of historical perspective that our present has imposed on their past.[4] The mood, Hale seems to say, was one of comfortable security, ebullient hope, and dynamic creativity. Those years were indeed "The Gay Nineties," or *La Belle Epoque,* an era when the Western world bathed for the last time in self-satisfied optimism and looked forward to both material and spiritual improvement. The evidence Hale produces is impressive. But it too bears the mark of the commonplace, for faith in prosperity and progress remained an important *Weltanschauung* in the Western world at least until the advent of the Great Depression. To assert that either one mood or the other was dominant misses the point. The question that ought to fascinate historians and students of human behavior is the question of how different men living in the same ambience confronting the same experiences and assessing the same evidence could come to such different conclusions. The question that ought to interest us is the question of why one perception seemed so much more prophetic—and in retrospect, so much more correct—than the other.

Rilke's mood was a consistent one. He saw death, illusion, and corruption at the heart of European society. His observation of European life led to no complacence and no optimistic expectation. In the fifth of the *Duineser Elegien* he wrote:

> Squares, o square in Paris, infinite show-place,
> where the modest Madame Lamort
> winds and binds the restless ways of the world,
> those endless ribbons, to ever-new
> creations of bow, frill, flower, cockade and fruit,
> all falsely colored, to deck
> the cheap winter hats of Fate.[5]

The problem then is not which attitude was in fact the zeitgeist, for very obviously they coexisted. The historian must explain, rather, how two such different views could arise out of the same experience; what the sources of pessimism, decadence, and cultural despair were, what their history had been, and how they came to play a role in the cultural complexities of past and present Europe.

One must observe immediately of historical pessimism and theories of decadence that perspective and social and cultural determinants play an enormous role in the perception of historical reality. Whatever Hale may mean when he says of European society at the turn of the century that "the real mood was broadly optimistic and anticipatory," the fact is that the mood of pessimism and decadence was as "real" as the religion of progress. The word "real" has little or no meaning used in this sense.

At the very moment in the European past that decadence emerged as a historical problem, eighteenth-century humanists and social theorists believed that they had discovered in the primitive societies that Western man had encountered in his exploration of the world men living in Paradise uncorrupted by luxury and unsurfeited by civilization, men living in accordance with the laws of nature in societies not yet decadent. The marks of virtue were clearly evident in these societies, the golden age of sex, nudity, heroic oratory, the lack of an elaborate culture, the absence of a priestly caste, a permissive morality, and the absence of great differences of wealth. The "noble savage" was seen as antithetical to the corrupted and decadent European. However, the savages saw themselves in very different terms.

Mircea Eliade points out that "[t]he savages, for their part, were also aware of having lost a primitive Paradise. In the modern jargon, we might say that the savages regarded themselves, neither more nor less than if they had been Western Christians, as beings in a 'fallen' condition, by contrast with a fabulously happy situation in the past."[6] As in the Hans Christian Andersen story of the happily married old couple, the history of the human race seen in a mythical perspective is "always downhill but merry all the way."

Myth and history in the Western world interpenetrate, and there is a constant temptation both to explain the historic past and to evaluate present discontents in terms of myths of degeneration, decadence, and apocalyptic regeneration. The perception of decadence need have little to do with the facts of overt reality. Its content is nearly always a subjective evaluation.

This easy mixture of myth and contemporary history is typical of the remarks of President Nixon in July 1971, when he observed in a thoughtful and depressed mood; "Sometimes when I see those columns [the National Archives building in Washington], I think of seeing them in Greece and Rome, and you see only what is left of great civilizations of the past—as they became wealthy, as they lost their will to live, to improve, they became subject to the decadence that destroys the civilization. The United States is reaching that period."[7] Then Nixon, taking heart, added significantly, "I am convinced, however, that we have the vitality. I believe that we have the courage, I believe that we have the strength out through this heartland and across this nation that will see to it that America is not only rich and strong but that it is healthy in terms of moral and spiritual strength."

In this statement, present difficulties of a political nature led the president to lapse into the mythical mode. He of course is not alone in his temptation to see the marks of decadence in contemporary American society. Even those who recognize the vast power and potency of contemporary America, as does Andrew Hacker, are apt in the light of current difficulties to speak as though the moment of America's decline is at hand. Hacker describes that potential power when he observed in 1968 that the U.S. possessed a GNP which exceeded $700 billion, 16,000,000 young men between the ages of eighteen and 30, and a military technology that could produce greater firepower than any other nation in the world.[8] He makes the further point that the empires of the past, Roman, British, and Nazi, were built on a base meager by comparison.

Yet having said all of this Hacker went on to point to a failure of will that in a book appearing a short time later is taken as clear evidence of America's impending decline.[9] Nor does he hold out the hope that President Nixon seemed to offer:

> Such a stance would at least be realistic. For the United States
> no longer has the will to be a great international power, just as it
> is no longer an ascending nation at home. We have arrived at a
> plateau in our history: the years of middle age and incipient
> decline. We are now at that turning-point ancient philosophers
> call *stasis,* a juncture at which it becomes pointless to call for
> rehabilitation or renewal. Such efforts would take a discipline
> we do not have, a spirit of sacrifice which has ceased to exist.

What immediately strikes the reader of the book in which these de-
spairing lines are lodged is the fact that their author offers so little by way
of substantive evidence to demonstrate his case. No doubt the Vietnam
War had a major impact on the subjective image most Americans held of
themselves and their society at this time. The disastrous Franco-Prussian
war had an equally devastating effect on the image Frenchmen held of themselves and the role of France in the world.[10] Historically, however, military
defeat does not necessarily usher in an era of decline, as witness the defeat
of England in the American Revolution, nor does military victory inevitably sustain a decaying power.

The perception of decadence in contemporary America is particularly
interesting because its onset has been so sudden and the critique of American society has come in large part from those members of the liberal and
Left intelligentsia who have played a dominant and determinate role in the
past four decades in the formation and shaping of present-day American
society. Only ten years ago, when the liberal hegemony was at its peak,
those voices who spoke of decadence in American society were very few in
number and were traditional-conservative and religious in orientation. The
great bulk of America's intellectuals viewed the transformation of American life that proceeded on all fronts with satisfaction and approval. Much
of the initial appeal of the Great Society programs derived from the rhetorical resonance these programs found in the liberal programs of transformation and amelioration in the previous half century.

Nor, indeed, in this period did technology figure as a source of impending decadence. Technology was seen by the liberal intelligentsia in
the first third of the twentieth century in essentially Marxian terms; terms
of approval. Technology, it was thought, transformed and revolutionized
society, its function was essentially ameliorative, and finally and perhaps
most importantly, it ratified the Promethean myth upon which Marxism
and modernity in general were based.

Moreover, the perception of decadence is not shared by a substantial
number of Americans. For them the problems that inhere in contemporary
American life are not manifestations of pathology or evidence of the slow

unwinding and unraveling of the American system but at most problems of discontinuity and social dissonance;[11] problems to be solved through the application of increased rationalization and technology.

Both foreign and domestic observers from diverse political backgrounds and ideological commitments have asserted that the present American era, far from being one of stagnation and characterized by the onset of the recession of the American dream, is one of extraordinary achievement and creativity. Zbigniew Brzezinski cites an OECD study demonstrating in terms of scientific papers, international scientific prizes, and patents for technical applications of basic science to fields of manufacture most heavily dependent on technical innovation, the commanding lead that the United States holds.[12] Facts of this sort led J. J. Servan-Schreiber in his book *The American Challenge* to see the United States as the model for future European development.[13] Another Frenchman[14] observing American society from the perspective of the Left has praised it as the only truly revolutionary society in the world today. "To my mind," he writes, "present-day America is a laboratory of revolution—in the sense that eighteenth-century England was to Voltaire." He further notes, "The stuff of revolution, and its first success, must be the ability to innovate. It must be mobility with respect to the past, and speed with respect to creation. In that sense, there is more revolutionary spirit in the United States today, even on the Right, than there is on the Left anywhere else."[14]

For the moment, the problem is not to determine which of these perceptions is the correct one but rather to point out that theories of decadence perennially exist alongside the most intense expressions of historical optimism. Any historical narrative that discards either the one or the other as not being consonant with reality leads to historical distortion.

Ortega y Gasset remarked on the coexistence of feelings of "plenitude" and the onset of feelings of decadence.[15] He remarks, "Let it not be forgotten; our time is a time which follows on a period of plenitude. Hence it is that inevitably, the man living on the other bank, the man of that plenary epoch just past, who sees everything from his own viewpoint, will suffer from the optical illusion of regarding our age as a fall from plenitude, as a decadent period." Then Ortega adds, significantly, "But the lifelong student of history, the practiced feeler of the pulse of the times, cannot allow himself to be deceived by this system of optics based on imaginary periods of plenitude. . . ."

By "plenitude" Ortega meant that sense of fullness, completion, and consummation which characterize certain cultural epochs. It is then that men feel themselves to be living at the very summit of the ages, having achieved what other eras could only aspire to and long for. Ortega sees "plenitude" and decadence as two separate moments. But in fact they are fused in one and the same time. They are the Janus faces of superfluity and fulfillment. Those ages of grandeur, those Augustan times, those gay, prosperous, powerful, and beautiful decades are perceived, at least by not a few creative and style-determining figures in every society, as decadent and ripe for dissolution.

They do not believe, however, that the times are bad, but only that they are out of joint. Their anxieties do not arise from problems of scarcity, deprivation, nor even political disorder. They are rather ontological anxieties rooted in the very perception of plenitude and superfluity. Their ontological anxieties, moreover, usually precede political disorder and provide an essential causative element in that disorder.

It has often been observed that Gibbon in *The Decline and Fall of the Roman Empire* dealt in a most unsatisfactory fashion with the concept of decadence. It was not, however, because the conception was unknown to him. Indeed, decadence was a great focus of eighteenth-century social and historical debate, the other side, as it were, of the eighteenth-century preoccupation with progress. Montesquieu, in *The Grandeur and the Decadence of the Romans,* had at least provoked the thought that the marks of grandeur need not always be signs of social health, and the eighteenth century, preoccupied as it was with the ideas of simplicity, innocence, and economy, held luxury to be the most socially fatal of all vices. Given these preoccupations it is surprising that Gibbon's analysis of the transformation of Rome's empire contains so little of the cant language of pessimism and is so inconclusive in its discussion of the causes of Rome's transformation. Every edition of Gibbon falls open of its own accord to his chapter "General Observations on the Fall of the Roman Empire in the West," in which he describes and explains in a summary fashion Rome's decline. It comes close to Ortega's concept of "plenitude," though, to be sure, it lacks Ortega's developmental sense.

> The rise of a city, which swelled into an empire, may deserve, as a singular prodigy, the reflection of a philosophic mind. But the decline of Rome was the natural and inevitable effect of immoderate greatness. Prosperity ripened the principle of decay; and the causes of destruction multiplied with the extent of conquest and, as soon as time or accident had removed the artificial supports, the stupendous fabric yielded to the pressure of its own weight. The story of its ruin is simple and obvious; and instead of inquiring why the Roman empire was destroyed, we should rather be surprised that it had subsisted so long....[16]

In short, Rome fell of its own weight, or as a less literate critic than Gibbon has observed, "When you'r up, you'r up, and there is nowhere else to go but down."

The notion of "plenitude" would no doubt have appealed to a generation that had read Voltaire's *Age of Louis XIV*, but those eighteenth-century historians lacked a vocabulary that would have enabled them to sharpen their perceptions. However, such problems belong to the concerns of historiography. What must interest us is that the eighteenth century, which felt itself Augustan and prosperous, powerful, enlightened, and creative as no previous age had been, should take the problem of decadence, decline, luxury, and superfluity so seriously. Nor will it do to explain the matter by saying that the age was only harking back to the quarrel between the ancients and the moderns that had animated the previous generation. The coexistence of ideas of prosperity and fulfillment with fears of decadence and decline is not so easily explained.[17]

Perhaps then, the preconditioning perception is not one of "plenitude" but rather one of superfluity. To return to Rilke's "Autumn Day," "Now God, is the time. It's been a big summer," catches the note of superfluity, of "too much," and suggests an autumnal fatigue as one stands in the warm sun on the verge of winter. The attack of Jean-Jacques Rousseau on the culture, prosperity, and luxury of his age is an attack upon superfluity, and the cultural revolution that he mounts is, like the cultural revolution of bourgeois radicals generally, a revolution of satiety rather than a revolution that has its origins in deprivation. The old order is attacked because it has provided too much rather than because it has provided too little. Of course, such revolutions of satiety are class phenomena and, unlike political revolutions, rarely cut across class lines.

The perception of decadence is frequently associated with strong feelings of satiety and superfluity, a satiety and superfluity that does not characterize the society as a whole but usually a narrow but socially determinative class. Man's evolutionary past has, as the ethologists have recently demonstrated, provided a considerable number of the determinants of human behavior. Is it not possible, even though the evidence is lacking, that historical environments characterized by superfluity are essentially incompatible with a human organism whose evolutionary development took place in the most extreme of marginal situations, where there was, in fact, never enough and where a little more or a little less meant the difference between survival and death? Such an explanation is at best a guess, but it is clear that superfluity produces ontological anxieties of the most acute kind characterized above all by a sense of decadence, disorder, drift, and guilt. It should come as no surprise, then, that historical situations which one portion of a society will regard as halcyon and the antechamber to utopia will be regarded by other elements in the same society as decadent and the vestibule to death. Seen in this light the perception of decadence is the price a society must pay for continued prosperity.

Of course such an explanation is not exhaustive and other, perhaps more important, factors play an important role in the perception of decadence. One of these, clearly, is the historicization of life and society that has taken place in the Western world. Eliade has called our attention to the preoccupation of the Western world with the problem and burden of history. He then adds:

> Let us now look at this passion for history from a standpoint outside our own cultural perspective. In many religions, and even in the folklore of European peoples, we have found a belief that, at the moment of death, man remembers all his past life down to the minutest details, and that he cannot die before having remembered and relived the whole of his personal history. Upon the screen of memory, the dying man once more reviews his past. Considered from this point of view, the passion for historiography in modern culture would be a sign portending his imminent death. Our Western civilization, before it foundered, would be for the last time remembering all its past, from protohistory until the total wars. The historiographical consciousness of Europe—which some have regarded as its highest title to lasting fame—would in fact be the supreme moment which precedes and announces death.[18]

Although Eliade does not use Hegel as an example, Hegel's dictum that "The owl of Minerva takes its flight at twilight" clearly demonstrates the close ties between historicism and the belief in a final historical consummation.

Desacralized time is the great problem for modern life and thought. The historical sense in Western society was sharpened in almost direct proportion to the degree in which society was secularized. Jerome Hamilton Buckley remarks appositely, "The appeal to time denied the sanction of eternity."[19] Time divorced from eternity must always be seen as defective and inadequate, unworthy and incomplete, and the effects of time as erosive and destructive. Things fall apart, men grow old, and institutions decay. One need not formulate the destructive character of secular time in the superficial sophistication of Henry Adams's reference to the second law of thermodynamics in order to come away from the study of private and public histories a convinced pessimist. Divorced from the eternal context that gives secular time its meaning, all human doing and making is devoid of meaning. With the secularization of time and history, meaning, once given to history by its eternal context, must now be discovered as immanent in history. If the meaning of history lies within the processes and unfolding of history itself then there is, indeed, no salvation from time.

Some strong-hearted men took courage from theories of history that supposed that the total movement of time was progressive and salvific; that the discontents and evils of the present moment were not to be compared with the glories that were to come. But most ordinary men, discontented with the present, were often unwilling, and more frequently thought themselves unable, to do anything now to assure a happier future later. "Why should I do anything for posterity; what's posterity ever done for me?" Hegelians, social Darwinists, and Marxists were alike in their devotion to a future that would make the depressing present meaningful, but there was an equal or greater number of historicists who perceived historical unfolding not as progressive and fulfilling but as a biological or systemic process that ended in defeat, failure, dissolution, dissipation of energies, and death. At the *fin de siècle,* theories of decadence based upon biology were nearly as numerous as theories of progress based on biology. Marxism, with its insistence on class decadence when a dominant class has at last exhausted all of its progressive and creative potentialities, did as much to propagate notions of historical decadence as the historical theories of the reactionary Right. Exhausted races, reactionary classes, and other potential occupants of the "dustbin of history" found little to cheer them in the progressive faith that the unfolding of desacralized history would ultimately cauterize and heal the wounds which time itself had made. The sadness of Oswald Spengler is the sadness of a man who has ceased to believe in the salvific processes of immanentized history. Spengler was the flower of the line that reaches back through Nietzsche and Burckhardt to Ernst von Lasaulx, rather than a uniquely creative man thinking his thought in isolation and without precedents.[20]

The sheer weight of history was in the course of the nineteenth century perceived as an unbearable burden. Increasingly all of life and culture was historicized. The medieval renaissance that was such an important aspect of romanticism was only one of the stylistic revivals that emerged as a result of the frantic search through past life and past styles for authenticity and creative potency. Even the most casual observer must have been struck by the incongruity between an age endlessly creative in its technical and scientific aspects but imitative and historistic in its art and value structure.

To Nietzsche the preoccupation with history was evidence of impotence, decadence, and death.[21] For him, the burden of the past was the single great reality of contemporary culture. "Man is always resisting the great and continually increasing weight of the past; it presses him down and bows his shoulders; he travels with a dark invisible burden that he can plausibly disown, and is only too glad to disown in converse with his fellows."[22]

More pointedly still he writes, "Historical culture is really an inherited grayness, and those who have borne its mark from childhood must believe instinctively in *the old age of mankind.* To old age belongs the old man's business of looking back and casting up his accounts, of seeking consolation in the memories of the past—in historical culture."[23]

Nietzsche sees this historicist preoccupation with a world grown old as a consequence of the secularization of medieval Christian eschatological ideas. "The *memento mori,* spoken to humanity as well as to the individual, was a sting that never ceased to pain, the crown of medieval knowledge and consciousness."[24] More important still as a source for the historicization of culture and the belief that mankind is living in some final era of consummation is Hegelian philosophy. "I believe that there has been no dangerous turning point in the progress of German culture in this century that has not been made more dangerous by the enormous and still living influence of this Hegelian philosophy. The belief that one is a latecomer in the world is, anyhow, harmful and degrading; but it must appear frightful and devastating when it raises our latecomer to a godhead. . . ."[25]

Moreover, Hegelianism is destructive, not only because it is in love with consummation and old age, but because the man who accustoms himself to genuflecting to the "world-process" will bow his head to every tyranny. In short, the age of history becomes the era of tyranny.[26]

No one in the *fin de siècle* period saw more clearly than Nietzsche the link between the perception of decadence, historicism, and the historicization of culture. One hundred years later those Nietzsche attacked with such assured genius still dominate the intellectual life of the Western world.[27]

The cure for decadence that Nietzsche offers in this essay of 1874 is both prophetic and instructive concerning the covert content of most decadence theories. Theories of decadence are usually if not always associated with youth movements and rejuvenatory efforts. *Renovatio* is the Janus-face of decadence. "Youth," Nietzsche instructs us in the final pages of his essay, will redeem culture and save humanity.

> And in this kingdom of youth I can cry Land! Land! Enough, and more than enough, of the wild voyage over dark strange seas, of eternal search and eternal disappointment! The coast is at last in sight. Whatever it be, we must land there, and the worst haven is better than tossing again in the hopeless waves of infinite skepticism. Let us hold fast by the land; we shall find the good harbors later and make the voyage easier for those who come after us.[28]

Youth, indeed, has become the great redemptive hope. However unclear its direction or its cultural program, youth, Nietzsche insists, possesses the power to reinvigorate society and to re-create culture precisely because it has jettisoned history.

> "Give me life, and I will soon make a culture out of it"—will be the cry of every man in this new generation, and they will all know each other by this cry. But who will give them this life?
>
> No god and no man will give it—only their own *youth*. Set this free, and you will set life free as well. For it only lay concealed, in a prison; it is not yet withered or dead—ask your own selves!
>
> But it is sick, this life that is set free, and must be healed. It suffers from many diseases, and not only from the memory of its chains. It suffers from the malady which I have spoken of, the *malady of history*."[29]

It is interesting to discover in Nietzsche's perception of decadence an anticipation and defense of the later youth movement. It was not altogether accidental that two decades later the youth movement drew so heavily upon Nietzsche's thought in rationalizing its own rather inchoate ideas.

However, in the 1870s few Germans read Nietzsche and he was unknown to the wider audience of informed Westerners. All of which, of course, did not mean that Nietzsche's pessimism and his reasons for that pessimism were not widespread. More important perhaps than the weight of secular history and the historicization of culture was the fact that the mystic capacity for regenerating time was lost when time was desacralized.

So long as time and history stood within the context of the eternal archaic society, its successors had ways in which to accomplish its regeneration. Time's erosion is the commonest of human perceptions.[30] Eliade writes:

> This need for a periodic regeneration seems to us of considerable significance in itself. Yet the examples that we shall presently adduce will show us something even more important, namely, that a periodic regeneration of time presupposes, in more or less explicit form—and especially in the historical civilizations—a new Creation, that is, a repetition of the cosmogonic act. And this conception of a periodic creation, i.e., of the cyclical regeneration of time, poses the problem of the abolition of history. . . .

It is the break with the eternal context of time, the desacralization of history, which poses enormous problems for a mankind that still, however, perceives the necessity to regenerate time and to restore the primal potencies. Either individuals and human societies abandon hope and live within the negativities of the void, or mankind secularizes the return to chaos and the regeneration of time that plays such an important role in archaic thought.

The secularization of time's regeneration usually takes the form of the institution of a "new" political order, the inauguration of a "new" era in human history, and the renovation and rejuvenation of mankind. Thus, the "Third Reich" is a thousand-year Reich, the beginning of another great cycle inaugurating an age that is "golden" at its inception. The "new" Soviet man and the "mutant type" of the age of expanded consciousness are both modeled on the innocent, unalienated, and potent humanity characteristic of regenerated time. Youth movements, pastoral idylls, and the dream of alienation abolished and innocence restored are all characteristic of the secularized attempt to restore time and regenerate potency. They are secularized attempts to deal with time's erosion and the burden of history.

More interesting still for the historical examination of the perception of decadence is the fact that the archaic myths all presuppose a period of decadence to usher in the beginning of a new and restored cycle of time. The appearance of Antichrist precedes and anticipates the Second Coming.[31] Regeneration and eschatology are linked in the most intimate fashion.[32] Speaking of the pre-Buddhistic Indian consciousness in its apprehension of the problem of time, Eliade writes:

> The conception of the four juga [ages] in fact contributes a new element: the explanation (and hence justification) of historical catastrophes, of the progressive decadence of humanity, biologically, sociologically, ethically, and spiritually.
>
> Time by the simple fact that it is duration, continually aggravates the condition of the cosmos and, by implication, the condition of man. . . .[33]

The return to chaos can be seen more explicitly if orgiastic behavior associated with the inauguration of the New Year is observed. Eliade's description of the Roman Saturnalia becomes in fact the classical description of the social phenomena of a "decadent era."

> Even if, as a result of successive calendar reforms, the Saturnalia finally no longer coincided with the end and the beginning of the year, they nevertheless continued to mark the abolition of all norms and, in their violence, to illustrate an overturning of

values (e.g., exchange of condition between masters and slaves, women treated as courtesans) and a general license, an orgiastic modality of society, in a word a reversion of all forms to indeterminate unity. The very locus appropriated to orgies among primitive peoples, preferably at the critical moment of harvest (when the seed was buried in the ground), confirms this symmetry between the dissolution of the "form" (here the seed) in the soil and that of "social forms" in the orgiastic chaos. On the vegetable as on the human plane, we are in the presence of a return to the primordial unity, to the inauguration of a "nocturnal regime in which limits, contours, distances, are indiscernible."[34]

This confusion of the orders, inversion of values, and return to social and cultural chaos has been built into the very fabric of Western historiography and political and cultural history. Aristotle's cycle of political forms, which terminates in regenerative anarchy, is repeated by Polybius and through Polybius mediated to Machiavelli. It reappears as a basic constituent of Vico's *New Science* and through Vico becomes one of the commonplaces of Romantic and neo-Romantic cultural criticism. There is not the least doubt that the symbolic world and the vocabulary of twentieth-century decadence harks back to the archaic myths. It is much more difficult to assert with certainty that any degree of self-consciousness in these matters exists in contemporary intellectuals who are preoccupied with theories of decadence.

Cyclical historical theories that account for cultural decadence as the onset of the final period in the life of a culture have been both influential and widespread in the recent past. These explanations have come largely from the Right and were given most complete expression by Oswald Spengler and in a modified form by Arnold Toynbee. It is important to point out once more that these expressions of pessimism were contemporary with interpretations of historical process that envisioned the onset of a golden age and the inauguration of utopia in the immediate future.

All perceptions of decadence, however, are not manifestations of the political Right. Herbert Marcuse in *One-Dimensional Man* offers a picture of Western society that is, according to his description, "decadent."[35] It is a picture that does not differ markedly from that offered by another Marxist, Michael Harrington, in *The Accidental Century,* and that Harrington characterizes as "decadent."[36] It ought not to surprise us to find the Left nearly equally as interested in the idea of decadence as the social and cultural theorists of the Right. The theory of class decadence has been an essential element in Marxism since the publication of the *Communist Manifesto.* More interesting is the fact that with Georg Lukacs, Herbert Marcuse, Michael Harrington, and many others, including every Soviet newspaper editor, the evidence offered to demonstrate the decadence of Western society is substantially the same evidence offered by the decadence theorists of the Right. That such agreement should exist poses a major historical and sociological problem. The fact that Right and Left theories of decadence and apocalyptic renewal are congruent has assisted in making it possible for members of the Left to move Right easily and without major ideological dislocations.[37] Thus, George Grosz depicts in stomach- and conscience-churning detail a decadent bourgeois society. At bottom most German social critics on the Right were not in fundamental disagreement with the observations Grosz made, though they confused the Communist artist as a cause with the effects that he reported.

This is not to suggest that there has not been the widest variety of meanings attached to the word "decadence."[38] Nor is it to suggest that there is even any agreement as to the primary evidences of or causative factors in decadence. The fundamental perception common to all theories of decadence is the notion that the currently existing configurations of culture and society are in a state of decay and dissolution and that the world as it is presently known is either dying or dead. Death and the iconography of death furnish the symbols to the decadent painter and poet and those periods of the past which have been haunted by feelings of impotence and senility are favorite subject matter for its historians and novelists. Marxist historians are particularly adept at bearing the corpse of bourgeois culture to the burning-ghats of class conflict and apocalyptic warfare. Their language is usually casual, as though in fact they are alluding to a commonly accepted and well-known fact, as in the following *aperçu* from George Lichtheim's history of Europe in the twentieth century: "Debussy arrived at similar results by a more complex route, against the background of a tired romanticism that had ceased to convey hope to a sick civilization, shadowing catastrophes yet to come."[39] The thought is muddled, the history is schlock-culture, and the sentence is totally lacking in syntax. None of this is important, however, as its impact derives from its relationship to poetry rather than its accuracy as history or its clarity as prose.

It is perhaps easier to see among the Marxists than it is the cultural critics of the Right the relationship between theories of decadence and the radical critique of society. All theories of decadence, from the prophetic denunciations of the Hebrew prophets to the literary wish-fulfillment of the Marxists, are a not so thinly disguised warrant for change.

Those theorists of decadence such as Maistre or Lasaulx who argue for a "restoration" of previous social and political forms are nearly always advocating social and political revolution, for the past that they seek to restore is a past that exists only in their imaginations.[40] These backward-looking utopias, whatever their validity as social criticism, are always falsifications of history.

Most theorists of decadence are, however, quite self-conscious innovators. Their perception of decadence is accompanied by a blueprint for regeneration or at least a program designed to arrest decay. The greatest symbolic painting of contemporary disorder is Picasso's *Guernica*. It is a powerful transformation of the manger scene at Bethlehem in which the promise of new life and the images of natural and cosmic order have been turned into terrified chaos and symbols of death. The ass and the ox have become symbols of frightened brutality and the angel of announcement has been transformed into the loveless and mystery-less electric lamp. Shepherds no longer adore but fall in panic, victims to the anguish that a modern Mary expresses in mourning her dead son. No single work of contemporary art so adequately depicts the wreckage of lives and culture by war in modern society or, indeed, the horror of a society that gives rise to such inhumanity. Instead of a new beginning Bethlehem becomes the symbol of the apocalypse.

But note something interesting. Picasso is not only portraying the end of a culture, he is also depicting the end of a style in art. His art tells us that the way in which artists have viewed and interpreted reality in the Western world since at least the Renaissance is dead. Art too is involved in the universal destruction. Critics have seen in *Guernica,* however, not an expression of hopelessness and pessimism so far as art is concerned but rather the affirmation of the "beginning of a new pictorial era." Sir Herbert Read quotes an essay by Juan Larres: "For when there is an end to the pitiless deluge of fire which has leveled to the ground the buildings of the ancient world, we shall see, outlined at the horizon, a new alliance of Heaven and Earth; within the pregnant round of the rainbow, a new Phoenix is preparing a rebirth in peace from the ashes to which *Guernica* has reduced all that was dead in painting."[41]

One of the most interesting aspects of theories of decadence is the fact that they are so often associated with notions of historical inevitability. They represent an abdication from human responsibility and a willingness, almost an eagerness, to be caught up in an enormous, uncontrollable process that lies beyond the possibilities of control through individual or collective action. While the hope of regeneration is an aspect of decadence theories that see history, the *mort main* of the past, as an intolerable burden, other theorists of decadence welcome the inevitability of apocalypse that the historical process in their theories comes to represent.

Wyndham Lewis, in his study of *Time and Western Man,* called the theorists of inevitable decadence "revolutionary simpletons" and "time children," and he recognized that the conception of time to which they sub-scribed had a profound influence upon both their cultural and political activity.[42] Romanticism, activism, the psychologization of all experience, and the bourgeois cult of left-wing and fascist revolution was, in Lewis's thought, closely connected to contemporary ideas about time.

They were also connected, Lewis believed, with the development of democracy in culture and politics. Enthusiasms for historical movements that are both revolutionary and inevitable flatter the mediocre participants in such movements into believing that they have become the motors of history, that they who were by nature and calling truly insignificant have become the hinge of fate and are an integral part of a process which is destined to reshape the world.

No doubt the enthusiasm of many fascists, Marxists, and bourgeois cul-tural revolutionaries for theories of inevitable and unarrestable decay is associated with their personal historical ambitions and their nearly reli-gious joy in being caught up in a movement that is so much larger, ampler, and potent than they are. The wave of the future is always attractive to those incapable of doing more than riding a rubber life-raft through the troubled waters of human history.

But perhaps there is something more than romanticism and democracy at work in the subscription to inevitable historical process. Perhaps there was, in the passive act of surrender to inevitable movements and processes, a thrill, a thrill to which intellectuals are often tempted.

Writing of Bertolt Brecht's association with communism, Otto Friedrich recently observed:

> One suspects that Brecht was drawn to Communism not just because of fighting in the streets, and not just because the radi-cals claimed to have a concrete program to deal with the eco-nomic crisis, but because Communism demanded the submis-sion of the individual to the organization, and because many intellectuals seem to find a peculiar kind of satisfaction in the act of submission. From *The Jungle of the Cities* to *The Measures Taken*, and on to *Galileo* and *Mother Courage*, Brecht, the radical, dramatized not revolt but stoicism and surrender.[43]

The very same observation could be made with even greater force about Oswald Spengler. Of Spengler, Wyndham Lewis wrote:

> He thinks, for instance, that he notices "The West" rapidly "de-clining"—and in any case it is about time it did; to satisfy the periodic principle, and to satisfy chronology, it is about *time* the

West "declined"! So he writes *The Decline of the West.* The last thing that it would ever occur to Spengler to do, even if he were able, would be to interfere with this process, to challenge *this historically fated* "Decline" for which he entertains the profoundest fatalistic respect. This fatalism should be particularly noted, for it characterizes most Time-thought. . . . With this you arrive at what is certainly the greatest paradox in the mass of time-doctrine taken as a whole: namely that, advertising itself as "creative," "evolutionary" and "progressive," it is yet the deadest system, productive of the least freedom that you could imagine.[44]

When the evidence is fairly assessed it is, however, very difficult to deny that certain eras are more orderly, creative, life-affirming, and buoyant than others, and that some eras bear the distinctive mark of misfortune and spiritual disease. One is always tempted to dismiss subjective agonies of any kind as the products of overly sophisticated and overwrought imaginations, and one must admit the role of imagination in all schemes of cultural pessimism. But troubled societies lack the philistine confidence necessary for ignoring the trumpets of the apocalypse. One's attitude is rather like that of a survivor of the London Blitz who hears a practice siren test. Maybe, just possibly, the sirens are announcing a real and unexpected raid. And so the marks of civic disorder and spiritual and cultural ill health, although they are as old as mankind, are in the present moment difficult to ignore and more difficult still to explain away.

Worlds do come to an end, though the world endures. Debates concerning eternal Rome must indeed have seemed academic when the Visigoths stood at the gates. Yet, from the standpoint of the historian, both perspectives were correct. Rome was eternal and Rome fell. St. Augustine, in spite of the decay and cultural rubbish that he saw piled so high everywhere about him, could discern a vitality and renewal that was hidden even from Gibbon, who replied to the *City of God* so unsuccessfully nearly fourteen hundred years later. It is the temporal perspective that ultimately determines the legitimacy of a theory of decadence or a doctrine of progress. As nations and as individuals men rarely assume as a group that their community and their society is moribund and that they are failed evolutionary experiments. Vitality finds such notions unacceptable. But individual men and social groups within historic societies have often felt themselves to be doomed and have occasionally put the impress of their gloomy vision, at least momentarily, on their societies.

Their perception of doom has usually been accurate. While the nation and the society survived, the individuals, their peculiar institutions, their groups and classes, their styles and the unique ambiance that characterized the minutiae of their daily lives—all that died, not suddenly and without warning, but after a long, lingering illness. Meanwhile other groups and institutions made their way forward and exerted their influence in the renewal of society. One need not offer metaphysical explanations, but the course of events fits easily into the pattern of the archaic myth of renewal and regeneration.

The world does not grow old, men do not grow effete, classes do not lose their potencies to creativity through nullifying internal contradictions. What happens is that dominant intellectual elites (establishments, as we prefer to call them these days) cease to project the established myths, cease to believe in themselves, and cease to compel belief on the part of the masses. One is tempted to argue that the perception of decadence is always accompanied by ideological exhaustion. The slogans and theological formulations that once produced nearly unanimous assent or at least a widespread consensus are questioned and found completely irrelevant. The social, political, religious, and cultural structures that had crystallized around these ideological or theological formulations suddenly find themselves in the process of dissolution and transformation.

From an objective standpoint—that is, a standpoint outside the threatened system, or a historical position outside the endangered era—this process of ideological and theological dissolution is not a sign of death but a sign rather of vitality and renewal. It is only when the process is perceived from the perspective of the dominant intellectual elite that it is conceived of as decadence and a sign of social disease and decay.

Periods of rapid cultural and social change transform in wholly unexpected ways basic myths and assumptions and the dominant elites who rationalize and organize social activity. In any period rising and falling individual and family fortunes lead some men to see the world as inherently unstable and doomed to disaster. *Apre moi le deluge* is a frame of mind in addition to the *bon mot* of Louis XV. Henry Adams and his brother Brooks perceived decadence everywhere, but its perception in the vigorous, dynamic, and prosperous America of the late nineteenth century was, of necessity, personal in its origins rather than social. Outmoded intellectual elites and decaying establishments have always filled history with their dying laments and the opalescent color of their futile lives.

> "Nowadays all the married men live like bachelors," said Lady
> Narborough, "and all the bachelors like married men."
> *"Fin de siècle,"* murmured Lord Henry.
> *"Fin du globe,"* answered his hostess.
> "I wish it were *fin du globe*," said Dorian Grey with a sigh.
> "Life is a great disappointment."

Bankrupt of every important idea except sensibility and subjectivity, these men of Florence and Siena after the black death, of the Burgundian and Venetian nobility, of eighteenth-century papal Rome, of the leading circles of French society on the eve of the revolution, of the late-nineteenth-century European literary intelligentsia, of the contemporary Left-liberal establishment, turn inward to the private worlds of "metaporn" and fantasy. But they also turn outward to "radical chic" and pseudorevolution. The flight to art and fantasy (because the interior world is more easily manipulated than that of everyday reality)—this flight is understandable.

The flight to art and fantasy by displaced elites is often accompanied by a movement away from ideological systems based on rationalized myths to utopian enthusiasms based on sentiments. Wyndham Lewis in a profound remark points out, "It is the same as in disbelief of the reality of life; the more absolute this disbelief is, as a formulated doctrine, the more the sensation of life (which we all experience impartially whatever our philosophy) will assume a unique importance."[45] An example, selected at random, must suffice. It is well known that extreme ritualism in religion often is characteristic of the unbelieving heart. Such indeed was the case with Walter Pater. In view of Pater's agnosticism his High Anglican ritualism seems if anything contradictory. Graham Hough asks, "What are we to make of all this?" and then does his best to explain the contradiction away.[46] But in fact it need not be explained away. For Pater the sentiment, the sensation of religion was more important than its truth, its reality.

The belief that "that's the way the world is" is replaced by the sentiment of "how nice it would be if that's the way the world were," or "we must make the world of recalcitrant reality conform itself to our vision of what the world should be." Reality, however, is a rather unbudgeable fixity, and so the sentimentalist (a man who often fancies himself a revolutionary) is distinguished not by his ability to transform the world, but rather by his lifestyle and the purity of his intentions. This emphasis upon lifestyle as a substitute for total transforming commitment or engagement with the environmental or social realities of one's time is a clear evidence of ideological or theological exhaustion. Genuine revolutionaries pay precious little attention to lifestyle. They have no time for striking poses. Behind this rejection of reality lies not a revolutionary consciousness nor manipulative sophistication but rather counterrevolutionary romanticism.[47]

"Everything that is deep wears a mask," Nietzsche once observed, to which he might have added with equal validity, "and everything that is superficial wears a disguise." The politics of an age of ideological dissolution, the religion of an age of theological decay, is a series of postures and poses; grand acting rather than elemental ritual. Its object is to fill the void of a lost faith. It is Easter Bunny Christianity and New Left revolution.

In this matter there is much historical evidence and many historical precedents. At the end of the medieval period, when the substance of faith and feudalism had given way, the response of the medieval aristocracy was very, shall we say, contemporary. Johan Huizinga writes of the Burgundian aristocracy of the fifteenth century,

> The life of aristocracies when they are still strong, though of small utility, tends to become an all-round game. In order to forget the painful imperfection of reality, the nobles turn to the continual illusion of a high and heroic life. They wear the mask of Lancelot and of Tristram. It is an amazing self-deception. The crying falsehood of it can only be borne by treating it with some amount of raillery. The whole chivalrous culture of the last centuries of the Middle Ages is marked by an unstable equilibrium between sentimentality and mockery. . . .[48]

At the Burgundian court there was incessant talk of great crusades, fervent vows, pledges, and grandiose plans, and no one, especially their authors, believed in them. They were a part of a lifestyle, or rather of a sentimental mood, rather than a commitment to action. The ironic hero, as Thomas Mann demonstrates over and over again, is the decadent hero par excellence. In order to dwell out of time in either Arcadia or Camelot one must, as did J. K. Huysmans's decadent hero of *A Rebours,* have resigned oneself to a stylish and mocking impotence. It is precisely at such moments and among such groups that sexual libertinism is confused with political revolution.

The confusion of metaporn and supersex with political revolution extends even to those who comment disparagingly on this development. Ronald Berman in an effort to explain the mood of America's intellectuals in the sixties notes this identification of sex and politics.[49]

> Consciousness has been made into an ethical value and sexuality into an ideological weapon. The most alarming thing about modern sexuality is not its heightened sensuality; indeed it is frigid, academic, and symbolic. The strained rendition of homosexual ecstasy—like the less ambivalent but equally didactic love of man and woman—has been in the largest sense political. Whether in the pages of the novelists or in the handbooks of the Bohemian left, sexuality has been unjoyous and serious. It has been radicalized so that we may see it as the sole property of the deserving Negro. It has been politicized, so that we may see it as the natural characteristic of the emancipated left. Perhaps

most ironically, it has been held up as the standard of natural
relationship and realism even as it has been turned into a kind
of religious formalism.

It is characteristic of the sexuality that Berman describes that it has lost
both its sexual and its political function and belongs to the world of make-
believe. It is, in fact, pretend revolution. In James Baldwin's *Fire Next Time*
all the themes of ideological exhaustion, political confusion, apocalyptic
yearning, and sexual inversion are combined and explored. The revolutionary landscape is no longer that of exterior reality but rather that of
consciousness. These "revolutionaries" do indeed have a program for the
regeneration of society. It is, however, an expression of their own feeling of
alienation and impotence, a dimension of their inability to transform reality. Wyndham Lewis displayed his usual prescience when he noted in 1928
that "[w]hen Revolution—that is simply the will to change and to spiritual
transformation—ceases to be itself, and passes over more and more completely into its mere propaganda and advertisement department, it is apt,
in the nature of things, to settle down in the neighborhood of sex, and to
make the moral disease its main lever."[50]

The connection between revolution and millennial and apocalyptic
enthusiasms has, in the recent past, been frequently noted.[51] When the world
is wholly spoiled, when innocence is wholly corrupted, some great apocalyptic or catastrophic event (such as a great earthquake, which will sink
California west of the Sierras into the Pacific) is called for to restore the
pristine purity of the natural order. Apocalyptic thought is not only the
refuge of the powerless and the oppressed. It is the refuge of the excluded,
the alienated, and the threatened generally. The outburst of millennial
thought in the French revolutionary and Napoleonic era clearly supports
this contention. The cultural and political importance of this movement is
revealed by the support it gained from intellectual figures such as Joseph
de Maistre and Franz von Baader and political leaders such as the Baroness
von Krudener and Czar Alexander.

In this instance apocalyptic enthusiasms were clearly generated by
threats to the political and social order, and the response was overly reactionary. Threatened elites may respond by recourse to revolutionary rhetoric
as well, especially when the threatened elite thinks of itself as the custo-
dian of a revolutionary tradition.

It should not be assumed that the sources of the perception of decadence are everywhere and always the same, or that the perception originates in the same individual type or social or cultural configuration. Indeed, decadence theories as critiques of society may originate in diametri-
cally opposed social groupings and may compliment and enhance one an-

other. Their validity rests almost exclusively in their self-fulfilling character. Every theory of decadence generates its penumbra of social disorder, which when associated with intellectual or cultural leadership may pose an acute social problem.

Nevertheless, the world endures, though private and social worlds may die. "But in history as it actually happens," R. G. Collingwood wrote, "there are no mere phenomena of decay: every decline is also a rise, and it is only the historian's personal failures of knowledge or sympathy—partly due to mere ignorance, partly to the preoccupations of his own practical life—that prevent him from seeing this double character, at once creative and destructive, of any historical process whatever."[52]

Part Two: Equality

Tonsor published several essays in *Modern Age* on the history of equality. Few of his readers knew, however, that Tonsor had proposed a book-length study of the idea—which, like his book on decadence, was never published. The chapters in this section contain three of the published essays from *Modern Age* as well as Tonsor's introduction to the unpublished manuscript. These essays began as course lectures and were later reshaped for publication. Tonsor's manuscript on equality drew interest from many publishers, but he never pursued its publication.

4

A Few Unequal and Preliminary Thoughts

No set of ideas has played a larger role in the history of the past two centuries than the notions we express through the use of the word "equality." But few ideas have been more complex, have meant more different things to more different men, have changed meaning as much over the course of time and through careless usage than the idea of equality. Few ideas are so rooted in historical experience and have been so transformed by the events of history as the idea of equality. The notion of equality is multiform and never abstract. Arithmetical measures of equality, with their indifference to human complexities, have been among the most important reasons the discussion of equality so often proves arid and unproductive. Philosophers, of course, continue to spin out their ethereal theories. They are interesting and not altogether unproductive, but as they lack a *Sitz im Leben* they are always less than satisfactory either as descriptions or as imperatives to action. To be sure, such abstract philosophical conceptions have played a very important role in stimulating men to action. Still, formulations of claims to equality such as those of John Rawls (to cite a modern instance) are usually claims made after the fact. They stand at a remove both from history and political theory. Historical development provides the arena in which the notions of equality manifest themselves, and only history can provide us with an understanding of equality and the influence it exerts in contemporary society.

How odd, then, that there has been no systematic historical exploration of the idea of equality in recent times.[1] There have been useful and interesting discussions of the idea of progress, and J. B. Bury, who first explored the idea of progress, wrote a *History of Freedom of Thought*. Lord Acton entertained the hope of writing a history of liberty in a day when men still thought it more important to be free than to be equal. How odd then that equality, an idea that historians have recognized as providing the key signature of the modern world, has not provoked a historical account.

Not only has equality no history but most contemporaries have neither a definition nor a satisfactory rationale for equality. Christopher Jencks noted this fact when he wrote in the first lines of his book, *Inequality: A Reassessment of the Effect of Family and Schooling in America*: "Most Americans say they believe in equality. But when pressed to explain what they mean by this, their definitions are usually full of contradictions."[2] Perhaps there is a relationship between the inability to say what one believes equality to be and the fact that historians have failed to provide an account of the development of the idea of equality.

Political scientists have long been in the habit of dividing works dealing with the organization of human society into two classes, the one called "prescriptive," the other "descriptive." The former seeks to establish an ideal pattern of politics, a prescription of how life in society ought to be. To a greater or a lesser extent all these normative formulations, from Plato's *Republic* to Aldous Huxley's *Island,* have been utopian. Their objective is not the description of how things are but rather what they might become, what they might be. Descriptive works in the field of politics, on the other hand, deal with what the writer conceives the political structure of society to be.

Now of course, few works in either social or political theory, ethics or government, are either wholly prescriptive or descriptive. Most works of prescriptive theory bear some important relationship to the facts, the realities of human existence in society. Aristotle studied 158 constitutions of cities before he wrote the *Politics,* and, moreover, he grounded the *Politics* in what he thought to be the observed realities of human nature. Marx and Engels held a theory concerning the condition of man in primitive society that colored and reinforced their notions of desirable social and political organization. The truth still holds, however, that there is a major gulf between the world of "is" and the world of "ought," and this gulf is one which is especially marked in the question of human equality.

When we look about us the fact is that we see very little equality. In a day when demands for equality are at an all-time high, when the rhetoric of equality is at a fever pitch, when the promise of equality is a staple of political life, the fact is that while certain kinds of equality have increased markedly over the past two centuries, there is, overall, little enough by way of genuine equality. A glance at Jencks's book, which is devoted to the educational dimensions of the problem, may serve as a slight indication of the scope of the situation. The chapter headings in his book read as follows: "Inequality in the Schools," "Inequality in Cognitive Skills," "Inequality in Educational Attainment," "Inequality in Occupational Status," "Income Inequality," and "Inequality in Job Satisfaction." These, I remind you, apply only to the field of education. We all know, however, that other important inequalities exist, including inequalities of beauty and strength;

Muhammad Ali is what he is and earns what he earns because of a peculiar combination of genetics, metabolism, training, and opportunity that can only be described as extraordinary. Genius in music and mathematics, even perfect pitch, are very unusual gifts that defy assertions of human equality. Wealth and ability, whether in business or sex, is something not everyone has, something in which, in fact, there is little human equality. Even intuitive understanding seems unevenly distributed. Our word *charisma,* which we use to describe those qualities of leadership that derive not from office or official position but seem rather to be a gift from the Gods (the Greek word *kharis* = grace, favor), is little understood by men, and the word itself suggests the inequalities associated with it. Finally, divine grace is inexplicably and unequally distributed, and the transcendent order as conceived by Jews and Christians would seem to be as inequalitarian as this-worldly human arrangements.

And so it is that our experience of human society is not an experience of equality but rather the experience of the most intense and pervasive inequality. Not only is inequality the mark of all contemporary societies, inequality, so far as the historian can discern, has characterized all the societies of the past. In fact, until the eighteenth century nearly all men regarded inequalities of wealth, status, and power as in the nature of things, an unalterable given. It was not until the eighteenth century and the great revolutions in America and France that any substantial number of men questioned inequality from the standpoint of political and social justice.[3] If one were to argue that the experience of history constitutes a prescriptive norm, then one must confront the fact that the great bulk of human experience constitutes an argument against equality.

Yet the founding fathers in the Declaration of Independence asserted, "We hold these truths to be self-evident; that all men are created equal and that they are endowed by their creator with certain inalienable rights. . . ." Surely there is a contradiction, then, in American political theory in particular and Western political theory as a whole, between descriptive and prescriptive social and political analysis. Did the founding fathers really mean that "all men are created equal"? And if so, "equal" in what sense? It is conceivable that the founding fathers meant something very different by the word "equality" than what we mean by that word. After all, the meanings of words may change in even so little a time as two centuries. This is especially true of words used by politicians.

Did the founding fathers mean by "created equal" the same thing that residents of south-central Illinois, the boyhood home of Abraham Lincoln, mean when they assert equality by saying, "I am just as good as anybody else"? It must be admitted that this is usually said as though there were some doubt in the matter. Often the statement is made even stronger, as for example, "I am just as good as those high muck-a-mucks." These statements are no doubt an appeal to the spirit of the Declaration of Independence, an appeal to the ideal of the universal equality of mankind. It is not clear, however, what precisely is meant by "good" ("I am just as good as anybody else"). "Good," surely, as it is so often used in this statement, is a curious and muddy word. If we compare this predicate adjective—good, better, best—we are immediately faced with meanings and consequences that the speakers I have just quoted never intended. Indeed, the speaker would be very reluctant to move from the good to the better and thence to the best. Moreover, "good," in whatever context we find it, is an evaluative term frequently ethical in its content. It is not a right nor a category bestowed on us indiscriminately by virtue of our humanity, even though it is often asserted that such is the case. Just as it has been asserted that all men are born "equal," so too it has been asserted that all men are born "good."

Of course there are sound reasons for this equation of the good with the equal, for all social stratification, as Talcott Parsons long ago pointed out, is a consequence of socially recognized values.[4] Stratification from high to low is simply a dramatic representation of the goals and values of any society. So it is that "the good" is always associated with "the best" and manifests itself in the formation of elites. Consequently, all claims to radical equality assert not only that all men are fundamentally the same in essence but that they are all equally good.

Talcott Parsons's analysis of social stratification and its relationship to value is not an altogether novel or original insight. Werner Jaeger, the great student of classical Greek culture, wrote in volume one of *Paideia: The Ideals of Greek Culture*:

> It is a fundamental fact in the history of culture that all higher
> civilization springs from the differentiation of social classes—a
> differentiation which is created by natural variations in physi-
> cal and mental capacity between man and man. . . . The nobility
> is the prime mover in forming a nation's culture. . . . All later
> culture, however high an intellectual level it may reach, and
> however greatly in content it may change, still bears the im-
> print of aristocratic origin. Culture is simply the aristocratic ideal
> of a nation, increasingly intellectualized.[5]

Both those who insist that all men are by nature equally "good" and those who, like Jaeger, believe that nature produces physical and mental capacities of transformative cultural and social importance only in certain men, appeal ultimately to "nature" as justification for their line of argumentation. This appeal to "nature" usually takes the form of an effort to discover the condition of man in the "state of nature" before his character and social institutions had been transformed by convention. "Nature" as the ultimate justification is the most powerful argument in the whole intellectual armory of both the equalitarians and the inequalitarians. The classical formulations of the state of nature as we find it in the Stoics, in Hobbes, in Locke, in Rousseau, in Marx-Engels, and in Freud are arrived at by stripping away the cultural and the conventional. Once we have subtracted the distinctively human, that is to say the conventional and the cultural, we are told, we arrive at the natural man. This is basically Rousseau's argument in his "Discourse on the Origin of Inequality among Men."

Rousseau believed that human inequalities were of two kinds: those originating in nature, such as inequalities of strength and intelligence, and those arising from convention, such as power and wealth. The former Rousseau believed to be of little importance, while the latter he thought were determinative in the society of his day.

This argument, once very convincing, has lost much of its luster if for no other reason than that it appears increasingly difficult to separate "nature" and "convention." They seem, in fact, to meld imperceptibly into one another, not indeed in a Lamarckian or Lysenkoist fashion, but in the complicated psychocultural relationships that have become the subject of study for the sociobiologists.[6] Much of human behavior, from altruism through aggression and the manifestation of sex roles, which was once thought to be culturally determined is now seen to be clearly evolutionary-genetic in origin and expression. Differences in status appear to be a *sine qua non* of both animal and human societies. Indeed, humanity would be unthinkable, purely in animal terms, without differentiation in degree and place.

Aside from the fascinating work of the sociobiologists, however, there are compelling reasons for our inability to distinguish between the "natural" and the "conventional." Our very humanity, our natures by any reasonable definition, is dependent upon what Rousseau would have described as a convention. Speech and language, demanding as they do the acceptance of rules common to the whole group, are by definition conventions and yet they are conventions that have become human nature itself.

Similarly, few would wish to dispute Aristotle's contention that man is by nature a political animal. It is difficult to conceive of man outside of society. Those interesting reports, legends, and studies of feral man all point clearly to the fact that man outside of human society is not man. That complex set of conventions and rules which make human society possible determine to a very considerable degree the "nature" of man.

Consequently, the useful distinction between nature and convention that dominated so much of the debate concerning inequality in the past appears now as invalid and false. The definition of "nature" and the "state of nature" in order to provide a satisfactory basis for argument will have to be less abstractly rational and far more empirical and historical.

I have made this excursion in order to indicate that "good," "nature," "convention," and "equality" are extraordinarily complex ideas. Most Americans, when they use the term "equality," mean equality before the law and equality of opportunity—or at least what they believe to be equality of opportunity. However, in Europe "equality" has generally been taken to mean equality of condition. These ideas have had a long and complicated history. It is a history far from its conclusion. What Plato said on the subject of equality has been echoed by nearly every defender of aristocracy since Plato's day. It should not surprise us that in the antebellum South the apologists for and defenders of slavery used arguments gleaned from Aristotle's *Politics* and quoted the famous Pauline dictum "Servants be subject to your masters" with relish. The vocabulary and the intellectual baggage of the "equality" debate reach back through history to the very origins of civilization. Few issues or ideas, not excluding theological notions, have had such a complex and convoluted career.

There is a natural temptation to turn away from complexity and to seek the simple and the pragmatic. Why bother with history when we all know our own minds and have achieved some clarity of opinion? The fact is that both history and the conflict of personal opinion and interest have ruled out the retreat to simplicity. We must study the idea of equality if for no other reason than that a familiarity with the complex vocabulary of equality is necessary to the debate.

Moreover, it is important to remember that equality is the fundamental idea that lies behind the American Revolution and the extraordinary society we in America have created. More important still, the idea of equality has transformed not only the political life and society of the United States but the life and society of the world. The notion of equality has been the single most potent revolutionary force the world has seen. Over and over again in the course of the past two hundred years mankind has defied tradition and status, blood and accumulated usage, in the hope of regenerating and recreating society. More often than not these revolutions have ended in failure and a diminution rather than an increase in equality.

Still, it is equality that has provided the dynamism, the moving force that has energized modern history. The great revolutions of the past two centuries have all been made in the name of equality, and even the counter-revolutionary movements of the Right have insisted on their own strange brand of equalitarianism, striking out at the traditional forms of status and the domination of the political order by wealth even while insisting on racial and biological inequality and the necessity of elite leadership and hierarchical structures.

In his introduction to *Democracy in America* (1835), Alexis de Tocqueville, having lived only through the American and French revolutions, was able to discern the importance of this great movement toward equality. He wrote:

> It is evident to all alike that a great democratic revolution is going on among us, but all do not look at it in the same light. To some it appears to be novel but accidental, and, as such they hope it may still be checked; to others [Tocqueville among them] it seems irresistible, because it is the most uniform, the most ancient, the most permanent tendency that is to be found in history.[7]

In the paragraphs that follow Tocqueville demonstrates in a cascade of words and historical examples that, "[i]n running over the pages of our history, we shall scarcely find a single great event of the last seven hundred years that has not promoted equality of condition."[8] He reminds us that this development has not only been true of France but rather that "[w]herever we look, we perceive the same revolution going on throughout the Christian world."[9]

> The various occurrences of national existence have everywhere turned to the advantage of democracy: all men have aided it by their exertions, both those who have intentionally labored in its cause and those who have served it unwittingly; those who have fought for it and even those who have declared themselves its opponents have all driven along in the same direction, have all labored to one end; some unknowingly and some despite themselves, all have been blind instruments in the hands of God.
>
> The gradual development of the principle of equality is, therefore, a providential fact. It has all the chief characteristics of such a fact: it is universal, it is lasting, it constantly eludes all human interference, and all events as well as all men contribute to its progress.
>
> Would it, then, be wise to imagine that a social movement the causes of which lie so far back can be checked by the efforts of one generation? Can it be believed that the democracy which has overthrown the feudal system and vanquished kings will retreat before tradesmen and capitalists? Will it stop now that it has grown so strong and its adversaries so weak?

If Tocqueville places in his introduction this most quotable tribute to providential determinism in a tone worthy of Karl Marx, he introduces enough doubts and qualifications in the remaining bulky two volumes to minimize the effect of most of what he has said. Tocqueville's fine print suggests that not equality but tyranny stands at the end of the long equalitarian revolution. To be sure, it is a tyranny that grows strong as the result of the claim to equality, but it is tyranny nonetheless. All the other side-effects of equality seem to Tocqueville bearable, if regrettable: the decay of the heroic, the decline of the arts and manners, the alienation and isolation of the individual. But the tyranny of the majority and the growth of the powers of the state, absorbing all the energies of society through the enlargement of the bureaucracy and the centralization of state power, is to Tocqueville an unbearable price for society to pay for the debatable benefits of equality.

Tocqueville's prophecy is confirmed by the developments of contemporary history. Those who believe the march of equality to be a providential and unstoppable movement need to be reminded that the really inevitable movement in the contemporary world has been the movement from limited and divided power to integral and centralized tyranny. No doubt claims to equality have played an important role in this development. Only Tocqueville could appreciate the full delicious irony of George Orwell's *Animal Farm*, in which "All animals are equal, but some animals are more equal than others."[10]

The fact is that equality can never be studied in abstraction as a single factor. In human societies equalities of various kinds are always lodged in an organic matrix of related and competing factors. Increases in a particular equality are always purchased at a social cost and involve the limitation of some alternative social value. This fact was, of course, apparent to Tocqueville, though it seems to have escaped some of the theorists of an abstract equality.

It is for this reason that a meaningful analysis of equality is necessarily a historical analysis.

5

Equality in the New Testament

It is not wide of the mark to argue that most religious revolutions derive at least a part of their dynamism from the fact that they are so conservative. Tradition and the past are not rejected but transcended. Even when Jesus attacks institutional religion he is very careful to distinguish in his attack the essential from the accidental, as when he says (Matthew 23:2–4), "The scribes and the Pharisees have established themselves in the place from which Moses used to teach; do what they tell you then, continue to observe what they tell you, but do not imitate their actions, for they tell you one thing and do another." Earlier in Matthew's account, he quotes Jesus as saying:

> Do not think that I have come to set aside the law and the prophets; I have not come to set them aside, but to bring them to perfection. Believe me, heaven and earth must disappear sooner than one jot, one flourish disappear from the law; it must all be accomplished. Whoever, then, sets aside one of these commandments, though it were the least, and teaches men to do the like, will be of least account in the kingdom of heaven; but the man who keeps them and teaches others to keep them will be accounted in the kingdom of heaven as the greatest. (Matthew 5:17–19)

Jesus' loyalty to the law was fundamental. However, it was, as Rudolph Bultmann describes it, a "radical obedience."[1] By this Bultmann means that it went beyond legalisms to demand, without quibbles or rationalizations, the surrender of the whole personality to the will of God. Legalism is not radical enough. It contents itself with the letter and is unable to penetrate to the spirit of God's commands. The legalistic loopholes and the ritualism of traditional Judaism must be, Jesus demands, transcended if man is to do the will of the Father and really observe the law. The Mosaic law concerning divorce and the interpretation Jesus gave it is quite instructive in the matter of Jesus' "radical obedience" to the law:

> Then the Pharisees came and put him to the test by asking him, whether it is right for a man to put away his wife. He answered them, "What command did Moses give you?" And they said, "Moses left a man free to put his wife away, if he gave her a writ of separation." Jesus answered them, "It was to suit your hard hearts that Moses wrote such a command as that; God from the first days of creation, made them man and woman. A man, therefore, will leave his father and mother and will cling to his wife, and the two will become one flesh. Why then, since they are no longer two, but one flesh, what God has joined, let no man put asunder." (Mark 10:2–10)

Thus, in Jesus' teaching, the law is at one and the same time reduced to its primal intention and given an inclusiveness that reaches beyond the particular case. In the explication that follows the Beatitudes in Matthew's Gospel, Jesus follows each command of the law with an expanded and sharpened interpretation: "You have heard that it was said. . . . But I tell you. . . ." In this "radicalization of obedience" to the law Jesus continues the prophetic tradition but goes well beyond it. It is also well to point out that the Dead Sea Scriptures offer no parallels to this radical interpretation of the law.

At the heart of Jesus' attitude towards the law are two fundamental ideas to which he returned again and again in his teaching: his messiahship, and the resolution of law and ritual in the demand that men show their love for one another as God has demonstrated his love for man.

In the past one hundred and fifty years Christology has been the focus of New Testament biblical criticism. The effort begun by David Friedrich Strauss to divorce the "Jesus of history" from the "Christ of theology" has been intellectual and theological busy work, as windy as it has been unproductive. By the beginning of the twentieth century it had become clear even to some theological liberals, such as Albert Schweitzer, that not only did Jesus claim to be messiah, but that unless this claim is recognized as the claim of Jesus and not the pious invention of the early Christian community we cannot understand Jesus' behavior as it is reported to us in the Gospels. No amount of textual and form criticism can dissolve the messianic claims that Jesus makes, divorce them from the context of apocalyptic and messianic anticipation that was the hallmark of the intertestamentary period, or reduce their significance for contemporary Christianity. "The time is fulfilled and the kingdom of God is at hand" (Mark 1:15).

Jesus' preaching of his eschatological messiahship was a matter of the greatest importance to the development of the social and political ideas of the early Christian church. Christian ideas of equality cannot be separated from their apocalyptic context. Christian political philosophy is nothing more than a series of prudential arrangements to govern the exterior of the life of the Christian in the time between the ages.

Unlike that of his Jewish contemporaries, the eschatological content of Jesus' teaching does not involve the national glorification of Israel, the reassembling of the twelve tribes, the reestablishment of peace and prosperity in Israel, or the projection of universal monarchy. Jesus' eschatology is based on a renunciation of the world and a transvaluation of the role of the messianic king: "My kingdom," said Jesus, "does not belong to this world. If my kingdom were one that belonged to this world, my servants would be fighting, to prevent my falling into the hands of the Jews; but no, my kingdom does not take its origin here" (John 18:36). The messianic king has come not in the role of the conquering Davidic monarch but in the role of Isaiah's "suffering servant." The kingdom, on the eve of whose establishment we stand, is left unidentified by Jesus. Similarly, he rejects the idea that we can know the day of its accomplishment. Unlike the prophesies of the Dead Sea Scriptures he neither gives dates nor describes with clarity the coming of the kingdom.[2]

In recent years it has been popular to argue that Jesus' teaching concerning the kingdom had a specific social and political content, indeed that it constitutes a "theology of liberation." Those who advance this thesis, in spite of the evidence of the New Testament, argue that Jesus came not only as spiritual savior but as social revolutionary whose purpose was the establishment of political and social justice and material well-being. No interpretation could be more remote from the facts as they are presented in the New Testament.

The discussion of the political and social intentions of the Gospels is not a recent matter. Already in 1911, when Christianity was in danger of becoming a pawn of politics and ideology, Ernst Troeltsch in his magisterial work *The Social Teaching of the Christian Churches* pointed out that the "message of the kingdom" was not an effort to perfect the mundane and the secular. Troeltsch wrote:

> Jesus began his public ministry, it is true, by proclaiming the kingdom of God as the great hope of Redemption, and this hope was cherished in the Early Christian Church as a whole; this "kingdom," however, was never regarded as a perfect social order to be created by the Power of God rather than the skill of man. The "Hope of the Kingdom" was not an attempt to con-

sole those who were suffering from social wrongs by promising
them happiness and compensation, perhaps even to the extent
of complete revolution, in another existence—an assurance given
by the Gospel to the destitute over against the dominant forces
of contemporary society. . . .[3]

Even the most superficial and cursory reading of the New Testament
reveals the complete absence of any concern with "the social question" or
with such ideological constructs as "class conflict."[4] Jesus simply did not
concern himself with the social and political structures of a world that
stood under God's judgment and was passing away. When Jesus says in
Matthew's gospel, "Why then give back to Caesar what is Caesar's and to
God what is God's" (22:21), he meant quite literally that the social, economic, and political arrangements of a world that stood on the threshold of
the last day was not a matter of ultimate concern to the believer.

Moreover, political, social, and economic concerns were not the moti-
vating factors in the conversion of Jew and Gentile to Christianity in the
early Christian world. If anything, there was in that world a general revulsion against politics and materialism and the strongest and most ardent
quest for spiritual salvation. The great time of troubles in classical civilization that marked the era in which Christianity was born led men to despair
of political solutions. It was the era of a vast "migration to the interior" in
that men sought in philosophy and religion the certitude, hope, and salvation that they could not discover in the politics of their time. Christianity
from Jesus to the present has involved a "renunciation of the world" rather
than a commitment to a doctrine of secular salvation.

All of which does not mean that Jesus and his disciples did not have a
social teaching or that they were unconcerned with the state of men living
in this world. No Old Testament prophet was so sharp and skillful in his
denunciation of the rich and the powerful or so respectful of the poor, the
humble, and the lowly as Jesus: "But woe unto you who are rich; you have
your comfort already. Woe unto you who are filled full; you shall be hun-
gry. Woe unto you who laugh now; you shall mourn and weep. Woe upon
you, when all men speak well of you; their fathers treated the false prophets no worse" (Luke 6:24–26). Jesus preaches a radical contempt for the
world not out of asceticism or a denial of the claims of the body but out of
a severity and austerity that prepare men for the coming of the kingdom.
Jesus welcomes a joyous affirmation of life but it must be within the context of "purity of heart" and preparation for the kingdom.

The highest motive within the eschatological community that he founds
is not political justice but love, love of God and love of neighbor, a love that
refuses to recognize the limitations and confines of mundane justice.[5] In

this, God's grace itself negates the human estimate of a rationally conceived justice and fills the measure even of the undeserving, as in the parable in Matthew (20: 1–16) of the workmen in the vineyard. In God alone are love and justice fully expressed and reconciled. Without love of God and neighbor one cannot penetrate to the spirit of the law and fulfill its demands. Jesus' radical obedience to the law is based on the fact that he transcends the human interpretation of the justice of the law and demands that the new covenant, the new bond of community be based on love and not human definitions of justice.

Humility and purity of motive are the characteristics of this new community. Humility is the response of the man who recognizes his littleness in the presence of God and his sinfulness against God and his fellow men. The equality among men that follows directly from this humility is not an equality based on political or legal definition. Christ demands that the community share its joys and pains, its benefits and its sufferings. Christ demands that the eternal take precedence over the temporal, that men be indifferent to material possessions and enjoyments, that they practice self-restraint and that their eyes be turned to the unseen and the everlasting rather than the superb and the transitory. Money, pomp, and status are all devalued, and humility, self-sacrifice, and service to one's fellow men are put in their place.

In short, gospel Christianity is radically otherworldly. Jesus simply did not discuss what the relationship of believers ought to be to culture and politics. He did not because he saw the community as one which had cut its ties with the world and lived in expectation of the coming of the kingdom. He did not discuss minimum wage legislation. He did say, "Consider the lilies of the field." If such is the case, equality as an idea determining political and social behavior in the world of culture and politics loses much of its meaning. Equality is central to the definition of man that early Christianity accepted, but it is an equality that lies beyond political definition. The mood and values of the gospel community survived in monasticism and the communitarianism of the sects. But Benedictines and Mennonites are alike in that they are communities that have abandoned the world.

Nevertheless, it is important to realize that the call to asceticism, humility, and the sharing of God's gifts, while not necessarily producing equality of status and equality of condition, moves strongly in that direction. The impact of such ideas on society as a whole, coming as they did from a small and despised group, was at first minimal, but after the third century AD the otherworldliness of Christianity began to have an important influence on this world. Christian behavior within and outside the community could not help but be translated into everyday political and cultural terms. Christianity tended to reduce differences between men and to put a pre-

mium on loving service to all, especially to the less fortunate and the oppressed. In a certain sense it is wrong to speak of equality as operative in
the values and structure of the Christian community. God's order and preferences are not simply egalitarian, rather they turn the values and the status
hierarchies of the world upside down, "for the last shall be first and the first
shall be last." The rich and the powerful find salvation difficult and the meek
and the poor are exalted. This inverted status structure is Mary's explanation of God's choice of herself as an instrument in his plan of salvation:

> He has mercy upon those who fear him, from generation to gen-
> eration; he has done valiantly with the strength of his arm, driv-
> ing the proud astray in the conceit of their hearts; he has put
> down the mighty from their seat, and exalted the lowly; he has
> filled the hungry with good things, and sent the rich away empty
> handed. He has protected his servant Israel, keeping his merci-
> ful design in remembrance, according to our forefathers,
> Abraham and his posterity for evermore. (Luke 1:50–55)

Finally when we consider the matter of sexual equality, we can see clearly
what a transforming influence Christianity had on human attitudes. To be
sure, the Old Testament is filled with extraordinary women; Sarah, Miriam,
Ruth, Judith, and Esther among them, and the women of the New Testament are not different in kind. However, the New Testament does include
more extraordinary women in a shorter period of time, and they play a
most important role in the foundation of the Christian community. That
role did not diminish with the passage of time, and Mary and her cult assumed in the church a position only slightly inferior to that of Jesus.

It was quite natural that, even though the values of gospel Christianity
were transcultural and transpolitical, they would impinge on and influence
the non-Christian community, for the Christian community, even in its
most extreme expressions, such as the hermit monastics of Egypt, remained
embedded in culture and politics.

It is clear that for many within the Christian community the great events
in the life of Jesus constituted "a realized eschatology."[6] Time had been
fulfilled, the messiah had come, and the great events of his life had transformed the character of human existence. One thing yet remained. The
second coming of the Lord would finally draw history to a close and usher
in the kingdom of God. For these believers, and the Apostle Paul is the
chief among them, the decisive events had already taken place. The last
days pale into insignificance in comparison with the events related in the
gospel narratives. There is a "meanwhile" that intervenes between the resurrection and ascension of Jesus and his triumphant return at the end of

time. This "meanwhile," even for those communities of withdrawal from the world, is filled with and dominated by a culture that is partially or even wholly non-Christian in its values.

A considerable portion of the community, however, expected an immediate end of time or at least believed that the end would be an event in the very near future. The Apostle John in the Book of Revelation and in his First Epistle articulates this hope. This radical Christian otherworldliness and expectation of the immediate dawning of the eschatological era has always involved a particular attitude toward time, culture, and politics. For these groups there is in fact no "meanwhile." John says repeatedly that the Christian community must live in the knowledge that the end of time is at hand: "My sons, this is the last age of time. You have been told that Antichrist must needs come; and even now, to prove to us that this is the last stage of time, many Antichrists have appeared" (1 John 2:18). "The world," by which John means society outside the church, must be rejected and abandoned. "Do not bestow your love on the world, and what the world has to offer; the lover of this world has no love of the Father in him. What does the world offer? Only gratification of corrupt nature, gratification of the eye, the empty pomp of living; these things take their being from the world, not from the Father" (1 John 2:15–16). "The world" lies about us in the grip of evil (1 John 5:19). For these members of the community of withdrawal there can be no discussion of life in the world or of participation in its secular concerns. This has been one of the most active, continuous, and dynamic groups within the whole of Christian history. To a greater or lesser extent the hermits and monastics have belonged to this tradition—Tertullian is one of the great exponents of its attitudes, and the sects, particularly the millenarian sects of the post-Reformation period, have lived in its tradition. The tradition is both anticultural and antipolitical.

A much larger group within the Christian community has concerned itself with its relationship to the world in the "meanwhile" between the events of Christ's life, death, and resurrection and the end of time. For two thousand years the great bulk of the Christian community has lived with the problem of what to do while waiting for the apocalypse.

In the generation after the death of Jesus one of the most important concerns of his disciples was the translation of his teachings into both a coherent theology and a coherent social program. The development of the institutional church as we find it described historically in the Acts of the Apostles is accompanied by a wide-ranging discussion as to the nature of the Christian community and the relationship of the community to the politics and the society in which it is embedded. Clearly, opinion among the disciples differed as to the stance the individual Christian and the Christian community ought to adopt toward the world.

C. H. Dodd draws attention to the familiar observation that "there is a certain tension or even contradiction between ethics and eschatology."[7] No doubt, he adds, it is possible to defend eschatology from the charge of neglecting ethics. Those who wait in expectation will want to be ready, as were the seven wise virgins who awaited the bridegroom. Still, it is true that the emphasis on eschatology tends to devalue the present and minimize, if not negate, attention to culture, the claims of society, and the human need and desire to participate in the everyday world. When the eschatological moment is defined and concretized as it is in the Book of Revelation there is little incentive to action or to reshape and reform the world.

So long as a distinction between the two comings of Christ had not been clearly made, the doctrinal, ethical, and cultural implications of the distinction between "already" and "not yet" could not be drawn.[8] As Jaroslav Pelikan observes, "once the dialectic of already/not yet is permitted to emerge from the texts, the magnitude of the change may become visible. It was nothing less than the decisive shift from the categories of cosmic drama to those of being, from the Revelation of St. John the Divine to the creed of the Council of Nicea."

If the emphasis on cosmic eschatology is most clearly represented in The Book of Revelation and St. John's epistles, the recognition of the "not yet" of the second triumphant coming of Christ and an accommodation with the world is to be seen most clearly in St. Paul's epistles and the Book of Acts. In Acts, which has sometimes been called "the Gospel of the Holy Spirit," Luke argues that the Spirit of God—the comforter, the sign that the new age has already dawned, the Paraclete sent by Jesus—moves and is active within the church, restoring and re-creating a sin-disordered mankind. The great work of restoration is already in progress even before the final apocalypse. The church, in the world, has become the vehicle of the restorative and saving work of the Holy Spirit. In a very real sense the church is the messianic community and the restoration of the covenant community, but it is now also the community of fulfillment in which the consequences of the Redemption and the gift of the spirit are manifest. Apocalyptic expectation is not abandoned, rather it is deemphasized and merged in the theological and organizational concerns of the community.

The Apostle Paul, who looms so largely in the Book of Acts, provides in his letters a commentary that illuminates the nature of this shift in emphasis. It must be asserted once more that Paul and Luke have not abandoned the expectation of the Second Coming in the near future, rather they have shifted their emphasis to the here and now and the immediate effects that the events of Christ's birth, death, and resurrection have on the individual and the community. For those who believe that history will be rolled up as a scroll immediately and that Christ is on the point of returning in glory to judge the world, organization, theology, and even ethics are meaningless. For them the great hope and the great emphasis is on an event that is to take place in the immediate future. For others, such as Paul, the great event has already taken place, and Christ's second coming will simply be the final act in a drama already well toward its conclusion. These two sets of attitudes had very important consequences for the social and political attitudes of Christians.

Paul's thought must be seen as an accommodation and not a synthesis. The followers of Christ live "in the flesh" but not "after the flesh." Christianity remains for Paul transcultural and transpolitical even though the Christian lives in the world of culture and the world of politics. Paul could claim, not without a touch of pride, it seems to me, that he was a citizen of Rome (Acts 22:26–30), although in contrast he would assert: "All you who have been baptized in Christ's name have put on the person of Christ; no more Jew or Gentile, no more slave or freeman, no more male or female, you are all one person in Jesus Christ" (Galatians, 3:27–28). He recognizes the needs of nature even while he asserts: "Thus, brethren, nature has no longer any claim upon us, that we should live the life of nature. If you live a life of nature, you are marked out for death; if you mortify the ways of nature through the power of the spirit, you will have life" (Romans 8: 12–13).

As with the teaching of Jesus so in the teaching of Paul the world is not so much condemned as it is transcended and transvalued. Nature, by the infusion of grace, is made to serve a supernatural purpose, and everything becomes acceptable that is "just, pure, lovely, of good report, of any virtue or any praise."

No doubt many of the teachings of St. Paul are related to ideas current in the Greek philosophy of his day.[9] His conception of asceticism, of organicism, his discussions of nature and natural law all have a close relationship to contemporary Greek thought. However, the differences are greater than the similarities. Paul's sense of the pervasiveness of sin in all human endeavor, even within the church, and his belief in the Redemption as the only path to human and cosmic salvation is strikingly different from the thought-patterns of Greek humanism. Greek thought, while it provides some of the language in Paul's letters, does not become a force until the century after Paul. Paul develops neither the teaching of an order of nature that has its source in the creator God and can be known through right reason, nor the idea that through the ordering and creative action of the Holy Spirit all culture participates in God's creative and conserving activity.

For Paul, the political and social order are gifts from God—institutions that arrest the tendencies to degeneracy in an unchecked nature. They possess no intrinsic merit and indeed they may become a snare for those who are insufficiently Christocentric. Paul's accommodation of the realms of nature and supernature, consequently, maintains the division between the two. This is a position which was to have enormous consequences for the development of political and social theory in the history of Western society.

The object of the social and political order, of ethics and the internal organization of the church, is negative. Its purpose is neither to secure natural happiness nor salvation but rather to maintain the perishable fabric of human existence until death shall usher the Christian into a transnatural realm. All arrangements that are a part of this social and political order are consequently temporary and have of themselves no intrinsic value.

Paul, like Jesus before him, is both radical and conservative. His claims of equality among men in the sight of God are absolute. Again and again he admonishes his readers that within the Christian community there can be no distinctions of worth or worthiness. "We too, all of us, have been baptized into a single body by the power of a single Spirit, Jews and Greeks, slaves and free men alike; we have all been given to drink at a single source, the one Spirit" (I Corinthians 12:13–14). "There are no human preferences with God" (Romans 2:11). Tribes and races, slaves and free men, women and men are all equal before God.

This equality is not simply the negative equality of universal human unworthiness in the sight of God, as Ernst Troeltsch so elaborately argued.[11] Rather, it is a consequence of Paul's Christ-mysticism. Paul argues that unworthy and sinful men are baptized into Christ's mystical body and become members of that body. From unworthiness they are raised to the status of ultimate value. Men put off the isolation and alienation of sin, the individualism and egotism of nature when they are baptized, thereby gaining for themselves a new corporate identity. For Paul, the recognition of universal unworthiness is important not as a source of equality but because it serves to destroy a false pride of person and of place and to prepare men for merging into the corporate identity of Christ.

When the doctrine of universal unworthiness, however, is associated with the doctrine of election, as it is in Troeltsch and in Protestant thought in general, it tends to distort Paul's Christ-mysticism and introduce a new and very important source of human inequality. The grace of God is the source of all human equality, mediated to mankind as a whole in Christ, in the church and in the sacraments. All share equally in God's love and glory, and man's claim to this love and glory is not as a consequence of nature or works or status, but rather by the appropriation of Christ's reconciling sacrifice to the Father. Christ takes on the status of a slave and suffers a slave's death in order to win for mankind a transmundane glory. As Christ shared all things with mankind, so men are called to share all with their fellow men. The sacraments and the life of the Christian community, as Paul sees it, are corporate in nature, and through them men and women acknowledge their equality in the organic unity of Christ's mystical body.

However, since grace is the source of this equality is it not possible that God may distribute that grace unequally, that he may predestine some for his love eternally and others he may reject out of hand? In this view of grace, so important in the Calvinist tradition, inequality is not something that originates with man but is rather the consequence of God's choice, of God's election. Paul argues that God gives special grace to some men and to all men grace sufficient to their need. Love stands at the center of Paul's teaching as it was later to be central to Luther's, and it is a love that manifests itself in the miracle of grace freely given that makes faith possible. As Troeltsch correctly points out, for Paul, while God's will

> sets before itself the goal of goodness and grace, the unequal distribution of the calling will presumably relate only to the distribution of destinies in relation with the history of salvation, it will only mean an "earlier" or a "later," a longer or a shorter period of being given over to error and sin; finally, all will be gathered home, and God will be all in all. This is how in his [Paul's] own mind he accounts for the destiny of his people, for the apparent rejection of Israel.[12]

If, however, one imposes an extreme predestinarian interpretation on Paul's words, these words have enormous importance for the idea of inequality. As Max Weber was later to argue, the Calvinist conception of election was to play a major role in the development of capitalism and to exert great influence on the politics of Calvinist communities and states.

Paul's Christ-mysticism and organic corporatism provide the justification for the social structure that he finds in the Christian community. His language may have Stoic echoes in it,[13] but the social structure he defends is older than Christianity itself and has parallels in the community of the Dead Sea Scrolls. Paul never abandoned the eschatological hope. However, he knew that life of necessity had to continue in the "meanwhile." He says of himself: "I long to have done with it [life], and be with Christ, a better thing, much more than a better thing; and yet, for your sakes, that I should wait in the body is more urgent still" (Philippians 1:23–24). While the whole church "waits in the body," the church requires not only an organizational structure but also a theology of social order.

It should not surprise us that while Paul's conception of grace is radical his social theory is conservative. He combines, both in the church and in civil society, the teaching of radical equality with an emphasis on hierarchical structure, authority, cooperation, and obedience. He does so because these, regardless of theology, hierarchy, and authority, are the *sine qua non* of social order. Paul writes his missionary communities repeatedly warning them against those disruptive anarchic, antinomian tendencies which threaten to dissolve the community. Not only the sins of the flesh but social disorganization and corrupt doctrine threaten the Christian community in the first generation after the Lord's life on earth.

The possibility of combining equality with hierarchy has been the basis of the social organization of the church for the past two thousand years. The baptismal charism of the priesthood of believers does not in any way abolish the necessity for an ordered and hierarchically organized clergy.[14] Paul writes:

> The body, after all, consists not of one again but of many; if the foot should say, I am not the hand, and therefore I do not belong to the body, does it belong to the body any the less for that? . . . As it is God has given each one of them its own position in the body, as he would. If the whole were one single organ, what would become of the body? Instead of which, we have a multitude of organs, and one body. . . . Thus God has established a harmony in the body, giving special honor to that which needed it most. . . . And you are Christ's body, organs of it depending upon each other. God has given us different positions in the Church; apostles first, then prophets, and thirdly teachers; then come miraculous powers, then gifts of healing, works of mercy, the management of affairs, speaking with different tongues, and interpreting prophecy. Are all of us apostles, all prophets, all teachers? Have all miraculous powers, or gifts of healing? Can all speak with tongues, can all interpret? (I Corinthians 12:14–31)

Just as differences of office within the church are based on function, so sexual distinctions as to role are based upon functions. Here again hierarchy and equality are harmonized. What today may seem to us sexist language in Paul is more accurately viewed as the language of liberation, in that Paul claims for womankind rights that were hers by reason of equality and were not hers either in the Jewish tradition or in classical culture. Above all, Paul casts over all human relationships the cover of love so that subject and object outgrow their human limitations and ego impulses and are transformed by charity. Yes, Paul argues that women are different from men and in the marriage bond should be subject to man's authority. Yes, Paul urges women to play a subordinate role in the church and insists that they maintain a seemly dignity and modesty. This, however, is not a reflection of inequality but rather a distinction of function and is based on mutual respect and concern. Just so, parent-child relationships are relationships of mutual respect (Ephesians 6:1–5).

It is interesting that in Ephesians Paul moves from speaking about parent-child relationships to a discussion of master-slave relationships. Like the Jew and Greek of his day, Paul considered the slave an integral part of the household, and here too the relationship was determined by function and was, Paul urged, to be governed by love and mutual charity.

> You who are slaves, give your human masters the obedience you owe to Christ, in anxious fear, single-mindedly; not with that show of service which tries to win human favor, but in the character of Christ's slaves, who do what is God's will with all their heart. Yours must be a slavery of love, not to men, but to the Lord; you know well that each of us, slave or free, will be repaid by the Lord for every task well done. And you who are masters, deal with them accordingly; there is no need to threaten them; you know well enough that they have a Master in heaven, who makes no distinction between man and man. (Ephesians 6:5–10)

The final line of the above verses drives home the essence of Paul's social teaching: distinction in role and function, authority exercised under God's direction, and absolute equality. Here we should draw attention to the distinction Paul makes between relative and absolute goods and relative and absolute evils. The commitment to the absolute good (the love of God) is fundamental. The pursuit of relative and subordinate goods insofar as they contribute to the attainment of the absolute good is not only admissible but desirable: "In eating, in drinking, in all that you do, do everything for God's glory" (I Corinthians 10:31). Evil, too, according to Paul, falls into these two categories. Absolute evil, sin, must be avoided, relative evils that are the consequence of man's fallen condition or the given of a particular social structure, such as slavery, are to be tolerated either because they are inescapable or because they are a part of the divinely instituted social order given by God for the preservation and protection of mankind.

All civil authority possesses this divine mandate. One must remember that Paul is talking about the Roman state, which will eventually execute him. Here is what he says:

Every soul must be submissive to its lawful superiors; authority comes from God only, and all authorities that hold sway are of his ordinance. Thus the man who opposes authority is a rebel against the ordinance of God, and rebels secure their own condemnation. A good conscience has no need to go in fear of the magistrate, as a bad conscience does. If thou wouldst be free from the fear of authority, do right, and thou shalt win its approval; the magistrate is God's minister, working for the good. Only if thou dost wrong, needst thou be afraid; it is not for nothing that he bears a sword; he is God's minister still, to inflict punishment on the wrong-doers. Thou must needs, then, be submissive not only for the fear of punishment, but in conscience. It is for this same reason that you pay taxes; magistrates are in God's service, and must give all their time to it. . . . (Romans 13:1–8)

The arrangements of civil society are interim arrangements. They, like the structured hierarchy of the church, provide an order for the "meanwhile." We should note that Paul follows the above passage concerning obedience to civil authority with a discourse on the nearness of the last days.

The New Testament is thus a further development and radicalization of the idea of equality found in the Old Testament. The church has become the new covenant community, the covenant community of early Israel restored. It continues the equalitarian tradition of early Israel and of the Jewish eschatological communities but it universalizes that tradition and transforms the old law into the new law of love. Because it is transpolitical and transcultural it behaves with conservative indifference to human political and social institutions, seeing in them a manifestation of God's providential order. Thus Christianity, formed in the school of the New Testament, has created a series of orders that while radically equalitarian have been also hierarchical, reverential to authority, and socially conservative.

6

The New Natural Law and
the Problem of Equality

An appeal to the condition of man in the state of nature has always been among the most powerful arguments pro or con concerning equality. "Doing what comes naturally" is the conclusive argument in support of all human behavior. For theists the argument from nature has usually borne the stamp of divine approval, for such behavior has its origin "in nature and nature's God." To prove that an action is natural is to demonstrate that it is licit. All of the great theoretical formulations of the idea of human equality or inequality from the Greeks to Freud have appealed to the condition of man in the state of nature as their ultimate justification.

It is important to note too that all the classic formulations of the "state of nature," with the exception of Freud's, stem from the pre-Darwinian era. They are often formulated in terms of the myth of the age of gold, when, as Virgil predicts in the Golden Eclogue, "the goats, unshepherded, will make for home with udders full of milk, and the ox will not be frightened of the lion, for all his might." Alternatively, they are imperfect inductions based on faulty or incomplete ethnological evidence. Even after the discovery of the New World the image of man in the state of nature continued to be heavily idealized and romanticized.[1] When, in the seventeenth and eighteenth centuries, primitive man was closely observed, the sources of his behavior were ill understood and faulty interpretation of the evidence often produced a picture as inaccurate as that produced by idealization and romanticism.

Most of these theoretical reconstructions of the condition of man in the state of nature posited a benevolent and nonaggressive human nature living in a state of equality, virtue, and abundance. Even when the equality was a negative equality—that is, even when mankind was seen as equally degraded, depraved, or sinful—these inherent weaknesses of condition gave no one a real advantage over another.

Darwinism, from the date of the publication of *On the Origin of Species* on November 24, 1859, to the present, has transformed both our conception of man in the state of nature and our knowledge of what "human nature" is and how it came to be. The easy simplicities of earlier views have been contested and abandoned, and although "Darwinism" in its many formulations was from the outset filled with scientific controversy, a new conception of human nature and of "natural law" gradually emerged.

Although the theory of evolution through natural selection is over a century old, the earlier ideas of a harmonious and nonaggressive human nature not only remained intact but continued to dominate the social sciences. As late as the 1960s, Donald Symons remarks,

> the chimpanzee (the customary model for early man) was a peace-loving, promiscuous, Rousseauian ape, and students of human evolution emphasized tool-use cooperation, hunting, language and "innate" needs for long-lasting, intimate relationships. Today, however, the chimpanzee is a murderous, cannibalistic, territorial, sexually jealous, Hobbesian ape; sociobiologists promote a cynical view of human life; and an evolutionary perspective on human beings as well as the concept of human nature are intensely controversial.[2]

This fundamental shift in conceptions of "human nature" is of the greatest importance for the debate concerning equality.

When Darwin published *On the Origin of Species* he dealt with the evolution of organic forms generally and except for a few cryptic allusions he made no reference to the evolution of man. Nonetheless, his essay would have had a tremendous impact on the idea of equality even had Darwin not followed its publication with a second essay, *The Descent of Man, and Selection in Relation to Sex*, on February 24, 1871. The earlier book, taken by itself, would have been important because it accounted for the development of animal species in terms of variation and the impact of the environment in sorting out those biological differences which in a particular environment gave a particular animal an advantage in the struggle for survival. The theoretical emphasis in Darwin's explanation of organic development lay not with the group, or harmony, cooperation, and a fixed, determined nature characterized by a rough equality of abilities and predispositions. Rather, Darwin emphasized surprising and sometimes extraordinary differences in biological makeup, differences that made for important inequalities between individuals and groups. His emphasis on struggle and conflict flew in the face of the theories of natural harmony and goodness, of cooperation and balance, that dominated the thought of most previous biological and social theorists. After Darwin, conceptions of an equality rooted in "human nature" lost their commanding position in Western thought.

The revolution, however, did not halt with the general application of evolutionary theory to organic development. In *The Descent of Man,* Darwin applied his evolutionary theories to humans in an effort to explain their origins and development. Darwin himself explained his objectives in the introduction: "The sole object of this work is to consider, firstly, whether man, like every other species, is descended from some pre-existing form; secondly, the manner of his development; and thirdly, the value of the differences between the so-called races of man...."[3] By emphasizing the continuum that existed between man and the other animal species, Darwin made possible a genuine science of man based on empirical rather than wholly theoretical material. The implication is clear that the same dynamics which shaped and transformed the lower animals were also causative forces in man's development.

Because Darwin observed, reported, and even emphasized the role of cooperation and what some sociobiologists have come to call "altruism" in evolutionary development, it has been argued that Darwin was no "social Darwinist," that, in short, Darwin refused to apply the principles of human biological evolution to the development of society. Ashley Montagu, among many others, has argued that Darwin was "not a muscular Darwinist" (whatever that imprecise description means).[4] Montagu argues that Darwin's theory had the misfortune of being born at the wrong time; that Tennyson had already colored "Nature, red in tooth and claw," and that in a world filled with conflict and in which the "dog-eat-dog" philosophy was widely held, it was easy to misunderstand Darwin's key phrases—"the warfare of nature," "the struggle for survival," "competition," and "the survival of the fittest"—when they appeared so frequently in the *Origin of Species.* But Montagu goes on to argue that in *The Descent of Man* "Darwin endeavors to show that cooperation, the 'social instincts,' love, the emotion of sympathy, of community, were principal factors in the evolution of man as a human being. It is this important aspect of his argument that has been so widely overlooked...."[5]

Any close reading of Darwin will not permit the total acceptance of Montagu's views. While not entirely incorrect, they must be qualified and footnoted, for they obscure the issues and questions that had arisen in the mind of Darwin himself. While Darwin, to be sure, did stress such elements in man's social behavior as cooperation, love, morality, and patriotism, he also wrote in *The Descent of Man*:

> With savages, the weak in body and mind are soon eliminated;
> and those that survive commonly exhibit a vigorous state of health.

We civilized men, on the other hand, do our utmost to check the process of elimination; we build asylums for the imbecile, the maimed, and the sick; we institute poor laws; and our medical men exert their utmost skill to save the life of everyone to the last moment. There is reason to believe that vaccination has preserved thousands, who from a weak constitution would formerly have succumbed to small-pox. Thus the weak members of civilized societies propagate their kind. No one who has attended to the breeding of domestic animals will doubt that this must be highly injurious to the race of man. It is surprising how soon a want of care, or care wrongly directed, leads to the degeneration of a domestic race; but excepting in the case of man himself, hardly anyone is so ignorant as to allow his worst animals to breed.[6]

A catalogue might be made of Darwin's smug but worried concerns regarding inferior races, inferior morals, inferior religions, and the absence in many groups of any enthusiasm for the evolutionary upward path. To be sure, Darwin's observations are more guarded and different in kind from those made by his contemporary, Herbert Spencer. That, perhaps, is due chiefly to the fact that Spencer was a sociologist rather than a biologist.

For Darwin there was an implicit difficulty in his evolutionary theory. The mechanisms of natural selection as he understood them seemed to point in the direction of selfish individualism (survival and reproductive success), while much of the evidence from the observation of animal and human behavior seemed to point in the direction of self-sacrifice for the benefit of the group. Darwin himself was puzzled by the appearance of altruistic behaviors when, in fact, these behaviors might lead to the death of the individual and reproductive failure.

Darwin first encountered this problem with respect to colonial insects. In *The Origin of Species* he writes: "I will not here enter on these several cases, but will confine myself to one special difficulty, which at first appeared to me insuperable, and actually fatal to the whole theory. I allude to the neuters of sterile females in insect-communities; for these neuters often differ widely in instinct and in structure from both the males and fertile females, and yet from being sterile, they cannot propagate their kind."[7] Darwin's clarification, while it points in the direction of "group selection," is not very satisfactory. The problem of forms and behaviors that benefit the group rather than obtaining the reproductive success of the individual reappear in Darwin's account of human evolutionary development. Darwin was puzzled by the rise of social and moral qualities that seemingly could not be explained in terms of individual survival. "It is extremely doubtful," Darwin noted, whether the offspring of the more sympathetic and benevolent parents, or of those who were most faithful to their comrades, would be reared in greater numbers than the children of selfish and treacherous parents belonging to the same tribe. He who was ready to sacrifice his life, as many a savage has been, rather than betray his comrades, would often leave no offspring to inherit his noble nature. . . . Therefore it hardly seems probable, that the number of men gifted with such virtues, or that the standard of their excellence could be increased through natural selection, that is, by the survival of the fittest; for we are not here speaking of one tribe being victorious over another.[8]

These difficulties in Darwin's theory were smoothed over by Darwin rather than resolved. Indeed, in Darwin's day they could not be resolved in the absence of a satisfactory explanation of the nature of heredity and in the absence of important new bodies of empirical evidence. Darwin and later evolutionary theorists who argued that "group selection" explained the appearance of altruistic behavior did so by ignoring the imperatives of evolutionary biology. Since Darwin the most important problem in evolutionary biology has been the formulation of a hypothesis that will harmonize natural selection with the appearance of seemingly "altruistic" behaviors.

In the 1930s Konrad Lorenz and Niko Tinbergen, both of whom have received the Nobel Prize in biology, pioneered the new science of ethology. Perhaps this new scientific discipline was poorly named, for "ethology" conveys very inadequately the fact that the new science concerned itself with the careful examination of innate patterns of animal behavior. The development of ethology would have been impossible had it not been for the revolution that took place in genetics and the growing volume of careful work and observation in the field of ecology. As the field of ethology developed it became apparent that a great deal of animal behavior which had previously been assumed to be learned behavior was, in fact, genetic in origin and a response by the species to environmental circumstance. Ethology, moreover, threw important new light on the question of "instinctual behavior" and its sources. It became clear that innate behavior was an adaptive response by the animal to the environment and that these responses had developed from more rudimentary ancestral behaviors. It was also obvious that there were certain unifying strategies and behaviors which characterized life generally and which were not peculiar to specific species.

The fact that these behaviors and strategies characterized life generally was an observation of the utmost importance. It was not only tempting but essential to fit human behaviors into the ethological framework. It was also necessary to resolve, in the case of social animals, the seeming contradiction between evolutionary selfishness of the survival of the fittest and the seeming "altruism" of social behaviors. The discipline of sociobiology advanced both new empirical data and new theoretical formulations that sought to resolve this contradiction.

Edward O. Wilson, the leading exponent of sociobiology, defines the discipline in the following fashion: "Sociobiology is defined as the systematic study of the biological basis of all social behavior. For the present it focuses on animal societies, their population structure, castes and communication, together with all the physiology underlying the social adaptations. But the discipline is also concerned with the social behavior of early man and the adaptive features of organization in more primitive contemporary human societies. . . ."[9] If the argument of the sociobiologists is correct, then it is apparent that a close scrutiny of animal behaviors and animal societies can tell us much that is both revealing and of value concerning human societies. Sociobiology has the capacity of transforming the social sciences and providing a unifying theoretical framework for sociology, anthropology, political science, and economics. As a life-science, sociobiology is no more nor no less deterministic than the life sciences in the past have been. It denies neither the existence nor the importance of culture and free will. It does establish the boundaries of social behavior. Sociobiology need not be thought of as determining the moves in the chess game of social development. It does establish the pattern within which those moves can be made. Such a theoretical situation is not new either to ethics or the social sciences. Sociobiology does not destroy human responsibility. It does, however, clearly demarcate what the limits of our social expectation ought to be.

As with all life, the evolutionary key to human behavior is the attempt by the organism to assure reproductive success. The formation of cooperative groups, the communication of alarm, hostility, hunger, status and rank, kinship, and the division of labor all aim at the achievement of the paramount objective of reproductive success. Genetic continuity seems to be the first and outstanding objective of life.

One of the most important ways of reconciling the selfishness of the "survival of the fittest" with the "altruism" of behavior conducive to the welfare of the group is the process known as kin selection and nepotism. It has been repeatedly observed—see particularly the work of Richard D. Alexander of the University of Michigan and W. D. Hamilton[10]—that genetic tendencies evolve so as to foster assistance to one's kin and that the measure of helpfulness is related to the nearness of kinship. Put quite simply, animals assist their kin. They do so, sociobiologists argue, because of the degree of genetic identity that exists within kinship groups. It has been argued that an uncle who shares one quarter of his genes with a nephew or a niece will be as willing to help two nephews or nieces as he will be willing to assist one of his own children. Genetic continuity thus applies to the kinship group as a whole rather than direct descendents alone. Nepotism is a determined tendency of animal and human behavior.

The self-sacrificing call of danger that may result in the animal's death will save, if the kinship group escapes, nearly the whole of the self-sacrificing animals' genetic material as it is embodied in other members of the group. Moreover, reciprocity within the kinship group reinforces nepotism. Consequently, what appears to be altruism is genetic selfishness, allowing for the fact that it is inappropriate to apply either the term "altruism" or "selfishness" to a process which is nonethical.

The human adaptive strategies whose aims are genetic continuity and reproductive success are patterns of behavior developed by big-brained hominid toolmakers and users over the past million years. In the relatively great length of time from the advent of *Homo erectus* to *Homo sapiens* the basic genetic patterns for contemporary men and their societies were laid down. The invention of agriculture, the smelting and smithing of metals, the development of urban life and complex political systems are events of the recent past that have, as yet, left behind no evolutionary residues. The genetics and the behaviors of modern man are those of paleolithic hunters and gatherers. Lionel Tiger and Robin Fox put the matter well when they write,

> We remain Upper Paleolithic hunters, fine-honed machines designed for the efficient pursuit of game. Nothing worth noting has happened in our evolutionary history since we left off hunting and took to the fields and towns—nothing except perhaps a little selection for immunity to epidemics, and probably not even that. "Man the hunter" is not an episode in our distant past: we are still man the hunter, incarcerated, domesticated, polluted, crowded, and bemused.[11]

What, precisely, were the characteristics of these early human societies, how is their genetic content manifested in contemporary societies, and what light does this information throw on the debate concerning equality?

We know a great deal about the societies of paleolithic hunters who have survived into the present.[12] The testimony of ethnology and anthropology generally, together with the sociobiological analysis and explanation of animal and human behavior, permits us to describe these behaviors with some confidence. Even were we to reject the theories of sociobi-ologists altogether we would have to take cognizance of the great weight of evidence that is now available concerning animal and human behav-ior, past and present, as it bears on the issue of human equality.

One of the most obvious and widely observed behaviors in animal and human societies is what ethologists call the "pecking order," "hier-archy," dominance systems, or more simply, "the peck order." Edward O. Wilson defines hierarchy in sociobiological usage as "the dominance of one member of a group over another, as measured by superiority in aggressive encounters and order of access to food, mates, resting sites, and other objects promoting survivorship and reproductive fitness."[13]

In one of the early ethological classics, *Social Behaviour in Animals,* Niko Tinbergen describes the movement from aggression to the establishment of a hierarchically ordered society in which dominance actually reduces rather than increases fighting:

> Animal species living in groups sometimes fight over other is-sues than females or territories. Individuals may clash over food, over a favorite perch, or possibly for other reasons. In such cases, learning often reduces the amount of fighting. Each individual learns, by pleasant or bitter experience, which of its compan-ions are stronger and must be avoided, and which are weaker and can be intimidated. In this way the "peck-order" originates, in which each individual in the group knows its own place. One individual is the tyrant; it dominates all the others. One is sub-ordinate to nobody but the tyrant. Number three dominates all except the two above it, and so on. This has been found in vari-ous birds, mammals, and fish. It can easily be seen in the hen-pen.
>
> The peck-order is another means of reducing the amount of actual fighting. Individuals that do not learn quickly to avoid their "superiors" are at a disadvantage both because they re-ceive more beatings and because they are an easier prey to preda-tors during fights.[14]

Aggression and self-interested cunning bravado, bluff and elaborate sig-naling behaviors enable certain animals within the group to establish domi-nance over others. The establishment of dominance is the key to reproduc-tive success, and while dominance may appear to be simply a quest for status, it is linked indissolubly with access to mates and those other factors which will result in genetic continuity for the dominant animal.[15] On the basis of this established order in societies a political system emerges. Its source is not altruistic cooperation or rationalistic contract-making but rather aggression and coercion. The Marxist assertion, based on ideology and faulty nineteenth-century anthropological thinking, that in his primitive state man was noncompetitive, nonaggressive, and practiced a form of "primitive communism" is simply wishful thinking. The universal presence of the dominant male is the most startling fact to emerge from the study and comparison of primitive societies.

The impact of intergroup aggression and the drive for dominance is mitigated by the fact that the group faces outward on a predatory world as well as inward on the group. Cooperation and reciprocity as well as competition are essential to survival and reproductive success. It is in the achieved balance between the interests of the individual and the success of the group as it ministers to the needs of the individual that politics takes its rise. Tiger and Fox describe the genesis of politics eloquently when they write:

> Competition for scarce resources—food, nest sites, mates—is the basis of society and the stuff of politics. But the simple nest-site competition is not very complex; no really ingenious political system can be seen to come out of it. The basic processes, however, are there—competition, inequality, exclusion, bonding. In any competition, someone wins and someone loses; a relationship of dominance and subordination is set up. If the subordinate is excluded, the matter quickly loses interest as far as the forging of political systems is concerned. But if the dominant and subordinate animals remain in some relationship to each other, and if dominance and subordination continue to be recognized, and if, further, the subordinate animal is itself dominant over yet another animal, then the rudiments of hierarchy emerge and a political system now exists. It is a system of inequalities in that those at the top get more than those lower down (including such intangibles as freedom of movement); it is a system of politics in that changes in status can take place—indeed, this is what political systems are about.[16]

The determinants of dominance are numerous and all of them are associated with reproductive fitness.[17] Adults are dominant over juveniles and males are usually dominant over females. Size, aggressiveness, and hormone levels all play an important role, and in the more complex animal societies experience and cunning are of great importance. Human females are almost universally attracted to high-status males,[18] and this attraction can be explained "because such males are more likely than low-ranking males to produce reproductively successful sons." Moreover, much female and juvenile status is a reflection of connection with a high-status male. "Lorenz found in Jackdaws that when a female of low 'rank' got engaged to a male high up in the scale, this female immediately rose to the same rank as the male, that is to say that all the individuals inferior to the male avoided her though several of them had been of higher rank than she before."[19] Status in childhood often relates to the mother's rank.

Dominance is overwhelmingly a male attribute. Males on the average are simply bigger and fiercer than females. They are the hunters, the fighters, the choosers. Now of course it will be said that up to this point there has been much talk of animal societies and very little discussion of human societies. Does the evidence suggest that human societies are innately nonaggressive, cooperative, and equalitarian, as theorists from Rousseau to Marx have argued? Is there evidence of a stage of matriarchal dominance in early society, as Johann Bachofen and Lewis Henry Morgan argued and Marx-Engels popularized? The biggest, the strongest, the most clever, and the most aggressive dominate the chicken-pen and the buffalo range. Is what is true of chicken-pens and buffalo ranges also true of human behavior and human societies?

Casual observation, scientific empirical evidence, and sociobiological theory all suggest that what is true of animals in general with respect to aggression, territoriality, and status hierarchies is also true of man.[20] To be sure, the manifestation of these behaviors differs from the manifestation of status and dominance, for example, in the buffalo herd or among Paleolithic men. In modern human societies demonstrations of physical strength, for the most part, have been replaced by what Desmond Morris describes as "inherited power, manipulative power and creative power."[21] "Instead of showing off his bulging muscles," Morris adds, "the inheritor shows off his ancestry, the fixer his influence, and the talent his works." Status displays are among the commonest and most easily observed of human behaviors. Indeed, human beings like animals have developed an elaborate repertoire of signals that reveal, even when we wish to suppress the evidence of our feelings, the inherited impulses of the old Adam. Not only are the behaviors characteristic of the Paleolithic hunters manifested on every hand, but even our secret inclinations are overtly signaled in the symbolic language of physiognomy and gesture. Those who, for example, attend leading business schools are shown slow-motion moving pictures that reveal the tell-tale gestures which accompany confidence, anger, deceit, bluffing, and submission in negotiating sessions.

As in animal societies, so in human societies there is the widest variety of means available for, on the one hand, ordering and ranking the society, while, on the other hand, holding competition and aggression within allowable bounds so that community and cooperation will not be destroyed or even impaired. These behaviors are universally present and readily recognized in contemporary primitive societies. In our technological, scientific, bureaucratic society they have their equivalents in virtually all our day-to-day dealings, including the board meeting of the local YMCA and a cabinet meeting of the executive officers of the United States. In every contemporary situation in which power is exercised, status considerations are of primary importance. The contest for status is as pronounced, if not more pronounced, among the men in the Kremlin or the members of university faculties as it is in Eskimo society, though, alas! we seem to have taken most of the fun out of the contest. Henry Kissinger is said to have observed with respect to the intense status conflicts that rend faculties, "University politics are vicious precisely because the stakes are so small."

And so it turns out that neither ethology nor sociobiology produce evidence of any equality in animal or human societies. In fact, just the opposite is the case. Animal and human societies can survive and prosper only so long as major inequalities and differences are preserved. These inequalities are the essential building blocks of biological and sociocultural advance.

All of which is not to say that competition is more important than cooperation and that the individual is more important than the group. The race, the species, seems to be the thing that interests the anthropomorphized entity we call "nature." Obviously, "nature" does not exist, and when men speak of "Mother Nature" or say that "nature" does this or that, we can depend on it that they are describing a mysterious process which they do not fully understand or else understand not at all. They are simply substituting "nature" for God as a covering word to describe the mysterious. Competition and cooperation, individualism and group benefit are held in tension in all biological and social processes. However, the existence of inequality, an inequality that redounds to the benefit of the group, is one of the preeminent facts of animal and human societies.

Inequality enters into every major social or biological activity: in competition for mates, in pair bonding, and finally in competition, which results in dominance hierarchies; all of these are based on inequalities and result in dominance and submission. The idea of a noncompetitive golden age characterized by total equality and prelapsarian innocence is a fantasy, a kind of social and political pornotopia whose correspondence with biological and historical reality is nil. Similarly, the myth of matriarchy and female promiscuity is simply not borne out by the evidence. Evolution has favored male dominance and female chastity.[22]

Assuming that the contest for dominance is the single most striking aspect of human societies, how, we are forced to ask, does this essentially inequalitarian ethos accord with the ideals and mechanisms of democratic government? Are tyranny and aristocracy the natural constitutional forms for political systems? Are the fragility and rarity of democratic governments due to the fact that they are essentially unnatural?

The question is worth considering, for it may provide an important insight into the "natural" values of a democratic polity. Aristocracy is based on the translation of physical strength and cunning, aptitude for aggression, reproductive vigor, and capacity for cooperation and leadership into an inherited status that does not regard biological and mental endowment. Galton's famous law of filial regression, that the children of distinguished parents are apt to be less distinguished than their parents, is particularly applicable to aristocracies. The biological and intellectual road aristocracies travel seems to be downhill all the way. It is for this reason that aristocracies must be propped up and held in place by the symbols of divine approval and the trappings and dramaturgy of authority and power. Even so, aristocracies are fragile constructions constantly threatened by envy, interior decay, and the challenges that arise from the strong and capable in the social order at large. Thersites always challenges Agamemnon, and when Agamemnon is named Nicholas II, Thersites, in spite of his limitations, usually is the victor.

Aristocracies are especially vulnerable to the process that Max Weber described as "demystification," through which the symbolic props of aristocratic power and authority are dissolved by unbelief, the substitution of new forms of political order (such as bureaucracy), and the growth of the power of money. Moreover, the internal quest for dominance within an aristocratic system leads to political anarchy and the destruction of the weak. Even marriage alliances cannot wholly mitigate the rivalry of aristocratic magnates. That the hereditary principle is an inadequate basis for monarchy has been widely recognized in the past, and elective monarchy was the constitutional form of both the Holy Roman Empire and the papacy. Hereditary aristocracy does often achieve the long-term stability characteristic of the dominance hierarchy because there is enough fitness in the system as a whole to outweigh its peculiar and particular weaknesses. Finally, hereditary aristocracy survives in the circumstances that characterize feudal ages and the societies that developed from protracted feudal periods.

Democratic policies overcome many of the weaknesses of hereditary aristocracy by opening up the competition for dominance to all comers.[23] Hereditary aristocracy effectively reduces competition by limiting the field and denying access. Restriction of entry into the arena of power and the substitution of the symbolic trappings of authority for the actualities of power are methods of aristocratic self-preservation. There is in this right of entry a measure of equality, of what we have come to call "equality of opportunity." But note that "equality of opportunity" can achieve its objectives only because men do not generally believe that equality exists. As Tiger and Fox put it, "In theory, the perfect system would be a true democracy, not because it renders all men equal, but because it gives them an equal chance to become unequal."[24] "Equality of opportunity" is a method by which society recruits greatness, energy, vitality, and talent. It is a method by which the maintenance of the dominance hierarchy is ensured.

The problems that arise from democratic polities are not due, as some have observed, to an increase in instability. It is rather the fact that, once having achieved dominance, the democratic politician always seeks to close off the entry ways to the arena of power. He achieves this not by appealing to his achievements but by substituting for them the symbols of authority and the appeals of ideology. "Don't debate the issues but have the band strike up 'Hail to the Chief!'"

But what of the assertion that "all men are created equal"? Surely its meaning must be attenuated and diluted by the facts of life as described by the ethologists and sociobiologists. The facts of the matter are never nearly as important as what men have thought these facts to be. The visions of what primal man, man in the primitive state, was like have been far more important in determining human conduct and political behavior than have the actual facts of primitive existence. Hobbes, Locke, Rousseau, and Marx-Engels all held elaborate theories of man's condition in the state of nature. These theories were not based on empirical evidence but were in a very real sense wish-projections and rationalizations of ideological positions. Nonetheless, it is these theories which have dominated human behavior for the past three centuries.

Finally, to say "is" is not to say "ought." It may well be that there is no sanction for radical equality in the "state of nature." It may also be that there are very good reasons why equalitarianism is essential to the survival of contemporary society. However, our knowledge of the past will help us to understand why the achievement of equality is so extraordinarily difficult.

7

Liberty and Equality as Absolutes

Of the revolutionary triad of "Liberty, Equality, and Fraternity" only liberty and equality have, in America, achieved constitutional status and genuine political visibility. Moreover, even liberty and equality have remained largely undefined and their consequences unexplored. In America we have always tended to vagueness, fudging the issues and glossing over the differences. There is evidence in the recent past that this evasion of discussion and debate, this pragmatic indifference to definition, is coming to an end. One of the consequences of the "age of ideology" in which we live is that the issues have generally been sharpened and the public polarized around competing alternatives.

This has been particularly true of the questions of liberty and equality and the public policies which involve their definition. It is not an exaggeration to say that nearly every important problem which we face, internationally or domestically, has at its heart either one or both of these two guiding principles of American political life. And suddenly we have discovered that either liberty or equality if pursued to its ultimate expression involves costs that we cannot afford or are unwilling to pay.

In the past, as I stated, it was possible to fudge the issue either by disguising or evading the costs or by pretending with the help of happy circumstance that it was not true that every increment of equality involved a diminution of liberty. Let me offer a few examples of this, to use a Marxist phrase, "sharpening of the antitheses," this growing unease with liberty and equality conceived as absolutes.

In a remarkable book, *People of Plenty: Economic Abundance and the American Character*, David Potter argued in 1954 that America had never really faced up to the question of equalitarianism because America had been able through natural abundance and technological tricks to evade that issue, had been able to fudge and gloss over this hard question.[1] He wrote:

Not only has the presence of more than enough seats, more than
enough rewards for those who strive, made the maintenance of a
democratic system possible in America; it has also given a characteristic tone to American equalitarianism as distinguished
from the equalitarianism of the Old World. Essentially, the difference is that Europe has always conceived of redistribution of
wealth as necessitating the expropriation of some and the ag-
grandizement of others; but America has conceived of it primarily in terms of giving to some without taking from others. . . .
Occasionally, one encounters the statement that Americans believe in leveling up rather than in leveling down. The truth of
the assertion is more or less self-evident, but the basic meaning
is less so. Clearly, if one is leveling a fixed number of items, say
personal incomes, the very process of leveling implies the reduction of the higher ones. But in order to raise the lower without reducing the higher, to level *up*, it is necessary to increase
the total of all the incomes—that is, to introduce new factors
instead of solving the problem with the factors originally given.
And it is by this stratagem of refusing to accept the factors given,
of drawing on nature's surplus and on technological tricks, that
America has often dealt with her problems of social reform.[2]

But let us suppose that the number of seats is not indefinitely ex-
pandable, that nature in her gifts of resources is not endlessly bounte-
ous, that scientists and technologists are not infinitely ingenious. What
then? Then one might assume that the debate as to the nature of equality would be sharpened and that in America it would take the same
forms of class conflict as it has taken in Europe.

Another American historian, David Donald, has recently suggested that
this is precisely what has happened. America's bounty, America's good luck,
has been running out, according to Donald. The energy crisis is only the
tip of the iceberg. According to Donald, America's future is dark and apt to
be filled with social commotion, disappointed hopes, and class conflict. I
happen to disagree with David Donald and all those other prophets of gloom
who suggest that America is moving from an era of abundance into an era
of scarcity. Nonetheless, it is obvious that in some areas of our national
lives there will be fewer seats and there will be less abundance than our
intensified demands for equality will accept. The great danger in a democratic society of too many chiefs and no Indians is, moreover, no longer a
chimera.

Let us take the example of fewer seats, in this case seats in medical
school, in law school, or in status or prestige locations generally. What-

ever the Supreme Court has decided or may decide, our society is deeply divided over the question of whether status may be divorced from performance, as to whether achievement may be penalized in the quest for equality. It does indeed seem to me that the mood of the '70s is one in which the older easy assumptions that liberty and equality cost nothing more than political rhetoric have gone by the board. Moreover, the relationship of equality to abundance raises another set of interesting problems. If the American attitude toward the achievement of equality has in substantial measure been determined by abundance, as Potter maintained, we now find ourselves in the curious position of being increasingly aware that abundance is dependent on inequality.

Although David Potter was a great social scientist and one of the first among historians to develop the implications of social-scientific evidence and theory for the study of history, he never dealt with the relationship of the quest for dominance and hierarchical status systems to democratic society. In Potter's day the revolution produced by ethology and sociobiology in the social sciences was only beginning to make itself felt.[3] Today it seems obvious to many social scientists that both order and abundance are dependent upon the efficient functioning of dominance systems in human society. So much is this the case that Lionel Tiger has described dominance systems as the "spinal cord of the human community."

The American economist Arthur M. Okun, chairman of the president's council of economic advisors in the administration of Lyndon B. Johnson, in a recent book, *Equality and Efficiency,* has adumbrated for us a rule that we should "promote equality up to the point where the added benefits of more equality are just matched by the added costs of greater inefficiency."[4] One is forced by the evidence to argue that productivity is at least in substantial measure due to differential status and material rewards; that in society there is a point of diminishing returns at which every increase in equality results in a decline of social utility or productivity. It is possible to argue with great cogency that in the Western world we have reached the point at which increasing equality can only be purchased at great cost to the commonweal.

I have called attention to these two instances only in order to point out that the debate concerning liberty and equality has reached a new level of intensity. This new level is not the consequence of theoretical and philosophical interest alone but is a reflection of the economic, political, cultural, and moral problems that confront our society. It is increasingly clear that life in a society where the hands of the craftsman and the artist have lost their cunning because skill goes unrewarded, where excellence and performance are penalized, and in which low status is equated with entitlement may not be life in the good society. One might, however, as easily have given innumerable instances where the claims to absolute liberty have been challenged by the need for social utility or the pragmatic values of the commonwealth.

Even though we have entered on an era in which the level of the intensity of the debate over liberty and equality as absolutes has reached an unprecedented height, the discussion is not a new one. No one foresaw the ultimate implications of this question more clearly or assessed the costs of liberty and equality more accurately than did Alexis de Tocqueville when he published the first part of *Democracy in America* in 1835. In that work Tocqueville raised the perennial problems associated with liberty and equality with a greater sharpness and clarity than any American observer of his own or later times. This sharpness was possible only because Tocqueville's European experience prevented his fudging and glossing over the question.

For Tocqueville the development of democracy was inevitable and ineluctable. Here is what he said in the introduction to *Democracy in America*, expressing the belief that if God is for it who can be against it?

> The various occurrences of national existence have everywhere turned to the advantage of democracy; all men have aided it by their exertions, both those who have intentionally labored in its cause and those who have served it unwittingly; those who have fought for it and even those who have declared themselves its opponents have all driven along in the same direction, have all labored to one end; some unknowingly and some despite themselves, all have been blind instruments in the hands of God.
>
> The gradual development of the principle of equality is, therefore, a providential fact: it is universal, it is lasting, it constantly eludes all human interference, and all events as well as all men contribute to its progress.[5]

One might assume that in view of Tocqueville's assumption of God's approval of the increasing liberty and equality of mankind no problems remained to bedevil the democratic era into which mankind was entering. Quite to the contrary; it was precisely the uninterrupted and unlimited extension of liberty and equality, the absolute claims of liberty and equality in democratic society, that Tocqueville saw as the fundamental threat to the civil order in the Western world.

At the very end of *Democracy in America* Tocqueville returns to those doubts and fears which he has expressed throughout the two volumes of his work. His conclusions are expressed in the strongest and most alarmed language:

I think then that the species of oppression by which democratic nations are menaced is unlike anything that ever before existed in the world; our contemporaries will find no prototype in their memories. I seek in vain for an expression that will convey the whole of the idea I have formed of it; the old words *despotism* and *tyranny* are inappropriate: the thing itself is new, and since I cannot name, I must attempt to define it.

I seek to trace the novel features under which despotism may appear in the world. The first thing that strikes the observation is an innumerable multitude of men, all equal and alike, incessantly endeavoring to procure the petty and paltry pleasures with which they glut their lives. Each of them, living apart, is a stranger to the fate of all the rest; his children and his private friends constitute to him the whole of mankind. As for the rest of his fellow citizens, he is close to them, but he does not feel them; he exists only in himself and for himself alone; and if his kindred still remain to him, he may be said at any rate to have lost his country.

Above this race of men stands an immense and tutelary power, which takes upon itself alone to secure their gratifications and to watch over their fate. That power is absolute, minute, regular, provident and mild. It would be like the authority of a parent if, like that authority, its object was to prepare men for manhood; but it seeks, on the contrary, to keep them in perpetual childhood; it is well content that the people should rejoice, provided they think of nothing but rejoicing. . . .

Thus it every day renders the exercise of the free agency of man less useful and less frequent; it circumscribes the will within a narrower range and gradually robs a man of all the uses of himself. The principle of equality has prepared men for these things, it has predisposed men to endure them and often to look on them as benefits.

After having thus successively taken each member of the community in its powerful grasp and fashioned him at will, the supreme power then extends its arm over the whole community. It covers the surface of society with a network of small complicated rules, minute and uniform, through which the most original minds and the most energetic characters cannot penetrate, to rise above the crowd. The will of man is not shattered, but softened, bent, and guided; men are seldom forced by it to act, but they are constantly restrained from acting. Such a power does not destroy, but it prevents existence; it does not tyrannize, but it compresses, enervates, extinguishes, and stupefies a people, till each nation is reduced to nothing better than a flock of timid and industrious animals of which the government is the shepherd.

I have always thought that servitude of the regular, quiet, and gentle kind which I have just described might be combined more easily than is commonly believed with some of the outward forms of freedom, and that it might even establish itself under the wing of the sovereignty of the people.

Our contemporaries are constantly excited by two conflicting passions; they want to be led, and they wish to remain free. As they cannot destroy either the one or the other of these contrary propensities, they strive to satisfy them both at once. They devise a sole, tutelary, and all-powerful form of government, but elected by the people. They combine the principle of centralization and that of popular sovereignty; this gives them a respite: they console themselves for being in tutelage by the reflection that they have chosen their own guardians. Every man allows himself to be put in leading strings, because he sees that it is not a person or a class of persons, but the people at large who hold the end of his chain.[6]

I have quoted Tocqueville at length in order to reveal the full force of his argument. He asserts boldly that the tendency in democratic societies is to pursue equality so relentlessly that meaningful liberty is abandoned and all that remains of freedom is plebiscitary democracy affirming in an all but meaningless fashion the will of the state. It is often argued that Tocqueville's great fear was the tyranny of the majority. Yes, indeed, he did fear the tyranny of the majority, but more than that he feared the power of the centralized, bureaucratic state exercising enormous power over the naked and defenseless individual citizen. He saw, moreover, that this power resulted from the unchecked quest on the part of the individual for equality of condition.

Both liberty and equality, precisely because they are such essential goods, in a sense like the very air we breathe or the water we drink, seem to us unproblematical, beyond the hazards of superfluity and without cost. How dismaying, then, to hear that one can have too much liberty, that equality may dissolve the structures of society, and that every increment of equality implies the diminution of someone's liberty.

We seldom think long or seriously about the fact that the intrusive and destructive power of the modern authoritarian and bureaucratic state is a reflection and implementation of the desire for equality of condition on the part of the citizenry. From time to time we are permitted to rattle our bureaucratic chains, and we all rejoice, as Tocqueville pointed out, that we are enslaved to the people rather than to a class or an individual, even though our status may be less free and more circumscribed than the status of our forefathers in oligarchic and class-dominated societies. We have now reached a point in our life as a people in which we shall be called with ever-greater frequency to assess the costs of added equalization. This is the case because, as I suggested at the outset, equality is becoming increasingly expensive in terms of the other values we shall have to sacrifice in order to obtain it.

One might assume from all I have stated thus far that the difficulties in the American polity all arise from the relentless quest for equality. Libertarians, especially those of Ayn Rand's persuasion, often seem to be arguing that if only we set equality aside and made liberty the relentless focus of our political and social activity, all would be well. The fact is that liberty is no less problematical as a political absolute than is equality. In 1941, Eric Fromm, close on the experience of totalitarian Germany, wrote a brilliant book: *Escape from Freedom.* In that book Fromm depicted what might be described as the psychic and social costs of freedom and offered the opinion that in the modern era these costs had been so high that many Westerners, unable to pay the costs of freedom, had retreated into authoritarianism and totalitarianism.

Historically, the same ineluctable forces that Tocqueville had described as having produced equality and democracy had thrown off the shackles of traditional society. When social status and hierarchy had been dissolved ordinary men were liberated, but liberated for what and at what cost? Anomie and alienation are the key words of the contemporary era, and both of these psychological and social states are the direct consequences of this liberation.

Let us look more closely at the process of liberation and the consequences of freedom and then attempt to assess whether or not freedom is absolute or only relative. Permit me to call attention once more to a book by the American historian David Potter. When Potter died in February 1971, the field of American history lost one of its most creative, responsible, and original thinkers. In January and February 1963 Potter had delivered the commonwealth fund lectures at University College, London. He had chosen as his topic for the series, "The Compulsions of Voluntaristic Society: Individual Freedom and Its Limitations in American Life."[7] The topic was not a new one to Potter. Indeed, the question was the steady preoccupation of his intellectual and personal life. (It is well to remind ourselves before I quote from this book that David Potter alone among prominent American historians publicly endorsed Senator Barry Goldwater in his unsuccessful candidacy for the presidency of the United States in 1964.)

In his commonwealth lectures Potter describes at length the long process of liberation from the forms of traditional society, the transition from custom to contract, from status to alienation. His description was not new and can hardly be called original. At the end of the nineteenth century Jacob Burckhardt, in his essay *The Civilization of the Renaissance in Italy*, had recognized as the distinctively modern note the dissolution of corporate identities and the substitution and growth of individualism. Nineteenth-century German sociology, particularly the work of Savigny, Tonnies, Sombart, and Weber, recognized the socially transforming nature of the dissolution of community.

Potter describes the cohesiveness of medieval life with its articulated pattern of customary obligations and community integration. To be sure, men and women living in such a tightly woven community were not fully "individuated." There was a cost, but there were also rewards of a very considerable nature. The Reformation, the Renaissance, and particularly the evolution of capitalism disrupted these age-old patterns of traditional society. Here is the culminating passage in which Potter describes this process of social dissolution:

> These developments tended to set men in impersonal and antagonistic relation to one another. They forced each man to realize that he stood apart from other men. If he was a resourceful person, this realization would probably foster his individuality by emancipating him from the network of ties with which society held him in his arbitrarily designated role. It would provide him maximum room for psychological growth and make him, in the fullest sense, a free man. But if he was a weak person, he would probably see such changes, not as presenting him with an opportunity to be free, but rather as threatening him with unbearable insecurity. And there would be a disposition to flee from such a threat by submitting himself to some kind of comforting authority.[8]

Potter's argument has been made for nearly two hundred years by historians, theologians, social theorists, sociologists, and economists, by men of the Right as well as of the Left and all points in between. Even allowing for the fact that this picture of the medieval past which Potter presents may be (in fact, is) a romantic idealization, we are compelled by the weight of the evidence and the force of the testimony to admit that there is a great deal of truth in this account of the way in which the collapse of community and the fall from status and hierarchy has not freed men but has isolated and alienated them.

Perhaps in no other society has the impact of these great social changes been so pervasive as in America. The dominant themes in our literature have been the quest for freedom and the fear of isolation. The American landscape—powerful, immense, diverse, but unarticulated and undefined—has only served to exaggerate both our freedom and our isolation. The fate of Europeans who entered into this landscape, often from finely articulated peasant communities, and found that the freedom of this strange new land dissolved their loves and their communal ties is one of the great themes of our literature. Willa Cather speaks most eloquently in her novels on this subject.

In the American character the desire for freedom, freedoms of the most radical nature, is held in tension by the great and compelling fear of isolation. The followers of John Humphry Noyes sought to dissolve the marriage bond and abolish the nuclear family, but they sought to do so within the confines of community. Nowhere else in the modern world has the desire for radical freedom been so often expressed in communitarian and sectarian terms. Even those who fled the restrictive atmospheres of Sauk Center and Spoon River for the liberty and bright lights of Minneapolis and New York, those who fled Main Street in the Twenties for the greater freedom of the Left Bank—even they thought they would find in New York or Paris a community of the pure-thinking and the like-minded, and they frequently did.

This tension between liberty and community has been much heightened in the period since World War II. Even the primary certainties and the primary communities of family and religion have threatened to give way. The value structures of previous millennia have either been abandoned or systematically questioned, and our America may be on the point of becoming the world's first antinomian culture. Rapid geographical and social mobility have threatened to dissolve the last vestiges of political community. It is ironic that the individuality produced by the dissolution of traditional society has increasingly been swallowed up in mass institutional, economic, and political forms. No one doubts that there has been an enormous increase of freedom accompanying these developments, but it has been a freedom purchased at the cost of anomie and alienation. David Potter quite perceptively asks: "The question is whether this urge to escape has become a willingness to surrender—whether the American has freed himself from formal authority only to enthrall himself to other, perhaps more insidious tyrannies."[9]

It may very well be that we have come to the awareness in the United States that freedom aside from the context of community is meaningless. If we men are indeed, as Aristotle affirmed, "political animals," then liberty, which is purchased at the price of the common good and at the expense of commonly perceived values, can only result in anomie and isolation. If this is true, the great social debate in the next decade will center on the reconciliation of liberty and equality and the definition of the social limits of freedom.

It has generally been assumed in the contemporary era that equality of condition has been more important to men than the condition of assured status. That is to say that both political and economic equality are more important than a communal role defined by status. The fact is that individuals and societies are dependent for their orderly functioning on status and are very reluctant to abandon status either in the name of liberty or equality.

In primitive societies where levels of consumption throughout the group are roughly equal it is interesting to note that differences in status remain very great. After all, the consumption of goods is a very inadequate way to designate status, if for no other reason than that the human organism is capable of only limited consumption. While the consumption of goods is limited, the desire for status is nearly infinite. In the eighteenth and nineteenth centuries, scarcity on the one hand, and superfluity because of economic concentration on the other, made it possible to define status and hence political power in terms of the ability to consume. It is because of this that Thorstein Veblen could speak of "conspicuous consumption" as one of the demonstrations of status in the nineteenth century. The transition from relative scarcity to relative abundance in the twentieth century has made it increasingly difficult to define status, and consequently power, in terms of consumption. This accounts for the fact, I believe, that the children of the rich—the Rockefellers, the Kennedys, the Heinzes, and numerous others—have attempted in our day to translate nineteenth-century status based on wealth and consumption into twentieth-century status based on politics. This particular maneuver is very tricky and difficult, and there is no great possibility of success, but the fact that the rich bother at all to make it indicates that equality of economic condition or equality of consumption are not the most important considerations either for individuals or society as a whole.

To fall out of status, to be isolated and alone, may be perceived as a social evil far greater than either inequality of condition or loss of liberty. Libertarians and men of the Right need to take this matter seriously lest in the name of liberty they create a world where no liberty can exist.

Both liberty and equality, whatever their status as ideal concepts, are social creations. They cannot be divorced from the social reality, the contextual matrix in which they are embedded. When they are considered in abstraction, as the absolutes of closet philosophers, they lose their meaning. Edmund Burke realized this long ago when he wrote in a much-quoted passage in which he discussed the natural-rights philosophy of the French revolutionaries:

> Government is not made in virtue of natural rights, which may and do exist in total independence of it—and exist in much greater clearness, and in a much greater degree of abstract perfection; but their abstract perfection is their practical defect. By having a right to everything they want everything. . . . But as the liberties and restrictions vary with times and circumstances, and admit of infinite modifications, they cannot be settled upon any abstract rule, and nothing is so foolish as to discuss them upon that principle.

This, it seems to me, is the great defect of John Rawls's *A Theory of Justice* and Robert Nozick's *Anarchy, State and Utopia.* They belong to the shadowy world of abstract philosophy rather than to the realms of ethics, politics, and history. Their abstract perfection is indeed their practical defect.

Liberty and equality are what some philosophers call "grading" terms, that is, terms comparing quantities or the availability of some commonly held good or commodity either available or accessible. It is at least questionable, in my mind, whether or not they can be discussed at all intelligently in abstraction from particular instances.

Edmund Burke went over this ground frequently but nowhere more eloquently than when he wrote in his *Appeal from the New to the Old Whigs* (1791):

> It is not worth our while to discuss, like sophisters, whether, in no case some evil for the sake of some benefit is to be tolerated. Nothing universal can be rationally affirmed on any moral or any political subject. Pure metaphysical abstraction does not belong to these matters. The lines of morality are not like the ideal lines of mathematics. They are broad and deep as well as long. They admit of exceptions; they demand modifications. These exceptions and modifications are not made by the process of logic, but by rules of prudence. Prudence is not only the first in rank of the virtues political and moral, but she is the director, the regulator, the standard of them all. Metaphysics cannot live without definition; but Prudence is cautious how she defines. . . .

If I am not mistaken we Americans are now embarked on an exploration of the limits of liberty and equality. The debate will stretch at least over the next decade. No one can now foresee the end or anticipate the passion and intensity that it will generate. Perhaps the time has come, while the political passions are still gathering momentum, to remember that our object in civil society is the common good, and that the common good can only be achieved by the exercise of prudence rather than the pursuit of abstractions.

PART THREE: HISTORIOGRAPHY

Tonsor taught historiography for many years at the University of Michigan. As a scholar, he explored the Western historiographical tradition in much of his writing. The following section contains some of his essays on history and historiography from the 1960s through the 1980s. A European intellectual historian by training, Tonsor was well aware of the central debates and issues in American historiography. Some of the essays herein are concerned with issues concerning liberty in America and the nature of the historical discipline in the modern era. Tonsor's interests in historiography stemmed in part from his intellectual interest in "historicism" and his desire to move history away from the progressive concerns of Hegel and Marx. Such "moral history," as Tonsor's colleague John Higham once referred to it, represented a desire to bring the individual, rather than social forces, back to the center of historical study.

8

History: A Revolutionary or Conservative Discipline?

Historians, it would seem, have every cause to indulge in satisfied self-congratulation. It is true that no president of the United States since Woodrow Wilson has been a historian, but historians have recently stood near the center of power in the United States, a position shared by few others in the American intelligentsia other than economists and scientists. (There is a suspicion, however, that if they continue to play "kiss and tell," as Arthur Schlesinger Jr. has, they will fall from this high estate.) They are widely read and feel themselves to be highly respected. Alone among the humanistic disciplines they command attention and speak with assurance. And yet, there are some painful misgivings, some dreadful suspicions, some gnawing doubts among historians that all is not well and that what is taken today as the color of health and the flush of success is in reality the feverish symptom of disorder, disease, and decay.

In his inaugural address, "The Great Mutation," given before the American Historical Association on December 29, 1962,[1] Carl Bridenbaugh asked, "How much longer will Society continue to support History as a useful branch of knowledge?" He followed his question with a long series of reasons he felt helped to explain the decline of historical consciousness in our society. The address struck an elegiac note and Professor Briderbaugh seemed to be mourning not only the passing of an intellectual epoch but the passing of a way of life. It would be hard, however, to dismiss it as autumnal melancholy, for too many other historians have begun to raise the same doubts and ask the same questions. In a recent essay, *The Meaning of History*, Erich Kahler remarks:

> This essay was conceived as a defense of history. An apology is
> required, since history, or more specifically, the use of the his-

torical viewpoint for the clarification of problems and phenomena, has widely fallen into disrepute. The Great Books movement is not the only one to exhibit a basic aversion to the historical and evolutional approach. Positivism, Existentialism, the
American school of purely descriptive anthropology, the New
Criticism, and, especially in Europe, a trend of thought deriving from Nietzsche, all of them reject the historical point of
view. In fact, as will be seen later, a whole epochal mood has
found its expression in this anti-historical tendency.[2]

More recently still, Professor Hayden V. White of the University of
Rochester, reviewing a survey of American historical study in the Princeton
Studies in Humanistic Scholarship in America,[3] asserted bluntly, "The question for the historian today is not *how* history ought to be studied, but *if* it
ought to be studied at all. This is the question posed in literature from
Nietzsche to Sartre, in theology from Barth to Tillich, and in social theory
from Weber to Popper."[4] White criticizes the authors of the Princeton study
for failing to recognize this breakdown of historical consciousness.

> Beneath their qualified praise of current historiography there
> lurks, one senses, a genuine disquietude, a suspicion that the his-
> torian may not be up to the performance of the role that he once
> played in Western intellectual life: that of mediator between past
> and future. This disquietude is manifested most obviously in the
> nostalgia with which they note the passing of the giants of histori-
> cal thought of the late nineteenth and early twentieth centuries.
> It is also shown in their failure to examine critically their shared
> conviction that contemporary historiography is a creative syn-
> thesis of the scientific and artistic approaches to reality....[5]

However misstated and overstated the Kahler-White thesis of a decline in historical consciousness is (and there are elements of both overstatement and misstatement in the quotations above), historians and
humanists and most especially those who are concerned with establishing the diverse points from which the wind of the spirit blows would do
well to examine carefully these assertions, for there is an important element of truth in them. There is, today, a very real danger that in a
revolutionary era we will sever our last ties with the common humanity
and common experience that history represents and wholly surrender
ourselves to a nihilistic present or to a future empty of everything but
the most common materialistic beguilements; that we will forget what
being human has meant and will abandon any aspiration to what being

more perfectly human might mean. There is a danger that we will impoverish ourselves through a loss of both the past and the future, for the quality of the future is such that it cannot exist in any meaningful sense without the sustaining ground of past experience.

The winds of dogma that blow in the present hour are not favorable to history. History has become an unbearable burden for modern man. There is a sense in which we are all displaced persons whose familiar world of everyday reality has been put to fire and sword by historical forces that, in the course of the nineteenth and twentieth centuries, the very writing of history helped to generate. But even were contemporary man tough-minded enough and deeply enough schooled in the sublime character of historical experience to be able to comprehend and bear the burden of history, it is still possible that he would reject history because of its bewildering complexity. To a far greater degree than any contemporary discipline history insists on diversity, complexity, multiplicity, randomness, and in its most mysterious moments, general confusion. The demands for generalization, symmetry, unity, predictability, and utilitarian purposefulness that are so much an aspect of the present zeitgeist are cruelly rebuffed by history. Moreover, in spite of its confusion and multiplicity, history seems constantly to demand human choice, value judgments, and moral actions, insisting that the historical moment par excellence lies not in synthetic generalization but in the individuating moment of choice. Thus history demands an ethic of responsibility at the very moment when the most diverse intellectual and material forces are either on the point of overwhelming the power to choose or simply denying through a new positivistic, mechanistic worldview the validity of any free choice at all. Finally, there is good reason to assert that modern social theory, behavioristic political studies, theology, philosophy, social psychology, and cultural anthropology are a flight from the complexities and the uncertainties of the historical forms of these disciplines. Contemporary man has rejected tragedy, has rejected complexity and diversity, has rejected moral choice and ethical responsibility, has rejected continuity and organicism, which by their very nature impose baffling problems and admit unprecedented and unpredictable eventualities. Contemporary man seeks a secure, predictable, permissive world, and history stands in the way.

However, it may be instructive to recall that the present moment is not the first occasion on which historical consciousness has been threatened by revolution, presentism, and pseudoscience. Indeed, the birth of our contemporary historical consciousness is the result of a growing awareness in the eighteenth century of the inadequacies of a philosophy too scornful of the past, too naïve and simplistic and too exclusively fixed on the present and a highly schematized and rationalized future. In rehearsing the evolution of historicism, therefore, we will be able to confront directly not only the nature of contemporary historical consciousness but its value both as a creator of modernity and, as it seems to me, the only viable ground for contemporary religious, ethical, social, political, and scientific thought.

In response to the positivism and the mechanistic determinism of the mid and late nineteenth century, historians and philosophers sought to distinguish two disparate ways of knowing the world, each method legitimate in its own sphere of inquiry, each false when applied to the phenomena of the other. Each was equally recognized as science, as ordered inquiry or *Wissenschaft*, to use the original German term, and each yielded pragmatically valuable knowledge. One of these "sciences" conceived of "the world as nature," the other conceived of "the world as history."

When, shortly after 1900, Oswald Spengler expressed this distinction in the following words, he was echoing the position of the most advanced German historicists.

> We have before us two possible ways in which man may inwardly possess and experience the world around him. With all rigor I distinguish (as to form, not substance) the organic from the mechanical world impression, the content of images from that of laws, the picture and symbol from the formula and the system, the instantly actual from the constantly possible, the intents and purposes of imagination ordering according to the plan from the intents and purposes of experience dissecting according to scheme; and—to mention even thus early an opposition that has never yet been noted, in spite of its significance—the domain of *chronological* from that of *mathematical* number.[6]

This fundamental distinction had not been made until the end of the nineteenth century; it was opposed even then by the positivistic mechanists and it is rejected today by their counterparts. It is this difference in ways of knowing which separates "social science" from history. Indeed one might say that "social science" is history from which historical consciousness has been removed.

"Historical consciousness" is simply viewing the world as history. But this viewpoint is an extremely modern development. Classical civilization was without it, and however historical Christianity and before it Judaism were, they did not produce an articulated historical worldview. Indeed, the medieval period was essentially ahistorical, even antihistorical in its thinking. The rationalist tradition from the Renaissance through the Enlightenment shared the medieval quest for synthetic system and rejected implicitly the process that escaped neat logical or mechanical categories. (It is interesting to note that a representative "progressive" historian, Carl Becker, in *The Heavenly City of the Eighteenth-Century Philosophers,*[7] noted the kinship of the *philosophes* both to his own "progressive" school and to that of the medieval scholastics, while failing to note the profoundly antihistorical tendencies in all these three "philosophic" eras.) The development of historical consciousness was the onset of modernity and a response to an inadequate mechanical, rationalistic, and systematic worldview. The "modern" worldview, a view essentially conditioned by "historical consciousness," is a rejection of what Stephen Spender has designated as the worldview of the "Voltarian ego."[8]

The essential characteristic of this "Voltarian I" is its desire to transform the world. Spender writes: "What I call the 'Voltarian I' participates in, belongs to, the history of progress. When it criticizes, satirizes, attacks, it does so in order to direct, to oppose, to activate existing forces. . . ." In short, the "Voltarian I," in contradistinction to what Spender designates as the "Modern I," is a revolutionary force that aims at the transformation of society. Philosophical movements, whether Enlightened eighteenth-century, American "progressive," or the contemporary cybernated model advocated by that artful pontiff, Sir Charles P. Snow, all share a common desire to reform radically, to break with the past and in the process annihilate history.

John Higham has recently remarked on this aspect of American history in his discussion of the Progressive Era. "The crucial fact underlying both their [the progressives'] theory and their practice was a broad sympathy with the spirit of reform then developing in contemporary life. This sympathy induced an attitude toward change and continuity quite different from that of their conservative colleagues." Moreover, Higham adds,

> As progressives, the New Historians had a vivid sense that a great turning point had arrived in the American experience. They wanted to participate in the transformation and to explain it. Accordingly, they studied history with more interest in interpreting change than articulating continuity. Carl Becker spoke for his own generation when he commented that the eighteenth-century *philosophes* had little use for the concept of continuity in history, which nineteenth-century historians established: "The reason is that the eighteenth-century Philosophers were not

primarily interested in stabilizing society, but in changing it."
Moreover the kind of change that seemed important to the
philosophes of the twentieth century was not the slow unfolding of
institutions through an inner logic of their own, but rather the
kind wrought out of conflicts of interest and clashes of purpose.
To be progressive was to believe that the progress of society was
neither automatic nor secure, but had to be won at every step,
over entrenched opposition.[9]

Seen in terms of the Enlightenment of the eighteenth century or in
terms of the Progressive Era of American experience or in terms of our
contemporary "social-scientific" *philosophes,* history is regarded as a tool
whose purpose is the alteration of society, as a weapon to be used against
the old order, as a method for dispelling superstition and ignorance and a
challenge to every institutional form that has come down from the "bad old
past." This historical viewpoint insists, additionally, on conflict, crisis, and
radical discontinuity. "The world will not be happy," Voltaire remarked,
"until the last priest is strangled in the entrails of the last king." Whenever
we encounter the philosophical mind we find it expressing itself in terms
of a revolutionary historical position that seeks to employ history as a
weapon against the past and places the major emphasis in historical thought
on discontinuity and some form of mechanistic determinism. It was out of
a reaction to such a revolutionary, antihistorical viewpoint that the modern historical consciousness was born.

Eighteenth-century naturalism, with its roots in the conception of a uniform natural law, a universal human nature, an empirical and pragmatic history that derives its values from a uniform and universal human
experience, and finally, a set of aesthetic norms and tastes that were time-
less and universal in their validity, has frequently been described by the
intellectual historian. It is less commonly recognized that the rise of historical consciousness played a decisive role in the dissolution of this complex of ideas. The crisis in eighteenth-century thought was not only philosophical, ethical, religious, and political; it was also, at its deepest levels, a
crisis in the way in which men thought about history.

For the developing historical consciousness of the eighteenth century
attacked every fundamental notion held by the *philosophes.* The rise of organicism as both a biological and social idea, entailing as it did the concept of process, continuity, and genetic development, was perhaps the most
fundamental reorientation of eighteenth-century thought, destroying, as it
quickly did, the mechanistic model that had dominated Western cul-

ture from the seventeenth century.[10] Organicism not only swept away the mechanistic causality and the simplistic determinism of "Enlightened" thought, it also provided an ideological basis for a new social and political theory, a new theology, a new science, and most importantly for our considerations, a new history. Continuity rather than sudden and dramatic change seemed to be the essential characteristic of historical thought when it was conceived in terms of the new biological and organic model. Edmund Burke's famous statement in *Reflections on the Revolution in France* is the great statement not only of new social thought but of a new theory of history:

> Society is, indeed, a contract. Subordinate contracts for objects of mere occasional interest may be dissolved at pleasure; but the state ought not to be considered as nothing better than a partnership agreement in a trade of pepper and coffee, calico or tobacco, or some other such low concern, to be taken up for a little temporary interest, and to be dissolved by the fancy of the parties. It is to be looked on with other reverence; because it is not a partnership in things subservient only to the gross animal existence of a temporary and perishable nature. It is a partnership in all science, a partnership in all art, a partnership in every virtue and in all perfection. As the ends of such a partnership cannot be obtained in many generations, it becomes a partnership not only between those who are living, but between those who are living, those who are dead and those who are to be born. . . .

When in the preface to *The Nigger of the Narcissus* Joseph Conrad, three generations later, reflected on the nature of art, he phrased his comments in almost the same terms Burke had used many years before:

> [The artist] speaks to our capacity for delight and wonder, to the sense of mystery surrounding our lives; to our sense of pity, and beauty, and pain; to the latent feeling of fellowship with all creation—and to the subtle but invincible conviction of solidarity that knits together the loneliness of innumerable hearts, to the solidarity in dreams, in joy, in sorrow, in aspirations, in illusions, in hope, in fear, which binds men to each other, which binds together all humanity—the dead to the living and the living to the unborn.

It is this concern with continuity and organic relationships which lies at the heart of both conservative political theory and the historical consciousness. The revolutionary break in institutional continuity thus strikes not only at traditional institutions; it breaks the historic links with the past and negates the possibility of historical consciousness. Conversely, those who destroy historical continuity destroy with it the organic links that bind a society together, merging and harmonizing classes and interests. History is always the revolutionary's most dangerous enemy, not simply because experience of the past casts doubt upon the pat and ready solutions characteristic of the reforms of closet philosophers, but more importantly because history establishes larger loyalties, a more universal humanity extending backward and forward in time, and forges a closer link to the human reality in all its diversity that every culture represents.

Second only to organicism and its insistence upon continuity is the reverence for tradition that both the conservative and the historical consciousness exhibit. Indeed, this reverence for tradition is the common property of the conservative, the historian, and the literary humanist generally. Stephen Spender remarks:

> Language of its own nature repudiates a break between the past and the present. A "revolution of the word," in the sense of words changing completely their sense and becoming something else, is one kind of revolution that is impossible, a revolution in human nature being perhaps another. Dictionaries contain the material with which writers work, and they are overwhelmingly traditional. It may be theoretically possible to discover an entirely new form in which a poem might be written, but form is only one aspect of a poem, and its unprecedentedness would only make a superficial break with the unavoidable continuities of grammar and usage.[11]

And so it is that tradition is written into language, history, and society. It is sometimes assumed that the romantic conservatives invented tradition, organicism, continuity, development, and the other characteristics of the romantic and historicist worldview. Far from it: they simply brought them to the conscious awareness of Western man. The eighteenth century, with its attempted break in tradition, made men aware of the tenacity of the past and the burden of ideas and forms that we carry out of that past. The intense interest in classical and modern philology and the historical study of the law that contributed so much to the development of the modern historical consciousness is eloquent testimony to the power that the rediscovery of tradition exercised over the minds of men in the late eighteenth and throughout the nineteenth centuries. Again, historical consciousness, rooted as it is in the search for tradition, was in its inception and duration closely associated with conservative thought.

The third of the great complex of ideas that formed the historical consciousness is the idea of development. "What was the Revolution?" Lord Acton asked. He answered his own question; it was "The defeat of History, History dethroned."[12] Change is the stuff of history and holds as important a place in the historical consciousness as continuity and tradition, but it is change that grows out of past experience and past forms. The genetic principle does not admit of mutations, of fiat creation, or of the idea that there can be something totally new under the sun. In terms of the idea of development society and history are seen as slow unfoldings of potencies and forces—evolution and not revolution. So long as biology dominated the nineteenth-century worldview both society and history remained essentially conservative. The impact of the notion of development upon the study of institutions and ideas cannot be overestimated. Even the notions of progress and of revolution were found to possess a developmental tradition, and ideas that at first appeared to be a clean break with past history were seen as the products of centuries of growth and steady maturation.

Organicism, continuity, development, and tradition were all closely related ideas associated to a very considerable extent with biological and particularly with evolutionary ideas. The impact of problems and ideas stemming from theology, ethics, and German idealistic philosophy was no less great than the influence of biology in forming the historical consciousness. In rejecting the mechanistic and deterministic behaviorism of the eighteenth-century *philosophes,* the romantic conservatives moved away from natural causality as historical explanation to a study of choice and value. From Kant forward the distinctively human act was seen to be the act of ethical choice, and the historical moment was thought to be that moment of action when values are affirmed or rejected. Thus, the focus of historical study shifted away from natural causality and rationalistic science to the moment of choice and decision. To the idea of tradition and continuity, of organic development, the romantic conservatives added the dimension of crisis—that is, the moment when an individual or an institution, freighted with all the heritage of the past, finds before it alternative lines of action. These recurrent crises were seen as the great focal points of history, the moments when society or the individual becomes most fully aware of its past and most acutely conscious of the need for action. Note that, in contrast to the idea of revolution as the abolition of the past, the romantic-conservative view of the moment of crisis involves the conception of affirmation of the past in present action rather than abolition. In the moment of crisis, history affirmed its positive elements; it was the embodiment of spiritual forces, of ideas and ideals that came to it out of the past. The negative perished and was dissolved by the erosive action of time. Only that which possessed permanent value and moral validity survived. Consequently, while crisis and choice seemed at first examination to be contradictory to organicism, development, and continuity, they were, on nearer examination, seen to be complimentary factors.

Closely associated with the ideas of value and choice as elements of decisive importance in historical study is the conception of the unique and the individual. The romantic conservatives rejected the generalizing tendencies implicit in eighteenth-century rationalism and emphasized the importance of that which could not be described in terms of the universal. The conception of a universal human nature and universal aesthetic norms was swept aside and a time-conditioned ethic and aesthetic was affirmed. There were implicit in this shift serious problems of relativism, which increasingly bedeviled the historical consciousness as the nineteenth century wore on, but the new historical ethic and aesthetic was the only one possible once the appeal had been made to empirical data rather than to closet philosophy. Moreover, the focusing of history upon crisis and choice, value and ethical action, could only be accomplished through an emphasis on individuality and the unique. Out of this new historical interest came the emphasis on the heroic, the uniquely temporal, the distinctive, even the exotic in past times and in living institutions. The nineteenth-century cult of the hero and the genius, the romantic quest for the strange and the exotic, the romantic emphasis on difference—national, racial, religious, sexual—was a consequence of this emphasis, and the passionate commitment of the century to liberty derived as much from its respect for the unique and the individual as it did from its commitment to choice and ethical action. Here again the conservative impulse and historical consciousness sprang from the same source and shared a common set of attitudes.

Finally, the romantic conservatives adopted an attitude best described as the reverence that influenced in a decisive way the development of historical consciousness. This reverence was characterized by three separate but related actions: reverence before the fact, the event, the person in all its authenticity and integrity; reverence for the mystery implicit in history, which cannot be exhausted in terms of natural causality and determinism; and finally, reverence for the past as worthy in its own right of study without appeal to present value or future hope. Because the romantic historians valued individuality so highly, because they saw in individuality and uniqueness the handwork of the creator and the repository of the potencies of history, they wished to get the story straight. Generalizations, rationalizations, guesses were not good enough. The fables of the *philosophes* were a canard upon Providence, and only the most exact historical data derived from exhaustive archival study would satisfy this new priesthood.

Secondly, the historical consciousness believed that historical understanding was linked to the a-rational and that the historical process was ultimately mysterious. After everything had been explained, after all the forces and potencies had been exhibited, the unknown and the unknowable still—or perhaps more clearly than ever—intruded themselves into history. It is for this reason that von Ranke was a mystic as well as a historian, and for this reason that German pietism was so influential in the rise of German historicism. Again and again, Burke, Maistre, von Ranke, Tocqueville, Acton acknowledge the dimension of mystery that lies at the very heart of history—as, I might add, it lies at the very heart of every other science whether it is acknowledged or not. And, most especially, the past itself was reverenced in and of and for itself. The past was not simply prologue to the future, or a thousand years of error, priestcraft, and exploitation. "Every age," as von Ranke phrased it, "is immediate to God." This notion, closely linked to the Kantian teaching that the individual was to be seen as an end in himself, was reaffirmed and amplified by Fichte and the other German idealists. The integrity and freedom of history is thus an extension of the integrity and the freedom of the individual. The *philosophe,* the revolutionary, and the social scientist who see the past as something to be overcome are directly challenged by this reverence. It is, and must always remain, a most important source of antirevolutionary feeling. Nor do I mean here to equate reverence for a real past with nostalgia for an idealized past. Those who seek comfort in history are most frequently guilty of this nostalgic idealization. Alas, history is not a source of comfort in this sense. It is tragic and suffused with the anxieties and perplexities that are the marks of life and growth. Conservatism as nostalgia will find no support or comfort in history. Indeed, the radical conservative at the present moment is as decisively the enemy of true historical consciousness as is his revolutionary counterpart. Reverence does not mean idealization, and history is not hagiography.

Historical consciousness, which is a combination of these elements, developed, then, as a response to the antihistorical tendencies implicit in the eighteenth-century rationalist worldview. Its rise was paralleled by social and political movements we have come to call romantic conservatism. Indeed, the historical consciousness would be unthinkable aside from the general intellectual development that culminated in the establishment of the conservative temper and ideology as the dominant intellectual movement in Europe and America.

The question must be asked whether or not these two movements stand in some special symbiotic relationship. Is it possible for historical consciousness to exist in an essentially revolutionary society? Is it possible for the historian who despises the past, who wishes to transform society radically and abolish the past, to write history or even to think historically? Is not, indeed, the decline of historical consciousness related in an important way to the decay of conservatism as a valid social and political force?

While it is difficult to establish a completely clear relationship between the decay of conservative ideology and the decline of historical consciousness, evidence of the role history itself has played in this declension cannot be overlooked. It is comforting to historians to blame the state of society for the condition of the historical discipline. It is true that the revolutionary technological transformation taking place in every nation of the contemporary world has either broken or greatly weakened society's ties with the past. Institutional change, in an effort to keep up with technological transformation, has been so rapid in many cases that the integrity of those institutions is frequently threatened. One might produce an impressive list of disruptive dangers from technological revolution, and it seems incontrovertible that the very principles of organicism, development, continuity, and tradition are threatened by technological change.

But beyond this threat of change resulting from new techniques is the challenge to humanist values imposed by the technician and the scientist. Perhaps the most articulate statement of this challenge has been that of C. P. Snow in his essay *The Two Cultures.* Snow asserts that the humanistic artist and the scholar have failed, that they are, indeed, in the devil's camp and are enemies of human happiness. Only the scientist and the "scientifically" oriented creative artist and historian can understand and plan for the new world mankind is on the point of entering. Planning, automation, cybernation, and the rule of the scientific priesthood will usher in the technological millennium. It does seem strange that when mankind has at last shaken off the attachment to dialectical materialism a new and perhaps more dangerous variant of the materialist faith should assert itself. But this form of scientism, which at the moment is quite pervasive among the cognoscenti, is as clearly antihistorical, simplistic, and revolutionary as its "enlightened" counterpart.

Nor can we neglect the impact of a zeitgeist that seems wholly pragmatic and instrumental. Politics has ceased to conceive of itself in terms recognizable by traditional political theorists. Philosophers, either language analysts or existentialists, have ceased to think in terms related to traditional concerns or ultimate values. Situational ethics has displaced both the divine fiat and the categorical imperative, and the theological certainties of revelation have been dissolved into humanistic myths and social involvement. It is obvious that in such a world historical consciousness can hardly find acceptance as a dominant mode of thought.

But historical study itself is at least partially to blame for the decline of history as a worldview. In the second half of the eighteenth century the historicism that was then taking form was not only a reaction to the revolutionary Enlightenment, it was a social program that embodied the most vital and positive forces of the century in its outlook. It is mistaken to see romantic conservatism wholly as reaction, for this was not an integral part of its program. The organic model was the most decisive renovating force in Western thought in the past half millennium. There is no aspect of Western society that has not felt its beneficent impact. The recovery of the irrational and the rebirth of the religious dimension were events of the greatest importance. The growing enthusiasm for the study and sympathetic understanding of the Middle Ages, rejected by the eighteenth century and scorned by Voltaire as "a thousand years without a bath," was to influence Western politics, society, religion, and laws. The rise of nationalism, which took its inspiration in large measure from romantic conservatism and its historiography, was, in the realm of practical politics, the most dynamic force in nineteenth- and twentieth-century life and we have not yet seen its end. In all of these ways and in many others romantic conservatism and its historiography provided the transforming energies and ideas that dominated the better part of the nineteenth century. In short, the romantic-conservative historiography created a history that sought to reconstruct the political life of Europe on the basis of the dynamic heritage of the past. These historians rejected the eighteenth-century concept of the dead hand of the past that throttled and thwarted the present and the future. The conservative historian set for himself the task of discovering what elements of positive value could be rescued from time's erosion and set to bridge the gulf between the past and the future.

But from the 1870s onwards a transformation took place in historical studies. Increasingly history was professionalized and in the process the scholar came to regard history outside the cultural and political context, which had made it such a dynamic and positive element earlier in the century. History was written for history's sake. In the process, history came unstuck from the cultural and political concerns that had previously vitalized it. Conservatism, when it appeared as inspiration for historical writing, came to be increasingly backward looking, devoid of a concern with the present and the future. It has been because of this, as much as any other reason, that history has failed to speak effectively to our generation. Whatever other legitimate reasons there may be for the decline of historical consciousness, a major portion of the responsibility must be placed at the doorstep of the historian.

9

A Fresh Start: American History
and Political Order

Stephen Vincent Benét wrote in his uncompleted *Western Star*:

> Americans are always moving on.
> It's an old Spanish custom gone astray
> A sort of English fever, I believe,
> Or just a mere desire to take French leave,
> I couldn't say. I couldn't really say.[1]

The poet's perceptions are usually better than his explanations and we cannot fault Benét if he is unable to tell us why we have always moved on to the fresh start, to the primeval landscape, regaining in our adventurous movement our lost innocence and our betrayed virtue.

Geographic mobility, no doubt, has been a major factor in our history, making the fresh start possible. Over and over again we have moved on in quest of that perfect place. Having failed, we move down the road to the next city, take the steamboat up the river, and start over; take the train to the coast or change our names and our churches and invent a status for ourselves that only success as easy as our failure can justify. We have been a nation of transients, moving from choice as much as from necessity. Social status, institutions, and communities have all possessed in our New World that mercurial changeableness which some observers have ascribed to our continental climate and others have attributed to necessity. We have been a nation "on the road," and mechanisms of long-distance transportation from the steamboat to the spaceship have been the most characteristic of our technological creations.[2]

This "restless temper," however, was not simply the product of geography, of distances and space and the machines Americans created in order to conquer them. Nor was it simply climate or the understandable desire to improve one's lot. The experience of the New World was above all else a desire to escape history, an attempt to throw off the burden of the past and make a fresh start.

Thoreau, the archetype of the contemporary anarchist-individualist, expressed it with complete insight and awareness when he wrote in *Walden*:

> Furniture! Thank God, I can sit and I can stand without the aid of a furniture warehouse. What man but a philosopher would not be ashamed to see his furniture packed in a cart and going up country exposed to the light of heaven and the eyes of men, a beggarly account of empty boxes. . . . I could never tell from inspecting such a load whether it belonged to a so-called rich man or a poor one; the owner always seemed poverty-stricken. Indeed, the more you have of such things the poorer you are. Each load looks as if it contained the contents of a dozen shanties; and if one shanty is poor, this is a dozen times as poor. Pray for what do we move ever but to get rid of our furniture, our *exuviae*; at least to go from this world to another newly furnished, and leave this to be burned? . . . I look upon England today as an old gentleman who is traveling with a great deal of baggage; trampery which has accumulated from long housekeeping, which he has not the courage to burn; great trunk, little trunk, band box and bundle. Throw away the first three at least. It would surpass the powers of a well man nowadays to take up his bed and walk, and I should certainly advise a sick one to lay down his bed and run. . . .[3]

I have quoted this passage from *Walden* at length because in it Thoreau fuses completely the image of the immigrant on the road struggling with the accumulation of the past with the image of a society burdened by its history. To both the individual and society Thoreau offers a simple and easy solution, "lay down or burn down your burden; escape the past." In a perceptive and telling essay Richard Weaver clearly identifies the antihistorical tendency in Thoreau and links it to his contempt for politics and his anarchic individualism.[4] Indeed, Weaver virtually gives us the dictum that where there is no history there can be no politics.

The present perennially recognizes itself in some moment or movement glimpsed from the past. Thoreau speaks with such authority because he voices an enduring American theme. That the New Left seeks once more to escape from history should not surprise us and demonstrates, if demonstration were necessary, that the student radicals of the '60s were far closer to native American populism and Know-Nothingism than they were and are to the orthodox certainties of Marxism. In this flight from history, the student radicals are joined by the main tradition of American culture. Primitivism and nativism accord, as Leo Marx in his great critical essay, *The Machine in the Garden*[5] recognized, with a particular conception of history:

> Like all primitivist programs Gonzalo's plantation speech [in Shakespeare's *The Tempest*] in effect repudiates calculated human effort, the trained intellect, and, for that matter, the idea of civilization itself. It denies the value of history. It says that man was happiest in the beginning—in the golden age—and that the record of human activity is a record of decline. . . .

It is accurate to observe that the pastoral ideal which has provided so many of the symbols and themes of American literature constitutes an effort to escape into a landscape in which conflict and the ambiguities of the historically conditioned life are absent. In American literature, as in America, the geography and technology of mobility are wedded to the myth of the pastoral golden age, and the notion of "a fresh start" takes on the proportions of a national purpose. David W. Noble has viewed all of American history as dominated by this theme.[6] He argues that American history has been dominated by the worldview of the English Puritans who came to Massachusetts. In its secularized form in eighteenth-century enlightened thought, in nineteenth-century democratic romanticism, and in progressivism, the continuity with the Puritan ideal was preserved. This view, more than any other factor, determined the way in which Americans viewed the past. As Noble puts it:

> The American people believe that their historical experience has been uniquely timeless and harmonious because they are the descendants of Puritans who, in rejecting the traditions and institutions of the Old World, promised never to establish traditions and institutions in the New World. If history is the record of changing institutions and traditions, then by definition there can be no history in a nation which by Puritanical resolve refuses to create complexity. And the American historian is the Chief Spokesman for the cultural tradition. . . .[7]

Nearly every powerful American experience fed into and augmented the drive to eliminate and expunge history. The immigrant experience was such as to encourage the immigrant to strip off his European institutional and cultural past and to become a New American Man. The evangelical

Protestant conversion experience, with its emphasis on a decisive break with the past, encouraged the ideal of personal and cultural novelty. It would be difficult to underestimate the total impact of these cultural forces, but at their minimum they created a myth of American novelty and simplicity, virtue and harmony, that is constantly threatened with corruption and confusion from the forces of high culture and history.

But above all, the Jacobin element in American life has been unremittingly hostile to history. Speaking of the temptations confronting English democracy in the nineteenth century, Matthew Arnold wrote in *Culture and Anarchy*:

> Other well-meaning friends of this new power are for leading it, not in the old ruts of middle-class Philistinism, but in ways which are naturally alluring to the feet of democracy, though in this country they are novel and untried ways. I may call them the ways of Jacobinism. Violent indignation with the past, abstract systems of renovation applied wholesale, a new doctrine drawn up in black and white for elaborating down to the very smallest details a rational society for the future—these are the ways of Jacobinism.

The revolutionary component that Arnold identified by the shorthand of "Jacobinism" would like to abrogate history, and with it previous culture and politics, because these all stand in the way of the transformation of mankind. It does not matter whether the revolution is American, French, Russian, or Maoist; many of its partisans attempt the improvement of the future by the destruction of the past. At the present moment, no doubt that Jacobin attack upon the past is of equal importance with the more traditional American desire to let the dead past bury the past.

History, however, is not so easily disposed of. In the midst of the frustrating and gloomy opening years of the Civil War, President Lincoln in his Annual Message to Congress, delivered on December 1, 1862, said, "Fellow citizens, we cannot escape history." He meant, in the context of that message, that what Congress did would determine the future and how the future viewed the past "to the latest generation." But Lincoln's view of the impact of the burden of history on a later generation, its life and its politics, was even more tragic. Recall his Second Inaugural, in which he dwells at some length on the subject of national sin and its punishment in subsequent generations. Lincoln, more than most men, was aware that wishing does not make it so, and that a fresh start is made possible, not by an abrogation of the past, but rather through acceptance, charity, and reconciliation.

Lincoln is the outstanding example of the American statesman with a sense of history, but whatever the symbols of American literature and the clichés of American political life, he was far from being the only statesman with such a sense. *The Federalist Papers* exhibit an encyclopedic knowledge of the history of the past. Hamilton, Madison, and Jay do not see history as a burden from which the new republic must escape but rather as a source of political norms and experience concerning human behavior. Sir John Seeley's dictum that "history is past politics, and politics present history" is one they would have understood and approved.

However much by inclination and tradition we are tempted to jettison the past and make a fresh start, we as pragmatic political men ought to ask ourselves whether this is indeed a possibility or whether, as President Lincoln assured us, we will find that we cannot escape history. Our emotions and our wishes are all on the side of the visionary, the revolutionary, the young. We too would like to reorder and reconstruct human existence by destroying the past, or at least by inventing for ourselves a past that is more in keeping with our ideal of what we would like to be than the very tarnished and rather discouraging record of what we have been.

I do not believe that the past can be either abrogated or reconstructed. The past as we twentieth-century men perceive it is so closely related to our humanity and consequently to our politics that its abandonment or its reconstruction would result in depriving us of those very qualities which make us fully men.

No one dares challenge the basic proposition that it is speech which gives man his distinctive human character. Without speech man would in fact resemble all the other primates, bound to the iron necessities of nature by instinctual fiat. But speech and the world of symbols that it embodies is history. We cannot escape history because we are creatures of language, and language is always conservative and traditional in its influence. It is for this very reason that revolutions seek to strike at the cultural continuity that any linguistic formulation represents. George Orwell's vision in *Nineteen Eighty-Four* of a language debased and transformed to meet the needs of ideology is only a most extreme case of all revolutionary efforts to transform human behavior by changing the language. But these efforts are doomed to failure. Man cannot jettison history because he cannot evade language.

Language is the repository of history. In order to abrogate history it would be necessary first to destroy language. It is not sufficient that language be corrupted and barbarized: it must, in fact, be destroyed. However, the effects of corruption of language give us some insight into the nature of language and its relationship to history and politics. Dante lodges these corrupters and falsifiers in the tenth bowge of hell because they strike at the very order that makes society possible. Dorothy Sayers writes:

> The Valley of Disease is at one level the image of the corrupt
> heart which acknowledges no obligation to keep faith with its
> fellow men; at another it is the image of a diseased society in the
> last stages of its mortal sickness and already necrosing. Every
> value it has is false; it alternates between a deadly lethargy and
> a raving insanity. Malbowges began with the sale of the sexual
> relationship, and went on to the sale of Church and State; now,
> the very money is itself corrupted, every affirmation has be-
> come perjury and every identity a lie; no medium of exchange
> remains, and the "general bond of life and nature's tie" (Canto
> XI. 56) is utterly dissolved.[9]

Language is historical in nature. Its symbols are the distillation of man's
experience. It orders and classifies all later experience and makes the raw
data of experience capable of assimilation. It is for this reason that our
humanity is so completely a product of language and history and that all
subordinate ordering systems (political order, for example) are dependent
on the experience of order in history and the distillation of that order in
the symbols of language.

The distinction between the world of man and a human world is a fundamental one. The concept of man is biological. The concept of the human
is cultural. All of these characteristics which pertain to man are grounded
in the necessities of nature. In the realm of nature there are no obligations
and there can be no politics. The process of "becoming human," however,
is one through which culture is appropriated and superimposed upon biological development. Man belongs to the world of nature and instinct. The
human world is the creation of culture and the product of social experience. Cleanth Brooks made clear the distinction between these two worlds,
the world of nature and the world of culture, in his discussion of Robert
Frost's poem "Stopping by Woods on a Snowy Evening." Frost's horse,
Brooks remarked, had his own reasons, instinctive ones, for wishing to re-
sume the journey. They were not Frost's reasons, "promises to keep." The
horse had no obligations, no promises; those distinctively human preoccupations which are the ground of all politics belong to the world of culture.

Culture endows experience with meaning. Purpose in a human rather
than a natural sense is a social creation. It is important to recognize, however, that this socially constructed world is not an arbitrary creation. In the
measure that it is arbitrary it is useless or even destructive to human purposes. When the socially constructed world of culture serves human purposes best it is in agreement with the objective experience of the environ-

ment.[10] The world of culture is, above all, the world of order. The booming, buzzing confusion of raw sense data is subjected to a *nomos* or a meaningful order. The multiplicity of individually experienced worlds is given by culture a common meaning, and it is on the basis of this common meaning that politics in both its broadest and its most circumscribed sense is possible. Meaningful order (*nomos*) within society and culture is always related to a wider order in the *cosmos* and is perceived as congruent with that order.[11] That is to say, the central images and symbols of any culture are religious in nature, and these "tyrannizing images" (Richard Weaver) impose their forms, or seek to impose their forms, on the totality of experience.

Order in its broadest sense expresses itself in language and is related directly to the cosmological quest for meaning. This quest for meaning gave rise in the experience of primitive man to the great cosmological myths. In the Western tradition, conditioned by Hebrew-Christian revelation, those "tyrannizing images" do not derive from cosmological process but rather are related to historical experience. Consequently, not only is language, the ordinary tool of nomization, historical in structure and impact, but the cosmic images that it mediates are historical in nature. Buried in the structure of our language and in the fabric of our thought are those elements which make it impossible for us to make a "fresh start." Any order that is not arbitrary, any meaning that is not a trifling fiction or an inverted cosmos, is rooted in a total cultural reality that is historical in nature.

It is because of this that the precondition for overcoming history and for the transformation of the human predicament is not anomie or amnesia but increased and deepened historical understanding. It will not be by leaving the past behind us that we will discover our humanity and usher in a new, a better, era. Great political orders and cultural eras are born not in unconsciousness and barbarism but in the full light of historical understanding. The past is a burden only so long as it is not forced to pay its own way.

Language and art are objectifications of order. Order, however, is not an arbitrary or subjective creation but a response to existential reality. While the symbolization of order is always time-bound, historically contingent, and, because of this, "relativistic," the quest for that order is permanent. As Eric Voegelin has recently expressed it in an unpublished paper, "Equivalences of Experience and Symbolization in History," "What is permanent in the history of mankind is not the symbols but man himself in search of his humanity and its order." Men encounter order and participate in that order in three areas of existence: in the individual human spirit and its relationship to the transcendent, in the nature of experiential reality, and in the structures and experiences of human society. Consequently, revelation, natural law, and historical experience all possess a common commitment and are engendered by a common center.

While language and art are the objectifications of order, they may, and indeed often do, obscure and conceal the order they originally illuminated. The full meaning of words and symbols, once divorced from their engendering experience, is lost to succeeding generations or proves impenetrable even to contemporary minds. The experience itself, however, lives on and continues to exert its impact on later human behavior. Men act out of a past that is submerged below the level of consciousness. History as a living and dynamic force continues to exert its sway whether or not its symbolism is understood by a later generation and whether or not its creative forces are perceived at the level of consciousness by later actors in the drama. Far from being able to jettison history, history is most active in the affairs of men when they are least aware of its dynamism. It is precisely those who live in the eternal present who are most completely the butt of those buried historical forces which constitute the eternal order of justice.

The function of the historian and the function of the political scientist is to bring the buried but active past into the full light of consciousness, where its meaning can be apprehended and its consequences dealt with. Sir Lewis Namier touched on this problem when he wrote in 1952:

> A neurotic, according to Freud, is a man dominated by unconscious memories, fixated on the past and incapable of overcoming it: the regular condition of human communities. Yet the dead festering past cannot be eliminated by violent action any more than an obsession can be cured by beating the patient. History has therein a "psychoanalytic" function; and it further resembles psycho-analysis in being better able to diagnose than to cure: the beneficial therapeutic effects of history have so far been small: and it is in the nature of things that it should be so. Science can construct apparatus which the user need not understand: a child can switch on the electric light; nor does surgery depend for its success on being understood by the patient. But psychoanalysis works, if at all, through the emotions and the psyche of the individual; and history, to be effective, would have to work through those of the masses. . . .[12]

Namier had a profound insight in this passage into the role of the historian. But he leaves us with a puzzle and a problem. How, Namier asks, can political order be joined to history in such a way as to overcome history, not by abrogating historical experience, but rather through its transformation?

I believe that the answer lies in the role of the historian and the political scientist as political rhetoricians. The invention of political rhetoric, the formulation of the symbols of community, is the paramount task of those who explore political order, past and present. It does not take an age when the poets are silent or speak only in broken, corrupted, and ravaged dialects of a diseased and disordered culture and polity to recognize that "the poets are the unacknowledged legislators of the world." They and they alone can give to the dumb and the inchoate a voice and can enable men to see into the mystery of their existences.

To know the symbols that the past has created and the experiences that engendered those symbols is not enough. They must be made vividly present to this generation of men and their meaning must be translated into the experience of this present moment. When that act of understanding and reflection has taken place the past will indeed be overcome and its yoke will be sweet and easy to bear. But where political rhetoric is either wanting or is dominated by the symbols of what Eric Voegelin calls "deformed existence," the truth of the verse in Proverbs, "Where there is no vision the people perish," is all too apparent.

10

Freedom and the Crisis in Historiography

B ad books often raise important issues. Edward Hallett Carr in his recent book, *What Is History?*,[1] after fishing in the muddy waters of Hegelian
and Marxian determinism, at last lands what seems a large—if rather commonplace—truth when he writes,[2] "History properly so called can be written only by those who find and accept a sense of direction in history itself.
The belief that we have come from somewhere is closely linked with the
belief that we are going somewhere. A society that has lost belief in its
capacity to progress in the future will quickly cease to concern itself with
progress in the past."[3]

   It is difficult to quarrel with the assertion that a belief in progress, or at
least a compelling faith in movement toward some great divine far-off event,
is essential to the writing and the understanding of history. The conviction
that there is order and meaning in history is as essential to the study of
history as the conviction of natural order is for the study of the natural
sciences. But is it possible to find and to accept Carr's meaning? For though
he buttresses his arguments with quotations from Lord Acton, the voice we
hear is the voice of Marx. The implication of Carr's argument is unmistakable, and his definition of, and proof for, progress is clearly one not supplied by history itself but rather is a faith imposed upon the events of history. His book lacks the modesty of the self-consciously fallible human
formulation and bears the mark of the true believer in quest of certainty.

   And his book is all the more striking because Carr lodges his belief in a
faith that the intellectuals of the Western world find increasingly outworn.
The vast and intricately articulated religion of dialectical materialism, the
last great world religion, has in its historical and ethical formulations become unbearable for modern man. Abraham Tertz (a pseudonym for a contemporary Russian writer of great perceptivity) has described this rejection at some length in a powerful indictment of the type of thought that
characterizes Carr's book. Tertz explains in his essay *On Socialist Realism*,[4]

"The man who received a Marxist education knows the meaning of both past and future. He knows why this or that idea, event, emperor, or military leader was needed. It is a long time since men had such an exact knowledge of the meaning of the world's destiny—not since the Middle Ages, most likely. It is our great privilege to possess this knowledge once more."[5] Marxism-Leninism represents, therefore, the restoration of meaning, purpose, and progress in history. But by the end of the essay Tertz has suffered a significant loss of faith. Now he admits, somewhat disheartened, that "the strength of a theological system resides in its constancy, harmony and order. Once we admit that God carelessly sinned with Eve and, becoming jealous of Adam, sent him off to labor at land reclamation, the whole concept of the creation falls apart, and it is impossible to restore the faith. . . . Today's children will scarcely be able to produce a new God, capable of inspiring humanity into the next historical cycle. . . ."[6] And I need not add that Tertz's confession is symptomatic of a very widespread reorientation of the human spirit.

Is there not a real danger, however, that in the breakdown of teleological purpose in history, history itself, as Carr suggests, and the dynamic society of the Western world that is rooted in its peculiar apprehension of history, is threatened and endangered? Candor demands that we acknowledge the reality of the danger. The quest for meaning goes on apace. We all feel its attraction and its necessity. We all acknowledge that harmony, order, and purpose are somehow indispensable to historical study. It is all well and good to mock a system whose pretensions have been destroyed by the ethical monstrosities it has produced and the gulf that has opened between its theory of events and the events themselves. But suppose, only suppose, that this is the last great faith permitted man. What then?

But the Marxian metaphysic is not the only metaphysic that has been discredited in the explanation of purpose in history in the past two centuries. Obviously the crisis in historiography goes deeper than the intellectual crisis that confronts the Marxist historian. The crisis in the meaning and purpose in history is one which has endangered nearly every recognized school of historical interpretation.

Providential history, which saw God's visible and directing hand in the mundane events of secular history, perished two centuries ago. Bishop Bossuet was its last and perhaps its greatest exponent, and when, in the late nineteenth century, Lord Acton and his German mentor, Ignaz von Döllinger, attempted to prove God's existence by His action on the world, Acton's liberal and unbelieving friends acknowledged his daring and his learning but rejected this proof for the existence of God. It was nearly as dated at the end of the nineteenth century as the natural theology of St. Thomas's five proofs. One can imagine the daring, the learning, the majes-

tic reaches of thought that would have characterized a conversation between Henry Adams and Lord Acton on this subject were it to have taken
place, but Adams, with all his crushing melancholy, would have had the
better of the argument. He would not have proven Acton wrong, but he
would have established the fact that Acton's demonstration of Providence
no longer satisfied the modern mind.

For a time the enthusiasm of nationalism and the assumed superiority
of Protestantism, either singly or in combination, as a secularized version
of progress occupied the place once held by Providence. Progress was assured by the triumph of the German, or the Anglo-Saxon, or the Latin, or
the Slav, and history traced the genesis and unfolding of the national ideal.
Alternatively, the cultural values of Protestantism guaranteed the lifting of
superstition, the flowering of creative rationality, and the independence
and political freedom of the individual. It was a large and attractive myth
that thus disguised itself as history, and it required two world wars and the
breakup of Protestant certainty under the impact of historicism to lay its
ghost.[7] The masters of this school were significant historians, who, as was
the case with Parkman, produced history of a very high order. But whatever the merits of national and sectarian history, its scope was always too
circumscribed, its morality too narrow, its sympathies too parochial to bear
the weight that total meaning and the demands of progress placed on it. It
was difficult for an outsider to consider the Prussian state, as had Hegel
and Treitschke, a manifestation of God's providential order, evidence of
"the cunning of reason," or the most advanced state of a long cultural evolution. Increasingly, as the century wore on, institutional forms, even the
state and the Church, came to be feared as the avenues whereby men were
robbed of their liberties and deprived of their culture. Burckhardt could
not assume, as did even Meinecke, that the state was an ideal entity.

Nor could the broad, liberal sympathies characteristic of much historical writing in the past century-and-a-half bear either the exacting criticism and analysis of modern historical study or the impact of the moral
and political nihilism that characterizes our present age. The idea of
progress, which has been the most persuasive and pervasive idea in modern historical writing, was incapable of dealing with the tragic in history. It
was equally incapable of squaring itself with lost empires and lost cultures,
the agonies of damned souls and damned societies, the great chaotic wash
of events that in the objective, empirical realm so frequently result in the
choice of Barabbas over Christ, or shake down man's greatest cultural and
moral achievement in some convulsive upheaval. Even when the idea of
progress in history was combined with scientism, technology, and organic
evolution, it raised more questions than it answered, and while it might
explain the invention of atomic weapons it could not account in any satis-

factory way for either the rise of morality or man's not infrequent re-lapses into bestiality. To the historians who identified meaning and pur-pose in history with progress, history was a moral science, and when morality failed the meaning of history failed. Burckhardt, writing "On Fortune and Misfortune in History" and speaking of "moral progress," remarked: "Morality as a power, however, stands no higher, nor is there more of it, than in so called barbarous times. We may be sure that even among the lake-dwellers men gave their lives for each other. Good and evil, perhaps even fortune and misfortune, may have kept a roughly even balance throughout all the various epochs and cultures."[8]

From the outset,[9] progress defined either in terms of human happiness or moral improvement posed a difficult problem for the historical observer. Were progress to be demonstrated as certain rather than accidental, as-sured rather than tentative, absolute rather than relative, it was necessary to link progress to some great causal law. The mid-nineteenth century had been reached by the time Marxism and Darwinism appeared on the scene. The older metaphysics of progress represented by Saint Simon and Comte had proven themselves unequal to the task. It was the merit of Spencer and Marx to produce systems that made history purposeful by making it deter-mined. Organic evolution on the one hand and social evolution on the other, following the fixed and determined pattern of natural law, guaranteed a meaning and purpose to history that could not be discovered without the aid of science.

There was, however, a fatal flaw in the morality of the scientific theo-ries of progress. Historians soon saw that men were better than their his-tory, better than their societies or nature gave any reasonable hope of their being. "Yet the stronger," Burckhardt wrote, "as such, is far from being the better. Even in the vegetable kingdom, we can see baser and bolder species making headway here and there. In history, however, the defeat of the noble simply because it is in a minority is a grave danger, especially in times ruled by a very general culture which arrogates to itself the rights of the majority."[10]

Moreover, the struggle for survival, whether cast in biological or class terms, could not by its very nature be morally meaningful or historically purposeful. Natural and social law were blind and irresponsible forces that cast up species and social classes only to murder and dethrone them in their ultimately purposeless revolutions.[11] Nature, as de Sade recognized, guaranteed neither morality nor purpose in history.[12] Ultimately, natural, causal explanations of the historical process were more thoroughly relativ-istic than the movement that came to be called historicism.

Economic and biological determinism, which were at first welcomed as guaranteeing progress and meaning in history, were soon to demonstrate that they could with equal effectiveness be employed to demonstrate that history, far from achieving moral and purposeful ends, was moving inexorably toward a dark and ugly decadence. At the middle of the nineteenth century, a contemporary of Marx, Ernst von Lasaulx, announced a biological-historical pessimism nearly as stark and as shattering to human confidence as the much later theory of Oswald Spengler.[23] Determinist biology seemed, in the hands of the anxious and in a period of culture crisis, to move men to thoughts of the senility, decline, and death that inevitably afflict all biological systems. Nor could men view social and economic causal law with any confident hopefulness. Standing halfway between Marx and Spencer, Brooks Adams in *The Law of Civilization and Decay* consigned Western man and his society to a finished cycle that might be renewed only with an influx of energetic barbarian blood. Economics stood at the center of his system, but it would yield in its determined laws neither the utopia of Spencer nor of Marx. A more sophisticated historian, Michael Rostovtzeff, writing after the calamity of the Russian Revolution, saw in his *Social and Economic History of the Roman Empire* the history of Rome—and by implication the history of the Western world—as one of progressive economic and political decadence resulting from class warfare and the accompanying destruction of the social and intellectual elite. History, dominated by the immutable laws of economics and biology, stood not at the beginning of a great new age. Rather, Spengler bade it stand "like that Roman soldier whose bones were found in front of a door in Pompeii, who, during the eruption of Vesuvius, died at his post because they forgot to relieve him."[14] Commenting on Spengler's thought, Erich Heller writes, "Let us build aeroplanes, no matter what they carry; roads, no matter where they lead; weapons, no matter what 'values' they defend or attack. For absolute scepticism is our intellectual fate, and absolute engineering our historical Destiny."[15] And thus the evidence and the arguments by which men sought to restore belief in meaning and progress are turned against their advocates.

It is possible, of course, that the older determinisms were too gross and too unsophisticated to yield the results desired by their formulators. It is argued that systems more scientific and less metaphysical will produce the larger certainties that men desire. There has recently been a concerted effort to restore to history the status of a science of causes, and to find, if not progress, then determined regularities that will enable prediction and, hopefully, manipulation. The focus of the newer "social science" history is "quantification" and generalization, and it seeks to meet through circumspection and care the antipositivistic attacks that the historicists so effectively leveled against the older determinisms. What Professor Carl

Bridenbaugh has derisively called "that Bitch-goddess *quantification*"[16] is much more dangerous to a free and humanistic history than the older deterministic systems precisely because its claims are more modest and its methods more circumspect. The new "social science" history is written in the spirit of David Hume rather than of Karl Marx, but it shares with the older determinisms a contempt for personalities and values, and it bears within itself the same destructive desire to mitigate both the freedom and the mystery of human experience. It assumes, moreover, that history is science and nothing more, and that meaning in history is the meaning of the natural causal order rather than the meaning implied in value, in ethics, and in art. The older deterministic teleological systems saved purpose at the price of sacrificing value and freedom. The newer "revisionist" social science has abandoned purpose altogether and to that extent is an improvement over the older determinisms, but in doing so it has lent to history a meaning derived from the natural casual order that is insupportable on the basis of the evidence and unbearable in terms of its human consequences.[17] Again, as was the case with the older historical determinisms, it has shifted the locus of the historical movement away from moral choice or aesthetic judgment to causal law and the graphic presentation of statistical evidence. The result of the new history is to enslave man and at the same time to deny him any hope in his own ability to transform history and to rise above causality. Henry Adams pointed out the ultimate result of such a history when he wrote, "The kinetic theory of gas is an assertion of ultimate chaos. In plain words, Chaos was the law of nature; Order was the dream of man."[18]

However much the past century has weakened men's faith in metahistorical systems, the desire for certainty, for progress, and for purpose in history remains. The debate is still cast largely in terms that initiated the discussion in the eighteenth century. It is the debate between the eighteenth-century philosophers of the "heavenly city" and the Berlin academy.

In 1936, in his introduction to *Die Entstehung des Historismus,* Friedrich Meinecke remarked that "the kernel of historicism is the displacement of a generalizing viewpoint by an individualizing viewpoint in the study of historical-humanistic forces."[19] Meinecke considered this the greatest spiritual revolution in Western thought, and he added that such revolutions "once they have happened cannot be unmade or henceforth be rendered inoperative."[20] What Meinecke implicitly suggests is that the study of history has shifted decisively away from the analysis of causes alone and the attendant attempt to generalize, and instead interests itself increasingly in the individual, the unique, and that which is dependent upon free human choice and the assessment of value. The center of historical interest had become not the establishment of regularities or the development of laws but rather the study of individuality; not the analysis of causes but rather the assessment of values; not the indentification of uniformities but rather the apprehension of the unique. The multiplicity of personality and cultures and times displaced the quest for a law of progress or the discovery of a uniform human nature. The judgment of the past was to be made from the perspective of the past rather than the perspective of the present. Every age, as Ranke remarked, was "immediate to God." Furthermore, historical study was not a rational and scientific study of causes, but rather an imaginative and sympathetic identification of values and an understanding of personalities and societies. The ethical and the aesthetic outweighed the scientific, and the irrational was perceived to be a source of imaginative historical insight.

History, therefore, as seen by the historicist, poses to itself a wholly different set of tasks than those of generalization and rationalization. And it does this not as a matter simply of choice, but rather as a matter of necessity. It is not that the historicist does not find generalization useful, even necessary, at a certain level of his historical enquiry. Rather, it is because the historically interesting and historically valid transcends the realm of causality and generalization.

In a famous indictment of the metaphysical in history, Karl Popper in *The Open Society and Its Enemies*[21] explores at length and with great precision the inability of the historian and the social scientist to arrive at predictive generalizations. He rightly denies that any system of progress can be derived from the study of history. In *The Open Society* and a later book, *The Poverty of Historicism*,[22] however, he uses the term historicism in a very special sense that does not accord with the meaning generally accepted by historians and philosophers.[23] Moreover, in his attack on metaphysics in history he moves to a position that insists that there is and can be no meaning in history other than the meaning men arbitrarily impose upon it, and that in fact, as Popper expresses it, there can be no "concrete history of mankind."[24] This is surely a gross overstatement of the case. We would be safe in assuming, I believe, that Popper is close to the conventional position of historicism, though certain ideas borrowed from crisis theology and neo-orthodoxy lead him to overstate his position. He quotes Karl Barth with approval and at great length in his assertion that there can be no history in a Christian sense, no providential proofs, no certainty. Popper accepts this position because it makes possible, as he believes, a moral history, a history that reaffirms the freedom of man's existential position. In doing so Popper is both correct and mistaken. It is obvious that man is both bound and free, that he is touched by natural law and the regularities of history, and that he transcends in his ethical choices those laws. For Barth, working within the traditional Protestant theology that assumes a radical disjunction between the world of Nature and the world of Grace, this reaffirmation of man's existential freedom is totally consistent. However, in terms of Popper's theory it leaves something to be desired.

Popper's insistence that meaningful history cannot be written is just as questionable. His rejection of political history is understandable. But it too falls short of the realization that politics is a moral science, and that the ethical and the unique embody themselves in the state, even the state that, as frequently happens, becomes an ethical monstrosity. It is true that history as seen by the historicist shifts the focus of history away from the political and the nexus of power in any society. It does not, however, eliminate the fact that the ethical always embodies itself in institutional forms, whether these institutional forms are political, religious, artistic, or economic. In fact, the strength of an ethical, religious, or artistic idea determines the speed with which it makes its way to the centers of power in any society. In the process it is undoubtedly transformed, brutalized, and betrayed, but to deny the role of the ethical in political history is simply to misread the facts. It is simply not true that "the history of power politics is nothing but the history of international crime and mass murder."[25] Reviewing this problem in terms of Germany's historical destiny and in the light of the two great unsuccessful wars of the past half century, Friedrich Meinecke in an essay "Irrwege in Unserer Geschichte" (Mistaken Paths in our History) deals with the same problem of the relationship of political power to the ethical ideal and comes to some strikingly different conclusions.[26] It is true that the conscience stands above the state and the culture. It is equally true that the conscience must affirm itself, if necessary through revolution. It is true also that the state can completely pervert an ethical ideal. It is, however, undeniable that the ethical impulse is the basis of political life. History is not so completely a question of "either-or" as Popper conceives it.

Historicism, in fact, as interpreted by Meinecke, never rejected the role of a treatment of causes as a valid part of historical study. No historicist today denies the value of generalizations; if anything, we need more and better generalizations. There is a valid social science upon which history depends. The world of nature, form, and causal law everywhere impinges upon historical study. It is precisely when causes are most thoroughly known that their inadequacy to explain historical events becomes most apparent. It is true that causal relationships are the ground of every individuality and that individuality can be comprehended only through them. It is equally true that historical study is interested not in the generalization but in the individuality, the realm of value, the event in and of itself.

Historicism solves one set of problems only by introducing another.

Will not the historicist who begins his quest in the pursuit of values rather than purpose soon discover that values are always in conflict and that history offers a bewildering array of causes, good and evil, for which men have given their lives? Will he not discover that history offers no touchstone or guide by which evil may be discerned or good identified? Will he not confess that good and evil are inextricably mixed and combined in history, that they are masked and disguised and indistinguishable, and that the only law present in history's flux is the dictum of Heraclitus that "Whirl is king"? It is not simply enough to affirm that values exist in history; these values must, if they are to possess any meaning, be tested and questioned, "judged" by the historian.

Baron von Hügel described the tragic position of many modern historicists when he described the position of the great German historian Ernst Troeltsch. Of Troeltsch he wrote,

> Midas died of hunger from his fatal gift of turning all he touched into gold; so also Troeltsch, *qua* vehement individualist, finds himself incapable of deriving spiritual force and food from those entrancing historical perspectives which everywhere arise under his magical touch. Since each such scene is utterly unique, we are left without common standard, or common ideal—the entire collection, however intellectually interesting, can afford no aid towards the establishment of an act and habit of faith.[27]

And so in historicism the ancient problem of the conflict between freedom and meaning reappears in a new and very acute form. If determinism is abandoned, is it absolutely necessary to go over to an unconditioned relativism?

There has been a tendency on the part of historians to retreat before this problem. As in the lines from Goethe's *Faust*, the historian is proclaimed "Zum Sehen geboren / Zum Schauen bestellt . . ." ("born to watch, appointed to observe"). His tower is an ivory tower, and he views history, as Ranke said, under "a species of eternity." His is not to judge, or to evaluate, but only to observe. "If only we could shake off our individuality," Burckhardt wrote, "and contemplate the history of the immediate future with exactly the same detachment and agitation as we bring to a spectacle of nature—for instance, a storm at sea seen from land—we might perhaps experience in full consciousness one of the greatest chapters in the history of the human mind."[28]

But not even (and perhaps least of all) do academic historians live in ivory towers, and to play God is a role for which human beings are singularly unfitted. And yet, the historian must stand above judgment, must retreat from the narrow morality of his time, must be broad and generous in his sympathies if history is to tell him anything. Lord Acton expressed the historian's dilemma when he noted, "Life is not worth living if one can do nothing for one's country, for religious truth and the relief of pain. Yet a historian must be indep.[endent] of his pract.[ical] object. It takes a very exalted view of history to renounce all that."[29]

And if the reason is somehow to be brought into harmony with the will, ethical commitment and the contemplative act must somewhere find reconciliation. Is it possible to construct a history that recognizes man's limitations and his existential condition, that rejects neither knowledge of causality nor value judgment, neither contemplation nor an active and refined morality? Must human history necessarily lapse into a determined slavery on the one hand or a relativistic chaos on the other? Is it possible to construct a history that is both moral and contemplative, both free and scientific?

This question is being raised, particularly among American and British historians, with increasing frequency. Increasingly they are unhappy with a history that is divided against itself and poses problems for itself with which history cannot deal. In a recent and very important article, "Beyond Consensus: The Historian as Moral Critic," John Higham has called for a "moral history."[30] Writing from a historicist viewpoint, he gropes his way in a series of brilliant intuitions towards a position that is in important respects like the view advanced by Friedrich Meinecke a generation ago. It would be totally incorrect to think of Higham's article as in any way derivative, but it is important to realize that it stems from problems to which Meinecke offered a tentative solution.

But Meinecke is not popular at this moment. He is neither widely read nor highly considered. H. Stuart Hughes, in his book *Consciousness and Society*,[31] says of him that "ultimately he had succumbed to his own vaporous brand of metaphysic," and later in the same chapter Hughes remarks that "like his master Ranke, he was incapable of reasoning about history in any unambiguous fashion." But the difficulties lie not in Meinecke, but rather in the ambiguities of history and in the condition of man. His vision was a clear and distinct one, and one grounded in the realities of historical experience. If we are to achieve a more satisfactory conception of history than that which he advocated we will first need to master his position and exploit the lines of thought that Meinecke opened up.

It is obviously quite impossible within the scope and argument of this essay to develop with any thoroughness the richness and complexity of Meinecke's thought.[32] It is possible, however, to sketch boldly and inadequately the outlines of the solution that Meinecke offered to a number of the major problems raised in this essay, particularly the problem of teleological history, the problem of progress, the problem of history as a causal science, the problem of freedom and ethical value, and finally the problem of the relativism to which historicist thought seems to be particularly subject.

Perhaps Meinecke's greatest contribution to historical study was to make explicit all the implicit elements and tendencies in the historicist revolution. In effect, he made that revolution constitutional, and so far as possible reduced to a system a living entity that had previously functioned at the level of intuitive practice. In his treatment of historicism he not only explored the lines of continuity and development and identified the elements brought together in synthesis, but he raised in explicit form the problems inherent in historicism's outlook and established the boundaries within which historicist thought must confine itself. If Meinecke's system ends in mystery, "in vaporous metaphysics," this is the end of the ultimate questions of life generally, and only an unconscious metaphysician, a messianic scientist, would dispute the fact.

For Meinecke, the world of teleological history, the idea of progress in history, the notion of history as the analysis of mechanical causal laws, the notion of history as an attempt to discover a universal human nature, have been swept away by the historicist revolution. There were many elements in this revolution, and it was a major aspect of the rise of modernity, but historicism triumphed largely because history seen in other terms would not bear the metaphysical weight placed on it.

Historicism introduced two major new concepts to fill the gap left by the destruction of the older histories: the idea of the unique individual and the idea of development. Today neither of these notions seems particularly startling but their implications have still not been comprehended, much less acted upon.

History, Meinecke repeatedly affirmed, was not a mechanical or a rational, logical system. History and life are one, no less than history and the present (*Geschichte und Gegenwart*) are one. Monistic systems that separate life into its constituent elements and deny the free volitional elements in human choice destroy the unity of purposive individuality. A denial of the unity of historical experience, of the weight of the present and the heritage of the past, ignores the reality of the way in which life is rooted in cause, environment, continuity, "external and internal necessity." It is only within the mystery and unity of the human personality that the polarities of individuality and development are reconciled. It is only within the unity of life that freedom and necessity are harmonized, that past and present merge. Meinecke has repeatedly been accused of "dualism" because he cast his thought in terms of dialectical antitheses. But it should be remembered that these antitheses were always merged in the larger unities which individuals constituted.

From the viewpoint of Meinecke's system much of the civil war presently raging in history is a ghostly battle fought over issues that are either dead or nonexistent. A history that restricts itself to causality, to necessity, is false, but a history that neglects either "external or internal necessity" is equally false. In short, the reconstruction of history in our time will follow upon the recognition of history as a humanistic discipline rooted in the unity of human experience. It is not enough simply to affirm the power of man to choose, to give meaning to history as Karl Popper suggests. History is not only individuality, it is also continuity and development.

But just as history is a living unity that takes for its study the individual and the unique, so too its ways of knowing are rooted in the whole man. Historical understanding is not a subject-object relationship. History perceives through a primary intuition resulting from the total individuality of the historian. To be understood, history must be comprehended as a unity. Much that is false and simply misleading in modern "social science" history follows from its lack of understanding the relationship of historical knowledge to the unity of human personality. "The attempt to master historical materials exclusively with causal means, when it is carried out with radical imprudence, does violence to the stuff of history, leads to the extinction of one causal imprint by the others—and when it is undertaken with tactful prudence must soon stand helpless before the stuff of reality," writes Meinecke. "Only a path no longer purely scientific, that is, no longer purely causal, can lead us a step further into the depths of reality."[33]

Meinecke knew that beyond causality lies the realm of value. "Behind the search for causalities there always lies, directly or indirectly, . . . the search for what is called culture in the highest sense, i.e., breakthroughs and revelations of the spiritual within the causal complex of the natural."[34] History, like life itself, is rooted in choice, value, creativity. The role of history lies not only in identifying these values but in actively assessing and judging them. It is as impossible for history to divorce itself from value as it is for life to abandon ethical judgment.

Because the object of life is the realization of values, the actualization of the ethical, the religious and the aesthetic impulse, history—as life itself—moves toward goals. In this sense there is movement and direction in history. However, this movement is not teleological, nor can it be defined in terms of progress or of providential purpose moving through all history in some grand linear pattern. Value is individual and immediate to the source of value, and if there is identifiable movement in history, that movement is vertical rather than horizontal and general.[35]

This movement is not implicit in history, however, but rather in life.

History is, considered aside from the values life imposes upon it, mean-ingless and tragic. It is the realm of the accidental and the contingent, it is the province of fate. And it is precisely because of this that freedom and value assume such importance in Meinecke's system. "Most stag-gering of all," writes Meinecke, "is the fact that both spheres are linked by a very close causal bond, the fact that great and blessed cultural val-ues often have a commonplace and impure origin and have struggled upwards from the depths of darkness as though God needed the devil to realize Himself."[36]

This reconciliation of freedom and necessity, of value with the tragic and purposeless in history, has many elements in common with Sir Isaiah Berlin's rejection of historical inevitability.[37] Ultimately, freedom in both Meinecke's and Berlin's system is dependent on man's necessity to believe that he is free. Moreover, both Berlin and Meinecke reject the relativism that has bedeviled historicist thought. But while Berlin rejects relativism on the basis of commonsense empiricism—that is, on the basis that relativ-ism simply does not accord with our experience—Meinecke goes beyond this to a more elaborate metaphysical justification.

Meinecke writes, "To the realization of Heraclitus that 'all is flux' must immediately be appended the demand of Archimedes, 'Give me a place to stand.' But then the tasks the individual works to achieve and the ideas for which he fights must actually contain something enduring."[38] In short, both eternal change and the demand for certainty and purpose are primary ex-periences of human life. Do values exist that stand beyond the reach of relativism? We can, Meinecke argues, escape relativity of values by absolutizing the values of the past—by romantic flight—or by absolutizing the future. But both romantic piety and futurism destroy the present and negate the identity of eternity and the moment.

A third avenue of escape offers itself. Relativity can be avoided only by absolutizing all values. "In every epoch, in every individual creation of history spiritual powers bestir themselves and strive to rise out of inert nature and pure egoism into a higher world. Their flight may be more or less successful, but what they achieve at any given time is completely indi-vidual and differentiated from any previous or later value in history."[39] Seen from this perspective, all the values of history have become absolute val-ues, irrespective of their position in the temporal sequence or their success or failure. Meinecke, one is tempted to say, wrote "inner-directed" history.

But these values are not arbitrary and subjective, and they are not de-pendent on place or time.

> In the voice of conscience all that is temporary and relative be-comes fixed and absolute. . . . The content of that which the conscience disclose to individual men is in many respects indi-

vidual and time-bound. But every self-examination discloses
that the conscience imposes at the same time exact limits on
pure subjectivity, arbitrariness or still worse temptations.... And
so the conscience is the mighty cement of human society—and
at the same time it is mankind's real metaphysical source.[40]

Even after the shattering experience of the total collapse of values
occasioned by the rise of National Socialism and the disaster of World
War II, Meinecke wrote, "Goethe said in an ode: 'Man alone is capable
of the impossible. He discriminates, chooses, judges.' How the appar-
ently impossible nevertheless becomes possible, how we in our observation so often see good and evil growing into one another and in our
moral actions are able to discriminate and work for the good—that can
never be fully comprehended through logic, but must be experienced
in life in order to be understood. . . ."[41]

In Meinecke's assessment of German history there was much that
was temporary, contradictory, mistaken.[42] But the enlarged vision that
he brought to the study of history possesses an absolute value. His solutions, tentative and incomplete though they are, offer the only viable
solutions to the problem of historicism, and the historicism that he so
critically explored is the only historical system valid for modern man.

11

The United States as a "Revolutionary Society"

The assertion that, two hundred years after a revolution reluctantly made and the adoption of a Constitution that strengthened rather than weakened the conservative character of American political institutions and arrangements, American society and politics are still revolutionary is, I suggest, a rather daring thesis. Other revolutions have run their courses from high hopes to Thermidorian reaction in the passage of a few brief years, and while the Russians and the Chinese have talked of "permanent revolution," they have exhibited only too clearly the ways in which revolutionary elites, while proclaiming themselves the handmaidens of popular revolution, have become in fact new privileged and exploiting classes. It is odd and very nearly contradictory that a conservative revolution now two centuries old should be the only "permanent revolution" history has known, a revolution that has perennially transformed the structure and the nature of life in the United States.

It is not obvious to everyone at the present time, however, that the United States is still a revolutionary society. There have been a good many recent assertions that American society has hardened into a totalitarian mold, that repression is the chief characteristic of American political life, and that there is both less liberty and less social justice in America than in many contemporary Marxist states. Perhaps, then, I would not be ill advised were I to first present my reasons for believing America to be still and increasingly revolutionary before I go on to explore the reasons why I believe America has been able to maintain and broaden its revolutionary base.

It is important that we demonstrate clearly the truly revolutionary character of the events of 1776 and their continuing impact upon American society. It has become fashionable on the Left to assert that there was no genuine revolution, or that if a revolution took place it was strangled by the ensuing conservative reaction. The study of American history has produced many stern judges and doubting Thomases. None was tempted to take a more critical attitude than were Charles and Mary Beard. When, however, they came to make an assessment of the American Revolution in their *Rise of American Civilization,* they pointed unhesitatingly to the truly revolutionary character of the events they described:

> If a balance sheet is struck and the rhetoric of the Fourth of July celebrations is disconnected, if the externals of the conflict are given proper perspective and background, then it is seen that the American Revolution was more than a war on England. It was in truth an economic, social, and intellectual transformation of prime significance—the first of those modern world-shaking reconstructions in which mankind has sought to cut and fashion the tough and stubborn web of fact to fit the pattern of its dreams.

But even without the Beards' respected view we know that there was a genuine revolution because we live out its enduring consequences and its continuing ramifications. Indeed, one of our least admirable contemporary attitudes is our retreat from the novelty and the implications of our revolutionary heritage and our search (a vain one to be sure) into what we think to be the quiet reaches of the past for a golden age of tranquility. Surfeited on change we imagine that at some golden moment in some magical American Camelot men were free of the necessity to choose and to change—the necessity that the initial revolutionary transformation of our society has imposed on all of us. While the Left sees insufficient change of a particular socioeconomic and political type, the Right rejects those changes which necessarily follow from the principles of the revolution.

That the American Revolution was indeed a "world-shaking reconstruction," as the Beards insisted it was, is borne out by the testimony of diverse observers of American society. Several years ago, for example, John W. Holmes, director general of the Canadian Institute of International Affairs, was interviewed by NBC News. In that interview Holmes made the following important point:

> The United States is a pioneer society even in its adversities. In spite of what many young Americans say, it is not counterrevolutionary—it is still a revolutionary society. It seems to me that you are going through a further and very turbulent extension of democracy. All sorts of people are participating in the policy-making process who never did before, and this is a trial other countries have yet to cope with.

Holmes's observations concerning the revolutionary character of contemporary American society are not entirely original. Much the same observations were made by Jean-François Revel, a Frenchman and a man of
the political Left, in his book *Without Marx or Jesus,* published in 1970 at the
very peak of our recent "time of troubles" and self-doubt: "To my mind,
present-day America is a laboratory of revolution—in the sense that eighteenth-century England was to Voltaire. . . ." "The stuff of revolution, and
its first success, must be the ability to innovate. It must be mobility with
respect to the past, and speed with respect to creation. In that sense, there
is more revolutionary spirit in the United States today, even on the Right,
than there is on the Left anywhere else."

One might enlarge both the number of quotations and the number of
authors. The fact is that America is a revolutionary society; has been such
from the outset and derives a great deal of its revolutionary élan from the
events and ideas of its initial revolutionary movement.

But even if we admit that the United States is a revolutionary society in
which the processes of political, economic, and social transformation are
constantly at work we must, in search both of historical and self understanding, ask the question "why?" There have been other revolutions in
other places and other times and the consequences have been far more
ambiguous, far less clear, far less progressive and optimistic. If one studies
the history of France in the nineteenth and twentieth centuries it becomes
clear that a well-intentioned and successful revolution is not enough to
energize permanently the forces of progressive change in a society. For the
past two centuries France has vacillated between the poles of anarchy and
authoritarian Caesarism. There have been brief and extended periods of
liberal and even democratic government but these have not been characterized by any high degree of certainty and self-assurance.

England alone has shown throughout this whole period of the past two
centuries the continuity of development in the direction of liberal and
democratic institutions comparable to the American experience, but that
development has at best been tardy, grudging, and complicated by ancient
social and cultural encrustations and deep-seated class divisions and an-
tagonisms. One is tempted to argue that innovative and democratic societies do not often arise from liberating revolutions.

And so we must return to the question of why the revolutionary tradition has maintained its vitality in the American setting, why America in
this respect has been so much more fortunate, so much more creative, and
so much more dynamic than other societies that have passed through a
revolutionary experience.

And no doubt good fortune, pure luck played a role. "Amerika, du hast
es besser," the German poet Goethe wrote in 1823. Freely translated, he

said, "America, you're lucky," though he hastened to add as his reasons "the lack of inner confusion, a useless fixation on the past, and vain conflict." Others have adduced different reasons for considering America a fortunate, a lucky land. There were the nearly empty continent, the favorable geographic and climatic factors, the untapped and abundant natural resources, the immense land area, the promise and the actuality of El Dorado even though the fountain of youth and the earthly paradise remained a dream. And yet it could not have been luck alone, or even chiefly, that accounted for the peculiarly American progressive dynamism. The Great Russian peoples entered the underpopulated and resource-rich vastness of Central Asia and Siberia and their authoritarian institutions were not transformed. Latin America was not so different geographically from North America and yet its political and cultural experience was wholly different. It too had liberal revolutions, often modeled on the revolution that had taken place in the Thirteen Colonies, yet these relapsed very shortly into political patterns of authority and tyranny. Even Australia and New Zealand seem stodgy and conservative in comparison with the cultural, social, and political experimentation that has characterized the United States. The existence, then, of a great, empty, unexploited land is not the answer to our question of why the United States has been characterized by a revolutionary dynamism.

Long ago men identified a "restless temper" with the private enterprise of democratic societies, societies in which men gloried in being thrown upon their own resources and encouraged to make their own decisions. Thucydides, on the eve of the outbreak of the Peloponnesian War (Book I, Chapter 6), puts into the mouths of the Corinthian ambassadors to Sparta a speech concerning the Athenians that must remind us at nearly every point of peculiarly American characteristics.

> Then also we think we have as much right as anyone else to point out faults in our neighbors, especially when we consider the enormous difference between you and the Athenians. To our minds, you are quite unaware of this difference; you have never yet tried to imagine what sort of people these Athenians are against whom you will have to fight—how much, indeed how completely different from you. An Athenian is always an innovator, quick to form a resolution and quick at carrying it out. You, on the other hand, are good at keeping things as they are; you never originate an idea; and your action tends to stop short of its aim. Then again, Athenian daring will outrun its own resources; they will take risks against their better judgment, and still, in the midst of danger, remain confident. But your na-

ture is always to do less well than you could have done, to mis-trust your own judgment, however sound it may be, and to as-sume that dangers will last forever. Think of this, too: while you are hanging back, they never hesitate; while you stay at home, they are always abroad; for they think that the farther they go the more they will get, while you think that any movement may endanger what you have already. If they win a victory they fol-low it up at once, and if they suffer a defeat, they scarcely fall back at all. As for their bodies, they regard them as expendable for their city's sake, as though they were not their own; but each man cultivates his own intelligence, again with a view of doing something noble for his city. If they aim at something and do not get it, they think they have been deprived of what belonged to them already; whereas, if their enterprise is successful, they regard that success as nothing compared to what they will do next. Suppose they fail in some undertaking; they make good the loss immediately by setting their hopes in some other direc-tion. Of them alone it may be said that they possess a thing al-most as soon as they have begun to desire it, so quickly with them does action follow upon decision. And so they go on work-ing away in hardship and danger all the days of their lives, sel-dom enjoying their possessions because they are always adding to them. Their view of a holiday is to do what needs doing; they prefer hardship and activity to peace and quiet. In a word, they are by nature incapable of either living a quiet life themselves or of allowing anyone else to do so.

Thucydides, as Herodotus before him, had no doubt that this "restless temper" which characterized Athens was a consequence of her democratic institutions. Of course democracy did play a major role both in Athens and in America in energizing the forces of innovation. But democracy alone was not the explanation, for Sparta too was, in its strange way, democratic, and there are contemporary democratic societies that one could hardly describe as dynamic. The explanation for our peculiar dynamism is not democracy alone but democracy coupled with the spirit of enterprise. That "restless temper" was most manifest when it was coupled with the desire for unique individual expression and the compelling drive to self-advantage. Self-fulfillment and free choice have been in America extended into every aspect of life. From the abandonment of primogeniture, titles, and heredi-tary status to the right of every man to build the biggest, costliest, and ugliest house in the neighborhood or to live in the meanest, shabbiest shack in town, the motive has been the same. Americans have believed that every man should be free to seek his bliss and his advantage on his own terms. The basic liberal assumption that private advantage redounds to public benefit has been the essential and fundamental assumption. From the outset democratic politics was related directly in fact and in theory to freedom of enterprise in economics. John Stuart Mill, after reading Tocqueville on *Democracy in America,* quoted with approval the lines in which Tocqueville expressed his belief that the links between capitalism and democracy were fundamental:

> As soon as land was held on any other than feudal tenure, and personal property began in its turn to confer influence and power, every improvement that was introduced in commerce or manufactures was a fresh element of the equality of conditions. Henceforward every new discovery, every new want that it engendered, and every new desire that craved satisfaction, was a step toward the universal level. The taste for luxury, the love of war, the sway of fashion, the most superficial as well as the deepest passions of the human heart, co-operated to enrich the poor and to impoverish the rich. From the time when the exercise of the intellect became a source of strength and wealth, it is impossible not to consider every addition to science, every fresh truth, every new idea, as a germ of power placed within the reach of the people. Poetry, eloquence, and memory, the grace of wit, the glow of imagination, the depth of thought, and all the gifts of providence which are bestowed by providence without respect of persons, turned to the advantage of democracy; and even when they were in the possession of its adversaries, they still served its cause by throwing into relief the natural greatness of man; its conquests spread, therefore, with those of civilization and knowledge; and literature became an arsenal, where the poorest and the weakest could always find weapons to their hand.

Tocqueville saw in this movement such evidence of inevitability that he assumed it to be the work of providence. Today we are less certain of the inevitable march of equality, however basic the drive for equality may be as an element in human behavior. It is clear, however, that the energies released through the free exercise, not only of the franchise, but of every human gift and talent unencumbered by tradition and unimpeded by society or the state has transformed and continues to transform the very conditions of human existence. No doubt there are many Americans who would be delighted were that "restless temper" to be quieted, were the revolutionary energies of our society to be stilled or stopped. Sometimes as I walk across the campus I yearn to see the year when the approach of spring does not mean that the grounds will be dug up, that old buildings will come down and new buildings rise, that old ideas will not be in the discard and a band of young turks will not be pressing for change and innovation— and the campus is our society in microcosm; change is the overriding aspect of our existence. It is the most characteristic feature of our society. My purpose is not to praise or to laud change or even to assert my admiration for a society that is constantly in flux. Indeed, my own conservative sympathies lead me to mistrust change and to feel uneasy when I am caught up in some rapid transition. My personal feelings, however, are of little importance; what is important is that we recognize what the full consequences of freedom have been in our society. No doubt some of the consequences have been unacceptable to many men, but we cannot doubt that there has been revolutionary change. Those who have lived through a revolution know it well enough. Things are simply different than they were before. The color, the texture, and the mode of life have changed and these changes have drawn us all into their circle.

We all know, moreover, that freedom has been either the remote or the immediate cause for these changes. Revolutions have a way of petering out; their mighty currents sinking into the sand in the course of a few decades at most. That this has not happened in the United States has been due to that "restless temper," and that in turn has been in substantial measure the reflection of a peculiarly American economic and intellectual pattern. In each generation the drive to innovation and the recasting of our institutions has been due, above all, to the institutions of a market economy and the spirit of enterprise. In the intellectual sphere, it has been a reflection of our dedication to freedom of the press and general access to education. We have continued to be a revolutionary people, then, because we have maintained a free market in goods and a free market in ideas.

Many of the complaints that thoughtful men have lodged against private enterprise are the same arguments, or arguments parallel to those, which they have lodged against a free press. They have said that it is wasteful, that it produces a society that is materialistic, vulgar, corrupt in taste, and indifferent in morals; that it produces a world in which the mediocre rather than the best prevail, that it rewards indifference to the truth and the fast-buck artist, the con-man, and the literary hack. And no doubt all these charges are true. The competition of goods and the competition of ideas are no doubt in the short run wasteful, and their effects lead some men to mediocrity and vulgarity. But this system, which rewards innovation and guarantees it through free and open competition, is the only method any society has of arriving in the long run at both the truth and abundance, at not only those things which are good but those things which are the best available. The central dictum of the philosophy of Charles Sanders Peirce, the key to his philosophy of science, was, "Do not block the way of inquiry." As theorists of market economics have demonstrated over and over again, the market is not simply an economic device but a discovery mechanism as crucial in its way for knowing as the work of scientific laboratories. We have remained politically resilient because we have rewarded innovation and difference, because we have encouraged men to do their own things, and because we have asserted always that the long-range welfare of the individual is more important than the short-range welfare of the group. In short, the founding fathers gambled on the desirability and the permanency of change.

Although the frontier alone neither produced liberty nor ensured its survival, it did provide the habitat in which freedom flourished. One need not subscribe completely to Frederick Jackson Turner's thesis in one of its variations in order to accept the evidence of the impact of the American landscape and American conditions on the political and social institutions of the United States. It was precisely in this environment, where geographic mobility paralleled and fostered social mobility, that our "restless temper" found its expression eased and strengthened. There was, in the very facts of geography, an invitation to expansiveness, and the abundance and bounty of the land encouraged men to what must at times have seemed a wasteful experimentation. Men were induced by nature to try their luck, and lifestyles that were both innovative and impermanent appeared and disappeared with bewildering rapidity. Of course, experimentation was not always rewarded; there have been tragedies enough in the American past to remind us of that; but there have always been the bonanzas too, the big but seemingly foolish idea that paid off handsomely. Ours is a landscape that has encouraged the far-out, the grandiose, the individual, the deviant, the violent, and the unusual. It has been a landscape that has seemed in natural league with the other forces of liberty to assure the continued existence of freedom on this continent; a landscape rich enough to encourage the wildest hope and the most magnificent of ambitions, yet challenging enough to ensure that the dictum of Darius, which we find in Herodotus, that "soft lands make soft men," would never be applied to the American scene.

Perhaps the most important characteristic of that landscape in its impact on politics and society has been its diversity. By diversity I do not mean the "regionalism" that has played such a large role in the explanations of American politics and history, particularly in the form given those explanations by Turner and his followers. Regionalism has been based on dividing and defining differences, and I am concerned with those smaller gradations and shades which make the garden I grow in my backyard different from that of my friend who lives only two hundred miles away. In Europe, we take the impact of those differences for granted, for there variety has been entrenched in history. In our new land, with its endless variations and differences, we often fail to see our daily encounter with a complex and variegated environment as a source of the most profound differences in character and mood in American political life. In periods characterized by the rapid shift of population, such as has taken place during the past three decades, we fail to note the influence of those differences inherent in the landscape. It is likely those great movements of population are now drawing to a close and we shall once more discover how widely we differ from one another rather than how like one another we are.

Diversity, even the subtle diversity of the landscape, is an important source of liberty and an important fount of change. One of the most important theoretical questions debated by Americans in the years of the republic's foundation was the question of whether or not republican institutions could survive in an extended and sizeable state, or, to put the question in the words of Alexander Hamilton in *Federalist* 9, "the necessity of a contracted territory for a republican government." Ancient precedent and modern opinion seemed to agree that republican institutions could survive and prosper only in the narrow territories of the small state. *The Federalist Papers* turn to this question again and again, with Jay, Hamilton, and Madison each in turn denying the validity of the assertion. Their reasons for denying it are all interesting and correct, but one in particular commands our attention at the present time. The chief threat to liberty in the view of the writers of *The Federalist Papers* was the concentration of power, especially as it is reflected in an unchecked and tyrannical majority. In *Federalist* 51 either Hamilton or Madison argues that the chief way of preventing such a concentration of power is through diversification of interest. The argument runs as follows:

> It is of great importance in a republic not only to guard the society against the oppression of its rulers, but to guard one part of the society against the injustice of the other part. Different interests necessarily exist in different classes of citizens. If a majority be united by a common interest, the rights of the minority will be insecure. There are but two methods of providing against this evil: the one by creating a will in the community independent of the majority—that is, of society itself; the other, by comprehending in society so many separate descriptions of citizens as will render an unjust combination of a majority of the whole improbable, if not impracticable. The first method prevails in all governments possessing an hereditary or self-

appointed authority. This, at best, is a precarious security. . . .
The second method will be exemplified in the federal republic
of the United States. Whilst all authority in it will be derived
from and dependent on the society, the society itself will be
broken into so many parts, interests and classes of citizens, that
the rights of individuals, or of the minority, will be in little danger from interested combinations of the majority. In a free government the security for civil rights must be the same as that for
religious rights. It consists in the one case in the multiplicity of
interests, in the other in the multiplicity of sects. The degree of
security in both cases will depend on the number of interests
and sects; and this may be presumed to depend on the extent of
country and the number of people comprehended under the
same government. . . .

Consequently the greatest and most telling defense of size in the republic is the fact that size itself will help to guarantee diversity and multiplicity. It is diversity alone that in the long run will prevent the tyranny of
the majority in any society and guarantee that freedom which has always
been the great boast of our American polity. The drive to diversity in the
actuality of American life was even greater than its theoretical formulation
in *The Federalist*. It has been a drive, moreover, that has not slackened with
time but in our own day has taken on a sharp and powerful new meaning.
The racial and ethnic claims to full and distinctive participation, not as
individuals but as members of an identifiable minority group, participation in both the culture and the polity, has created a wholesome check on
what threatened to become an unexamined consensus. Submerged minorities—cultural, political, sexual, and social—have emerged within the last
few decades to challenge an older complacency and to demand the right to
participate fully after their own unique fashion in the shaping of American
life. They represent a vast potential for the renewal of the American system, and they provide, as the founding fathers anticipated, a dynamic with
which to drive the engine of liberty.

It is apparent, even from what I have so far said, that a powerful tension
exists in the American polity and American society between the ideals of
complete liberty and full equality. I am highly unoriginal in pointing this
out. We have chosen to absolutize neither the ideal of liberty nor the ideal
of equality, chosen not to sacrifice the one to the other, as happened in the
French, Russian, and other revolutions. Rather, we have tried to have it
both ways; demanding achievement and status and yet insisting, perversely
perhaps, upon equality; boasting of our liberty yet willing from time to
time to see that liberty attenuated and diluted in order that we may all

enjoy a bit more equality of condition. So much I think has often been observed and remarked on. It has not been so often pointed out, however, that this relationship of tension and reciprocity in the American system is one of the major sources of its ability to transform and to change the conditions of American life. We have remained in a state of flux because we have refused to become totalists with respect to our ideals. We have refused to succumb to the beguiling power of a single good idea and have alternated in an unseemly but very practical fashion between liberty and equality. In questions of class conflict, race, education, and minority rights in recent times we have sacrificed a measure of liberty in order to secure a greater degree of equality, but there are limits—as evidenced by the busing controversy and the question of open admissions to colleges, to cite only two examples, chosen at random—beyond which the American people will not go in sacrificing liberty to equality. A shifting adjustment between liberty and equality is always in process in American life and we have managed because of it to become both more free and more equal. Whether or not in the years ahead we shall be able to maintain this feat of social prestidigitation remains to be seen. Should we lose it I believe the system itself will falter and slow and we will find ourselves like so many other political systems and sects ruined by one good idea taken to its extreme.

We now stand at the end of a decade in which anti-institutionalism has been a major force. Political, cultural, social, and religious institutions during the past ten years have not only had a bad press, they have been vigorously attacked and denounced by the trendy intellectual elites of the Western world. That has happened before and is not necessarily a sign of danger. More important, however, is the fact that ordinary men and women have lost faith and confidence in those institutions, often not without reason. The courts have not functioned well. The holder of the highest office in the land has laid himself open to charges that, if true, exhibit a contempt for the values of our system almost unprecedented in our history. To argue that these developments came at the end of a period during which governmental powers had been surrendered by the states and concentrated in Washington; that in this period the office of the presidency moved from republican simplicity of manner to imperial grandeur; and that during this time more and more of the everyday decisions of our public lives were made at a great remove from the people whom those decisions effect—to say this and to add that other recent presidents appear to have acted no better simply compounds the problem and deepens public pessimism. Nor do Congress, state legislatures, and state administrative officers fare better in the public estimate.

It may seem presumptuous, then, to argue that the basic structure of our institutions as set forth in the Constitution is sound and functioning

and that the self-correcting powers of the system have asserted themselves and are, in fact, even now producing the necessary changes.

For the Constitution, conservative in temper, liberal in principle, has
been, it seems to me, one of the chief reasons for ordered change in our
society. That conservative temper of the Constitution is reflected in its
evaluation of men and their motives and its ability to employ even self-
interest in the pursuit of the common good. *Federalist* 51 (which surely is
one of the most remarkable documents in all of the American state papers)
puts the case in the following words:

> Ambition must be made to counteract ambition. The interest of
> the man must be connected with the constitutional rights of the
> place. It may be a reflection on human nature, that such devices
> should be necessary to control the abuses of government. But
> what is government itself, but the greatest of all reflections on
> human nature? If men were angels no government would be
> necessary. If angels were to govern man, neither external nor
> internal controls on government would be necessary. In fram-
> ing a government that is to be administered by men over men,
> the great difficulty lies in this: you must first enable the govern-
> ment to control the governed; and in the next place oblige it to
> control itself. A dependence on the people is, no doubt, the pri-
> mary control on the government; but experience has taught
> mankind the necessity of auxiliary precautions.

Those "auxiliary precautions" have been written into the fabric of the
Constitution. They lie at the heart of our self-correcting system. Even and
particularly at the moments of greatest crisis, they have enabled us to proceed in our public and private lives with a measure of assurance in making
those changes—in the sum revolutionary—which have enabled us to live
in ordered freedom. How sad, then, "the fact," as Irving Kristol recently
pointed out, that "at our major universities it is almost impossible to find a
course, graduate or undergraduate, devoted to *The Federalist*." (How important those essays are may be determined by anyone who cares to read
number 65, written by Alexander Hamilton on the subject of impeach-
ment.) And so, in the final analysis, it is our basic institutions and the founding instruments of the Declaration of Independence and the Constitution
that have perpetuated our values and given our system its elasticity and its
dynamism.

The men who made the American Revolution were reluctant rebels.
They did not deliberately set out to create an ideal society and forge the
fabric of a new nation in the fires of war. They were surprised at their own

audacity and fearful of its consequences. And when they sought to justify their actions to themselves and to the world at large they rested their arguments on an appeal to the British constitution and a demand that their traditional rights as Englishmen be recognized. Few if any revolutions have been so conservative in their inspiration.

Yet once those liberties and historical rights were taken seriously, once they had become the central principle of a new polity, they changed and transformed the whole texture of American political and social life. It was, indeed, as though the American Revolution had salvaged the great vital principle that stood at the heart of the English historical experience and had given it new life and meaning. Far from being a break with the past and its institutions, the new American nation sheltered, preserved, and quickened political ideas, constitutional forms, and political institutions that were temporarily in eclipse in Europe.

Sometimes an act of conservation is a truly revolutionary action. The concrete realization of specific liberties, no matter how partial or incomplete, was in the instance of the American revolution the great device by which liberty permeated the totality of American life in the years that were to come. That process has not ended and I would like to remind you that success as well as failure exacts a price.

PART FOUR: INTELLECTUAL HISTORY

This section reflects the range of ideas with which Tonsor was concerned throughout his career. His interests ranged from the philosophical (especially continental philosophy), including the impact of Marx on modernity, to the prosaic, such as the role of myth as an agent in human affairs. He also wrote widely on topics ranging from science fiction to poetry. An unpublished—and somewhat incomplete—lecture on socialism is published here for the first time.

12

Socialism

"Socialism," you must have realized by this time, is a very elastic term, so elastic, in fact, that by constant stretching it has lost much of its meaning. Any term which can be stretched to cover George Bernard Shaw, Virginia Woolf, F. D. Maurice (the founder of the Christian Socialists), Henry George (who introduced the idea of a single tax on undeveloped property), William Morris (one of the founders of the Arts and Crafts movement), Charles Fourier (who was described by Marx as a "Utopian Socialist"), and Karl Marx (who liked to call himself a "scientific socialist") is surely one which is so elastic as to be able to stretch no further. Are we then to say that unlike conservatism and nineteenth-century liberalism, socialism has no coherent set of social perceptions and contains no integral body of doctrine?

This, of course, is not the case, but to get at the meaning of socialism we shall have to turn to what I will describe as the engendering experiences and then work outward from these experiences to a body of doctrine and plan of social action which, in broad terms, is described as socialist. Which, then, were the engendering experiences which gave rise to a distinctively socialist viewpoint?

I believe that fundamental to the rise of socialism was the decay or transformation of community as human beings had hitherto perceived community. The natural community of the village, a community in which peasants and craftsmen were enmeshed in a set of reciprocal relationships, was by the end of the eighteenth century being dissolved by capitalistic agriculture, the industrial process, and urbanization. Sociologists of the nineteenth century often spoke of the progressive development of society as a movement from custom to contract, by which they implied that the dissolution of natural community was both inevitable and humanly fulfilling. At the beginning of society stood the spontaneous development of mutual obligation and the instinctive social solidarity of the extended family and the village community. No one lived alone or totally pursued his own purposes. Custom was king and dependence was the mark of the good society rather than a badge of inadequacy. This set of mutual dependencies, reciprocal obligations, and status based upon hierarchy and aristocracy was to be swept away and replaced by contract, an elite based on achievement, and a community that had been transformed into the marketplace and the cash nexus.

Moreover, the social cement of supernatural religion was weakened and dissolved by the thoroughgoing rationalism which characterized advanced urban-industrial, technological-scientific configurations. The Lord of life and death, the God of seedtime and harvest, the giver of rain in due season, the refuge of the sick and afflicted, the aid of the poor, despised, and exploited seemed distant, remote, and unreachable in the cities, mines, and factories of the new age.

It was easy for the Romantic poet to find God in nature, even to equate God with nature. No one attempted to equate God with the industrial process or to find God in the dark alleyways of London, Manchester, or Birmingham. William Blake spoke of "England's dark, Satanic mills" and it was generally agreed that the city and the factory were the devil's own place, if indeed they belonged to any supernatural power. Consequently both the idea of community of the spontaneous, natural variety, and the cement of community that religion provided were by the opening years of the nineteenth century breaking down and disappearing.

Those who were uprooted from the older patterns of community and deprived of the consolations of religion felt the loss most acutely. Nationalism, which was in part a surrogate religion and which attempted to provide a substitute community, was a poor compensation for the lost feeling of belonging that traditional society provided. The nineteenth-century liberal substitute for community in the marketplace and the cash nexus had little appeal to those accustomed to the certainties of traditional society and the sense of place and assured status such a society was able to give.

We must not paint too rosy a picture of pre-capitalistic, pre-industrial society. There were many dark shadows in that set of social relationships, too. Perhaps, indeed, they were even darker than the conditions that characterized urban and industrial development. However, human beings had learned to live with that set of limitations and deprivations through thousands of years of human experience. The new conditions simply cut them adrift and exposed them to the experience of anomie and purposelessness.

There were new images of community on which socialism was based and from which it derived much of its appeal, and these images of community were reflections of the experience of industrial and urban life. The natural community of the agricultural village was replaced by the new social experience of the factory. The cement of supernatural religion was replaced by the perception of a common class enemy and the solidarity of a common class identity. Now, the meaning of this experience was not immediately apparent to the new urban and industrial masses. Their consciousness had to be formed by the theorists of socialism, who pointed out the meaning implicit in this new set of experiences.

First of all, then, I wish to argue that socialism was a response to the quest for community and the discovery of new forms of community in the factory and in the rise of class consciousness. The fact that workers have rarely found community in the factory or in the labor union hall does not of course mean that they did not look for community there.

Secondly, socialism was a response to the wealth and productivity that resulted from the new factories and the new highly developed and complex interworkings of human purpose that characterized capitalistic and industrial society; wealth and productivity came to be viewed as social creations rather than the consequence of private enterprise. John Locke had argued that property was the consequence of the individual's having mixed his labor with the common store of the earth's resources. That property was private, the creation of an individual laborer. However, in a factory it is extremely difficult to describe wealth as the creation of an individual. In a manufacturing process characterized by a high degree of division of labor, the manufactured good is the creation of many hands and many talents. Wealth appeared to many of those who created it to be social rather than individual in character.

In such a process, all who participate are indispensable to the creation of the good. If wealth is social in this sense, there is no possible way to allocate goods on the basis of productive contribution, and so the distribution of goods must be in some sense equal. Because wealth cannot be created aside from society, all private wealth—that is, wealth appropriated for private purposes—is, as Proudhon said, "theft." Private property is theft. If one follows this line of reasoning it becomes clear that private property must be abolished and all participants in the productive process must be entitled to equal shares in the goods produced. Such reasoning does not recognize differing weights to the factors of production, nor does it recognize differing contributions of talent, energy, and skill.

No doubt this particular view of wealth as social was caused at least in part by an enormous increase in wealth. From the beginning of the nineteenth century in Europe and America, it was clear that the environment was being transformed at an unprecedented scale. Great cities rose, engineering works such as the Suez Canal and the American transcontinental railroads changed the face of continents, and industrial enterprises and extractive industries dramatized the suddenly released energies of the age of coal and iron. The cult of conspicuous consumption among the old and the *nouveau riches* of the nineteenth century, consumption and power that made the wealth of kings seem petty in comparison—all of this led the workers who were the creative sources of such wealth to question the legitimacy of a system that rewarded capital and enterprise with what appeared to be a disproportionate share of the newly created wealth.

Socialism has always insisted that wealth be distributed according to need, and that as wealth is created by all so should all own the means of production. But socialism no less than liberalism is unable to banish scarcity. Recall that economics is the science of scarcity; need alone is therefore hardly a justification for a claim on the common store. Whose "need" is the greatest? What sort of needs ought we to seek to satisfy? Ought food to come ahead of education, housing ahead of art, public structures ahead of private housing, investment capital ahead of consumption? Socialism seeks to solve the problem of scarcity in two ways. In a market economy the satisfaction of needs and the direction of economic development are left to market forces and individual decisions. Market forces are impersonal and for the most part are made outside the political arena. In every socialist system, on the other hand, economic decisions are not made by market forces but are determined in the political arena. The economy is politicized and the people as a whole or a party elite make economic decisions. Moreover, since socialism cannot banish scarcity socialist systems must always resort to rationing. Of course, rationing does not necessarily involve the use of ration cards. It may simply be a tax on certain items, or it may be a subsidy which keeps the price of certain items below the cost of production, or it may be the failure of state enterprises to produce particular items or satisfy a particular market. Capital is rationed and directed; labor cannot move freely or advantageously. Rationing and direction rather than the free flow of market forces determines the shape and size of the economy.

Of course, until the 1917 revolution in Russia no socialist government exercised power in Europe. (I do not count the brief experience of the Paris commune in 1870.) Consequently the particular form that productive and distributive mechanisms would take in socialism was unclear. Still, there was enough experience from utopian socialist communities and cooperative societies, together with a great body of theoretical writing, to make clear the main outlines of socialist economies. They have scarcely changed either in objective or policy up to this time.

Planning, in some form, was to replace the interaction of market forces. When we go to the stationer's shop we know that there will be on the shelves the kind of paper we wish to buy. It is there because a complex of market forces and spontaneous decisions has placed it there—at a market-clearing price. In the command economies that characterize socialism, however, goods appear in the marketplace because a central planning body has anticipated need (note that I did not write "demand").

It was assumed in the nineteenth century that planning would be a much more efficient and effective way to produce goods than the wasteful mechanisms of private initiative and free competition. There would be no gluts or surpluses, there would always be full employment, and resources would be used effectively. We know today from actual experience with socialist economies that such planning rarely achieves the goals planners set for themselves, and often enough when we go to the stationer's in the Soviet Union there is no paper to be had. But, theoretically and viewed from the outside, market forces and free competition seem a terribly inefficient way to produce goods, and there can be no doubt that this perception played a very important role in the development of socialism.

Planning and the utopian dimensions of socialism appealed in particular to intellectuals. By the middle of the nineteenth century, the universities were producing larger and larger numbers of intellectuals, many of them unemployed, many of them alienated and hostile to the society in which they lived—a society that did not recognize their talents and had not made a place for them. In a certain sense socialism has always been far less a workers' movement than it has been a movement of alienated intellectuals.

Thirdly, socialists believed that the victory of the working classes would eliminate poverty—the grinding poverty of the nineteenth century—and replace it with plenty. The hope was a utopian one and helps to account for the secularist and frequently antireligious tone of socialism. You must recall that Christianity reverenced poverty, that the poor were considered especially blessed by Jesus, that St. Francis embraced "Lady Poverty" as his ideal companion. The basic assumptions of socialism were quite contrary to this ideal. The ascetic ideal and voluntary poverty were incomprehensible to those who joined the socialist movement.

Furthermore, socialist doctrine held a conception of the progressive development of human history in which the final and last stage of history would be a golden age in which poverty and alienation had been eliminated. Often, socialists believed that the historical process itself made this development inevitable. Christian socialists held a variant form of this teaching of progressive development. According to the Christian socialists, the last age of the world would see the establishment of the kingdom of God on earth. The work of redemption would be completed and the reign of sin would be abolished. Whether the socialism was secular or Christian it contained a marked component of millenarian and eschatological anticipation.

As a part of that expectation socialists believed that the class struggle and national economic competition were the chief causes of war. It was assumed that as soon as an international classless society appeared war would vanish from the earth. Militarism and military budgets were, said the socialists, merely means by which capitalists kept themselves in business. Competition within particular capitalistic societies and competition between capitalistic societies in the international sphere would both disappear with the advent of the international proletariat.

Finally "alienation" would be abolished. Marx wrote in the *Economic-Philosophical Manuscripts* of 1844:

> What constitutes the alienation of labor? First that the work is *external* to the worker, that it is not a part of his nature; and that consequently, he does not fulfill himself in his work but denies himself, has a feeling of misery rather than well-being, does not develop freely his mental and physical energies but is physically exhausted and mentally debased. The worker, therefore, feels himself at home only during his leisure time, where as at work he feels homeless. His work is not voluntary but imposed, *forced labor.* It is not the satisfaction of a need, but only a *means* for satisfying other needs. Its alien character is clearly shown by the fact that as soon as there is no physical or other compulsion it is avoided like the plague. External labor, labor in which man alienates himself, is a labor of self sacrifice, or mortification. Finally, the external character of work for the worker is shown by the fact that it is not his own works but work for someone else, that in work he does not belong to himself but to another person.

What Marx calls alienation was a common enough experience in the nineteenth century and is, indeed, a common enough experience today in both capitalist and socialist countries. Striking Polish workers must be driven back to their machines and into the mines with rubber truncheons and bayonets. But the perception of work in the nineteenth century was filled with a pathos and anxiety which it has in part lost in the last one hundred and fifty years. Recall that the new industrial masses were only a few miles away from the agricultural villages in which they had been born. Recall that the factory bell and whistle were new experiences, that the labor discipline demanded by the industrial process was unknown in agricultural life. Recall that the laborer worked twelve- and fourteen-hour days, six days a week, that the life of labor began in childhood and ended at the relatively early death of the laborer, and that wages were painfully low. It is this experience of labor—given the fancy name "alienated labor" by a German intellectual—which made socialism a great hope for many nineteenth- and twentieth-century workers.

If community is the key to the thought of nineteenth-century conservatism and liberty the key to the thought of classical liberalism, equality is the key to the thought of socialism. Men are moved to action by a few key words rather than complicated ideological formulations, though, indeed, these simple words may embrace a wide context of experiences and meanings.

Socialism was fortunate in that it was not put to the test of the exercise of power for nearly eighty years. True, those little microcosms of socialist society, the utopian socialist colonies, all ended in a fairly short time in failure—sometimes spectacular failure. They were usually broken on the hard stone of the nuclear family or the passions of greed and self-interest. But for eighty years socialism on a national or international scale remained a great and thrilling hope.

When it did come to power it faced, oddly enough, the same set of problems faced by classical liberalism. Men were less rational and behaved less rationally than most socialists believed they would. Socialism was as little a method for obtaining social harmony and social equilibrium as classical liberalism had been. Competition for power and status did not disappear with the advent of the socialist state. The socialist state failed in a most significant way in the achievement of equality. "Alienated labor" did not disappear. International conflict between socialist states became a commonplace (witness the conflict between the Soviet Union and China). Finally, scarcity was a problem at least as intractable in socialist as in capitalist societies, and many would argue that if one desires material plenty and a wide and free choice of goods, life in a nonsocialist society is to be preferred.

13

The Use and Abuse of Myth

So long as myth was thought of as the inconsequential and childish imaginings of the human race, and so long as myth was considered as essentially decorative, it was not and could not be taken seriously. When Thomas Bulfinch, the American mythographer, put his *Age of Fable or the Beauties of Mythology* into print in 1855, he did so in order that "our readers may thus at the same time be entertained by the most charming fictions which fancy has ever created, and put in possession of information indispensable to everyone who would read with intelligence the literature of his own day." Bulfinch had already pointed out in his preface that "[s]uch stories and parts of stories as are offensive to pure taste and good morals are not given. But such stories are not often referred to, and if they occasionally should be, the English reader need feel no mortification in confessing his ignorance of them." Bulfinch saw mythology as a source of "elegant and suggestive illustration," and little more. Its content was the product of fancy and was by its very nature untrue, fantastic, and unreal.

The rebirth of myth in the course of the eighteenth and nineteenth centuries, however, led men to see that far from myth being untrue, it was "truer than true"; it led men to see that the truth of myth was a living, experiential truth which escaped the neat categories of logic and rational analysis. Myth possesses that higher kind of truthfulness which characterizes the typical rather than the particular: that symbolic transparency which enables the essential character and quality of human experience to shine through the confusion of ordinary events.

Bulfinch was concerned about the fact that myths contained materials which were offensive to "pure taste and good morals"; in short, he was troubled because myths concerned themselves with life. One need not take decoration seriously, but life—and that most important aspect of life, sexuality—is another matter. The nineteenth century, you will recall, was quite willing to talk about love, but not about sex, quite willing to talk about death, but not about dying.

But it is exactly the quest for life that lies at the center of all religious and mythic thinking.[1] Whatever else has been corrected and super-ceded in J. G. Frazer's *Golden Bough*, Frazer's demonstration of the relation-ship of the quest for life with religious experience and thought has stood the test of criticism. Jesus had argued the same point much more succinctly when he said of his mission, "I have come to let them have life, and to let them have it in abundance" (John 10:10).

Myth enables mankind to participate ritually in the abundance and or-der of the cosmos. The mythic and religious are manifest to men in those moments of crisis in which life is threatened or in the process of transfor-mation; at those times when the conditions for life become insecure or when the order upon which social and individual life is dependent threat-ens to collapse. The leading contemporary student of myth, Mircea Eliade, has described these critical situations in the following way:

> Every existential crisis brings once again into question both the reality of the world and the presence of man in the world. The crisis is indeed "religious" because at the archaic levels of cul-ture "being" is fused together with the "holy." For all primitive mankind, it is religious experience which lays the foundation of the World. It is ritual orientation, with the structures of sacred space which it reveals, that transforms "Chaos" into the "Cos-mos" and, therefore, renders human existence possible—pre-vents it, that is, from regression to the level of zoological exist-ence. Every religion, even the most elementary, is an ontology: it reveals the *being* of the sacred things and the divine Figures, it shows forth *that which really is*, and in doing so establishes a World which is no longer evanescent and incomprehensible, as it is in nightmares, and as it again becomes whenever existence is in danger of foundering in the "Chaos" of total relativity, where no "Centre" emerges to ensure orientation.[2]

It is precisely because religion and myth accomplish the ordering of experience, particularly in the moment of crisis when we confront life's border situations with a sense of anomie and loss of reality and identity, that mythic thinking in its great variety has reappeared with such intensity in the Western world at the present time. The great cultural and civilizational crisis of our times has driven the human spirit back to the basic ordering patterns of archaic man. There anomie, death, and nightmare are put to rout and life, in both a quantitative and qualitative sense, is ensured.

To be sure, one must enquire why the more sophisticated theologies of Christianity and Judaism do not serve, at a popular level, the need to keep anomic terror at bay. For many in Western society these traditional religions do serve this purpose, but for many more the doctrinal and theological formulations, the institutional structures, separate experience from belief. It has not satisfied most theologians to "see in a glass darkly" and to await in hope the time when they shall see "face to face." Theirs is a hubristic confidence that everything can be defined and that the spiritual man is distinguished by his knowledge rather than his love. That men fall away from the high religions, contenting themselves with the imperfect perceptions of archaic religion, is not an unusual circumstance in the history of religion. It usually follows an inordinate expansion in the intellectual and institutional claims of religion.

If the purpose of the mythic-religious generally is that of life-giving meaning and order, the mythic consciousness achieves its objectives in a particular way. Here let me quote once more from Mircea Eliade:

> Briefly stated, it is my opinion that for members of archaic and traditional societies, myth narrates a sacred history, telling of events that took place in primordial time, the fabulous time of the "beginnings." Myth is thus always an account of a "creation" of one sort or another, as it tells how something came into being. The actors are supernatural beings, and myths disclose their creative activity and reveal the sacredness [or simply the "supernaturalness"] of their work. Thus the history of this activity is considered to be absolutely *true* [because it is concerned with realities] and *sacred* [because it is the work of supernatural beings]. The cosmogonic myth is "true" because the existence of the world is there to prove it; the myth of the origin of death is equally true because man's mortality proves it, and so on.
>
> Since myth is always related to a "creation" [the world, man, a specific institution, etc.], it constitutes the paradigm for all significant human acts. By knowing it one knows the "origin" of things, and hence can control and manipulate them at will. This is a knowledge that one "experiences" ritually, either by ceremonially recounting the myth or by performing the ritual for which it serves as both a model and a justification. In traditional societies, one "lives" the myth in the sense that one is seized by the sacred, exalting power of the events recollected or reenacted.[3]

We can understand from this how important the divine paradigm is for all making and doing, how the cultural and civilizational process is bound up with religion, how every act of creation becomes, in fact, an act of worship.

More than forty years ago, when the relation between religion and culture was first being systematically explored, Christopher Dawson wrote in the Gifford Lectures of 1947:

> The complete secularization of social life is a relatively modern and anomalous phenomenon. Throughout the greater part of mankind's history, in all ages and states of society, religion has been the great unifying force in culture. It has been the guardian of tradition, the preserver of the moral law, the educator and the teacher of wisdom.
>
> And in addition to this conservative function, religion has also had a creative, conative, dynamic function, as energizer and life giver. Religion holds society in its fixed culture pattern, as in Plato's *Laws*, or as in the hierarchic order of Sumerian and Egyptian culture; but it also leads the people through the wilderness and brings them back from captivity and inspires them with the hope of future deliverance.
>
> Religion is the key of history. We cannot understand the inner form of a society unless we understand its religion. We cannot understand its cultural achievements unless we understand the religious beliefs that lie behind them.[4]

At that moment when the divine paradigm fades from consciousness, art ceases to be art and becomes the tracings of the absurd, music becomes cacophony and accidental noise, dance a spastic convulsion, and politics either a monstrous ideology or a futile effort to harmonize anarchic passions. The technological works of civilization are subordinated to no larger purposes and serve no universally human objectives. Little wonder then that in poets such as Yeats and Eliot there has been such a powerful resurgence of mythical thought; that in James Joyce and Thomas Mann the return to the myth has been made the distinctive note of modernity. The myth was reborn just at the moment in Western history when the full implications of a desacralized society were making themselves apparent.

There is, however, a danger in the recognition of the role of myth in the creation and preservation of culture. The abuse of myth in this regard is a real and powerful one. Put quite simply, it is that men confuse cultural achievement with the "holy" itself. While it is true that you cannot have culture without religion, culture is not religion. While it is true that you cannot have politics without religion, politics is not religion. As the creative power that resides in the myth is increasingly recognized, the danger grows that man will confuse his creative activity with the "holy." This confusion will produce, as it has produced in the past, an idolatry in which man worships himself in the form of the culture which man produces.

As we study myth comparatively and come to a deeper knowledge of the history of religion, particularly as religion is expressed by archaic man, we discover the common elements of our humanity. The best definition we can give of our humanity is constituted by those common elements which emerge in symbolic form in the depths of the soul as a consequence of the soul's experience of transcendent Being.

Whatever the equivalences in myth that the comparative analysis suggests, no one ought to believe that in a thoroughly relativistic fashion all myths are equally revelatory, that all myths share an equal symbolic adequacy. When Nietzsche created the symbolic figure of Zarathustra and made the "myth of the eternal return" the key to understanding Nietzschean teaching, he created a myth that obscured rather than illuminated the truth of the soul. Those who disorder their lives by placing themselves in congruence with this myth experience a fall from being. They do not become, as Nietzsche suggested, *Übermenschen*, but rather diminished men. Similarly, those who attempt to take the pseudo-Celtic mythology of Yeats seriously are surely less capable both of dealing with the soul's encounter with the divine and with the conditions of existential reality which are the givens of everyday life.

Not all myths possess the same degree of that quality which Eric Voegelin has described as "transparency." A myth must not obscure or distort the truth of the soul. It must serve to illuminate that truth. It must be truer than true. In terms of our contemporary predicament, a racial myth based upon the revival of Germanic paganism can only deprave and degrade. Similarly, a revival of the pagan myths of sexuality as we find them expressed in the works of D. H. Lawrence or Norman O. Brown can only deprive us of our full humanity. The satisfactory models of womanhood are Eve and Mary rather than Hera and Aphrodite.

A part of the "transparency" of the symbol, of the symbol's adequacy, is that it does not conceal or distort essential aspects either of the soul's experience or of everyday reality. It is very important to bear this in mind in discussing the contemporary revival of the mythic mode of thought.

God is always experienced either in the cosmic order or in the depths of the soul as power. In Judaism and Christianity particularly, as well as in classical mythology and philosophy, the power of God is embedded in a matrix of complementary qualities: love, justice, and harmony. It might, indeed, be argued that there are two great categories of myth: the myths of power and the myths of love. The myths of power, which symbolize the divine in terms of overmastering and unloving power, are extremely common. It is both easy and tempting to separate the power of God from the love of God. To appropriate power without appropriating love is the ambition of every magician, of nearly every technician, and all but a few politicians. The power of God is, in the matrix of the divine ground, a power that moves and governs through eros. The unmoved mover moves the world through love.

When the mythical deals with the power of the gods as separate and distinct from love, that power always has a demonic dimension. Satan is power, and the quest for power is always satanic in character. That is why the occultist seeks to accomplish through magic what the religious man seeks to achieve by prayer. In the nineteenth century those who meditated deeply on the subject of power—Lord Acton, Jacob Burckhardt, Max Weber, and Max Picard—all saw the demonic character of power. When, in his final temptation, Jesus was carried up to a high place, "from which he [Satan] shewed him all the kingdoms of the world and the glory of them, and said I will give thee all these if thou wilt fall down and worship me" (Matthew 4:8–11), the bait was power.

In classical mythology and its contemporary reworking, the theme is a familiar one. The tale of Philemon and Baucis, as it appears in Book Eight of Ovid's *Metamorphoses* and as it is elaborated at the close of Part II of Goethe's *Faust*, is very instructive. These two narratives taken together constitute a marvelous continuity of mythical insight and meaning. Bulfinch has paraphrased Ovid's story in the following words:

> On a certain hill in Phrygia stands a linden tree and an oak, enclosed by a low wall. Not far from the spot is a marsh, formerly good habitable land, but now indented with pools, the resort of fen-birds and cormorants. Once on a time Jupiter, in human shape, visited this country, and with him his son Mercury (he of the Caduceans), without his wings. They presented themselves as weary travelers, at many a door, seeking rest and shelter, but found all closed, for it was late, and the inhospitable inhabitants would not rouse themselves to open for their recep-

tion. At last a humble mansion received them, a small thatched cottage, where Baucis, a pious old dame and her husband Philemon, united when young, had grown old together. Not ashamed of their poverty, they made it endurable by moderate desires and kind dispositions. One need not look there for master or for servant; they two were the whole household, master and servant alike. When the two heavenly guests crossed the humble threshold, and bowed their heads to pass under the low door, the old man placed a seat, on which Baucis, bustling and attentive, spread a cloth, and begged them to sit down. Then she raked out the coals from the ashes, and kindled up a fire, fed it with leaves and dry bark, and with her scanty breath blew it into a flame. She brought out of a corner split sticks and dry branches, broke them up, and placed them under the small kettle. Her husband collected some pot-herbs in the garden, and she shred them from the stalks and prepared them for the pot. He reached down with a forked stick a flitch of bacon hanging in the chimney, cut a small piece and put it in the pot to boil with the herbs, setting away the rest for another time. A beechen bowl was filled with warm water, that their guests might wash. While all was doing they beguiled the time with conversation.

On the bench designed for the guests was laid a cushion stuffed with seaweed; and a cloth, only produced on great occasions, but ancient and coarse enough, was spread over that. The old lady, with her apron on, with trembling hand set the table. One leg was shorter than the rest, but a piece of slate put under restored the level. When fixed she rubbed the table down with some sweet-smelling herbs. Upon it she set some of Chaste Minerva's olives, some cornel berries preserved in vinegar and added radishes and cheese, with eggs lightly cooked in the ashes. All were served in earthen dishes, and an earthenware pitcher with wooden cups, stood beside them. When all was ready, the stew, smoking hot, was set on the table. Some wine, not of the oldest, was added; and for dessert, apples and wild honey; and over and above all, friendly faces, and simple but hearty welcome.

Now while the repast proceeded, the old folks were astonished to see that the wine, as fast as it was poured out renewed itself in the pitcher of its own accord. Struck with terror, Baucis and Philemon recognized their heavenly guests, fell on their knees, and with clasped hands implored forgiveness for their poor entertainment. There was an old goose, which they kept as the guardian of their humble cottage; and they bethought them to make this sacrifice in honor of their guests. But the goose, too nimble, with the aid of feet and wings, for the old folks, eluded their pursuit, and at last took shelter between the gods themselves, they forbade it to be slain; and spoke in these words: "We are Gods. This inhospitable village shall pay the penalty of its impiety; you alone shall go free from the chastisement. Quit your house and come with us to the top of yonder hill." They hastened to obey, and staff in hand, labored up the steep ascent. They had reached to within an arrow's flight of the top, when turning their eyes below, they beheld all the country sunk in a lake, only their own house left standing. While they gazed with wonder at the sight, and lamented the fate of their neighbors, that old house of theirs was changed into a *temple*. Columns took the place of the corner posts, the thatch grew yellow and appeared a gilded roof, the floors became marble, the doors were enriched with carving and ornaments of gold. Then spoke Jupiter in benignant accents: "Excellent old man, and woman worthy of such a husband, speak, tell us your wishes, what favor have you to ask of us?" Philemon took counsel with Baucis a few moments; then declared to the Gods their united wish. "We ask to be priests and guardians of this your temple; and since we have passed our lives in love and concord, we wish that one and the same hour may take us both from life, that I may not live to see her grave, nor be laid in my own by her." Their prayer was granted. They were the keepers of the temple as long as they lived. When grown very old, as they stood one day before the steps of the sacred edifice, and were telling the story of the place, Baucis saw Philemon begin to put forth leaves, and old Philemon saw Baucis changing in like manner. And now a leafy crown had grown over their heads, while exchanging parting words, as long as they could speak. "Farewell, dear spouse," they said together, and at the same moment the bark closed over their mouths. The Tyanean shepherd still shows the two trees, standing side by side, made out of the two good old people.

We encounter Philemon and Baucis once more in Goethe's *Faust*, Part II, Act V. The old Faust has undertaken the final great project of his life, the ultimate adventure in his quest for power. That adventure is nothing less than the transformation of nature and society, a project so often undertaken by ideological leaders and movements of our own time. Faust hopes to regenerate and transform society through a gigantic land reclamation project. The power to carry through this gigantic undertaking is, however, demonic power. Mephistopheles and his minions enable Faust to achieve his goal. One thing stands in his way. One thing denies him complete success. That one thing is an old couple, Philemon and Baucis, and their hut, church, and garden.

> Philemon: Who will Majesty accuse?
> 'Twas the Emperor gave the shore:
> Herald's trumpet brought the news,
> Sounding as he passed our door.
> Stroke of tools then struck our
> hearing. Near our dune the start was made;
> Huts and tents, then high upreaving
> Stood a palace in the glade.
> Baucis: Day-work failed, though never quitting
> Pick and spade men toiled away;
> But where fires at night were flitting
> Stood a finished dyke next day.
> Nightly rose a wailing sorrow,
> Sacrifice of human blood;
> Trim canal was seen the morrow,
> Where had ebbed the fiery flood.
> He is godless, long has lusted
> To possess our home and glade;
> Claims to be a neighbor trusted,
> Yet by us will be obeyed.[6]

The only thing standing between Faust and the total achievement of his objectives are these two old lovers of the gods, though in this version the temple has been transformed into a church and the swamp that once covered at divine command the inhospitable inhabitants has now been transformed into a gigantic reclamation project.

Mephistopheles advises Faust:

> Since might is yours, you'll have the right.
> You ask not *How* but *What* is done.

To be sure Faust is only half culpable. He orders Mephistopheles to remove Philemon and Baucis. Had he lived at the present time no doubt Faust would have had them sent to a well-run nursing home. Instead, they are to be transferred to a new homestead. Of course, once one enlists the aid of the demonic there is no possible way to check the degree of power either sought or applied. And so it happens, quite naturally enough, that Mephistopheles and his minions murder Philemon and Baucis and burn the hut and chapel. When the godly myth of love is displaced by the demonic myth of power, there is a near certainty that the consequences will be disastrous. And yet that precisely is the mythic displacement which increasingly characterizes the modern world. The most extreme forms of this cosmological quest for power are to be found in occultism and witchcraft, mythic religions which have achieved widespread followings in the twentieth century. More important still are those secularized versions of the great transformational myths of alchemy, smelting, and forging.[7] Smelting and forging, like the alchemy to which they give rise, are magical arts. They are arts of transformation so powerful that they very frequently require human sacrifice. The sword and the plow are magical tools and they gain their special qualities only through the powerful rites of the smith. Eliade writes: "'To make' something means knowing the magic formula which will allow it to be invented or to 'make it appear' spontaneously. In virtue of this, the artisan is a connoisseur of secrets, a magician; thus, all crafts include some kind of initiation and are handed down by an occult tradition. He who 'makes' real things is he who *knows* the secrets of making them."[8]

When Oswald Spengler wrote the *Decline of the West,* the scientific study of myth was still in its infancy. He could, however, have learned much from the works of Ernst von Lasaulx and particularly from Johann Bachofen. Myth did not bulk large in Spengler's theoretical analysis of cultures. Nonetheless he did discern the distinctive character of Western culture, which he named Faustian because of its unceasing though ultimately unsuccessful effort to conquer and transform nature.

We must not suppose that the quest for power and transformation is characteristic of contemporary ideological systems alone. In fact, it is a most common theme, running through the whole of Western history. Eliade makes this very clear when he writes in *The Forge and the Crucible*:

> The survival of the alchemists' ideology does not become immediately evident just when alchemy disappears from the pages of history and all its empirically valid chemical knowledge is being integrated into chemistry. The new science of chemistry makes use only of those empirical discoveries which do not represent—however numerous and important one may suppose them to be—the true spirit of alchemy. We must not believe that the triumph of experimental science reduced to nought the dreams and the ideals of the alchemist. On the contrary, the ideology of the new epoch, crystallized around the myth of in-

finite progress and boosted by the experimental sciences and the progress of industrialization which dominated and inspired the whole of the nineteenth century, takes up and carries forward—despite its radical secularization—the millenary dream of the alchemist. It is in the specific dogma of the nineteenth century, according to which man's true mission is to transform and improve upon Nature and become her master, that we must look for the authentic continuation of the alchemist's dream. The visionary's myth of the perfection, or more accurately, of the redemption of Nature, survives, in camouflaged form, in the pathetic programme of the industrial societies whose aim is the total transmutation of Nature, its transformation into "energy."[9]

The attitudes of the myths of power toward the world are consequently very different from those attitudes which derive from what I have called the myths of love. In the myths of power the world is transformed magically, while in the myths of love the world is transformed by a hero who struggles and suffers redemptively until evil is purged away and harmony is restored. It is difficult for us to understand just how important a role the classical heroes played: Theseus and Hercules, Oedipus and Orpheus, Jason and Achilles. They reaffirm the wholeness, rightness, and fitness of the divine ground. They do not separate power from love.

14

Modernity, Science, and Rationality

In a brilliant essay titled "The Importance of Cultural Freedom," Richard Weaver observes that a "poet who cannot show that he has felt the disillusionment of his own time as poignantly as other people cannot speak to his time."[1] If one applies this dictum to the topic under discussion, one must assume that any exploration of the antinomian, antirational, and antiscientific movement which is so markedly an aspect of modernity—or better said, contemporaneity—should come from someone who understands and at least shows some sympathy for the attitudes and arguments which mark the so-called "cultural revolution." If we are unable to bring to our topic that initial understanding we will be able neither to speak to our contemporaries nor overcome those anticultural and antirational forces which lodge not only in our society but are an important element in our own natures.

Let us begin by agreeing with Robert Frost when he wrote:

> Something there is that doesn't love a wall,
> That sends the frozen-ground-swell under it,
> And spills the upper boulders in the sun,
> And makes gaps even two can pass abreast.

Robert Frost was uneasy about walls, boundaries, rules, analysis, and order, fearing their impact on himself and on his world. He knew, of course, as we know, that life is impossible without all of these elements, though just where one should strike a balance Frost was uncertain, and his poetry is a long discussion about freedom and constraint. And we too are uneasy and troubled at the iron necessity of law and ineluctable order, the need for instinctual renunciation, the thought of a world in which all passion has given way to calculation and all feeling has become analysis. We all fear the loss of our humanity and think it just possible that the most important choices of our lives may be made somewhere outside ourselves on the basis of knowledge and information unknown to us. Worse still, we fear that we will be lamed in our vitality, that spiritually and physically we will find ourselves robbed of our potency and creativity, reduced to shadowy functionaries serving the mechanical necessities of a sterile robot culture.

Behind these well-founded fears and at a deeper level of our existence, unconscious but powerful, lies the strong human drive to anarchy and immediate and complete instinctual gratification. We want what we want when we want it, and what we want is nearly always to be had only at the expense of society and by endangering our own futures. The criminal, the conman, the delinquent are all men who have chosen what all of us are tempted to choose. As Jacob Bronowski writes: "Each of them is protesting against something in society which constricts him, and each of them wants to be a man after his own heart; yet each act of protest is more commonplace, and each conspiracy more uniform, than the society they would like to despise."[2]

"Something there is that doesn't love a wall," and yet the walled city, the walled garden, the enclosure made by the four walls of a house, all these are the very symbols of the exclusion of chaotic and anarchic nature. They are the ways by which men secure themselves and order their existences. Beyond the wall lies the insecurity and the violence of a world where the rules and purposes of civilized life do not apply. In myth and legend those anarchic and threatening forces outside the wall are depicted as dragons, Minotaurs, and Sphinxes. But they have allies in the city, allies who give them the power that they possess to work destruction on the city. Those allies are none other than the city's citizenry, who in their divided natures and wishes seek the destruction of order at the very same time as they desire its preservation. It is for this reason that the Minotaur is kept at bay by human sacrifice: a part of mankind, a part of human society is surrendered to him. Seven youths and seven maidens were sacrificed each year to the half-man, half-beast monster who lived in a labyrinth cunningly constructed by the first of the great technicians.

The image of the city with its protecting wall is more than the image of community life. It is the image of all order. That order is threatened by what lies outside the city wall, but the city is in even greater danger from what lies within. The Trojan horse of unreason, the lust for lawlessness and disorder, and the impiety of Alcibiades and his drunken friends are all a greater threat to the life of the city than the enemy outside. Order is bought at a great price. It is always provisional and unstable, and it is always enforced at the expense of individual men and their fondest desires. Law is necessary in all those instances where the common advantage is not coincident with the advantage of the individual. The theory of anarchism supposes that altruism and voluntary association will enable men to live without the law or the ordinary structures of organized community. But law exists, and community exists, precisely because the individual, left to his own devices, sees advantage in disorder and the triumphant will of the strong individual. Whatever the truth or the untruth in terms of historical accuracy of Freud's exploration of the development of community in *Totem and Taboo, Moses and Monotheism,* and *Civilization and Its Discontents,* his essays possess a profound mythic truth in their acknowledgment and affirmation of the drive to immediate instinctual gratification, their awareness of the social dimension of all culture, and their insistence that culture is created in the ceaseless war against nature and through instinctual renunciation. Man in his human rather than his animal dimension is a cultural creation. His hold upon order and civility is always precarious and threatened both by the natural exterior and by his own anarchic and ego-involved interior. Nature outside the gates and man inside both do not love a wall and would have it down.

But why, precisely, is that wall so important, and why is order so essential to any human activity? It is a fact that the very structure of our humanity is dependent on the ordered world of symbolic thought. Language, numbers, and the objectification of experience in art are all ways of ordering and structuring. Outside the world of symbols there is and can be no humanity.[3]

Even were we to discount the value of our humanity and assume that an unspoiled and unfettered animality is preferable to the world of culture, we men would still find ourselves trapped in the world of the distinctively human. As animals we are terribly ill prepared, aside from our superior intellectual capacity, for the unremitting struggle with nature which is the essential condition of the nonhuman world around us. It is precisely the ability to order, to symbolize, to organize, to deny present gratification in order to gain a distant or long-term advantage that enables the "naked ape" to succeed in this hostile and unfriendly universe. Were we to abandon this single advantage, man would cease to be the most successful biological organism on earth and would very possibly disappear altogether. The choice has been made. We may reject its implications. We may balk at the demands which the choice entails, but unless we are willing to hazard extinction there is no turning back.

Nor, indeed, are there many outside the satisfied and satiated classes of the Western world who are going to be willing to turn back. Some time before ecology became fashionable and antinomian irrationality became the vogue among our society's well-heeled cognoscenti, C. P. Snow made this point very ably. He wrote:

For, of course, one truth is straightforward, industrialization is the only hope of the poor. I use the word "hope" in a crude and prosaic sense. I have not much use for the moral sensibility of anyone who is too refined to use it so. It is all very well for us, sitting pretty, to think that material standards of living don't matter all that much. It is all very well for one, as a personal choice, to reject industrialization—do a modern Walden, if you like, and if you go without much food, see most of your children die in infancy, despise the comforts of literacy, accept twenty years off your own life, then I respect you for the strength of your aesthetic revulsion. But I don't respect you in the slightest if, even passively, you try to impose the same choice on others who are not free to choose. In fact we know what their choice would be. For, with singular unanimity, in any country where they have had the chance, the poor have walked off the land into the factories as fast as the factories would take them.[4]

More recently Peter Drucker made the same point in his impressive study, *The Age of Discontinuity*:

It does not even matter greatly whether the developed countries would prefer to call a halt to technological change and economic growth. There is no sign that mankind is ready to forswear economic growth and with it technological change. There is no sign that the majority of mankind is willing to take vows of poverty while the minority in the developed countries live in great wealth. Not only are the developing nations desperate for economic advancement; other developed nations, especially Western Europe and Japan (not to mention Russia), are eager to catch up with the United States and to push economic growth as fast as it can be pushed.[5]

The rejection of science and technology, economic growth and industrialization, are, however, perhaps only the most obvious aspects of the revolution against reason and order in the modern world. There can be no doubt that science and technology themselves have too often been caught up in the pursuit of irrational and antihuman goals and objectives, that science has too often confined itself to the realm of means rather than to the analysis of ends. That, however, is a subject for another time. Suffice it to say that the problem is not simply the rejection of science and technology but rather the rejection of rationality altogether.

Daniel Bell has explored at considerable length the cultural consequences of the triumph of the will over reason.[6] He regards the current wave of irrationalism in our society as a major cultural crisis. One need not be as pessimistic as Bell in order to recognize this development as a movement of major consequences to ourselves.

Although the development of rationality is a process that antedates the appearance of man, and although the technical manipulation and mastery of the environment is as old as man, the self-conscious employment of science, technology, and all the processes of rationalization do not extend back over a period of time longer than Europeans have been present in significant numbers on the North American continent. The really major changes in the organization of society, the growth of knowledge and the mastery of the environment through science and technology which mark off "modernity" from the past, have nearly all come since 1600. The decisive changes produced by these cultural and intellectual forces are even more recent. The process has been an accelerating one. You are all acquainted with the statistic that 90 percent of all the scientists who ever lived are alive at the present moment, and those of you who have browsed in the work of the "futurologists" know that further dramatic technical and social changes lie in the immediate future, indeed are already well underway.[7] Indeed, if we look back over that comparatively short time span since 1600, in comparison with the totality of human history, we will recognize that it accounts for greater changes in man's world and in humanity itself than any brief time span since the Neolithic revolution.

How are we to account for this enormous acceleration in the rate at which change impinges on us and in the manner in which events of world-historical importance pile in on us? It sometimes must seem that history is rather like a motion picture, that vast stretches of it are in slow motion (some societies, even today, live in this world of slow motion). But in the twelfth century, roughly, the projectionist began to speed up the picture, until today the figures dance a mad and uncoordinated jig, running about confusedly like the participants in certain well-known television commercials.

Why has this enormous acceleration taken place? What is the driving force behind the transformation of Western history since 1600? We know that Western society in that time span was unique, that no other society in history has exhibited such dynamism and such revolutionary energies. Indeed, all the non-Western societies we know are traditionalist—or were until the West touched them with its transforming energies. Many of them were stagnant and changeless, caught and encapsulated in the past as fossil flies are caught in amber. Or else change occurred in them in a random, meaningless fashion. The notion of progress, of unidirectional linear time, of development and progress are distinctively Western ideas. These days there is a great deal of discussion of the impact of the non-Western world on the West. There has been a return to the cult of *ex Orient lux,* that curious belief that the failed societies of the so-called Third World have some special humanity and spirituality which the non-Western world is lacking, and that we ought to renounce our rationality and science for the primitive but pure life of nontechnical society. No one can deny the tremendous influence which non-Western societies have exerted on the West nor the value of non-Western Culture to contemporary Western man, but the fact remains that it was and is the West which opened up the world and both destroyed and energized the traditionalist non-Western societies. Still, the question remains, why has the West been the changing, aggressive, energetic, innovating society it is? Why has history speeded up for us and why, finally, does it appear, as Spengler, Toynbee, and others have pointed out, that our culture is in a state of dissolution and decay?

Max Weber, in his introduction to *The Protestant Ethic and the Spirit of Capitalism,* points out that "only in the West does science exist as a stage of development which we recognize today as valid."[8] He goes on to insist that in every aspect of Western life a long-term and unique rationalization exhibits itself: in philosophy, religion, art, government, and, in short, the total structure of culture and the organization of life. Weber recognized that implicit in Western culture was an antitraditionalism, a rationalism, a calculating spirit that constantly and with ever-increasing momentum transformed Western life. The motive power of Western history, as Weber saw it, was the vision of a rationally ordered life that called forth an energetic and unremitting pursuit of its goal and eschewed all magical escapes.

Far from the spirit of Western man being the product of the material environment and being dominated by the mode of production, as vulgar Marxists insist, the spirit of Western man transforms and revolutionizes this material environment and the mode of production through its persistent quest for rationality. The history of medieval society is the story of the slow process of the rationalization of that society, the displacement and destruction of traditional institutions and ideas or their amalgamation with more rationalized forms and modes.

This rationalization of all the aspects of Western life has involved a successive elaboration of techniques and methods and the creation in those who employ the techniques of attitudes which can best be described as professional. Technique is a rational method applied to a particular problem. The problem may be totally intellectual or spiritual or it may be manipulative or mechanical. But in each case it involves the employment of rational means to achieve rationally conceived ends.

Now the essential characteristic of modernity is not simply that it is "the most recent" era, and certainly not that it represents a period of Western history that began in 1492 or 1600. The modern age rather is the period of Western history marked most decisively by the process of rationalization. If we are attempting to define an institution or idea as modern we will not inquire into its date but will simply ask to what extent its orientation is traditional—that is, to what extent it is rooted in customary behavior, poses for itself nonrational objectives, and acts through nonrational methods. Custom, fear, unpredictability, anxiety, and magic are the marks of the older, traditional, and especially non-Western cultures. To be modern is to seek, insofar as possible, the solution to practical and intellectual problems through the employment and expansion of rational means.

Essential to these developments is the professionalization of life, the increasing bureaucratization of every aspect of human existence. For professionalization and bureaucratization are among the most important techniques by which life is rationalized. The substitution of known procedures indifferent to personal status or influence by the arbitrary or baffling actions of government, teachers, doctors—these are all a part of the general development of professionalism and bureaucracy.

It is, of course, tempting to see the rational-innovating forces of our society as always on the side of progress—tempting to always approve of revolution if it is made in the name of reason; to forever transform without thought of consequences; to believe that reason is always right and that the heart, whatever its reasons, is always wrong.

But obviously not all of life is subject to rational manipulation; nor is the spirit exclusively rational. We are all aware, or at least I hope we are, that important areas of life are not so much irrational as arational. That is to say, they lie outside the purview of rational systems and rational methods. When rationalism becomes too exaggerated in its claims these aspects of life which lie outside reason, which lie beyond it, revolt and take their revenge upon rational systems. And that too is a part of the history of the recent past.

It is the fear of a totally rational society and its constraining and deadening impact upon human behavior that led Max Weber to the gloomy and pessimistic passage with which he closed his essay on *The Protestant Ethic and the Spirit of Capitalism* in 1920:

> No one knows who will live in this cage in the future, or whether
> at the end of this tremendous development entirely new proph-
> ets will arise, or there will be a great rebirth of old ideas and
> ideals, or if neither, mechanized petrification, embellished with
> a convulsive self-importance. For the last stage of this cultural
> development, it might well be truly said: "Specialists without

spirit, sensualists without heart; this nullity imagines that it has attained a level of civilization never before achieved."[9]

But this is not the only, and is perhaps not the most important, problem involved in the processes of rationalization and technological mastery. Surely one of the most threatening aspects of technology and bureaucracy lies in the separation of rational techniques from a rational spirit. The consequence of this separation is that rational means of a highly sophisticated nature are employed in the pursuit of totally irrational objectives. The processes of dehumanization and alienation are the direct effects of the pursuit of irrational ends. If the ends of life go unexamined and only the means are considered by our society, if we assume that everything is allowed so long as it is technically possible, then we condemn ourselves to a sophisticated barbarism.

15

The Inevitability of Tradition

On the beautiful Beaux Arts façade of the Clements Library at the University of Michigan, a library devoted to manuscripts and rare books in American history, the following inscription establishes the purposes of the library: "In the darkness dwells the people which knows its annals not." The architects did not find the inscription in *Bartlett's Familiar Quotations* or in *The Oxford Book of Quotations*; rather, it was concocted by a local historian. Its obvious truth strengthened its rhetorical resonance.

History, which is objectified tradition, makes possible individual and collective self-awareness, makes the discernment of selfhood possible. We are, indeed, our traditions, the distillation of our experience in the written word. It is for this reason that when the past is lost, when tradition is abrogated, the individual and the collective self are lost or distorted, culture is impoverished, and the humanity of the individual is diminished. The experience of hundreds of millions of human beings living under the domination of ideological totalitarian systems in the last half century bears out this observation. The personal, the political, and the historic past are expunged, and ideology presents a substitute reality, a substitute self, and a substitute history to replace the organic cultural tradition which had developed over millennia. Eastern and Central Europeans often do not know who their ancestors were. They kept no personal papers or correspondence for fear that family connections, personal experience, communal attachment, social and political evaluation might, if known to the political commissar or the secret police, prove fatal to them. The past, cultural tradition, and sense of self were to be buried in the files of the Stasi or some other police agency.

As we have observed following the decay and collapse of totalitarian ideological regimes, the surviving culture resembles a clear-cut forest floor, and the restoration of traditional cultural forms and a traditional sense of the self is a slow and difficult development not unlike the restoration of an ecological system. The ultimate destruction of tradition and the emptying of the self as depicted in dystopian novels such as Aldous Huxley's *Brave New World* (1932) and George Orwell's *Nineteen Eighty-Four* (1949) have, to date, never succeeded, and that for the very good reason that both nature and culture make nearly impossible the complete destruction of tradition.

As much as modernity respects change and innovation, nature and "nature's God" protect and foster permanence. The genetic code is a living record of the experience of the race. Certainly variety and uniqueness are insured by nearly infinite combination, but the basic pattern always remains intact even in the face of radical variation. It must be added that most variations prove lethal to the organism or at least constitute a reproductive disincentive. One is impressed with the remarkable stability of the human type since the appearance of Cro-Magnon man. The biological physical type maintains its integrity.

Equally important, the world of symbol and language, the basis of the cultural tradition, maintains its integrity and continuity. Long before the advent of cognitive science, the mystery of the ability of the child to learn the complex linguistic and grammatical structures that make speech possible puzzled scholars. Sometime between 1868 and 1885, Jacob Burckhardt wrote the first four chapters of *Reflections on History*. In chapter two, "The Three Powers," he observed: "The spearhead of all culture is a miracle of mind—speech, whose spring, independently of the individual people and its language, is in the soul, otherwise no deaf-mute could be taught to speak and to understand speech. Such teaching is only explicable if there is in the soul an intimate and responsive urge to clothe thought in words." Burckhardt continues in a passage that links mind to culture and emphasizes the stability and continuity of culture: "Further, languages are the most direct and specific revelation of the nations, their ideal image, the most perdurable material in which they enclose the content of their spiritual life, especially in the sayings of their great poets and thinkers."

This awareness on the part of Burckhardt of "the miracle of mind" has at the end of the twentieth century been reinforced by "cognitive science," which posits, on the basis of increasing evidence, the existence in the mind of tacit or unconscious grammars and logical structures which make the world of symbolization and speech possible. These neuron structures are biological in character and are the inherited property of all human beings regardless of sex, race, or class location. They are the permanent basis on which culture rests. They are incapable of transformation by revolutionary ideology.

It is of course true that culture is not biological, but, like the genetic code, culture develops on the basis of human experience; it is the distillation of experience and its realization in concrete form. Tradition exists and is handed on from generation to generation because it is life enhancing and life preserving. It does not possess quite the same durability and stability as the genetic code, but its patterns move in the same fundamental direction. Indeed, it is difficult to distinguish, especially in the lower animals, genetics from culture, as becomes increasingly clear from a review of the nineteenth-century debate concerning instincts and the much more sophisticated exploration of animal behavior by the ethnologists and sociobiologists. Territoriality may, for example, be instantiated in very elaborate human cultural forms, but it has the same biological basis that we observe in animals without a sentient culture. It is not at all clear that culture can be easily, or without severe damage to the human organism, transformed.

It is well to note, moreover, that the path of biological and cultural development is unidirectional. Once cultural change has taken place, once the traditional pattern has been altered, there is no returning to a previous stage of development. Whales may be mammals that have returned to the sea, but they do not become fish nor are they even like fish. Time's arrow is unidirectional in its flight, and development is a one-way street. As Boris Pasternak points out in the second chapter of *Dr. Zhivago*, once Christ entered time, the history and culture of mankind was transformed; there is no turning back to earlier religious, ethical, or cultural forms. The notion of Federico Fellini in his film *Satyricon* that he would return to the forms of a pre-Christian consciousness is as ridiculous as the film was unsuccessful in the achievement of its objective.

These great cultural mutations survive only if they are congruent with the essential structural patterns that manifest themselves in the tacit and unconscious traditions and basic biological givens of the organism and its society. The change is one that affirms what is already present, a change that gives life and gives it more abundantly.

It is to be noted too that stability and change, the formation of tradition and culture, are not the consequences of ratiocination and abstract reasoning. They are the consequences of what Edmund Burke described as "prejudice."

By "prejudice" Burke meant custom, unreasoned habit—very nearly, indeed, what a sociologist or historian means by culture, "the superadded ideas, furnished from the wardrobe of the moral imagination, which the heart owns and the understanding ratifies ... which are communicated by the circumstances of civil life."

Prejudice, Burke argued, was a "second nature." This "nature" manifests itself in unconscious action and is not the result of reasoning. It is an action as spontaneous as breathing and is not the consequence of thought and abstract analysis. Which is not to say that "prejudice" is unreasonable or antirational. Prejudice constitutes and manifests a higher ratio-nality which is the distillation of human experience. It is a social deriva-tive as essential to the common life of mankind as is language, to which it is closely related. Private reasoning, especially the abstract reasoning of the philosopher, is subject to error, indeed is very apt to be in error. The unconscious reason of the many is far more likely to be congruent with reality than is private reasoning or the reasoning of the few. Men tend for their own convenience or interest to reason falsely, to rational-ize a line of action that is in error. Of course, many men acting on preju-dice, even all men, are apt at times to fall into error, but this is less likely to be the case with the many than it is with the few or the individual.

What Burke describes as "prejudice" is tradition. Its power is so great and pervasive because it is a "second nature," because it is unconscious, and because it is the distillation of human experience. Like language, it is a convention, but it is a convention rooted in nature. It is the outer face of that quiddity which is humanness. It is for this reason that it is so difficult to abolish or to transform tradition. The great effort of ideological totali-tarianisms, using all the means of terror, corruption, propaganda, lies, and hatred, has been unable to expunge the self, to eradicate tradition, to re-write history, or to transform the language.

Language is the great fortress against which the waves of revolutionary ideology break themselves. It is for this reason that the commissars and the poets are inveterate enemies. The poets are "the unacknowledged legisla-tors of the world," but even Shelley, the greatest of revolutionary poets, could not fashion a language that was itself revolutionary, nor even a sensi-bility that broke decisively with the past, for language is the most conser-vative of all cultural artifacts. What the poet does is to fashion from the language of the past a vocabulary that will give meaning to mankind's in-choate dreams, longings, and perceptions. The language itself and the mean-ing that it symbolizes are as old as mankind. The language the poet uses is dipped from the wellsprings of primitive human utterance and shows forth the images of the aboriginal soul. It is for this reason that the Romantic theorists of language and literature came to believe that poetry was the original literature of mankind and that the age of prose, of analysis and reason, was the sorry cob from which all the kernels of the spirit had fallen.

Beginning with the French Revolution, ideologists have sought to se-cure a transformation of human behavior by revolutionizing language. The new order, it was believed, could not be successful until the souls of men had been changed, and the transformation of language was the key to that change.

Both the Bolsheviks and the Nazis debased and corrupted language in the belief that the revolution had first to take place in the souls of the people. This is the most profound meaning of Orwell's invention of "Engsoc" in *Nineteen Eighty-Four*. It is the meaning of that strange language of Marxist-Leninists called, derisively, "party-Chinese."

Stephen Spender, in his splendid but now-forgotten book *The Struggle of the Modern* (1963), points out the futility of such efforts at linguistic transformation. "Language of its own nature repudiates a complete break between past and present. A 'revolution of the word,' in the sense of words changing completely their sense and becoming something else, is one kind of revolution that is impossible, a revolution in human nature being perhaps another."

Language is innately conservative. The "mother tongue" that is drunk in with the mother's milk reaches back across the centuries to those grids of logic, symbol, and meaning through which we construct an ordered cosmos out of the booming, buzzing chaos of experience. The destruction of those fundamental orders introduces the nightmare world of anomie.

Does this mean that the spiritual world of culture, tradition, language, symbol, and value cannot be lost, that all efforts at revolutionary transformation must fail? To this question the historian must answer both "yes" and "no."

There have been in the historic past the collapse and destruction of cultures and their traditions, such as the destruction of American Indian civilizations. It is possible that, as in the case of Egyptian civilization, this destruction can only occur when the culture is severely flawed or when it has ceased to be a creative and developing culture and has lapsed into cultural petrification.

Evolutionary transformation rather than revolutionary change is the more usual, one might say the predominant, pattern. There is a real sense in which the cultures of ancient Greece and Rome live on in the contemporary civilization of the Western world. It often strikes one that we can understand well our own cultural situation only to the degree that we become the cultural contemporaries of the ancients. It is slow and unconscious change rather than ideological revolution that is the great danger to the integrity of tradition in the contemporary world. The erosion of tradition in the way in which a stone is worn away by the steady drip of water is the great danger in our age. It is not that new traditions, new languages, take the place of the old, but rather that there is an impoverishment, a leveling off of life. We can resist this only if we live beyond the world of easy and meretricious sensation, only if through language, religion, and art we remain in contact with the world of "prejudice," of unconscious spontaneous action, the deeper rationality that derives from the experience of the community over long periods of time.

16

Marxism and Modernity

Modernity has come to mean as many things to as many different men as has Marxism. Now that both have been consigned to the capacious dustbin of history, it is worth considering the essential characteristics of these movements and the possible relationship which existed between them.

One is immediately puzzled by the fact that modernist literature, art, and political theory seem, at first inspection, to have little or nothing to do with Marxism; are, in fact, reactionary to Marxism. The antipositivist revolt and the symbolist movement, the keys to understanding the rise of modernist aesthetics and politics, are clearly anti-Hegelian, antipositivist, and anti-Marxist in inspiration. "Socialism" was, for Nietzsche, the very symbol of Western decadence.

Socialists and Marxists themselves were aware from the time of the appearance of the first symbolist poems and novels, neo-Kantianism in philosophy, Schopenhauer in aesthetics, and neo-Machiavellianism in politics that these distinctive manifestations of modernity were incompatible with Marxism. Lenin's attack on "empirico-criticism" is of a piece with Stalinism's invention and elaboration of socialist realism as a substitute for modernity. The frantic efforts of the *Partisan Review* to be both Marxist and "modernist," and the tensions and debates that this effort engendered among American humanist intellectuals, is evidence enough of the deep and intractable problem which the relationship of Marxism to modernism presented.

Nor was it simply that men of the Left had moved Right or that men of the Right had moved Left, the extremes embracing on the common ground of fanaticism. There were important and essential differences which held Right and Left in tension, and these differences could not be bridged by the easy clichés of newspaper editorial rhetoric. There was, after all, some fundamental difference between the modernism of Ezra Pound and the cynical sentimentalism of Bertolt Brecht, even though they both admired and embraced bloodstained tyrants. The fundamental question remains: Was Marxism a modernist movement? And if so, was the association so deep and close that once philosophical and cultural modernism waned Marxism too was bound to depart from the scene of history? Are Marxist intellectuals, recently so numerous that their intellectual flights darkened the skies, about to go the way of the passenger pigeon?

Marx and Engels felt themselves to be the heirs of the Enlightenment and dialectical materialism to be the philosophical cutting edge of the progressive forward march of humanity. Mankind was on the point of departure out of the alienation and conflicts of the old society for a new and utopian society which lay, charted but undiscovered, in the future's expansive seas. Like the figures in Watteau's *Pilgrimage to Cythera* (1717), the new man had embarked on a Voyage to Cythera, an eroticized secular paradise. The presiding deities were to be Venus and Mars, for even Marx agreed that one could only make love by first making war.

There can be no doubt that the socialists of the nineteenth century thought themselves to be the most modern of men, the vanguard of the future. Traditional society and conservative politics were, according to them, the preserve of the reactionary past. In the transformation of society, both the intellectual and the artist were to play an indispensable role. One of the most interesting and important aspects of the development of the idea of progress from the eighteenth century to the present has been the relationship of morals and especially art to the idea of progressive development. As religion and the transcendent as a source of value and creative inspiration decayed, an invented morality and a culture rooted in the transforming desires of the new man became the source of artistic inspiration. The Enlightenment insisted that all of man's activities should be tested by the measure of utility. Art as conceived of in classical aesthetics, together with contemplative knowledge or prayer, cannot meet this test of utility.

Moreover, if art is to be socially useful, if it is to be responsive to the perceived needs of mankind, it must be developmentally progressive. However, taught by the romantics, we have come to regard a "masterpiece" as standing outside the temporal sequence and as endowed with an absolute validity. Nor, we may argue, is the quality of ethical action progressive. The moral imperatives and the supreme act of selflessness, of laying down one's life for one's fellow man, possess an absolute character.

The Enlightenment and socialism, the Enlightenment's successor, insisted that all human action is time-contingent and progressive in character. Aesthetic idealism and moral absolutism must be abolished, Marx wrote in his *Theses on Feuerbach,* "All philosophies have sought to explain the world; the point, however, is to change it."

However, from the standpoint of social utility, it is entirely conceivable that a man ought not to lay down his life for his friend. Perhaps the man who performs the act is a Nobel laureate and his friend is an intellectual mediocrity only marginally useful to society. Perhaps it would be more useful to our society were the money spent on art museums instead spent on slum clearance or in counseling delinquent teenagers. The fact is that the ideas of progress, political transformation, and social utility pose special problems for moral and aesthetic theoreticians.

The invention of the concept of the "avant garde" was the work of Saint-Simon, Pierre-Joseph Proudhon, and the French realist painter Gustave Courbet. Though initially socialist, it was not specifically Marxist, though Marxism borrowed its theoretical framework. Like Marx, both Proudhon and Courbet were revolutionary activists. Never mind that Proudhon was the father of modern anarchism, and despite the bitter attacks Marx made on Proudhon, one of the most important influences on the thought of the mature Marx. Marx nearly always repaid influence with denunciation and vituperation.

Art was to become a weapon in the class struggle, but more importantly the artist, the intellectual, and the moralist were to occupy a central position in society, for it is they who would formulate the social vision when the old priesthood and the old religion had been banished. They would invent the vocabulary of dream and aspiration; they would create the rhetoric of social and political life. They would have, in short, power over the forms of the secular myth. The myth of a secular paradise restored strikes one, now that we are at the end of the twentieth century, as romantic and sentimental balderdash, whether the object of the new myth is the classless society or the creation of the Nietzschean *Übermensch*. The Marxist myth of alienation overcome, sentiments of universal harmony and humanitarianism, aggression dissolved by sympathy and love, is indeed a kind of Rousseauistic religion intended to restore man to his lost paradise. It is difficult to believe that intellectuals and artists who supposedly gave their energies to close observation and analysis could espouse a doctrine so contrary to the empirical evidence. Such a conception, of course, places the artist and the intellectual in a very powerful but also very perilous position. We can understand why artists get into trouble in totalitarian societies.

Much has been written in the past decade and many brains have been spilled over whether or not the atheism of Marx was intrinsic to his system or simply a cultural and temporal accident. The notion that but for a cultural derailment Marx might have been a cantor in a London synagogue is too absurd to be humorous, too farfetched to be taken as a historical possibility. Any socialism that is more systematic than the compulsory distribution of alms presupposes a world in which the gods have been deposed and man, "come of age," is the master of his fate, a demiurge whose creative activity has displaced the flawed and imperfect creativity of God.

The essential character of modernity, whether it is the modernism of the Left or of the Right, is the displacement of God and the fashioning of a human order that transcends a providentially ordered history. "Atheist humanism," about which Henri de Lubac has written so illuminatingly, is the essential ingredient in modernism, whether Left or Right.

Insofar as the Enlightenment served as the seedbed out of which modernism grew, atheism was modernity's heritage from the Enlightenment. Paul Hazard, in *European Thought in the Eighteenth Century from Montesquieu to Lessing,* observed nearly two generations ago:

> First there were the critics in full cry.... It was the chorus of the new generation upbraiding their predecessors for saddling them with so ill-conceived a social order, an order which was the child of illusion and the parent of ill....
>
> Why, they asked, was this? Thereupon they preferred a change the like of which for sheer audacity had never before been heard of. Now, the culprit was dragged into open court, and behold, the culprit was Christ! ... What the critics were determined to destroy, was the religious interpretation of life....

The Promethean vision of a new age and a new society is predicated on the death of God. As Dostoyevsky clearly discerned, it is only after the death of God that everything will be permitted. The socialist vision of a heaven on earth and the aspiration of the nihilistic Right to create a heroic mankind unfettered by traditional moral concerns, untrammeled by conventional aesthetic norms, and liberated through violence and art, remold the givenness of life; both assume the necessity of deicide.

Modernism has little or nothing to do with the control of the environment and the amelioration of the human condition through the application of science and technology. Men have been doing that since the first man used a tool, and perhaps the greatest changes in the way men live were made at the time of the neolithic revolution from 9,000 to 6,000 BC. Modernism is rather the belief that all creatureliness, all limitations, all conventional values and beliefs have been abrogated, and sovereign man now disposes of his destiny with godlike power. Artistic creativity is no longer mimetic, no longer a reenactment of the divine creative gesture, but the arbitrary and self-sufficient enactment of the artist's personality, wholly new and completely individualistic. This arbitrary creativity could be either social drama, an expression of class, or it could be the powerful gesture of the *Übermensch.*

By 1870 it was clear that the socialist vision of a political avant garde, served by an artistic avant garde acting as a kind of propaganda arm (what was later called by the Bolsheviks "agitprop"), was unacceptable either as convincing politics or as persuasive art.

This shift had really taken place just after 1848, but it became very noticeable in 1870. The composer Wagner was, for example, an enthusiastic revolutionary in 1848. After 1848 his aesthetics led him to reaction and a rather typical blend of racist nationalism and neoromantic authoritarianism.

The Symbolist art that dominated the period after 1870 was an elite art, an art that sought its audience among initiates and the cognoscenti rather than among the politically awakened masses. It was an art of metaphysical anxiety and social alienation rather than an art of revolutionary affirmation. To be sure, many of the writers of the symbolist school and painters of the impressionist and postimpressionist schools espoused the avant garde social and political ideas of various revolutionary "Lefts," but their art was elitist and very nearly in contradiction to their social and political theory.

How did this happen, and what were the consequences? The problem arose because both bourgeois society and the movements of the Left— bourgeois liberalism and democracy on the one hand and socialism and anarchism on the other—were creatures of mass society and mass man. Nietzsche saw this clearly enough and said it over and over again. Indeed, most socialists were more bourgeois, in a cultural sense, than the bourgeoisie itself. What the elite artists and writers of the late nineteenth and the twentieth century were protesting were the values, tastes, standards, and enjoyments of mass society with its materialism and its anxious pursuit of comfort. Both the middle classes and the proletarian revolutionaries wished to create a society which was "snug" and *gemütlich*. Ideally, such a society would be neat, orderly, provide plenty of creature comforts, and not make many spiritual or intellectual demands.

Seen from the viewpoint of the elite artist or writer, the taste of commissars is not very different from that of capitalists. They are both, in fact, philistines who wish to employ art as decoration for a mediocre life or as a slogan with which to manipulate the masses. The elite artist, however, had something quite different in mind, and so while he might entertain revolutionary social and political enthusiasms because he felt keenly the injustice of the world, he no longer conceived of art as a weapon in the class struggle, as a Stalin or a Hitler was later to think of it. There was no patience among them for what H. G. Wells was to describe as a utopia of little fat men.

Symbolist and decadent alike rejected the passé materialism, the naïve belief that all reality might be explained by recourse to reductionist natural scientific ideas. Positivism and determinism left no scope for creativity, and even for those who rejected any transcendence the drive to free creativity ruled out the philistine platitudes of Marxism. We must realize that what the symbolists and decadents of the 1870s were creating was a counterculture. The source of this effort to create a counterculture was that all-purpose invention of the romantics, alienation. Here Marx, himself profoundly influenced by romanticism, found himself psychologically if not aesthetically in harmony with the romantics and neoromantics. He too saw *Entfremdung* as the root of the revolutionary dynamic. It was, however, a psychological perception which might in part be explained by dialectical materialism but could not be reconciled to it.

The evidences of alienation were numerous; the loss of community, boredom, satiety, powerlessness, and futility, the suction of the absurd together with the awareness of a terrible freedom. All these are constantly reiterated feelings on the part of the neoromantics and symbolist writers and artists. They are, moreover, perceived by these writers and artists both as man's essential condition and as a fate forced on them by society. Mass man, his pleasures, his comforts, his dreams and hopes—these are the sources of alienation and enervation, the impotence, despondence, and pessimism felt by the elite artist and poet. It is a revolution against the petty goals, the mindless pleasures, the dulled sensibilities induced by materialism. The poet and the writer become revolutionaries, though not revolutionary in the ordinary political sense. Their revolution is individual, personal, and cultural rather than universal and political. It is the revolution of Sinclair Lewis fed up with the pettiness and provinciality, the mediocrities and stupidities of Sauk Center.

Of course, this sense of alienation and rebellion can itself be turned into art, transmuted into high poetry. There must be chaos, Nietzsche observed, in order that a dancing star be born. There is no better description of the source, the engendering experience, out of which the early poems of T. S. Eliot developed than the above.

The alienation of the avant garde artist is, however, not a mysterious consequence of the materialist society in which he lives. It is the direct result of the elite and esoteric nature of his art and his conception of the creative act as a displacement of the divine creative gesture. Not only is the avant garde artist a revolutionary in his rebellion against his society, but he is also an even greater rebel in his rejection of the artistic expectations of his society. He refuses to create for a wide general audience. He deliberately chooses forms that will make his work inaccessible to ordinary men and women. And so, at one and the same time, he denounces a philistine society that rejects him, and deliberately separates himself from his society by an art that is inaccessible to all but a narrow public, or by an art that rejects the values and violates the sensibilities of the larger public.

Marxism was thus an early and incomplete form of modernism. Like the great bulk of the modernists, Marx assumed a world without God, a world marked by alienation, a world to be transformed by human action into a utopia. Man is man only insofar as he is self-sufficiently creative. To be sure, a considerable number of modernists were either pantheistic mystics or else turned from atheist humanism to religious orthodoxy. Religious modernists are modernists after the fact of modernism. Atheist humanism is the distinctive mark of modernism.

Thus, while twentieth-century modernists have for the most part rejected the naïve "science" of dialectical determinism and Marxism's preposterous aesthetic and political theories, modernism, like Marxism, is a system of ideas fashioned to deal with a world from which the transcendent is absent. This accounts for the centrality of Nietzsche to both contemporary modernists and Marxist survivors. It is no accident that the definitive scholarly edition of Nietzsche, only recently published, is the work of two Italian Marxists, Giorgio Colli and Mazzino Montinari.

Marxism as a system is not viable. It is quite possible that it will survive in a reborn Nietzschean form, godless, alienated, and promising social and political transformation. In the Soviet form, from Lenin through Stalin, it had already abandoned political Marxism to adopt the political mode of the modernist Right. The congruence of Stalinist and Hitlerite political forms was no accident, as Karl Dietrich Bracher has brilliantly demonstrated. Aesthetic and political modernism is totalitarian in its affinities.

It is possible that modernism will choke and suffocate on its own anxiety, despair, and hopelessness. If it survives, it will survive as a Nietzschean philosophy that seeks to transform the world through art and violence. The art and violence will not be justified and contained within the framework of dialectical materialism, but rather a fascism whose goals are set by a nihilist elite. The transformational myth will be preserved at the expense of dialectical materialism.

Of course, socialism will survive not as Marxism but rather as welfarestatism. The belief that there is a remedy, technical or human-manipulative, for every evil will not die easily. Statism is older than Marxism and will survive its demise. There are always many who will put their faith and hope in the "utopia of little fat men."

PART FIVE: POLITICS

———————————

Tonsor's writings on politics were usually scholarly and theoretical. Thus, in this section he deals with the question of political idealism and reflects on the nature of political order in a democracy. But he could also be quite practical and concrete when it came to politics. For instance, he discusses here, in an unpublished essay, why he is both a Republican and a conservative. Tonsor, while an articulate and erudite conservative intellectual, was attracted to strong leadership. He supported Richard Nixon and Ronald Reagan, even frequently writing them if he was perturbed by one of their policies. Unlike many older conservatives, he remained quite loyal to, and supportive of, George W. Bush. His political views remain quite conventional, and quite Republican, befitting the Midwestern upbringing and inclinations described in the following essays.

17

Political Idealism and Political Reality

One of the puzzles of democratic political life arises from the fact that while morality and political idealism are essential elements in any democratic polity, the excesses of political idealism and absolutist morals make democratic politics first unworkable and then destroy it altogether. In democratic societies there is both a constant temptation and invitation to moral athleticism and a constant betrayal and corruption of the ideal. The political idealists and the moral athletes attempt to transform the democratic polity into a French revolutionary–style "republic of virtue," and though America's real religion is a civic rather than a transcendent one, all public issues tend to assume the vesture of ideal absolutes and all debate of public issues is couched in terms of moral fervor. The campaign of Senator George McGovern is an excellent example of the way in which political issues in America are often translated into religious enthusiasms and clothed in the language of moral absolutism. In spite of the disastrous defeat suffered by McGovern at the polls, it is nevertheless true that this tendency, inherent in democratic politics, has enormous popular appeal. For this reason, among others, the great sin in the politics of exalted expectations is the sin of hypocrisy, which in America is not simply the tribute vice pays to virtue, but a technically perfected and universally recognized political skill. This may, in fact, be one of the dominant aspects of all democratic mass political movements that have a revolutionary origin, or at least a revolutionary bias. Michael Polanyi has remarked that National Socialism was not, as many men have believed, a political movement that was totally amoral in character. Indeed, Polanyi remarks, it was a political movement whose moral commitments were so great and so compelling that the Nazi movement brought the world to the brink of destruction in order to see its moral ideals realized.

From the tone of these remarks you may suppose that my politics are

Machiavellian and totally cynical, that they are operational in the worst sense of the word, and that I propose as a political ideal a system in which ideals are sacrificed and morals corrupted not out of necessity but as a matter of course. It is necessary, therefore, that I make emphatic my conviction that any and every politics is based upon a vision of the good and projects a political order that is both moral and idealistic. Wherever "the good" is defined narrowly in terms of impersonal and morally neutral forces such as "the market" or power political configurations, the long-term political response of the people has been in the past, and will be again, one of revulsion and protest. The fact is that men are extraordinarily jealous of their humanity, and when they see it threatened by impersonal and morally neutral forces they resort to protest and revolution. Morality and political idealism, especially in the mass democracies, are indispensable political forces. Nothing attests to this fact more powerfully than the moralizing tone and artifices of enthusiastic idealism which are so important a part of the propaganda effort of totalitarian states. In these propaganda efforts, politics has been reduced exclusively to its ideal and moral dimensions; the fact that the idealism is frequently fraudulent and the morality perverse ought not to blind us to the important role it plays. All too often we fail to properly gauge the moral impact of totalitarian propaganda simply because we have decided, and rightly so, that the propaganda is fraudulent and issues from a morally suspect source.

The fact that the energies and dynamics of politics are frequently and persistently moral ought to caution the political practitioner and the student of politics to suspect those easy and seemingly uncomplicated technical solutions to difficult social problems. Zero population growth, abortion, complete First Amendment protection for any and all kinds of publications and utterances, a national social policy based totally on the self-interest and self-sufficiency of the individual, a national economic policy that subordinates national defense and the public welfare to economic maximization are all public policies that in the long run will prove morally repugnant to the majority of the American people, and consequently they are always politically dangerous to the individuals and groups supporting these particular programs. Unless a program can be defended in moral terms, in terms of justice and charity and the general welfare, to argue that it is socially or economically efficient is to expose the program to general public opprobrium. While it is essential in any social or political situation that we start with the specific task at hand rather than a vague general ideal, it is no less imperative that we constantly check our solutions against the moral imperatives. Even so, morality, popularly defined, will often be defective. Politics without prophecy is always in danger of mistaking the wishes of men for the promptings of conscience. The tyranny of the majority is no greater than when it demands conformity to a defective but popular moral sense. Tocqueville spoke eloquently on this subject and it is one of the persistent problems of democratic societies.

The problem posed by morality and ideals in politics, then, stems from the fact that ethical and political ideals are often abstract, general, and without reference to conditioning historical factors and experience, rather than practical, specific, and derived from a particular historical and social situation. Neither political rights nor political obligations can be of a general and abstract nature. You will recall the powerful argument made by Edmund Burke in his *Reflections on the Revolution in France*. You will remember that Burke was attacking the French philosophers (who made the revolution) and their English sympathizers. When he came to justifications of the revolution based on the morality of "natural rights," Burke wrote:

> Government is not made in virtue of natural rights, which may and do exist in total independence of it—and exist in much greater clearness, and in a much greater degree of abstract perfection: but their abstract perfection is their practical defect. By having a right to everything they want everything. Government is a contrivance of human wisdom to provide for human *wants* [emphasis in the original]. Men have a right that these wants should be provided for by this wisdom. Among these wants is to be reckoned the want, out of civil society, of a sufficient restraint upon their passions. Society requires not only that the passions of individuals should be subjected, but that even in the mass and body, as well as in the individuals, the inclinations of men should frequently be thwarted, their will controlled and their passions brought into subjection. This can only be done by a power out of themselves, and not, in the exercise of its function, subject to that will and to those passions which it is its office to bridle and subdue. In this sense the restraints on men, as well as their liberties, are to be reckoned among their rights. But as these liberties and restrictions vary with times and circumstances, and admit of infinite modifications, they cannot be settled upon any abstract rule; and nothing is so foolish as to discuss them upon that principle.

It is interesting to speculate on the reason and the rhetoric Burke would bring to bear on both the anarchist Right and the Old and New Left. Burke's great and chief criticism no doubt would be that in their pursuit of absolute rights and absolute ideals they cut the ground out from under the possibility of attaining any rights at all and of achieving political ideals commensurate with the limitation-filled character of human nature. Burke's continuing injunction to politicians is to be practical; to fit long-term objectives and high ideals to the petty and not so petty needs of the moment; to wed the sublime to the immediate and the pragmatic. Here is Burke in his *Letter to the Sheriffs of Bristol* (1777):

> Civil freedom, Gentlemen, is not as many have endeavored to persuade you, a thing that lies hid in the depth of abstruse science. It is a blessing and a benefit, not an abstract speculation; and all the just reasoning that can be upon it is of so coarse a texture as perfectly to suit the ordinary capacities of those who are to enjoy, and of those who are to defend it. Far from any resemblance to those propositions in geometry and metaphysics which admit no medium, but must be true or false in all their latitude, social and civil freedom, like all other things in common life, are variously mixed and modified, enjoyed in very different degrees, and shaped into an infinite diversity of forms, according to the temper and circumstances of every community. The *extreme* of liberty (which is its abstract perfection, but its real fault) obtains nowhere, nor ought it to obtain anywhere; because extremes, as we all know, in every point which relates either to our duties or satisfactions in life, are destructive both to virtue and enjoyment. Liberty, too, must be limited in order to be possessed. . . .

These are cogent but unpopular words in an era of exaggeration, when restraints of any kind are perceived as galling and unbearable. Beyond what Burke says concerning the nature of liberty lies the more important and general principle of the limited and contingent nature of all political ideals and moral enthusiasms. Burke does not argue that we ought to dispense with ideals and morals in politics. Far from it: Burke believed that the feelings, or as he preferred to call them, "spontaneous natural affections," were the source of morals and the basis for social and political life. These "affections" Burke conceived to have been implanted in the human heart by God. But, more important still for our argument, civil society can never be the product of nature alone; it is not the consequence of abstract reasoning or the result of some enthusiastic action of the human will. Civil society is the consequence of "art." As Burke argued in the *Appeal from the New to the Old Whigs* (1791): "The state of civil society . . . is a state of nature; and much more truly so than a savage and incoherent mode of life. For man is by nature reasonable; and he is never perfectly in his natural state, but when he is placed where reason may be best cultivated, and most predominates. Art is man's nature. We are as much, at least, in a state of nature in formed manhood, as in immature and helpless infancy." Art takes cognizance of the workings of the practical intellect and is contingent upon and shaped by historical process. Men do not and cannot form their minds or govern their societies on the basis of abstractions. Extremes of every kind are evidence, finally, not that motives are pure and minds are noble but of political immaturity and an imperfect historical consciousness. Seen in the total context of history, many events, events in which we have taken an active interest and perhaps participated, will have a very different quality than the one that we ascribe to them today.

Take the currently much-debated question of America's role in the world. From the turn of the nineteenth into the twentieth century, a sizeable portion of the intellectual and leadership elites in the United States advocated a break with the traditional American policy of nonintervention in the affairs of other nations and nonparticipation in the alliance systems of the great powers. This policy of nonintervention came to be called, mistakenly, "isolationism." In fact, it was something quite different from isolationism, for it argued that America's revolutionary hope could be best taught by example rather than forceful intrusion. This traditional theory, however, came to be rejected by moral and political enthusiasts who argued that the world had to be made safe for democracy, that America had to impose its order and act as the world's policeman in the chaotic societies which lay beyond our shores. The "Fourteen Points," the "Four Freedoms," and "doctrines" by the dozens provided the slogans for this adventure into international morality and idealism. After long and continuous debate, most of the American people came to approve a policy which seemed to many little congruent with our traditional values. Those who persisted in rejecting these enthusiasms were denounced as narrow and provincial "isolationists" unfit to live in the sparkling new world which was about to come into existence. Now, at the end of three quarters of a century of exhausting warfare, the American people have begun slowly and uncertainly to reexamine the old arguments and to ask whether indeed our enthusiasm for establishing the reign of international morality was not the pursuit of a destructive chimera.

The historical context of any action is important both before and after the fact. All political action is a species of "situational ethics," just as all human action is contingent, in terms of rightness or wrongness, upon circumstance. Which is not to say, once again, that moral absolutes do not exist, but rather that they are poor guides to practical action. The revolutionary proclaims, "Let justice be done though the heavens should fall." Cardinal Newman is reported to have said that it would be better for the whole world to perish than that a single venial sin should be committed. Fortunately, God, who is the ultimate judge in such matters, has a somewhat less exacting standard. These are the extremes of moral and ideal enthusiasm, but there are many other examples of a less grave character. Looking back at the political causes of the past two decades, whether the causes of the Left or the Right, is discouraging because so little practical and pragmatic wisdom has gone into their formulation and execution. The great question in politics is not "what is right?" or even "what is desirable?" but rather "what is possible?" Of course, the "possible" changes from moment to moment and no political leadership can really be great unless it knows, quite exactly, what is possible. In his early years, intuition and a profound political sense led Adolf Hitler to a very clear and accurate perception of what was possible in Germany's international relations. After 1938, this sense, corrupted by a long series of successes, failed Hitler completely, and a war which Hitler chose and enormously complicated by the invasion of the Soviet Union finally led to his undoing and defeat.

The determination of the possible is closely related to the greatest of the political virtues: the exercise of prudence. Prudential considerations in politics and in individual morality have to do exclusively with means, never with ends. It is for this reason that the ideal and the moral as absolutes may be preserved intact even though the prudential solution may fall short of achieving the abstract ideal, may indeed be nothing more than the choice of the lesser of two evils. A more fortunate social dilemma exists when the choice is between goods, but nevertheless it is a choice in which the pursuit of one good often excludes the attainment of another. Situations of this sort are the everyday experience of economists, for the science of economics is a science of less and more, of scarce resources and infinite wants. Men who think politically and who determine the shape of civil society frequently do not recognize the fact that some choices always exclude others. They reject the realities of the world of either-or and insist, in spite of all the evidence to the contrary, that men can have both-and. The both-guns-and-butter policy of the Johnson administration, a policy that prevented us from seeing that we had a major war on our hands and kept us from acting accordingly, is an excellent example.

Perhaps the most serious political delusion of our times is this belief on the part of a great many Americans that their government can do everything simultaneously. A healthy respect for human and governmental limitations has been all but lost. In the guns-and-butter policy and the contradiction it contained we have a practical example, important but superficial, of the conflict of goods which bedevils all politics. Much more important and much more central to our democratic society are the conflicts that exist between liberty and equality and freedom and order. Both terms of these antitheses are essential elements to our polity. The pursuit of the abstract and perfected form of one of the terms excludes its antithesis altogether. It is obvious that men desire to live in a society where both perfect freedom and perfect order coexist. It is equally obvious that such a society does not and cannot exist on earth. How much freedom or how much equality men enjoy at any juncture of the temporal process depends upon a host of factors, including complicated individual and social choices. Political wisdom, manifesting itself in prudent action, cuts the mind loose from absolutes and abstractions and settles for the best possible combination.

What I am saying is the oldest kind of political theory. The observations are indeed so old and so ordinary that I am almost ashamed to make them. I may be excused, perhaps, when I point out that prudence, compromise, tolerance, and even "benign neglect" have recently been scorned by important groups in our society, who see them as the corrupting appeasement of evil and imperfection. The Democratic Convention of 1968 and the Democratic campaign of 1972 are excellent examples of the triumph of intransigent ideological abstraction and the danger posed by such a triumph to the politics of moderation and the human measure.

In a great book of an older generation, *An Essay on the Nature and Significance of Economic Science* (1932), Lord Lionel Robbins observes:

> There are cases when it is either bread or a lily. Choice of one involves sacrifice of the other, and although we may be satisfied with our choice, we cannot delude ourselves that it was not really a choice at all, that more bread will follow. It is not true that all things work together for *material* good to them that love God. So far from postulating a harmony of ends in this sense, Economics brings into full view that conflict of choice which is one of the permanent characteristics of human existence. Your economist is a true tragedian.

Exactly the same words might well be written of the political scientist, or if you prefer, the political theoretician. For this reason Burke observed in his *Speech at Bristol Previous to the Election* (1780), "The condition of our nature is such that we buy our blessings at a price."

Burke spoke with his accustomed eloquence and great good sense again and again on the subject of political prudence, and perhaps prudence is the most distinctive Burkean and conservative virtue. In a letter to Monsieur Dupont in October 1789, he wrote:

> Prudence (in all things a virtue, in politics the first of virtues),
> will lead us rather to acquiesce in some qualified plan that does
> not come up to the full perfection of the abstract idea, than to
> push for the more perfect, which cannot be attained without
> tearing to pieces the whole contexture of the commonwealth. . . .
> In all changes in the state, moderation is a virtue, not only
> amiable but powerful. It is a disposing, arranging, conciliating,
> cementing virtue. . . . Moderation (which times and situations
> will clearly distinguish from the counterfeits of pusillanimity
> and indecision) is a virtue only of superior minds. It requires a
> deep courage, and full of reflection, to be temperate when the
> voices of multitudes (the specious mimic of fame and reputa-
> tion) pass judgment against you. The impetuous desire of an
> unthinking public will endure no course, but what conducts to
> splendid and perilous extremes. Then to dare to be fearful, when
> all about you are full of presumption and confidence, and when
> those who are bold at the hazard of others would push your
> caution and disaffection, is to show a mind prepared for its trial;
> it discovers, in the midst of general levity, a self-possessing and
> collected character, which sooner or later, bids to attract every-
> thing to it, as to a center.

There have always been those in American politics who have urged
caution, prudence, and compromise; those who denounced the act of hu-
bris, of political overreaching, but they have been all too few in number,
and their appeal has never possessed that éclat or the grandeur of ideological denunciation and crusading fervor. Especially during these last few
decades one wonders what the complexion of American politics might have
been had there been only a handful more of men such as Robert Taft in the
United States Senate to urge compromise, caution, and distance from passion.

But of course, crusades are such fun, nevermind who must pay the price
exacted by virtuous sentiments acted upon to the exclusion of good sense.
And the conservative, behaving prudently, must be willing not only to see
others pay the price in waiting, in justice undone, and in rewards foregone.
He must, above all, be willing to pay the price himself.

Prudence is so important as a political virtue because of the very nature of political reality. In a splendid essay by Hans Buchheim, *Totalitarian
Rule: Its Nature and Characteristics* (1968), we find the following passage:

> Action is rooted in reality; it must accept reality's diversity and
> cannot fall back on the gradations of its own commitment; it

recognizes only the one alternative—that something is done or that it is not. Every practical decision must be taken in the light of the ambiguity of a situation, and it leads to consequences that in the last analysis are quite as ambiguous. Every theoretical statement, therefore, simplifies the infinite diversity of reality, while every practical decision destroys the spectrum of gradations of commitment over which theory ranges.

For this reason, though theory can serve as a guide to action, it can never be a blueprint for shaping political reality, and it certainly cannot become a guide for individual conduct. For if the simplified structures to which theory owes its clarity and comprehensiveness are applied immediately in practice they must deform the diversity of life and do violence to its historically conditioned individuality. It follows that politics will be the more artificial the more uncompromisingly it is subjugated to theory. . . .

Prudence and compromise have, moreover, not been uniquely conservative responses to the complexity of political reality. Even those operating within the revolutionary tradition have studied the advantages of a politics of moderation. I am reminded of Alfred Nacquet, one of the outstanding leaders of the Left in the early years of the Third Republic in France, though many others might be cited. Nacquet had begun his political life as a so-called "intransigent," a defender of the abstract ideals of the French Revolution, unwilling to bow to any of the political necessities and realities of his time. Nacquet came to realize, however, that politics could not be made on the basis of ideological abstractions. The whole latter part of his career was one in which he attempted to realize what was possible of his ideals, always believing that half a loaf was better than none. His new position earned him and the group of politicians who surrounded him the derisive designation "Opportunists," and in August 1882 an "intransigent" journalist attacked and denounced him for his inconsistency and the betrayal of his former ideals. Nacquet replied by saying:

> There are several manners of being consistent with oneself. One consists of affirming absolute metaphysical principles, divorced from facts, that one never abandons and from which one never departs no matter what happens; even if this affirmation leads to the death of the Republic.
>
> The other manner of being consistent with oneself is to pursue an ideal which does not change, but to recognize the ground on which one walks, to maneuver around obstacles, to some-

times accept something bad for fear of something worse, to avoid disasters, and to arrive as Spuller [a prominent Gambettist] said perhaps slowly but more surely at the desired goal than the seekers of the absolute.

Both the Right and the Left in American politics need to relearn the great political art of compromise and practice the great political virtue of prudence. For it is in the reconciliation of the ideal with the actual that we realize our full humanity and make possible a society in which both public and private morality have their origins in a common source, and in which it is possible to be a good man even while obeying the laws of the state.

18

What Is the Purpose of Politics?

I suppose that if one were to ask the question, "What is the purpose of politics?" of Mayor Richard Daley (in one of his candid and relaxed moments), he would say, "The purpose of politics is to get elected." And if one were to ask that same question of Mr. John Dean, lately of the White House staff, he would reply, "The purpose of politics is to get appointed." Now, however crass these answers may seem, they are not bad answers, for getting elected and getting appointed are political actions of great importance. They are not, however, the end or purpose of politics, even though they have come to seem the very essence of political life. Politics for the general public increasingly means "something," or better said, a set of activities engaged in by politicians to their own great advantage and to the general disadvantage of the public. Politics for many is no longer viewed as the source of community and order in society, but rather has come to be regarded as the preserve of professionals who have learned to make the system function to their benefit.

The state of mind that is frequently described as "political alienation," or more succinctly as "dropping out," derives at least in part from the feeling that politics is for politicians and that ordinary men and women can have little or no effect on their political destinies. It is better, or so many believe, to take refuge in a thoroughgoing cynicism and withdrawal from public life than to court the disillusionment that follows on the discovery of the political ineffectuality of the individual.

The characteristic mark of the age in which we live is an overwhelming skepticism with respect to the organized and institutionalized structures of our common life. The retreat into the private sphere is a reflection of this general distrust of politics, for politics reach beyond the governmental into every community activity. Survey research and public opinion polls reveal the steep decline of public confidence with respect not only to government but religion, education, medicine, labor, science, business, the press, and, significantly, even the family. All of these institutions have well-developed political structures, are in fact a part of politics, and so what we see so evidently manifested is the decline of politics, the massive desertion of the political and communal for the private and individual.

This underestimation of the effectiveness of politics is the mirror image of the overestimation of the possibilities of political action. In fact, the retreat to the private sphere has recently often been a consequence of the disappointed expectations men held with respect to their most honored and powerful institutions. As Henry Fairlee has pointed out in his book *The Kennedy Years,* the current mood of depression and dismay in American society stems at least in part from the grandiose dreams engendered by the New Frontier and the Great Society. In those years, American political leaders held out hopes and aspirations to men which simply could not be fulfilled through political action. Something of the same mood dominated the Roman Catholic Church during the pontificate of Pope John XXIII and in the brief period following the first session of Vatican II. When the inflated rhetoric had exhausted itself, when the great gestures had been made, when the eulogies had been organized and the money spent, when the manifestos had been issued and the council documents promulgated, the millennium had, alas, still not been achieved, and we discovered that we were still stuck with our recalcitrant and unregenerate human natures. It was a dismaying experience. We ought to have learned from it not that politics can do nothing but that it cannot do everything. Many, however, came to believe not that politics could not do everything but that the wrong sort of politics could not do everything. The belief is now widespread that if only John F. Kennedy had been purer in his intentions, had not been at heart a Cold Warrior, had been more deeply convinced on the issue of civil rights, had been more revolutionary in domestic commitments, then today we would indeed be living in a sort of Camelot.

These positions are the consequence of a defective knowledge of the nature of politics. Both those who cop out and refuse political action and those who hope for fulfillments that political action can never bring to pass fail to understand the nature of politics. Let us ask again then, "What is the purpose of politics?"

Politics is the institutional organization of society, whether the form is that of the family, the community, the factory, the voluntary association, or even that of business. Of course, much of the politics of these groups is informal, and only in the most highly developed communities does politics become organizational. Nonetheless, wherever the individual touches on or is connected with society, political life and political activity result.

Being fully human involves acting politically: this is the root of Aristotle's famous dictum. Nor can we as individuals avoid social or political involvement. Even Robinson Crusoe discovered that, although he was autonomous, he was not self-sufficient. It is an interesting fact that the more highly intellectualized and spiritualized, the more elaborately cultural human societies become, the more political they are. Diversity and complexity, both of which make autonomy not only possible but meaningful, can exist and be optimized where society and politics are highly developed. It has often been remarked that Thoreau was able to conduct his experiment at Walden Pond only because Cambridge lay nearby and his family and friends provided that infrastructure of community which permitted the full flowering of anarchistic individualism.

Much has been written during the past decade concerning "libertarianism" and "anarchism." Many poses have been struck. The roads and the parks, at least in theory, have been sold over and over again, and the defense establishment has been let out to contract. For the most part, libertarians and anarchists have not dealt realistically with either the problem of community or the problem of politics. Their recently invented social and political systems resemble nothing so much as the fanciful perpetual motion machines of the seventeenth and eighteenth centuries. Liberty is a reflection of social complexity and political sophistication. It does not result in anarchism. Rather, it always creates and it requires obligation. Consequently, the question is not whether one has the right to withdraw from society, to make the great refusal, to break the bonds that bind men together for purposes of mutual fulfillment; the question is not whether we shall be political or not, but rather, how we shall be political and what the ends of our politics shall be. To be fully human is to live politically. The condition of alienation is a reflection of the impossible dream of total self-sufficiency. The madman who invents and peoples a world in his imagination is the only unpolitical man.

Liberty and obligation are indissolubly linked. To be free to do anything means to be obligated to do something. We are free to choose; that is, we are autonomous, but the very possibilities of choice open to us are the products of the social matrix in which we have our being and in which we find our fulfillment. All politics and all community have their roots in the inadequacy of the individual, acting alone, to achieve the objectives he finds desirable. These objectives go to the heart of human existence, for human survival depends on man's ability to organize societies to meet the challenge of the environment. Beyond survival, all those things which make life worth living and offer us a foretaste of eternity are communal in nature. In this respect the Christian conception of the Trinity has always seemed to me, purely from a symbolic standpoint, a much more satisfactory representation of the Godhead than Aristotle's self-sufficient, self-contemplating unmoved mover. The image of the beatific vision in the Christian tradition is the image of community, the "communion of saints." But aside from these startling and profound images, it is apparent that we ought to view our individual insufficiency not as limitation and as frustration but as the key to fulfillment. As the French are reported to say, *Vive la différence!*

It follows from this that the bonds of obligation in society are not exclusively or even predominately contractual; that is, social structures and political forms are not simply arrangements in which the costs and benefits are calculated and nicely weighed, and when cost exceeds benefit the contract is nullified. Attempt running a family on that basis some time, or better still rearing a family of teenage children.

Having said this I must add that I reject the communitarian position which argues that unless there is a common religion, unless there are commonly shared political myths, and unless there are pervasive and commonly accepted cultural values about which there is no debate there cannot be an orderly and coherent society. This is neither logically necessary nor is it the experience of mankind.

Common action follows on the acceptance of a common task, the confrontation with a common challenge. Politics does not begin with contract or consensus. The origins of society do not lie in so ethereal a thing as community or so rational and calculated a thing as contract. Life is not quite so simple a matter. As soon as individual men, no matter how diverse they are in origins, heterodox in religion, pluralistic in custom, and different in culture, perceive a common need or confront a common challenge, politics is born. Community and contract are not antecedent to political action but derive from it.

Politics, then, takes its rise from individual insufficiency. Does it follow that men acting together can do all things? Does it follow that there are no limits to political action? We have been speaking, up to this point, of politics in very broad terms, the politics of the family, the politics of the office, the politics of the playing field. Let us now speak quite specifically of the politics associated with government. Whatever the objectives of political activity in the family, the church, the military, these politics are in a striking way different from the politics of government, or what we most frequently call simply "politics." Are there any limitations to the actions of government? What is the purpose of the politics of the "state"?

To ask that question is to raise a series of issues of the utmost consequence for contemporary society. The historical record in the Western world for the past one thousand years reveals the steady growth and concentration of the powers of the state, an enormous increase in its activities, and absorption into itself of all other political forms and structures.

The state has clothed itself with the mystique and liturgical forms of religion; it has become the moral arbiter of society; it has steadily drawn all the activities of the culture-creating elites into its ambit; it has assumed the dominant position in education; it has usurped many of the functions and roles of the family; it has continuously enlarged its activities in the economic sphere and threatens now to engulf all enterprise, production, and distribution of goods and income; it licenses and restricts and eventually will destroy (as Rousseau hoped and Tocqueville predicted) all intermediary groups and voluntary associations. The growth of the powers of the state has been the single greatest fact in modern European history. The French and Russian revolutions and the development of nationalism are only incidents in the history of the evolution of statism.

This growth in the power and authority of the state gives the politics of the state a wholly new meaning and imposes on it forms that in other eras would have been thought totally inappropriate. We have come to view these new political forms as authoritarian and totalitarian. They are political nonetheless, though the form of political participation may be very different from the forms characteristic of other eras and other political structures. For example, totalitarian politics casts itself increasingly in the religious and liturgical mold. Participation in the community is sacramental rather than conventionally political. The rites of solidarity on May Day or the anniversary of the revolution are a much more important form of political participation than casting a ballot or seeking electoral office.

Is genuine politics possible under such conditions? Has the evolution of Western governments been such that this is, in fact, the only type of politics possible? Is there a limit to what the state can and ought to do imposed by the nature of man and society? Or is the purpose of politics the augmentation of the authority and power of the state until it becomes the gigantic though rusty mechanism of which Ortega y Gasset spoke so eloquently in *The Revolt of the Masses?*

I assert that the politics of the state has one purpose and one purpose only, and that is to enable men to live together in civil society. The purpose of politics is not to make men good or holy, though that may be an indirect benefit which results from a properly ordered state. Politicians are not and can never become philosopher-kings. When politicians speak of philosophy their accents are not those of Plato and St. Thomas but Marx, Rosenberg, Sorel, and Marcuse. And this is the case because the very act of attempting to establish absolute rather than relative justice, the very act of making all men virtuous or holy, the very act of allocating goods on the basis of the concept of equality pose a range of problems that lie beyond the powers of governmental action.

While governments cannot make men good, they can create the conditions of peace and security that will enable men, singly and in groups, to seek the multiform goods that have always been characteristic of any sophisticated society. While governments cannot make men virtuous, they can maintain those conditions which make the pursuit of virtue possible. Above all, government will refuse the temptation to commit evil in the name of some higher and remoter good. Evil will not appear as a historical necessity pressed on mankind by the cycle of constitutions, by the invisible hands, by the cunning of reason or the next sequent step in the womb of time. "Historical necessity" is always another name for the abdication of moral responsibility. When politics attempts to achieve that which is beyond political action, it often resorts to evil, always believing it is temporary, always assuming that when the new dispensation has been ushered in, evil will have been forever banished.

The purpose of politics does not go beyond securing the conditions in which the creative potentialities of the individual, and the groups and communities he and others create, are liberated and facilitated. Note that such political action will always be concrete and related to the solution of specific and particular problems. It will not be general, vague, or ideological, nor will it be premised on the belief that either man's nature or his environment can be perfected. The world is a marvelous and complicated place and our natures even more complex. To believe that absolute justice, innocence, or the perfection of person, time, or place this side of the grave is possible is to indulge one of those groundless hopes which only idiots and revolutionaries entertain. Such notions are commonplaces with the monsters and deformities who serve as heroes in the novels of Dostoevsky. They are inexcusable in a world where every man's work is colored by ambiguity and tried by fire.

The great politicians of any age are not the dreamers and the idealists. They are practical men who have a vision of what is both desirable and possible for their societies. They are not the inventors of slogans such as the "classless society" or the "new frontier" or the "great society." They speak in terms of specific and concrete goals, and they have some estimate of what the costs, material and social, will be. They realize that in a world of scarcity and conflicting demands to do anything means not to do something else. They are aware, moreover, that those actions which benefit one member of a society may not, probably will not, benefit another. They believe, therefore, that only those actions which benefit the whole of society more than they benefit any particular individual or group in society ought to be undertaken by government.

Even so, it is extremely difficult to calculate benefits with any degree of accuracy. For example, does public education benefit the individual more than it does society, or is the opposite the case? Does public housing benefit society more than it does the recipient of the housing, or is the opposite the case? How exactly is one to calculate and weigh benefits? These are extremely difficult problems, but we might begin by making it a rule that individual welfare ought never to be the object of political action, just as private actions ought never to be the object of scrutiny by the police power or society as a whole. Individual welfare may be and ought to be the object of politics or institutions other than the state. That, in fact, is the role of the family, the church, the voluntary association. That the happiness quotient in my family should remain high should not become the object of state action. Aside from its ability to spend money (an action that in terms of happiness is very ambivalent) the state has little to offer that can increase our happiness. It can do a great deal, however, to make life for myself and my family a living hell. The language of political discussion ought to eschew discussions of private benefit.

One way in which the state can limit its actions to those which benefit society as a whole is to refuse any actions that can be performed by other institutions or groups within society. The state, following this rule, does not attempt to perform the functions of the family, does not attempt to provide education, does not organize charity, does not regulate the economy, and forgoes intrusions into the processes of production and consumption.

We have seen that the whole tendency of state action in the past five hundred years has been just the opposite of this. The state has constantly enlarged the sphere of its activity and increased the degree of centralization within society. I am not arguing that we need fewer social services, that individual need, dependency, helplessness are today less pressing problems than they were a century ago, though that may very well be the case. I am arguing that direct state action in these areas is inappropriate. I am arguing that these are not areas suitable for governmental politics. I am saying that governmental action is less apt to maximize welfare and liberty than are alternative social solutions. Only in those cases in which a desired social objective cannot be achieved except by the intervention of the state, and in the absence of alternative social institutions and structures, ought the state to undertake public action. The community has every possible interest in the world in the collection and safe disposal of garbage. It does not follow from this that garbage ought to be collected by city employees who are paid out of tax money. The same argument can and ought more often to be made with respect to the postal service.

However, we would delude ourselves were we to assume that all those needs essential to the orderly and satisfactory functioning of society are now or have ever been all met by voluntary associations and corporations and institutions other than the state. Libertarians have reason but not history on their side when they argue for the "night-watchman" concept of the state. Most men, even contemporary liberals, wish that a state of such limited powers were capable of meeting the needs of our society. But even in America, where the voluntary association has obtained a development unequaled anywhere else in the world, men are forced, repeatedly, to turn to the state simply because private agencies and institutions are unavailable.

Moreover, we have seen in the past half century, and that at an increasing rate of acceleration, the decay and dispersal of communities. Rapid and inorganic suburban growth, the movement of large populations from the farm to the city, the industrialization and economic development of the southwest, northwest, west, and south, rapid social mobility and the erosion of the mores and institutions that supported them in an older America: all of these factors have created an anomic and dislocated society in which the organs of community seem no longer capable of affording individuals and groups the services and protections they find necessary for survival. In consequence, when problems arise they devolve almost immediately upon the state. It alone seems to possess the organizational capacities, the experience, the skills, and the resources necessary to deal with many problems. Finally, it seeks to provide an ideology to replace the lost faiths and shattered myths which had at one time provided support for community.

The solution to this problem lies with the individual. He must deliberately choose to devote his time and talent to the location of community and to the solution of the problems that his society confronts through common action. The individual must become a participant in the common tasks of the community. He must increasingly devote himself to the common good and to activities that have as their objective the securing of the common welfare. Indeed, the individual will discover his humanity most completely in these activities, in which he brings to bear on the problems of his culture and time his gifts and insights. The alternative to participation freely and enthusiastically given is participation through the coercion of the state, participation often in solutions to pressing social problems that fly in the face of the moral, economic, cultural, and political views of the citizen. We do not have a choice as to whether we shall participate or not. In the early 1950s, when West Germany began the grim business of rearming, slogans suddenly appeared stenciled on the walls and pavements crying "*ohne mich*," "without me!" That, however, is in any society never really an option. We cannot choose whether or not we will participate; we can, if we are fortunate, choose the method of our participation.

Beyond the cooperative action of individuals in the creation of community, the state has a powerful and important role. It is in the interest of the state to encourage and foster voluntary associations and nongovernmental institutional forms. These powerful corporate groups and institutions serve in all good societies to stand between the great power of the state and the helplessness of the individual. They act to check the power of single individuals and the power of other corporate groups in society, but above all they alone are capable of challenging state power and authority. The state will be able to fulfill its mission best when its tasks are clearly delineated and when the boundaries of its powers and activities are constantly patrolled by strong and capable competing communities.

For its own health, therefore, the state ought not to undertake activities that go beyond the preservation of the civic order unless it can anticipate a time in the fairly immediate future when its intervention will no longer be necessary. It ought always to be the object of politics to make men and their communities autonomous and independent rather than to coerce them into dependency and servitude. There will always be moments when the resources of individuals and communities are insufficient to meet the staggering problems of the community. The state must then exercise special care that temporary assistance does not become permanent servitude.

Authority and its reflection in the exercise of power is ultimately based on the moral dispositions of citizens and on consent freely given. The moral character of the state, as Harold Laski pointed out long ago in his book *A Grammar of Politics* (1925), is no different from that of any other association: "It exacts loyalty upon the same grim condition that a man exacts loyalty from his friends. It is judged by what it offers to its members in terms of the things they deem to be good. Its roots are laid in their minds and hearts. In the long run, it will win support, not by the theoretic program it announces, but by the perception of ordinary citizens that allegiance to its will is a necessary condition of their well-being." There have surely been few better definitions of the state or the purpose of politics.

19

Why I Am a Republican and a Conservative

Every one of us ought now and then to be forced to give an account of the faith or faiths he holds. Each one of us ought to have to defend his commitments, give his reasons, and own up to his prejudices. Those of you who have teenage children must do it every day and so I excuse you from further obligation, but I suggest that the rest of us ought to ask ourselves just why we are what we are and not something else.

As a matter of fact, I have not always been a Republican, though I think it unlikely that I shall ever cease now to be one. I grew up in a family where the noun "Republican" was always prefaced by the adjective "black." The word "black" had no racial connotation, but it did convey the proper degree of distaste in which my father held the local establishment. It was not until I had married, completed my education, and, in fact, had become a fully political animal that I asked myself seriously for the first time why I voted as I did. My answer was a partial one and though it did not reassure me I continued to vote, at least in national elections, as a Democrat, down to the building of the Berlin wall. That did it. On that day in September 1961 I promised myself not only that I would never vote Democratic again in any election—local, state, or national—but, more importantly, I also decided to vote Republican. Of course my change of political behavior was not a whim of the moment, but a decision that had been ripening in my consciousness for some time. Why did I make that decision and why is it that I now urge my decision on other people?

I have said that my decision was crystallized by the building of the Berlin Wall, and looking back on the political events of the twenty years from the time I entered college in 1941 to the building of the Wall in 1961, I must confess that foreign affairs played the major role in my thinking. I served for three years in the Army in Asia during World War II, and after the war I attended universities in Europe, years when Cold War tensions were at their very peak. It is little to be wondered at that I was more cognizant of and more interested in foreign policy than I was in domestic affairs.

During those twenty years I came to see that our Democratically managed foreign policy was provocative without being principled, and utopian and idealistic when it should have been self-interested. Let me be specific.

For thirty years now the American people have been at war. We have poured out immense amounts of blood and treasure during that time, and in not a single one of these bloody and often fruitless encounters have the Democratic presidents who led us into war told us why and how our American interests were at stake. Not one of them has made a convincing case that American safety and America's future were in peril. Indeed, in the Korean and Vietnam wars the Democratic presidents in power so little trusted the judgment of the American people, so little regarded the provisions of the Constitution, and were so contemptuous of public opinion that they did not even ask Congress for a declaration of war, but rather fought these terrible conflicts on the basis of administrative fiat.

How is one to account for the itch that Democratic presidents from Wilson to Johnson have felt to exercise their powers as commanders-in-chief? Certainly it was not military talent. Not one of them had a capacity for military leadership. Their desire to lead America into war derived from their conviction that America had a messianic role to play in the world, that we should make the world safe for democracy, that we should extend to it the blessings of the New Frontier or the goodies of the Great Society. Republican foreign policy has, by contrast, never been ideological or interventionist. We have, as Republicans, always believed that we most convince the outside world of the blessings of the American system by our example rather than by force of arms. We have, as Republicans, always asserted that we must be prepared to fight, but only when our national interest is involved and our national safety directly challenged.

It would be unjust to assert that Democratic presidents have in the recent past won elections, fought depressions, and sought to dispel domestic crisis through a war-inspired consensus. No doubt those motives occurred to each and every Democratic White House tenant, but I am convinced that their reasons for intervention were never quite so crassly political as that. Their reasons for intervention were the messiah complex, the Napoleon complex, the Mr. Clean complex, which seem to get hold of every Democrat whether his name is Franklin Roosevelt, Teddy Kennedy, or— what is the first name of Maine's Senator Muskie? (I really doubt that it will ever become a household word). No matter what the cost, this messy world of ours must be set to rights, and all men must enjoy the dubious blessings of the Democratic ward politics of our urban machines.

But just as Democratic international politics have been interventionist, so their domestic politics have been meddlesome. To intervene and to control have been the undeviating purposes of every domestic political measure introduced by Democratic politicians since the days of President Wilson. Democratic politicians have assumed steadfastly that the American people can do nothing for themselves, indeed, should be permitted to do nothing for themselves. These politicians have been so convinced of this that they have been quite willing to forge those golden chains (made in Washington) which bind the poor so successfully to their poverty by making them dependent on politicians, rather than releasing the poor to opportunity and to the utilization of their own considerable resources.

Is there a problem in the community? For heaven's sake don't solve it at the local level, where men can identify the problem and possess the ingenuity necessary for its solution. Send for help to Washington, where the matter will be taken out of the hands of the people and where all the devices of administrative tyranny will be employed, not to solve the problem, to be sure, but to enlarge it with such enthusiasm and bureaucratic inventiveness as to make the old problem look petty, mean, and to use one of Washington's favorite words, "underdeveloped." Of course I have been using the word *problem.* However, Democrats never use that word. Their word is "crisis." With their cast of mind nothing can ever be simply said, simply stated, or simply solved. And it must be admitted that those things which would be problems under normal circumstances become, with help from Democratic lawmakers and officials, crises. To paraphrase the motto of the state of Michigan, "If you would see a mess, look about you."

In contrast, Republican domestic policy has been almost rigidly noninterventionist. It has insisted that the centralization of power and centralized management of the nation's political, economic, and social affairs is destructive to liberty, is harmful to political and social creativity, and, finally, will dry up the fund of goodwill men naturally show toward government and will replace it with doubt, distrust, and disillusionment. Republicans have always insisted that it is the role of government to help men to help themselves, to make opportunities rather than plans and programs, and most importantly, to create no program that does not anticipate a time when the success of that program in liquidating the problem will make the program redundant and unnecessary. How unlike the farm program of the successive Democratic administrations, the various poverty programs, the urban renewal efforts, the economic tinkering and meddling. Republicans do not believe that individual men or even local communities can solve all their problems, but neither do they believe that big government can solve those problems. Nothing that has happened in the past fifty years should lead us to believe otherwise.

Finally, Republicans believe that government ought to be truthful, open, and dignified. Republican administrations are dull when compared to the vulgarity of the Johnson years. Mr. Nixon is not a swinger when compared to the Kennedy brothers, but then I doubt that he will have difficulties with an unlighted bridge. But aside from the personal behavior of politicians, political office ought to be so employed as to educate the public in the choices which the public confronts. It ought not to be used to propagandize, to manipulate, to hide and evade. If there is any credibility problem for the Nixon administration, it is rooted in the fact that successive Democratic administrations have cynically and for petty political gains manipulated public opinion and practiced a policy of studied deception. Sound politics is possible only when the electorate is in full possession of the facts. It is for this reason that the campaign of the vice president for truth and honesty in the media is such an important part of current Republican political activity.

I have argued that I am a Republican in politics because I believe in nonintervention in foreign affairs, because I believe that most government action should be local in nature and control and limited in action, and because I believe that officials should not only provide the public with models of decorum and honesty but above all provide the public with information necessary to make intelligent choices. These are all pragmatic values which reflect themselves in the realm of political choice. The purpose of political parties, after all, is to win elections and to exercise political power. I vote the straight Republican ticket not because I believe that every Republican candidate is a model of political wisdom and principle but because politics, in America, is made by parties. I may not agree with particular features of the legislative program of President Nixon or Senator Griffin, but I know that legislative program is more apt to reflect my principles than the legislative program of Hubert Humphrey or Senator Hart. My Republican politics rarely wholly represent the principles that I hold, but Republican politicians nearly always represent those principles better than their Democratic opponents would. It is a fact that cannot be too often repeated that we do not vote for men if we wish to be politically effective, we vote rather for great political traditions as they embody themselves in a party. The party is never the embodiment of the ideal. The party is the creation of compromise and trimming, of those bendings and turnings by which we accommodate the demands of reality and the differences of opinion and honest doubts of the moment. The party does not embody the ideal and it is all the more useful because it does not.

There is a place for the ideal, however, in the life of every man and every organization, and that is why, in addition to calling myself a Republican, I describe myself as a conservative. By that, I mean that my political ideals, as distinct from my political accommodations, my political party, are conservative. In the realm of principle I make no concessions and no compromises. In that realm the absolute reigns supreme even though aspects of that ideal are mutually contradictory. Let me give you an example. I believe in the equality of all men. I believe it with sufficient conviction to work to see that equality realized legally, socially, economically. I also believe in hierarchy, natural aristocracy, and the right of excellence not only to honor but to privilege. I grant you that my belief in equality and aristocracy cannot be reconciled perfectly in the real world any more than free will and determinism can be reconciled. Still, at the level of the ideal I hold them both, and I believe my behavior would be less honorable and my world impoverished were I to abandon one of these contradictory ideals.

As a conservative I believe in freedom—not a limited and circumscribed freedom but an absolute freedom; but I also, as a conservative, believe in the ideal—yes the absolute necessity—of order. That there are areas in the practical, pragmatic realm where these ideals are in conflict seems to me not only self-evident but an unavoidable aspect of our humanity.

As a conservative, I believe in both individualism and community. Of course, in an absolute sense these two ideals are contradictory, and yet no good society has ever existed that has not struck a balance between the two.

Finally, as a conservative I believe in private enterprise, competition, and the market mechanism, but I also believe in values—human, moral, cultural—that cannot be expressed in economic terms, that cannot be defined by the competition of interests. And I do not, fellow Republicans, intend to abandon the one or the other. I intend to bring as much of my contradictory idealism to bear on my present political situation as possible, moving the practical as near the absolute as humans are capable of going.

And it is in this very aspect that we Republican conservatives differ from Democratic liberals. They do not believe that politics is the art of the possible, the sphere of compromise, the area of our existence where we always settle for half a loaf. They are utopians who believe that through some political magic the ideal, in spite of human imperfections, the demands of reality, and the conflict of human desires, can be enacted into everyday reality. For them ideals are never in conflict. In the conflict between the individual and the community they simply choose the community. In the conflict between aristocracy and equality they always choose equality. In the struggle between value and the market they always choose what they feel is value, even though the choice destroys the economic welfare of the state. In the conflict between freedom and order they seem in the present day always to choose freedom.

And so I urge you as fellow Republicans to hold fast to your realistic political commitments. Don't be tempted to sacrifice the world of practical politics to the absolute ideal. Political victories are not won in the realm of the absolute. Many conservatives of the present moment have succeeded in maintaining their ideological purity, but at the cost of rendering themselves totally ineffective in the political sphere.

However, in the recent past, and in Michigan at the present time, the greater danger is that in the desire to win elections, in the effort to compromise and trim, the Republican politician and his supporters will totally abandon ideals and completely surrender principles. That is the pattern followed by the Lindseys, the Javitses, and, to a lesser but an alarming extent, by our own Governor Milliken.

Politics is as contradictory, as divided, as ambiguous, and as imperfect as any of the other aspects of our humanity and our everyday behavior. Consequently, let us not only accept these inherent conditions but find some way to turn them to our advantage.

PART SIX: CONSERVATISM

Tonsor deserves to be regarded as a conservative intellectual of the first rank. He was deeply concerned about the nature of conservative thought and order. In his writing on conservatism, Tonsor discussed how conservatives were consistently searching for an identity, which they found, most typically, in their embrace of traditional social order and historic Christianity. He also felt most connected as an intellectual to the burgeoning conservative movement, supportive of not only its intellectual goals but also its politics.

20

How Does the Past Become the Future?

To what extent should the past determine the future? Only a few years ago it seemed to most intellectuals that the future would extinguish the past. The past in an "age of revolution" would become a museum of artifacts.

Perhaps the most potent and commonplace source of this abolition of the past lay in the idea of "youth" as a determinative force in present history. From Rousseau onward, "youth" ceased to be a formative stage in the achievement of maturity and became an autonomous condition. By the end of the nineteenth century, youth movements everywhere displaced the goal of maturity. Increasingly, men and women, aided by style, the cosmetician's art, the plastic surgeon's skill, and the physician's pharmacopoeia, provided extraordinary examples of arrested development. It is instructive to note that the ideological movements of the twentieth century had as their most important component youth movements. Their objective was human transformation and the abolition of the past.

From the French Revolution to the Russian and Chinese revolutions, the goal was the abolition of the past. Through the "Romantic" mumbo-jumbo of Hegelian sublation, the past was to be transcended and refigured in such a way as to provide mankind with a new dawn. The religions, social orders, ethical and artistic constructs of the past were to be bulldozed into the capacious dustbin of history and replaced by a utopian dream world.

It is difficult now to comprehend, even with the sophisticated tools of historical understanding, the Marxist dream world; a world in which human limitations were to be transcended by gigantic projects aimed at the total conquest of nature, beginning with the transformation of human nature. Schemes to water the arid reaches of central Asia were no less fantastic and abortive than schemes to create the New Soviet Man or, in Nazi ideology, the racially pure Germanic superman.

It is, of course, mistaken to assume that these transformational efforts to abolish history were limited to the ideologies of the nineteenth and twentieth centuries. Utopianism was not necessarily colored by ideology. The "Brave New Worlds" men constructed in their imaginations and to which they attempted to give the shapes of reality were often as not the products of Promethean presumption and pseudoscientific daring. It is well to remember that the eugenics movement, so closely tied to racism and middle-class humbug, antedated National Socialist dreams of creating a super-race.

"Scientism" was, and still is, as powerful as any political ideology. Its dreams of and blueprints for a perfected future have been a strong revolutionary force whose object is to overcome the past, to abolish tradition, and create new hedonistic values. That the givens of the human condition cannot be transformed but only ameliorated is a fact that does not seem to have occurred to the "scientist." That amelioration in one area of human experience is often purchased at the expense of deformation in another is an unexpected aspect of everyday experience. "The unanticipated consequences of rational action" is a cliché of twentieth-century speech.

Those postmodernist movements which have been born of a sense of ideological and "scientistic" failure nonetheless repudiate and denigrate the past. Deconstructionism is Voltaire's cynical remark that "history is the pack of lies the living play upon the dead" writ large. If we cannot make any truth statement, all assertions, including any analysis of the past, are acts of the will that conform to our advantage. Race, class, and gender, rather than a disinterested analysis of the past, are the sources of the fictions through which we manipulate the present and transform the past.

It is apparent now to everyone except tenured professors at our universities that the age of scientism and ideology is over and that the Pyrrhonistic claptrap of postmodernism is an expended force. The past cannot be abolished, amended, or appropriated by the causes of race, class, and gender.

The English poet Edward Thomas says in a poem, "Early One Morning," "[T]he past is the only dead thing that smells sweet. . . ." He surely is mistaken, for the past is not dead, and never dies, but lives on as a force in all of our daily lives and in the very constitution of the self. The past, as the power of grace and sin, exerts an energy and is a quiddity whether or not that past is known or regarded. The institutions of slavery may be abolished and abandoned. The fact of slavery in the past conditions every possible future.

Conservatives since Burke have held that history is the distillation of past experience, the awareness of past experience, of the sum of human trial and error. It is the fixed star by which the present and the future should be guided. Public interest is no more than an awareness of this body of tradition and its implications for present action.

Statesmanship is no more than an apprehension of the meaning of past experience.

It is clear, however, that today is not simply a replication of yesterday and that tomorrow will not be like today. The future cannot be shaped in terms of the past alone. All life has a novelty that transforms genera and species, ancestors, and location in the temporal sequence. Some lives and events possess an absolute character. Once the world-historical character has appeared, as Hegel realized, all future history bears his mark. He does not abolish the past but rather fulfills it and gives significance to its experience.

The abolition of the past that the past two revolutionary centuries hoped for has proven to be not within the realm of possibility. However, neither the restoration of the past nor the preservation of the *status quo* is a possibility either. Time is a one-way street and there is no turning back or any possibility of arresting forward motion. There is a note of unutterable pathos in a person or era that pretends its creaking joints have been limbered by drinking at the fountain of youth.

It is a matter of great interest that just at the moment in the eighteenth century when the abolition of the past became the object of revolution, historical consciousness became more acute. Modern historical science was invented just when the men of the Enlightenment thought they had strangled and trampled on the writhing body of the past. Niebuhr and von Ranke charmed history, phoenix-like, and caused its resurrection out of the ashes of the past. Moreover, the sciences of history and philosophy understood the process of becoming as developmental. History was conceived to be an unfolding of the character and content of the past. "Development" was not seen as amendment but rather as fulfillment. The future was seen as that which existed in potentiality transformed into that which existed in actuality. In this sense the future was the handmaiden of the past.

These notions were implicit in Aristotelian philosophy but were given their clearest formulation by Catholic nineteenth-century theologians who sought to express both the continuity of truth, *semper eidem,* and the clearer, ramified, transformed, and contemporary expression of that truth. The great question for these theologians and historians was the question of how the doctrines and structures of the primitive church became the complex and time-conditioned church of the nineteenth century.

The work of theology was not simply additive and adjustive. It was, these theologians believed, a development of those elements inherent in the deposit of faith. This work was essentially conservative but its end result was a more complex, comprehensive, and contemporary understanding of the deposit of faith. History was not simply a historical process, as Marxists believed, by which history itself was abolished.

These ideas were not simply theological but were in a broad sense historical, biological, and, as I shall argue, political. Developmental pattern was the stuff of history, theology, biology, and politics.

John Henry Newman and the Munich School were the chief exponents of historical theology. Newman's *Essay on the Development of Christian Doctrine* (1845) was the most important and comprehensive statement of these ideas. It led to his being received into the Roman Catholic Church and was to become a source of Roman suspicion as to the orthodoxy of his faith.

Newman argued that doctrine in a primitive, incomplete, undeveloped form was present in the early church. What appears to be change in the course of time is only amplification and the growth of understanding. Not all change, of course, is integral to the development of primitive doctrine. Heresy, often enough, is simply an index to the state of mind, the terms of debate, concerning doctrine within the church. It is not a doctrinal untruth but a portion of doctrine wrenched and sundered from the complementary context of doctrinal wholeness. "Corruptions," on the other hand, are manifest untruths and stand in bold contradiction to the doctrines held by the church. The problem for historical theology is one of discernment, a process aided, according to Newman, by certain tests of "authenticity." Newman's essay was an extraordinary effort to reconcile integrity and continuity of doctrine with increasing complexity and understanding and applicability to historic changes in mentality and perception.

At the very time Newman was expounding a theology of the development of Christian doctrine, Benjamin Disraeli was constructing a theory of the development of conservative political ideas. Disraeli was in search of an authentic "primitive Toryism," and he was interested in analyzing how this "primitive Toryism" could, in a contemporary, developed form, be instantiated in current policy and legislation. What were the basic doctrines of Toryism and how could these doctrines be made relevant to contemporary political situations? In 1835, Disraeli published his *Vindication of the English Constitution,* which attempted to do for Toryism much of what Newman was later to attempt for Catholic doctrine. The coincidence is not accidental, for the power of ideas, as they move through history, is contagious. This is especially true for those who have a bent for literature, who think of themselves as poets and novelists, as did both Disraeli and Newman.

Politics no less than theology involves belief resulting from a fundamental orientation to the experience of existence. This experience and these beliefs always have a historical dimension. They come to us out of a past that embodies the cumulative experience of mankind or a significant part of mankind.

Disraeli argued that "Toryism should be divested of all those qualities which are adventitious and not essential, and which, having been produced by the course of circumstances which are constantly changing, become in time obsolete, inconvenient . . ." It is this essential character which marks fundamental positions in theology and in politics. "Authentic" development is the unfolding of the content of these essential positions.

Disraeli's rethinking of the content of conservatism made possible the revival and eventual triumph of the Tory party. Today's British conservatives, as Margaret Thatcher acknowledged, owe him a great debt. However, Disraeli's policy of political expedience corrupted the purity of his theory. It remained for his great opponent, William Gladstone, close student of Newman, Ignaz von Döllinger, and Lord Acton—the great exponents of theological development and historical theology—to transform conservative political theory into practical politics in the parliamentary programs of the Liberal Party. It was Gladstone who rescued the authentic past and transformed the threatening present into its image.

These nineteenth-century theological and political theories have a pregnancy and meaning, however remote they may seem to the current dilemma of American conservatism at the end of the twentieth century. The essential conservative position is beguiled on all sides by "heresies" and "corruptions" which mask themselves as "authentic" developments of the classic conservative position. These heresies and corruptions develop out of mistaken legislative programs originating in expedience, enthusiasm, and political wrongheadedness. At the present moment, conservatives must ask once more who they are and what they believe before they present a program of what they intend to do legislatively.

Conservatism reenacts the past not as a past program but as a set of beliefs and values which are translated into the current idiom. The "authenticity" of this current idiom is demonstrable in that it does not contradict, corrupt, or attenuate the conservative goals, perspectives, or values of the past. Principles and not programs lie at the heart of conservatism.

Conservatism, then, is a set of beliefs, principles, and historical reflections which have come to us from the past. Everyday conservatism has become increasingly aware of this body of doctrine. Burke, Tocqueville, Mill, Burckhardt, and Acton are for conservatives the "Law and the Prophets." They are the reflective ordering of the experience of men living in modern society. They all lived in the shadows of the French Revolution, and all of them must be considered as responsive to the heresies, corruptions, and political deformations of the revolution. Conservatism lives out of a past, and that past is "the Revolution."

But beyond this body of doctrine and insight, there is what I would like to call the "vernacular architecture" of conservatism, the way in which these ideals and principles are translated into the politics of a particular time and place. Here, too, conservatism faces the danger of an accommodation that is, in fact, a corruption, a political deformation. In America, of course, the founding is determinative, and the Constitution stands at the very center of American political conservatism. It is for this reason that the questions of "original intent" and judicial activism are the most important questions in current American political thought. The "vernacular architecture" of American politics is conservative, even though liberalism and left-wing intellectuality have managed to build some shanties on the American political foundation.

Central to conservative doctrine, and the translation of this doctrine into the politics of a particular time and place, is the fear of unchecked power and its centralization. There is no room in the American system for an imperial presidency and its employment of revolutionary rhetoric and democratic bribery to sustain its quest for totalitarian dominance.

It is for this reason that the checks of a balanced constitution are so important. It is for this reason that the diffusion of power to the states and particularly to local communities is imperative. Education, welfare, and social control must be taken out of the hands of the central power and its instrumentalities.

It is for this reason that the budget of the federal government must be reduced, that taxes paid to the central power must be drastically curtailed and redirected to the states and local communities. Beyond the needs of defense and a limited federal police power, only those extraordinary needs of national communication, the alleviation of national disaster, and the control of corporate entities that are national or international in scope should be left in the hands of the federal government. The federal government should not subsidize culture, impose standards on education, or engage in any activity, however benign it may appear to be, that is more properly the activity of the states or local communities.

These are, of course, the commonplaces of contemporary conservative thought, and yet elective officeholders of the Left and Right, in spite of the wishes of the electorate, day in and day out increase the power and scope of the federal government. As Tocqueville was aware, the great engine for transforming and increasing the power of the central government was warfare and the growing scope and might of the armed forces. There cannot be an imperial presidency aside from an imperial America. It follows that the United States must disengage itself from any exercise of power which is not an expression of commanding American national interest. We must not become the policeman of the world. Our interest in the Third World must be predicated on the idea of benign neglect. Surely the people of East Peoria have little at stake in East Timor, however much we may grieve at the fate of the East Timorese and however much as private citizens we are bound, in charity, to assist the alleviation of their suffering.

Tocqueville and the founders were well aware that religion was indispensable to the prosperity and survival of democratic polities. The myth of the "wall of separation" between church and state was long ago refuted by Paul Kuyper, the great constitutional lawyer and historian. Established religions are bad, not simply because they compel the consciences of dissenters, but because they are harmful to religion itself. The fear of establishment and its consequences does not mean that the state must discourage or act antithetically to religion and its interests. Indeed, the state should do all in its power to acknowledge and encourage the role of religion in society and should act to foster those practices which have popular approval and which acknowledge man's dependence on God. Moreover, in those areas where the state and the church have a common interest, such as education and charity, the state should sustain and encourage religious communities.

It is clear that there is a marked division between conservatism and libertarianism. Political society has interests that are more comprehensive and responsible than those of a selfish individualism. Privatization alone is not the key to the good or even minimally functioning society. The general rather than the individual welfare must in most cases be paramount. The state should always act in such a way that its powers to tax foster the development of communal and personal initiatives in charity, the elimination of poverty, and the development of a vibrant culture.

The vernacular architecture of conservatism is the stuff of contemporary politics. In every area of individual and community concern, there are proposals and plans to achieve the goals of traditional conservative political doctrine based on the experience of the past. This vernacular architecture of political conservatism must be organic, decentralized, and rooted in past experience. Even here, however, not all developments will prove to be "authentic." There will be heresies, corruptions, and deformations masquerading as a politically desirable future.

21

The Conservative Search for Identity

Writing with all the Romantic appreciation of the dialectic of opposites and polarities, Walt Whitman said, "Do I contradict myself? / Very well then I contradict myself, / (I am large, I contain multitudes)." Whitman and the Romantics expressed eloquently and frequently the profound observation that the essence of life is polarity, opposition, contradiction, and that these warring forces, when integrated, harmonized, synthesized, and harnessed by the sovereign personality, institution, or society, enrich and energize the larger context of which they are a part.

However, the organic union of opposites is not today a central intellectual concern. "Things fall apart, the center cannot hold," wrote Yeats. The stern necessities of an age of ideology demand conformity, and, locked in his preconceptions, the liberal intellectual is impotent to do more than mourn the passing of an age in which variety and the dialectic of opposites produced a rich and dynamic society. He desires movement but refuses to pay the price for movement; he desires nonconformity and creativity but refuses to tolerate the divergences of viewpoint and the frequent eccentricity which are the price of nonconformity. He wishes creativity but is uncomfortable with the messiness of failed experiments and failed lives which creativity produces. For the organic reconciliation of opposites, which is the measure of a healthy society, he has substituted the myth of "pluralism," the dream of a multitude of mutually exclusive and hostile social units and individuals that coexist, but which fail either to stimulate to action or to enrich the common group. It is a classical age but, like all classical periods, it is both static and weary.

It would be false to assume that, unlike liberal thought, conservative thought has avoided the spirit of the age, that it is broader, more inclusive, more dynamic, and more creative than the doctrinaire liberalism that is its counterpart. The blunt truth is that most conservatives do not know what manner of men they are; they have no clear conception of the society they wish to create, have no organic relationship either to the present or the past, hold no grand design, entertain no enduring principles, and are responsible to no whole and healthy vision either of man or society. Their discourse consists of the platitudes of political criticism, and, however salutary and necessary this may be, it is neither a substitute for principle nor a guide for action.

The tendency of conservatism is to disintegration, for the centrifugal forces are much greater in it than in contemporary liberalism. Liberalism is a body of coherent doctrine deductively derived from a set of central propositions, while conservatism is a synthesis of contradictory principles, the principle of authority and the principle of freedom. These principles are ever held in precarious balance by individuals and by societies; the resolution of their forces is never final; their synthesis is never complete. The drive they impart to society is in a measure the product of their instability.

If conservatives are finally to achieve the common agreement necessary to the establishment of both principle and party, they must reconcile themselves to the dialectic of freedom and authority and must capitalize on the values of their divided heritage. They can achieve this in no better way than through an exploration of the thought of Alexis de Tocqueville (1805–59) and Lord Acton (1834–1902). Together their lives spanned the nineteenth century, and together they elaborated the soundest and most coherent modern body of conservative thought of which contemporary conservatives may avail themselves. They reconciled, in their lives and in their thinking, authority and freedom; they anticipated the modern world with all of its problems; and they worked towards viable and optimistic solutions. They both stood near the center of power, and they both mistrusted power and spoke repeatedly of its corrupting influence. Both were active in practical politics, but both were contemplative by nature, preferring the study of power to its exercise. Both were deeply religious men, but both stood near the edge of heresy. Both suspected the worst of human nature, but optimistically hoped for the best. Both were born to an aristocratic order that was in the process of dissolution, and both met the situation not with reaction but rather with an attempt to understand and to assimilate themselves to the new social processes transforming Western society. Both were ethical thinkers of the highest order who would tolerate no concession of principle to practical politics. Both combined in their thought and in their lives such a devotion to both principle and freedom as ought to distinguish the contemporary conservative.

Not only singular personalities, but history itself by slow conjunction unites the opposites that men so often find in contradiction. Providence, which has its own purposes, disposes, and wise men conform themselves to a world whose ordering was only partially theirs. It is difficult, once man accepts the basic proposition of historical purpose, to couple with this acceptance the necessity of individual and collective action. It is all too easy to assume, as others in the past have, that faith and hope make an active charity unnecessary. But it is only through historical understanding, through action, and finally through faith in God's Providence that the reconciliation of opposites becomes possible. Lord Acton and Tocqueville understood both the necessity of faith and hope and the necessity of immediate political action. Although both were pessimists about human nature, both were optimists largely because of their belief in an overriding Providence. Acton said, "Christ is risen on the world and fails not." Tocqueville wrote, "I cannot believe that the Creator made man to leave him in an endless struggle with the intellectual wretchedness that surrounds us. God destines a calmer and a more certain future to the communities of Europe. I am ignorant of his designs, but I shall not cease to believe in them because I cannot fathom them, and I had rather mistrust my own capacity than his justice."

But both Acton and Tocqueville recognized that if it is difficult to accept the necessity of action and understanding within the framework of a world ordered by Providence, it has been, for the past two and a half centuries, even more difficult to accept the concept of Providence itself. The attack upon Providence and purpose has been the distinguishing characteristic of modern society, the abandonment of hope and value its singular mark. Whether in Voltaire's *Candide* or in the antirational and antiprovidential works of the Marquis de Sade, the general conception of a creative Providence that establishes purpose and imposes meaning upon the events of history was denied by the eighteenth century. What has been described as the "revolt against the eighteenth century" was well under way before the eighteenth century was half over. It was only incidentally a revolt against reason, but reason, too, was forced to abdicate its sway once purpose had been banished. The era of nihilism and the totally absurd begins with a doubt as to the nature and purposes of God in history. The nineteenth-century attempts at the restoration of order, the restoration of value, the restoration of purpose, all revolved around the central problem of restoring meaning to history. Even Marxism is an attempt to restore purpose, to restore ends, to restore values to history. That it restores these to history without restoring Providence is the most telling reason for its failure. It is difficult enough to reconcile God's ways to man as they reveal themselves in the ambiguities, failures, and dilemmas of history; it is impossible to justify the course of dialectical materialism as it reveals itself in its subhuman and antihuman processes.

In order to escape from absurdity man must move into the realm of order, value, purpose, and belief. By the end of the eighteenth century this had become intellectually impossible except through an appeal to authority. At the social and the political level the appeal was to the authority of established social and economic institutions; at the religious level the appeal to authority was an appeal to orthodoxy and especially to established religious forms and institutions. The moment was antirevolutionary and antirationalistic; authority was to be reestablished by restoration of the throne and the altar. But note that those who sought authority from the conservative side were unyielding pessimists. Maistre, Bonald, Metternich all despaired both of human nature's and God's ability to produce a better world. Skepticism had broken through the barriers of rationality, the absurd had replaced the world of meaning and purpose, nihilism and the diabolical had replaced the world of value and of beauty. There is in Maistre's *Les Soirées de Saint Petersbourg* a terrible echo of the violence, despair, and ugliness of the vision of the Marquis de Sade. "Don't you hear the earth crying for blood?" writes Maistre, who then proceeds to paint the most terrible picture of the struggle of life against life depicted by any Western thinker. Darwin's picture of the struggle for survival is innocent because it is natural; Maistre's is diabolical because the struggle is metaphysical. He concludes in a dreadful passage: "The earth, continually drenched in blood, is only an immense altar where everything that lives must be immolated endlessly, without respite, until all things are used up, the evil is extinguished and death itself is dead. . . ."

The poet Nerval echoed the ruin which had fallen on the world when he wrote: "Seeking the eye of God, I only saw a huge black bottomless socket, whence the night that dwells in it radiates over the world and becomes ever more dense; A strange rainbow surrounds this dark pit, threshold of old chaos whose shadow is nothingness, a vortex swallowing up the Worlds and Days!"

Those contemporary "conservatives" who seek a conservatism that is not coupled to principle, a life not teleological in its orientation, a history devoid of meaning, have not studied mankind and do not know the meaning of the past. Both the Right and the Left these past hundred and fifty years have reflected the anguished efforts of men to regain the lost center, to reintroduce a principle of authority, to fathom the riddle of history. Lacking internal religious authority, society can exist only if an external secular authority is imposed. The nineteenth-century conservative alliance between the throne and the altar was a failure because neither throne nor altar retained any compelling power. Pessimism and a loss of faith is a poor beginning for conservative politics.

Writing in *Democracy in America*, Tocqueville predicted the consequences of the loss of belief:

> When the religion of a people is destroyed, doubt gets hold of
> the higher powers of the intellect and half paralyzes all the
> others.... When there is no longer any principle of authority in
> religion any more than in politics, men are speedily frightened
> at the aspect of this unbounded independence. The constant
> agitation of all surrounding things alarms and exhausts them.
> As everything is at sea in the sphere of the mind, they deter-
> mine at least that the mechanism of society shall be firm and
> fixed; and as they cannot resume their ancient belief, they as-
> sume a master.

From authority to authoritarianism is but a short step, and substitute
religions of force spring up where authentic religions of love fail. In a society where "the strong do what they can and the weak suffer what they
must," men are driven to the employment of force and coercion in order to
preserve the fabric of civilization. If John Donne's vision be true,

> And new Philosophy calls all in doubt,
> The Element of fire is quite put out;
> The Sun is lost, and th' earth, and no man's wit
> Can well direct him where to look for it.
> 'Tis all in peeces, all cohaerence gone;
> All just supply, and all Relation.

then indeed we are lost and must take such comfort as we can in the absolutism of the Right or the absolutism of the Left. We will act for good or ill
in the measure in which we retain some undestroyed bourgeois prejudices
or some undissolved illusions... for a time. And then even the human myth
will weaken and the uncontained forces of decay will complete their work.

Authority may be imposed from without for a moment; the fabric may
be conserved for a time, but the life expectancy of the empires of the absurd are rather less than a thousand years. At the vital center of man's experience stand the gods, and they alone can grant immortality, purpose,
and grace.

Faith, purpose, and value, while expressing themselves in social forms,
are never social in origin. It is because of this that religion can never be
legislated, and that authority can only endure when it is the result of assent
freely given. Authority and freedom are not only contradictory in human
society, they are interdependent. No true authority exists without unqualified freedom, and individual freedom is quite impossible without assent to
some generally held set of beliefs. "For my own part," wrote Tocqueville,
"I doubt whether man can ever support at the same time complete reli-

gious independence and entire political freedom. And I am inclined to think that if faith be wanting in him, he must be subject; and if he be free, he must believe."

However, the conception of the absolute inviolability of the conscience is a relatively new one. Not until the late eighteenth century did it occur to many men that the consciences of others ought to be respected; not until the nineteenth century did men generally assume that the purpose of the state was the extension of liberty rather than the preservation of religious orthodoxy. The mission of the state was to make men both good and happy, and it defined goodness in terms of a particular Christian orthodoxy. This conception of the state was an ancient one, reaching back to the Roman imperial ideal, and it was one only reluctantly abandoned. For the vast majority of men, the object of civil society has not been to make them free but rather to make them good and happy. An important part of the conservative movement, now as in the eighteenth century, conceives the role of the state in positive terms and the mission of the state as that of temporal and eternal welfare.

But to enforce orthodoxy, to establish religion, to guarantee security, or to legislate happiness forces the state to intrude itself into the consciences of individual men, to circumscribe their freedom and deny their liberty. And so, in the name of religion, freedom, the greatest gift of religion, is denied. Authority cannot stand without assent, and throughout history men have sought to compel what they could not win. Consequently, the links between political reaction and religious establishment have been constant.

However this may be, the fact is that only the internalized authority of the voice of conscience, prophetic and revolutionary, conservative and hopeful, possesses the moral and ethical energies necessary to secure religion and to extend liberty. The conscience lies outside the authority of either church or state. They can only resist it or bow to its demands.

Nevertheless, it was religion itself that slowly paved the way for the ascendency of conscience. Lord Acton, in his *Lectures on Modern History*, described the process:

> Yet the most profound and penetrating of the causes that have transformed society is a medieval inheritance. It was late in the thirteenth century that the psychology of conscience was closely studied for the first time, and men began to speak of it as the audible voice of God, that never misleads or fails, and that ought to be obeyed always, whether enlightened or darkened, right or wrong. The notion was restrained on its appearance, by the practice of regarding opposition to church power as specific heresy, which depressed the secret monitor below the public and vis-

ible authority. With the decline of Coercion, the claim of Conscience rose, and the ground abandoned by the Inquisitor was
gained by the individual. When it had been defined and recognized as something divine in human nature, its action was to
limit power by causing the sovereign voice within to be heard
above the expressed will and settled custom of surrounding men.
By that hypothesis, the soul became more sacred than the state,
because it received light from above, as well as because its concerns are eternal, and out of all proportion with the common
interests of government.

How important Acton thought the conception of conscience was, in
relationship to the establishment of liberty, is indicated in one of the thousands of notes he made for himself:

Importance of S[t]. Thomas's use of the term [conscience].
Why then did he not apply it to religion?
Because he denies that religious error is conscientious.
So long, there was no liberty.
If the state excludes all that, it does what it likes.
Extend the domain of conscience to religious error and then
only is liberty possible.

And in another passage Lord Acton summarized this relationship once more:

The Christian notion of conscience imperatively demands a
corresponding measure of personal liberty. The feeling of duty
and responsibility to God is the only arbiter of a Christian's
actions. With this no human authority can be permitted to interfere. We are bound to extend to the utmost, and to guard
from every encroachment, the sphere in which we can act in
obedience to the sole voice of conscience, regardless of any other
consideration.

Consequently, the authority that Acton and Tocqueville and the great
conservative libertarians of the nineteenth century sought was not the institutionalized authority of orthodoxy speaking in either church or state. It
was the authority of conscience, a conscience that had its source in God
and which was graven by Him on the human heart. "The moral law," Acton
wrote, "is written on the tablets of eternity." In another place, Acton quoted
with approval a passage from Alexander Vinet: "Conscience is not ourselves; it is against us; therefore it is something other than ourselves, what

can it be but God: And if it be God, we must give it the honor due to God: we cannot reverence the Sovereign less than the ambassador."

And just as conscience was not institutionalized in the secular or religious authority, so conscience and liberty could not stand uncorrupted if either secular or religious authority possessed power to crush it. If liberty was man's highest good, then governments ought to be so constructed that men might satisfy the demands their consciences make upon them.

There was no doubt in Acton's mind that liberty was man's highest good. He wrote: "The best things that are loved and sought by men are religion and liberty, not pleasure or prosperity, not knowledge or power. Yet the paths of both are stained by infinite blood."

Governments ought to enable men to act according to their consciences. In his "Inaugural Lecture," Acton noted that "duties are the cause of rights," that is to say, liberty arises from conscience. In an essay of 1861 in the *Rambler,* he wrote: "Liberty is not the power of doing what we like, but the right of being able to do what we ought." In a note to himself, he added, "Liberty enables us to do our duty—unhindered by the State, by society, by ignorance and error." Where, therefore, religion or the state stands in the way of conscience it is evil and must be resisted.

But the proposition that, whatever the objectives and intentions of the state, its actions frequently end in oppression and violation of the conscience, is one which has been demonstrated over and over again since the beginning of the nineteenth century. Only the conservatives of that century and the liberals of our own century have insisted that the action of the state, whatever the circumstances and whatever its purposes, was good. Even Karl Marx knew the state for what it was, an instrument of oppression, and his utopian politics called for its withering away in the name of freedom. He saw the tendency of the centuries as the destruction of the class state, which in turn would free the individual for the full development of all his potentialities. But the movement of the century did not liberate, educate, and humanize its offspring; rather, it brutalized and corrupted them. The state did not wither away; rather, it grew monstrously, intruding itself in the Soviet Union into every aspect of human life and thought. The revolution made in the name of conscience and against authority did not always free men but, just as the reactionary conservatives had warned, it simply led to the war of all against all. The reign of conscience and opinion led inevitably to the establishment of democracy, and democracy, unchecked by any influence and fired by the dreams of demagogues and messiahs, threatened the whole structure of society. The conception of man's relationship to the state and to authority suddenly changed, and many men found the system that they had destroyed in the name of conscience to be superior to that which took its place.

Thus, the problem of our age was to be a new one not previously faced by men. Democracy tended to bring absolute conformity and tyranny in its wake unless it was checked by churches, constitutions, economic interests, divided powers, and decentralization and plurality of authority. The movement of the age was not, as Marx's sociology predicted, towards freedom, but towards tyranny. Acton, a wiser man and a more discerning political mind, noted: "To reconcile liberty with an aristocratical society and a monarchical State was the problem, the striving of many centuries. To preserve it under absolute democracy is the special problem of the future. . . . [The modern danger] is state absolutism, not royal absolutism. . . . It is bad to be oppressed by a minority, it is worse to be oppressed by a majority. From the absolute will of an entire people there is no appeal, no redemption, no refuge but treason."

Nor was Acton alone in his vision of the dangers the future would hold. Tocqueville wrote in the middle of that optimistic century:

> When the state of society among a people is democratic—that is, when castes or classes no longer exist in the community and its members are nearly equal in education and in property the mind follows the opposite direction [away from liberty]. Men are much alike, and they are annoyed, as it were, by any deviation from the likeness; far from seeking to preserve their own distinguishing singularities, they endeavor to shake them off in order to identify themselves with the general mass of the people, which is the sole representative of right and might in their eyes. The spirit of individuality is almost obliterated.

"I think," Tocqueville wrote in *Democracy in America,* "that in the democratic centuries that are beginning, individual independence and local freedom will always be the product of art. Centralization will be the natural government."

Marx as well as Tocqueville knew the tendencies of his age. He studied and encouraged its centralizing tendencies, and yet his utopian expectations were completely out of keeping with his political and his sociological knowledge. He could not see that unless checks to the democratic tendencies in society were instituted, the banishment of inequality would mean the extinction of liberty.

Nor did he see that materialism provides a most inadequate base for the love and exercise of freedom. This was due, in part, to the fact that Marx saw freedom not as an end but rather as a byproduct of economic and sociological processes. For Acton and Tocqueville, freedom was an absolute end, a primary value to which all other objects and ends in society must be sacrificed if necessary. "Liberty is so holy a thing," Acton wrote, "that God was forced to permit evil that it might exist." On another occasion he said, "Liberty is not a gift or an acquisition; not a state of rest, but of effort and growth; not a starting point, but a result, of government."

Perhaps with the destructive and antiliberal tendencies innate in democratic society, it were better to follow the advice of those conservatives who would halt the economic and social developments that have overtaken our society and, if not set back the clock, at least prevent the further democratization of our society. Perhaps it were better to install in power, and support, class governments around the world in the hope that the tyranny of a class society would, at all odds, be less pervasive and efficient than the tyranny of a classless society.

Conservatives who think in these terms, aside from the basic immorality of the proposition, are living in a world of illusion. Conservatism, for good or ill, is the child of change as much as it is the child of tradition. From Burke to Buckley, it has combined conservative ideas with revolutionary politics and economics. Capitalism and personal freedom are the two most revolutionary ideas in modern society. Even more importantly, we live in a revolutionary society which will not be deflected from the course of change. Technologically and socially, we are in the grip of vast and constant changes. There is no turning back. Indeed, there has been no turning back in our dynamic Western society since the tenth century. Democracy and increasing social and economic equality are the givens of the society in which we live.

Tocqueville was quite certain of this one hundred years ago when he wrote:

> I am persuaded that all who attempt, in the ages upon which we are entering, to base freedom upon aristocratic privilege will fail; that all who attempt to draw and retain authority within a single class will fail. At the present day no ruler is skillful or strong enough to found a despotism by reestablishing permanent distinctions of rank among his subjects; no legislator is wise or powerful enough to preserve free institutions if he does not take equality for his first principle and his watchword. All of our contemporaries who would establish or secure the independence and the dignity of their fellow men show themselves the friends of equality; and the only worthy means of showing themselves as such is to be so: upon this depends the success of their holy enterprise. Thus the question is not how to reconstruct aristocratic society, but how to make liberty proceed out of that democratic state of society in which God has placed us.

And Acton, writing of William Gladstone, said:

> The decisive test of his greatness will be the gap he will leave.
> Among those who come after him there will be none who un-
> derstands that the men who pay wages ought not to be the po-
> litical masters of those who earn them (because laws should be
> adapted to those who have the heaviest stake in the country, for
> whom misgovernment means not mortified pride or stinted
> luxury, but want and pain, and degradation and risk to their own
> lives and to their children's souls), and who yet can understand
> and feel sympathy for institutions that incorporate tradition and
> prolong the reign of the dead.

Just so! The question is "how to make liberty proceed out of that democratic state of society in which God has placed us." To those conservatives
who would retreat from the tendencies of our democratic age, to those who
would stand still, the answer is the same. To those liberals who have asserted that there can be no genuine American conservatism because America
lacks a Tory class, a privileged aristocracy and establishment, the answer
is, "Thank God! We have nothing to undo." Conservatives will face the
issues of their times, and their enduring concern as children of authority
and children of revolution will be that the interests of liberty and the sanc-
tity of the individual be preserved.

The democratic revolution that was brought about by the introduction
of the principle of conscience has changed the nature of the problem of
government. Tocqueville wrote:

> The political world is metamorphosed, new remedies must
> henceforth be sought for new disorders. To lay down extensive
> but distinct and settled limits to the action of government; to
> confer certain rights on private persons, and to secure to them
> the undisputed enjoyment of those rights; to enable individual
> men to maintain whatever independence, strength, and original
> power he still possesses; to raise him by the side of society at
> large, and uphold him in that position; these appear to me the
> main objects of legislators in the ages upon which we are now
> entering.

The concern of Acton and Tocqueville and the concern of the legisla-
tors who would follow them was to be with the growth of centralized authority. The nineteenth-century state, whether dominated by liberals or
conservatives, continued the progress toward the centralization of author-

ity and the growth of absolutism which it had begun in the twelfth century. There was, by the second half of the nineteenth century, no mistaking the tendency in Western political institutions. Acton wrote: "In that society out of which modern European States have grown, the corporation was the first thing, the sovereign State the second. But the State gradually gained ground and took into its hands what was common to all." Increasingly, as corporate rights and obligations had been assumed and discharged by central governments, the liberties in which these rights were embedded disappeared. Moreover, the many competing forces and authorities that existed within the premodern state limited the power and authority of any one body. For this reason Acton warned repeatedly: "Never destroy a force. When it is not dominant it may serve to check dominion." But one by one competing authorities within the state disappeared. Churches were nationalized, assemblies decayed, and central authority grew; classes were impoverished or displaced; power shifted from status to money; and freedom increasingly was sacrificed to security. The drift of affairs was clear enough in Tocqueville's day. He wrote: "The unity, the ubiquity, the omnipotence of the supreme power, and the uniformity of its rules constitute the principal characteristics of all the political systems that have been put forward in our age. They recur even in the wildest visions of political regeneration; the human mind pursues them in its dreams."

But this tendency was absolutely inimical to liberty. So much Acton and Tocqueville saw even without the added experience of our generation. As libertarians, they both, therefore, detested any form of political organization that hastened the growth of absolutism, any form of political organization that by its very nature broke down those natural checks to absolute authority. What then of their attitude to democracy, for, patently, democracy paved the way to tyranny? Acton wrote: "[In the French Revolution] the people were quite resolved to be oppressed no more by monarchy or aristocracy, but they had no experience or warning of oppression by democracy. The classes were to be harmless; but there was the new enemy, the State. ... They were protected from government by authority or by minority; but they made the majority irresistible, and the plebiscite a tyranny."

Tocqueville and Acton recognized that democracy and the reign of opinion were but an extension of the principle of the absolute character of the dictates of conscience. Moreover, both realized that democracy was to become the dominant political form of their time, that its march was irresistible. Both believed this to be providential. But how was democracy to be prevented from destroying liberty? How was freedom finally to be reconciled with authority?

The answer was to come from America. Acton wrote in a note to himself:

> The great revelation of America was that of a revolution ef-
> fected by conservative politicians.
> Hamilton and Adams and Washington.
> In our days, Deak, Cavour.
> Nobody can measure their force.

Decentralization, multiplied authorities, and federalism were not only the natural checks on absolute democracy but were also the basis of good government. "Centralization," Acton wrote, "means apoplexy at the center and paralysis at the circumference."

Because federalism, multiplied authorities, and decentralization were at the heart of the American constitutional system, both Tocqueville and Acton hoped that in America the tendencies to tyranny implicit in democracy would be checked. Acton witnessed the first great disappointment to his hopes in the course of the American Civil War. During the twentieth century more and more of these natural and constitutional checks on democracy have disappeared.

Tocqueville was detailed and specific in his discussions of those aspects of American life and the American Constitution which kept democracy from fulfilling itself in tyranny. Of major importance to Acton and Tocqueville were the institutions of federalism, the separation of church and state, an educational system not wholly dominated by the central government, and a free-enterprise, market economy.

Local initiative and local authority constituted for these men the most important aspect of federalism. Charity and education, law and government, to be either effective or libertarian, must be local. Divided powers and divided authorities were no less important. Above all, both Acton and Tocqueville would have been depressed by the drift of all power and privilege to the central government in Washington.

But even aside from the checks of federalism, there were other important checks on democracy in the American system. It may be true that, as Acton said, "religion and liberty are more dear to men than prosperity or pleasure," but modern revolutions have been made at least as often in the name of social and economic justice as they have been made in the name of liberty. Tocqueville wrote:

> Almost all the revolutions that have changed the aspect of the
> nations have been made to consolidate or to destroy social in-
> equality. Remove the secondary causes that have produced the
> great convulsions of the world and you will almost always find

the principle of inequality at the bottom. Either the poor have attempted to plunder the rich, or the rich to enslave the poor. If, then, a state of society can ever be founded in which every man shall have something to keep and little to take from others, much will have been done for the peace of the world.

Lord Acton was no less certain of the necessity for a wide and just distribution of the material resources of life. He wrote: "There is no liberty where there is hunger. . . . The theory of liberty demands strong efforts to help the poor. Not merely for safety, for humanity, for religion, but for liberty." Property, if it is a natural right, must be so broadly based as to fall to all men who make a genuine contribution to their society.

The theory of democracy requires an ever-increasing degree of equality, and unless this can be achieved through the instrumentality of a market economy and an advanced technology, it will be achieved by the hand of the demagogue or tyrant. Tocqueville saw this clearly. "The foremost or indeed the sole condition required in order to succeed in centralizing the supreme power in a democratic community is love of equality, or to get men to believe you love it. Thus the science of despotism, which was once so complex, is simplified and reduced as it were, to a single principle."

Acton and Tocqueville's concern for a market economy complemented this preoccupation with equality and a wide distribution of property among the democratic masses. Tocqueville, particularly, was worried about the impact of state capitalism upon the enterprise and free institutions of the people. There was as much to fear in the nineteenth century and the period that followed it from a state that dominated the economic life of its people as there was from the dangers of an established religion. It seems odd indeed that the contemporary liberal who finds the thought of an established religion so disgusting because of its impact on personal liberty finds the thought of state capitalism so comforting. Both are absolutely incompatible with political liberty.

For Acton and Tocqueville it was obvious, however, that while economic and social equality were a *sine qua non* for a stable society, they were not the most important elements in that society. "Democracy," wrote Acton, "without a moral standard . . . could no more stand than a Republic governed by Marat." Tocqueville pointed up Acton's meaning by saying,

> Most religions are only general, simple and practical means of teaching men the doctrine of the immortality of the soul. That is the greatest benefit which a democratic nation derives from its belief, and hence belief is more necessary to such a people than all others. When, therefore, any religion has struck its roots deep into a democracy beware that you do not disturb it; but rather

watch it carefully, as the most precious bequest of aristocratic ages.

Conservatism ought not to confuse its cause with secularism. Neither ought it to confuse its cause with those who encourage a religious establishment.

The doctrine of the separation of church and state does not and never has implied the theory of a wall of separation, and conservatism ought to do all in its power to strengthen and encourage religion. Religious education, far from being divisive in a democratic society, can only strengthen and solidify the federalism of the state of which it is a part. Tax monies ought to be employed for the support of church schools; nonsectarian religious education should be a part of the educational program of the public schools; and faculties of theology should be associated with the state university systems. They will, by taking a large part of the educational structure out of the hands of the state, ensure an area of liberty and nonconformity to the popular prejudices of liberal secularism.

But just as certainly, the coercive power of the state ought not to be employed to enforce religion's observation or intrude itself into the realm of private as distinct from public morality. The enforcement of orthodoxy, even in the seemingly benign form of "blue laws," constitutes a danger to the individual's freedom of conscience. Religion can compel through an interior command; it cannot command through an exterior force and still retain its place in men's hearts. Nor should religion seek to usurp an authority that belongs to the state or to other community bodies. Its message is an eternal one, and it ought to divorce itself from the meddle, meddle, meddle of the pious Mr. Slopes and the ecclesiastical Uriah Heep. Tocqueville wrote:

> The more the conditions of men are equalized and assimilated
> to each other, the more important it is for religion, while it carefully abstains from the daily turmoil of secular affairs, not needlessly to run counter to the ideas that generally prevail or to the
> permanent interests that exist in the mass of the people. For as
> public opinion grows to be more and more the first and most
> irresistible of existing powers, the religious principle has no external support strong enough to enable it long to resist its attacks. This is no less true of a democratic people ruled by a
> despot than of a republic. In ages of equality kings may often
> command obedience, but the majority always commands belief;
> to the majority therefore, deference is to be paid in whatever is
> not contrary to the faith.

Religion is important to the democratic state not only because it preserves the fabric of society but also because it acts as the most important power to check the aggressive, centralizing, and totalitarian tendencies of the modern state. Without a strong religion, which remains outside and independent of the power of the state, civil liberty is unthinkable. The power of the state is, in part, balanced and neutralized by the power of the church. The freedom of the individual is most certain in that realm which neither church nor state can successfully occupy and dominate.

Finally, if contemporary conservatives cast their political sentiments in terms of Acton's and Tocqueville's libertarian conservatism, they will abandon pessimism for an optimistic and active faith. Acton wrote:

> End with the kingdom of God, which is liberty.
> How far from the end? Africa not begun, Asia how little
> But America and Australia, South Africa,
> Governed by the ideas of our revolution. The Ideas that went
> out there govern the world—Their reaction in Europe.

22

Gnostics, Romantics, and Conservatives

Henry Adams was fond of identifying his intellectual confusion by calling himself a "conservative, Christian, anarchist," a description later adopted by the less imaginative Pitirim A. Sorokin. For Adams, the description was inadequate. Perhaps it applied to what he might have been at one time. In reality he felt the pull of his age too strongly and verged on a secular gnosticism. Adams was not unaware of his position, though the vocabulary developed by Professor Voegelin was, unhappily, not available to him. Characteristically, in *Mont-Saint-Michel and Chartres* he reveals the pivotal question in Western history when he reports a witty aside by St. Thomas Aquinas:

> St. Louis' household offers a picture not wholly clerical, least of all among the king's brothers and sons; and perhaps the dinnertable was not much more used then than now to abrupt interjections of theology into the talk about hunting and hounds; but however it happened, Thomas one day surprised the company by solemnly announcing—"I have a decisive argument against the Manicheans!" No wit or humor could be more to the point—between two Saints that were to be—than a decisive argument against enemies of Christ, and one greatly regrets that the rest of the conversation was not reported, unless, indeed, it is somewhere in the twenty-eight quarto volumes; but it probably lacked humor for courtiers.

And no doubt it would lack humor or even cogency for twentieth-century intellectuals. Still, the question remains the same even though the "flower children" of the present do not recognize that they share a common faith with the Cathars of Albi.[1] This long and eventful war which Friedrich Heer describes as a "struggle between 'above' and 'below' in

Europe's inner history,"[2] and which finds its culmination in our own day, not only connects St. Thomas and Henry Adams but links the larger questions of the thirteenth and the twentieth centuries. The "pneumopathology" of contemporary secular gnosticism, especially as it appears in the thought of the nineteenth-century prophets Hegel, Marx, and Nietzsche, has been diagnosed and analyzed by Voegelin in two brilliant essays.[3] These essays carry us beyond a historistic account of gnosticism in terms of intellectual constructions conceived either in social or ideal terms to a discussion of gnosticism in terms of deliverance from loss of meaning and spiritual insecurity through the promise to transform a human nature that is inherently subject to limitations and constantly threatened by the loss of meaning. Voegelin would understand the excitement of St. Thomas at having discovered a decisive argument against the Manicheans.

Gnostic political and ideological movements were not in the thirteenth century, nor are they in the twentieth, simple and unitary in form. Then as now, complexity, variety, and disguise mark the gnostic movements. Surrogate churches, salvational political movements, and utopian ideological movements all have common spiritualist roots in the repressed heretical movements that are nearly as old as Christianity. Few of the gnostic theoreticians have been as successful in combining wish-fulfillment, contemporary sociology, anomic anxiety, and political salvationalism as Karl Mannheim. What Marx formulated as a relatively undeveloped gnostic science receives a systematic, contemporary, and sophisticated formulation at the hands of Mannheim in *Ideology and Utopia*.[4] It is the sort of book Marx would have written had he belonged to the first half of the twentieth century rather than the first half of the nineteenth. It is a book that was inspired by the now much admired "early Marx." In the early 1920s Georg Lukács, that great Marxist Talma who has played so many roles, turned the young Karl Mannheim's attention to the early Marx. Mannheim found in Marx a questioning spirit filled with Promethean ambitions and anomic anxieties. This Marx had been swallowed up in the mid-nineteenth century by the wave of positivism that swept over Europe. Lukács and Mannheim recognized, however, that at the beginning of the twentieth century the essential questions confronting Marxism were cultural, metaphysical, and ethical. From the top of his Mt. Nebo, Marx could not see into the deeps of the twentieth century, a century whose landscape had by the 1920s been transformed by Nietzsche, Kirkegaard, Dostoyevsky, Sorel, Freud, and the neo-Kantians.[5] The movement characterized by some intellectual historians as the "antipositivist revolt" left behind as one of its most enduring consequences its impact on Marxist thought. Mannheim's thinking likewise was conditioned in a most striking way by the re-conquest of Marxism by German romanticism and idealist philosophy. In the process, the latent gnosticism in Marxism becomes startlingly manifest, the "cultural problem" takes precedence over the economic, and ideology comes to be formulated in terms of its contradiction to gnostic content. That is to say that "ideology" comes to be identified in terms of its specific antiutopian content. It is for this reason, and in spite of the fact that Mannheim's name is all but unknown to the men of the New Left, that Mannheim is a prophetic figure anticipating and announcing the chief lines of thought in post-Stalin Marxism.

Ideology and Utopia is a brilliant tour de force. It has that lacy, airy, fretwork quality that only the most daring theological constructions possess. It is a bold and ingenious effort simultaneously to find a personal Archimedean point in a world where whirl is king and to salvage Marxism in a cultural situation that has made the conventional formulations of Marxism irrelevant. In developing his position, Mannheim helped to invent the sociology of knowledge, established the relationship of utopianism to the cultural crisis of our time, worked out an unsatisfactory definition of ideology that has been powerfully influential in contemporary thinking about ideology, and developed a totally misleading conception of conservatism.

Ideology, utopia, and conservatism are the three basic idea clusters in the thought of Mannheim. His historical conceptualization of conservatism is the most important and influential effort to explain the development of conservatism in terms of social dynamics. Mannheim's account is the only sophisticated Marxist explanation of conservatism as distinct from fascism. Moreover, although conservatives are not nearly so untheoretical as Mannheim (and even many conservatives) believe, his explanation of the nature of conservatism has become the standard—and, one is tempted to say, the only—accepted explanation of the phenomenon of conservatism. A recent conservative writer in *National Review* remarks that "[Mannheim's] essay on 'Conservative Thought' in *Essays in Sociology and Social Psychology*—while truculent and somewhat Marxist in motivation—is one of the most brilliant studies of conservatism ever written."[6] Clearly Mannheim's interpretation has been influential in many recent interpretations of conservatism and, more particularly, in both the typology of conservatism and the discussion of German conservatism offered in Klaus Epstein's exhaustive study, *The Genesis of German Conservatism.*[7]

The validity of Mannheim's thesis that conservatism is the "ideology" of a dominant but challenged aristocratic and traditional society, the reflection of a "class society" and an outgrowth of "class conflict," is, for conservatives, of the utmost importance.[8] If conservatism is a nonrational, antiprogressive force bent on the maintenance of the values of an outworn class, then, regardless of its positive contributions as a weapon against bourgeois rationalization, it must, of necessity, be swept into the rather large

Marxist dustbin of history. If, on the other hand, conservatism can be effectively progressive, if it represents a general human response rather than a specifically class response, and if conservatism is essentially "nonideological" in the Mannheimian sense, the possibilities of its playing a creative role in historical development are vastly improved. It is important therefore that conservatism offer some non-Mannheimian explanation of itself, for Mannheim's explanation falsifies not only the content and posture of conservatism, but also the historical and social circumstances associated with the recurrent rise of conservative movements.

The anomic condition of Central European social and intellectual life at the close of the nineteenth century and during the first decades of the twentieth century provides us with the key to an understanding not only of the sources of Mannheim's thought but of the genesis of conservative thought as a recurrent phenomenon. Antinomian tendencies were in the ascendant throughout Central Europe,[9] and although the institutional structures that had survived the intellectual revolutions and ushered in modernity were still dominant, every perceptive intellectual could discern the chaos of conflicting values and felt terror at the death of all but arbitrarily imposed meaning. Mannheim makes this epistemological predicament the Archimedean point of his philosophical reconstruction.[10]

It is important to stress here how deeply and keenly Mannheim felt these problems. The structure of the individual personality and the coherence and viability of a society are dependent on the establishment of order. This preoccupation with order and the sources of order in society not only has been, as Robert Nisbet demonstrated,[11] the overriding concern of sociology at the present time; it has also played a dominant role in the development of sociological thought.[12] Eric Voegelin, in his monumental work *Order and History*,[13] distinguishes the various sources of order within man's historic experience and the consequences contingent upon shifts in the symbolization of order. There can be little debate that the process of nomization is the fundamental social activity and that all that man is, and all the options open to him in the process of becoming, are dependent on a socially sustained nomos. The establishment of a normative order is, indeed, a "shield against terror."[14] These orders were, at least until the advent of the scientific cosmological views of the recent past, religious in nature.

Rationalization, secularization, pluralism, and revolutionary appeals to ethical ideals derived from the experience of the transcendent have shattered the older unities. This anomic movement has been strengthened by the transformation of the conditions of existence by technological innovation, though the rapid development of the technological sphere has been subsequent rather than antecedent to changes that have taken place in the spiritual order. All of this has been accompanied by the metastatic de-railment of Christian hope into secular fulfillment through the estab-lishment of gnostic political and social orders.

Nor was "science" able to serve the integrative function once pro-vided by religious symbolization, as so many had once hoped and not a few continue to believe is possible. "Science" is not only morally neutral but absolutely devoid of spiritual content. Today we are aware of this and the fear is quite generally shared that the triumph of the tech-niques of science may well lead to the dehumanization and destruction of mankind.[15]

The Central European consciousness in which these changes first mani-fested themselves most strongly responded in a number of ways. Much of the response remained at the unconscious level and expressed itself overtly in heretical and occult sectarianisms and political mass movements. At the level of individual consciousness a whole range of anomic psychological diseases developed. The more perceptive the individual, the more clearly he discerned the implications of a world devoid of meaning. Karl Mannheim was, without question, one of the representative figures of the Central Eu-ropean intelligentsia for the period between the two World Wars. His pre-occupation with the search for a universally valid meaning and a univer-sally valid ethic is the key to his Marxism, but at the same time it links him in a significant way both to his generation and to our own.

From the destruction of the Holy Roman Empire in 1806 to the present time, the European intelligentsia has concerned itself with the problem of decadence. The date of the destruction of the empire, however, was not the date of the onset of the problem. Vico's New Science and the "quarrel be-tween the ancients and the moderns" had raised the question in a period when bourgeois self-assertion and self-confidence were, in Mannheim's view, at their peak. Throughout the eighteenth century, the possibility of decadence was a nagging though never acute question. The fascination with mortality, the graveyard school, and the cult of ruins all built upon these preoccupations. The development of a manneristic-anomic style in the representational arts that emphasized nightmare and death was character-istic of the cultural mood. It is quite impossible to mask these anxieties by describing the eighteenth century as the "Age of the Enlightenment." In 1734 Montesquieu published his *Considerations sur les causes de la grandeur des Romans et de leur decadence*. It found a reply and an echo in Gibbon's *Decline and Fall of the Roman Empire*.

An uninterrupted and flourishing intellectual tradition concerned with mutability, decadence, and death conceived in both personal and social terms reaches from Vico to Toynbee.[16] There were many attempts to ex-plain the processes of decadence, and these explanations fall roughly into three categories: biological, social, and religious. Each explanation had its vogue, although today only the religious explanation appears to be viable.

By the 1880s the perception of decadence had given rise to an equally strong current of vitalistic, salvational rejuvenationism. The birth of occult and scientistic religions such as theosophy and anthroposophy and the revival of diabolism and orthodox Christianity were essentially efforts at individual salvation and cultural rejuvenation through religious revival. Biological rejuvenation through a pansexual vitalism and a pseudoscientific racism were commonplace efforts during the past eighty years. Mannheim chose the path to rejuvenation offered by the rise of a new and energetic class whose unconscious life was more exactly attuned to the deeper "rationality" of the historical process than was the unconscious life of its class predecessors. Utopia, which Mannheim sees as an oppressed group's effort to transform a satiated and content society through revolutionary action, is in reality an effort to save society from decadence and death. In *fin de siècle* literature, irrational politics, the youth movements, Jugendstil, and Art Nouveau, decadence and rejuvenation live out a symbiotic relationship. It is this historical moment which supplies the conditioning context for *Ideology and Utopia*.

At bottom, these concerns all reflect the "rage for order" in contemporary thought. The problem of modernity par excellence is the problem of religion. That these concerns were Mannheim's concerns has been adequately demonstrated in David Kettler's essay "Sociology of Knowledge and Moral Philosophy: The Place of Traditional Problems in the Formation of Mannheim's Thought." Kettler quite properly points out that in *Ideology and Utopia* and in the essays of the late '20s and early '30s, the disorientation of cultural life and the effort to reestablish a valid orientation are Mannheim's most important themes. It is no exaggeration to say that, in his effort to escape the relativism implicit in the historicist position, Mannheim was drawn into a Marxism that found its expression in the works of Georg Lukács. The summary of Mannheim's "Soul and Culture" that Kettler gives us makes clear that in 1918 the twenty-four-year-old Mannheim was concerned more deeply with the eternal verities than with the mechanical economic determinism which then characterized vulgar Marxism.[17] His description of alienated and unauthentic man reduced to cultural impotence by his feeling of estrangement sets the stage for his conversion to secular gnosticism.[18] Lukács showed Mannheim the way from "renovation of culture" by "immanent laws of cultural development" to a way based upon revolutionary social process,[19] and it is Marxism that henceforth provided a romantic-scientific patina of rationality for an irrational act of faith. In these early years, Mannheim's progress can best be described in Voegelin's phrase as a fall from "uncertain truth into certain untruth."[20] The motive in Mannheim's thought is religious; the symbolization is, however, pseudoscientific and applied as a façade.

The sociology of knowledge becomes for Mannheim an apologetic device rather than a scientific conception. The problem of alienation and reification, the antinomies of subject and object, the gulf between the world of man and the world of nature, the perennial problem of freedom in a world bound by causal determinism, and the seeming irrationality of history, coupled with the wish for a providential and rational historical order, are all reduced by Mannheim to problems associated with a class perspective and deriving from "bourgeois style." Mannheim escapes the contingent relativism of every historical perspective by absolutizing the judgments of the alienated and "free-floating" intellectual. The intellectual, standing outside the arena of class conflict, would be able, Mannheim assumed, to unmask every interest and uncover the seemingly irrational forces that "really" dominate the processes of history. At last this new incarnation of Auguste Comte's priesthood of scientists would actually wield power. The method of sociological analysis may be Marxist, but the philosophy of history in Mannheimian thought is Comtean. One is thrown back upon the law of the three stages through which all thought passes: religious, philosophical, and a new consensus that was to be achieved through a dedicated order of savant priests. As with Comte, social reconstruction was to be accomplished by the restoration of social consensus arrived at by a savant priesthood. One of the greatest of Mannheim's achievements was the synthesis of Marxist eschatological certitude with the egocentricity and ambition of the intellectual.

In the broad definition given it by Robert K. Merton, the sociology of knowledge is "primarily concerned with the relations between knowledge and other existential factors in the society or culture."[21] The sociology of knowledge, in terms of this broad definition, has gained increasing support from sociologists and historians in the past half century. But while there may be agreement about the relationship between knowledge and society, there is no agreement about the basis of this relationship or the degree to which knowledge is influenced by society and culture. Even in Mannheim, the veneer of Marxist certitude is somewhat chipped and reveals a disquieting degree of uncertainty beneath. Is scientific as well as ethical and social "knowledge" subject to ideological deformation? Mannheim seems never to have decided.

While an account of origins is manifestly no test of validity, an account of origins does tend to discredit that which appears earlier and to associate the label of "progressive" with that which is later in the temporal sequence.

Consequently, when the sociology of knowledge does not produce a completely relativistic conception of all truth it is apt to fall back into a Comtean scheme of progressive clarification, validation, and fulfillment. Mannheim manages to impale himself on both horns of this historicist dilemma.[22] He assumes that all knowledge is goal-directed, instrumental, exploitative.[23] It is an epistemology that has as its purpose utility rather than knowledge and aims at aggression against and violation of its object. This empirical approach to reality "corresponds to the practice out of which it evolves."[24] "To understand philosophy," Mannheim writes, "one has to understand the nature of the action which lies at the bottom of it."[25] Mathematics, of course, is not the only discipline which discovers knowledge and ultimately finds that knowledge to serve a utilitarian purpose. Undeniably, much knowledge takes its rise from the attempt to solve problems, but it is equally undeniable that much knowledge is the result of play and wonder.

Since for Mannheim knowledge is instrumental and aims, consciously or unconsciously, at the achievement of a particular objective, it is always related to society and to "class carriers." At first reading, the relationship of knowledge or ideas to social context seems complex, but it becomes increasingly clear that the relationship of the superstructure to the "real" substructure is that of the vulgar Marxist theoretician. "In a word," he writes, "traditionalism can only become conservatism in a society in which change occurs through the medium of class conflict—in a class society. This is the sociological background of modern conservatism."[26] Moreover, in Mannheim's explanation of the historical process, there are metahistorical "needs" of a Hegelian flavor that determine historical development. "The generation that followed Romanticism," Mannheim writes, "however, supplanted this conservative view with a revolutionary one as being in accord with the needs of the time."[27]

Instrumental social knowledge is described by Mannheim as "ideology." The class-rooted intellectual, whether his commitment is feudal-aristocratic, bourgeois, or proletarian, not only creates the theoretical structures that defend his social interests, but is also engaged in a "Nietzschean" task of "unmasking" the "real" interests that lie at the bottom of competing "ideologies." In the idea of historical analysis as a process of "unmasking," Mannheim seems to have been more influenced by Nietzsche than by Marx.[28]

Mannheim offers us no explanation of the psychological links between the determining existential social situation and "style" or "political ideas" or "knowledge." Indeed, once class behavior based upon conscious or unconscious interest is removed from his theories, very little by way of a historical explanation remains. Mannheim uses a wide variety of circumlocutions to express what at bottom is an intellectual determinism based upon class interest.

Like Hegel and Marx before him, Mannheim wishes to discover beneath the play of interest and the constructions of "false consciousness," which are inherently irrational, a deeper rationality. It is this metahistorical quest for a justifying purpose and an overriding meaning in the historical process which enables Mannheim to speak of certain forces as "progressive" and others that are status quo–oriented as "instruments used by those who profit from it, to distort, pervert, and conceal the meaning of the present."[29] In Mannheim, the cunning of reason masks itself with the language of existential free choice, just as class necessity is disguised as historicist sociology. Once the metahistorical *unterbau* has been removed from Mannheim's theories there is no method for determining what is status quo and what is progressive, no method for determining the more perfectly rational and the more adequate and appropriate action at any given historical moment.

The essential test of any theory, however, is its congruity with existential reality. Mannheim aspired to the role of historian, as had Marx. His only genuinely sustained historical work was his study of German conservatism. While Mannheim's essay is not an exhaustive treatment, he does develop the topic sufficiently to enable us to judge his prowess as a historian when he applies his theory to a specific body of empirical evidence and offers us a substantial amount of historical explanation. Mannheim himself regarded the essay on German conservatism as a test of his theory.[30]

In his essay Mannheim does not believe conservatism to be a recurring set of political postures but rather "a function of *one particular* [his emphasis] historical and sociological situation."[31] Mannheim's assertion is that conservatism is "indissolubly associated with feudalism, status, the *ancien régime,* landed interests, medievalism, and nobility; it becomes irreconcilably opposed to the middle class, labor, commercialism, industrialism, democracy, liberalism and individualism."[32] Not only, then, is conservatism a movement produced by a class society and taking its rise "through the medium of class conflict,"[33] but within that temporal context conservatism is nonprogressive, a remnant of the past rather than a polity that is yet to be. If one accepts either formulation, conservatism in a twentieth-century— and particularly in an American—context is political folly.

That conservatism is "nonprogressive" is easier to refute than the assertion that conservatism is the product of a particular moment in history and is *sui generis.* Perhaps this argument has been used more than any other in the hope of establishing the thesis that there has never been and can never be an "American" conservatism. Louis Hartz has demonstrated that since the United States lacked feudal institutions it could not produce a conservatism.[34] Klaus Epstein argues in *The Genesis of German Conservatism* that while liberalism is a general movement and as such lends itself to historical treatment, there is a specificity about conservatism that makes it impossible to treat it in general terms. Epstein writes,

> Many self-styled modern Conservatives—especially in the ranks of America's so-called "New Conservatives"—are highly arbitrary in identifying one specific historical form of Conservatism with Conservatism per se. They tend to canonize the admittedly great figure of Edmund Burke and attach an absolute value to the principles of eighteenth-century England (or the pre-1789 regime generally) which he defended against the Jacobin challenge. These Conservatives make themselves ridiculous when they try to apply the principles of Burkean Conservatism to a contemporary America where its foundations (a landowning aristocracy, an established clergy, and an ancient monarchy) do not exist now, have existed only in a vestigial manner in earlier times, and are quite irrelevant to the solution of contemporary problems.[35]

Peter Viereck pointed out the falsity of this line of argumentation when he wrote, "Our argument is not against importing European insights when applicable; that would be Know-Nothing chauvinism."[36] And Viereck is correct in sensing that there is a set of common conservative concerns that exist whether the society in which a particular conservative movement is generated is institutionally feudal or laissez-faire liberal, and that these concerns provide a common conservative identity, however much the programmatic content of conservatisms may differ from one historical situation to another. Consequently, Samuel P. Huntington's *situational* definition of conservatism as an "ideology arising out of a distinct but recurring type of historical situation in which a fundamental challenge is directed at established institutions and in which the supporters of those institutions employ the conservative ideology in their defense"[37] has much to recommend it. Huntington rightly observes that "conservatism is the intellectual rationale of the permanent institutional prerequisites of human existence."[38] However, his conception of established institutions is far too narrow in its emphasis upon the political. The appearance of conservatism usually signals a much deeper disturbance of normative and ordering values than those associated with the political sphere. No doubt it is at the level of the polity that many, especially at the present time, first sense these disturbances in ordering institutions. This is simply a reflection of the progress of secularization. These disturbances, however, are nearly always religious in point of origin, a fact repeatedly illustrated in the religious history of the eighteenth century. Not only was the disturbance of the normative processes first perceived in religion, but religion was the first to respond to the challenge of eighteenth-century secularism, deistic rationalism, and agnosticism. Long before conservative politics developed, religion in the churches and the sects had not only begun the process of restoration but had begun to revolutionize the content of the ancient creedal symbols. Thus, the romantic transition in the church's conception of itself as *Heilsanstalt* (means of salvation) to the conception of itself as *Glaubensgemeinschaft* (community of belief) is an attempt to restore order. But the restoration takes place in terms of romantic organic theory, which was revolutionary in its implications and at the same time appealed to the ancient model of the primitive church. The development of ultramontane theory in Roman Catholicism combined traditional forms with revolutionary content. Conservative and restorative movements not infrequently have a radically innovative face which it is quite impossible to square with the Mannheimian conception of conservatism as the static response of a satiated class.

The problem and morphology of restorative movements, closely associated as the latter are with conservatism, are extremely complicated.[39] It simply cannot be argued that restorations are nothing more than the reestablishment of old orders and old classes in their former positions. Nor can it be argued that revolutions are irreversible, for there is too much evidence that this is not the case. Conservative politics are various in the degree of restoration and revolutionary change that characterize their programs, and the classes from which they draw their support are as varied as their programs. What they all share in common is their reaction to a violent disturbance in the social and metaphysical realm. Conservative movements are the offspring of societies threatened with anomie.

It is a curious fact that in Epstein's *Genesis of German Conservatism*, a book running to 710 pages of text, there are only two references to romanticism and these are slight in the extreme. Although there is a considerably larger number of references to romanticism in Mannheim's "Conservative Thought" and "The History of the Concept of the State as an Organism," and although these references are more detailed discussions, neither Epstein nor Mannheim appreciate the total connection of these two movements. Had Mannheim understood romanticism, his conclusions concerning conservatism would have been very different. The link between conservative politics and the romantic movement is so commonplace that one must marvel at a treatment that does not make that connection a central feature of the historical explanation of the conservatism of the late eighteenth century.[40] Indeed, an analysis of romanticism reveals clearly that the root problem for both the romantics and the conservatives was not the continued existence of a particular social order but the existence of order in any form. Nor can it be assumed from this that romanticism was unitary. It was, on the contrary, diverse and complex, and if it can be said to have had a central tendency, that tendency was only superficially one which supported restoration and tradition. Heine was well aware of the revolutionary implications of German idealism. Heer writes, "German romanticism was a multi-leveled phenomenon. In its deepest dimension, it was a part of a European movement which had always tried to demolish the superstructures, the political systems and religious orthodoxies of old Europe."[41]

Moreover, the tendency in both Mannheim and Epstein to narrow the focus of their treatment to the specifically German aspect of the problem of conservatism and romanticism obscures an important fact. Both movements were essentially pan-European. Romanticism and conservatism appeared in diverse polities and in socioeconomic climates as widely divergent as the natural climates of the poles and the tropics. One can hardly imagine social situations more different than those of the England of Burke and the Russia which was the scene of Maistre's *Soirées de Saint Petersbourg*. Romantics who lived on the banks of the Hudson River adopted a *Weltanschauung* hardly distinguishable from that which characterized romantics living on the banks of the Danube.

Similarly, within particular societies socially differentiated groups helped to shape a common *Weltanschauung*. Pietism in its Methodist formulation had little in common either socially or intellectually with those Englishmen who created the revolution in epistemology, or the garden architects such as William Kent who taught an era to see nature anew, and yet romanticism forged a common body of belief out of these disparate elements. It is not enough to say that all these elements in society possessed a common "style" and shared a common hostility to bourgeois rationalization.

Moreover, Mannheim asserts that the romanticism in which conservatism was embedded was a product of "dialectics." "It is well known," he writes in the "well-known" style of Marxist theoreticians, "that romanticism developed from the Enlightenment as antithesis to thesis,"[42] and he quotes Franz Oppenheimer to the effect that romanticism is an "intellectual counter-revolution." Mannheim writes that "[t]he sociological significance of romanticism lies in its function as the historical opponent of the intellectual tendencies of the Enlightenment, in other words, against the philosophical exponents of bourgeois capitalism."[43]

To present romanticism as a revolt against "bourgeois rationalism" is to fail to apprehend the continuity romanticism has both with an earlier irrationalist tradition and, more importantly, with the Enlightenment. In epistemology, ethics, and aesthetics one simply cannot speak of an Enlightened thesis and a romantic antithesis. Romantic epistemology develops in terms of quite specific problems that were inherent in the philosophy of the Enlightenment. The same observation could be made for the development of romantic historiography. Simplistic class explanations, metahistorical "needs," and primitive dialectical schemes distort the many valuable insights Mannheim produces.

The Mannheimian definition of conservatism is inadequate (1) because it identifies conservatism narrowly as the product of class conflict and as the embodiment of class attitudes, (2) because it fails to construct a common definition of conservatism that embraces the full variety of historically conditioned conservatisms, (3) because it insists that conservatism is an "ideational ideology" (Huntington's term), and (4) because it insists that conservatism must, of necessity, be status quo–oriented.

23

Elites, Community, and the Truth:
A Little Story

History is a series of little stories, or so at least Herodotus, the "Father of History," thought. His stories were so fascinating that my mentor entertained his children with bedtime stories drawn from Herodotus. And so, dear friends, here are some little stories, entertaining or otherwise.

Lissy Voegelin once said that she could not hire someone to help her with the cleaning, for when the *Putzfrau* switched on the vacuum Eric Voegelin would emerge from his study in his bathrobe and in a tone of wounded and confused majesty inquire, "What! Today?" Ah! The power of that Anglo-Saxon four-letter word, "What!" "What! Today?" Yes, friends, Today!

I grew up in an Illinois town that was traditionally served by priests from Germany, or by priests who had been educated in Germany. When I was in grade school the pastor was a man ill-suited to his task. In those Depression years he permitted the parish to sink into chaos and ruin, and he was said to have loved men and boys too much. At last a committee from the parish went to the bishop and asked that he be removed. The bishop refused, saying that the committee had only hearsay evidence and that he could not take action. However, after a few years, that great Christian worker, Death, did what the bishop refused to do, and the long-suffering parish got a new priest.

He, too, was a German, a refugee from National Socialism, and a man who devoted the whole of his life—he died at age 93—to the people of his parish. A descendant of a prominent family, he had been instrumental in the founding of the Catholic Center Party, and was an intellectual who wore his learning with grace and ease. The farmers and small-town people hardly knew what to make of him. For a while his sermons were intellectual and theological exercises that stunned his parishioners into amused silence. Finally, one of his parishioners went to him and said, as Germans are apt to do, "Father, your sermons are too high for us. Just tell us a little story."

"A little story. What! Today?"

In 1954, the "conservative movement" was hardly more than a handful of people, a self-selected elite who knew something was terribly wrong with the politics, economics, and community life of the American republic. Though they were not political physicians, they could hear the death rattle of the Left-liberal old order. They set about to educate themselves, to argue, to discuss, to organize, and especially to recruit. The elder statesmen, none of them very old, were uniformly concerned with the recruitment of the next generation into the movement.

This elite, many of whom were disillusioned Communists or fellow travelers, knew from firsthand experience the power both of ideas and of organization. It was this consciousness of standing on the forefront of history, of battling at Marathon and Thermopylae, which gave this elite its special quality and its dynamic force. Many, like Whittaker Chambers, felt that the battle had already been lost. It was reported to me by someone who ought to have known that Henry Kissinger believed that the tides of history would carry Soviet power to the fore and that his role was simply to buy time. Not everyone was so gloomy, to be sure.

Aside from the Soviet threat and the fact of internal subversion, the conservative elite spent its time battling the growth and centralization of state power and restoring order and meaning to everyday life. In this respect the first generation of the conservative elite distinguished themselves from those who came to call themselves "neoconservatives" and who were anticommunist statists.

Moreover, that first generation of conservative elites participated in the religious revival of the 1950s and 1960s. Those who discovered the "Religious Right" in the second half of the decade of the 1990s are just about half a century too late. The essential character of that primal conservative elite was religious and value-oriented, and if conservatism has anything to say at the beginning of the new millennium it will embody the beliefs and values of that earlier elite. We are now more aware than ever that man does not live by bread alone.

Many in those early days of the movement liked to think of themselves as "individualists," and indeed there once was a society that called itself the "Intercollegiate Society of Individualists."[1] I always took that to mean that its members distinguished themselves from the schools of bottom-feeding liberals who dominated every campus, and every faculty, and who automatically assumed that unless one took one's politics from the *New Republic* and the *Nation,* one's aesthetics from *Partisan Review,* and one's entertainment from the *New Yorker,* one was intellectually unqualified to serve on a college or university faculty. Indeed these "individualists" paid dearly for the views they held and the ideas they defended.

The danger to the conservative elite, however, was not the stranglehold the Left-liberal elite held and still holds on the academy. The great danger to the conservative elite was, rather, the success that elite generated in the social, political, and economic world. Once the conservative intellectual entered the realm of power he surrendered himself and his motives to that power and its amassment through politics and bureaucracy. At that point, he traded his tweed coat for a pinstriped suit, caught Potomac fever, and went off to Washington to become a denizen of a think tank. The moral of this little story is that if the conservative movement is to be successful in the years ahead, it must cease to be dominated by policy wonks and must find a form of creativity other than writing position papers. The Weberian transition from the realm of ideas to the realm of power has very important consequences for the conservative movement and these must be recognized and confronted.

The conservative elite of forty years ago was not a happy band that suddenly found itself to be thinking "forbidden" thoughts and debating "undiscussable" propositions. The existence of this happy band was the consequence of deliberate recruitment. A handful of creative leaders said, in effect, "Come, follow me." Men such as Frank Meyer, Richard Weaver, Ludwig von Mises, Kenneth Templeton, Russell Kirk, M. Stanton Evans, Henry Regnery, and Don Lipsett, to name only a few, made it their business to identify talent, to recruit graduate students, to organize meetings, and to see that there was a next generation. They were intellectually diverse, with personalities as large and as contradictory as the issues with which they engaged. Increasingly, it has struck me that their like has disappeared from the conservative movement and that converts are made, if at all, from the printed page. This does not bode well for the future of conservatism.

Every great transforming movement in world history is essentially a movement of the spoken word. Jesus and Socrates did not write books. Books, indeed, are important, but they are afterthoughts. There must always be an original *kerygma* or proclamation. It may be Frank Meyer calling at 2:00 a.m. from Woodstock, or Kenneth Templeton sitting in the living room when the morning stars sang together and the fire had gone out, or students gathered at an ISI summer school talking—no, not talking but arguing—far into the night. When the *kerygma* ceases and the movement bureaucrats take over, the vitality of the movement is threatened.

Moreover, the early conservative movement was a community. Frank Meyer, who had been a Communist organizer in the Midwest, once remarked to me that the Communist movement, like the early Christian, was a movement in which no one was a stranger. One could come into a strange town and find immediate hospitality and companionship. And so it was with the early conservative movement. There was a bond of hospitality and friendship. I find this intense spirit of community lacking in today's conservative movement, and I wonder whether it is not another sign that we have grown sclerotic. A room full of five hundred people eating rubber chicken is no substitute for a night at Mecosta, Woodstock, or Three Oaks.

Finally, I wish to say a few words about the importance of the *truth* to the conservative movement. Conservatism developed essentially as a response to persistent and massive Left-liberal untruth. The problem was not simply Lillian Hellman, who, as it was observed, never wrote a truthful word in her life: "even the 'thes' and the 'ands' were a lie." Franklin D. Roosevelt was nearly equally incapable of the truth. He was the leader of the pack and many in it were more mendacious and artful than he was. Conservatism sought to banish the right to lie in the name of *reason of state, Staatsraison, raison d'Etat.* There is no greater enemy of community than the lie. It dissolves common purpose and mutual confidence. How terrible, then, that conservatives in power succumbed to lying.

I do not mean the sluggards among conservative writers who resorted, in a pinch, to plagiarism. I have known a number of them but it is not profitable to give the infamous fame by naming them.

In 1974, I attended a meeting in West Branch, Iowa, celebrating the one-hundredth anniversary of the birth of President Herbert Hoover. The conferees divided their time between the celebration of a noble and tragic figure in American history and the slow-motion televised abdication of a pseudoconservative liar, President Richard M. Nixon. In the person of William Jefferson Clinton we have seen how low the presidency can sink. Not only has the president behaved in a loathsome fashion but also he has lied more persistently than any other figure in American history—including Mike Fink.

Here I shall not speak of those supposed conservatives, the "Ravelsteins," who have practiced an intellectual dissimulation which permitted them to say, in the secret writing in which they indulged, one thing while intending another. No Athenian sophist was more adroit. Nor shall I dwell at length on the subject of a college president who did enormous harm both to the institution he guided and to the conservative causes he supposedly espoused.

There have also been those men who saw conservatism as a way to personal status and power, men devoid of any purpose other than, as one of my students observed, "an ego-splat." I knew well one of these dark men from the gutter. He lied to himself. He lied to his friends. He created a fictitious past for himself. He even lied in creating objects for his inordinate hatreds. He lied as to his purpose and beliefs and he harmed the movement and those in any way connected with him.

William Buckley—with a charity not unlike that of my wife, who believes that serial murderers are victims of a bad breakfast—observes that as Christians we must all recognize our fallen state and draw a veil of forgiveness over dark and unseemly deeds. This is nonsense, and Mr. Buckley knows it. Yes, we forgive the sinner, but it is equally important that we recognize that sinner and sinned-against must live out the temporal consequences of sin, the disruption of the social and natural order that sin produces. The road to recovery is an acknowledgement and a quest for remedies for those actions which are matters to be dealt with in the exterior forum.

And now, having told all these little stories, like the wise king advising his minions as he sends them off to heroic deeds, let me say, "Be good! Be smart! Be brave! And be gone!"

PART SEVEN: POLEMICS

Tonsor's most famous essays were polemics. Never shy in defending his position, Tonsor's sharp wit and intellectual sagacity found release in his pointed commentaries on topics ranging from education to conservatism. Like most of his articles, these polemics began as lectures or speeches and reflect his ability to hold the attention of an audience without skimping on substance. Such polemics grew more common as he aged; the essays in this section date from the 1970s and 1980s. His most famous essay, "Why I Too Am Not a Neoconservative" (the "too" refers to an essay published earlier that year by George Gilder with the title "Why I Am Not a Neoconservative"), is reprinted here. Tonsor's pointed criticism of neoconservatives drew many letters to the editors of *National Review*, including one from Werner Dannhauser claiming that Tonsor was anti-Semitic. The exchange, along with Jeffrey Hart's description of Tonsor's speech in *National Review*, convinced some that Tonsor was but a conservative relic. Regardless, the essay is a fine example of Tonsor's wit and style.

24

Alienation and Relevance

There is a striking parallel between the crisis in government at the national level in America and the crisis in the universities. In both cases, the institutional structure has recently increased gigantically in size and in the scale of operation. Along with this increase in size has gone a tremendous augmentation of power, both real and potential. However, it is a characteristic of this power that it is diffuse and focused only with difficulty, that it is all but impossible to bring this power to bear effectively on the problems of the state and the university. The problems that bedevil both the state and the university are frequently not problems that can be solved by the application of power. Along with the augmentation of size and power has gone a singular inability to match commitments with resources, so that the state and the universities, in spite of mega-dollar budgets, find themselves perennially impoverished. Finally, and most importantly, each finds itself alienated from its constituency. Each has discovered that it is increasingly difficult to project an objective that will move men to its single-minded pursuit. It is not that men no longer believe in government and education. Indeed, they believe passionately in both. It is rather that they no longer understand either the purpose or the designs of big government or big education. While the power of both institutions has steadily increased, their authority has declined. Ultimately, authority is far more important to education than power, and power without authority in the state soon gives way to tyranny. This parallel between the state and the university is instructive.

What is necessary in order to restore the institutional authority of higher education? How can higher education regain the confidence of those over thirty and command the respect of those under thirty who listen with reluctance and dissent without debate?

It would be false to assume that all our difficulties are institutional in origin, that they arise from the fact that the university has either done too much or too little. It must be said at the outset, and the fact faced with candor and resolution, that the most important problem higher education faces today is the growing wave of irrationality and anti-intellectualism that has caught up large numbers of both students and professors. Student and professor activists inside the university and certain ideological groups outside the university no longer believe that truth must be the essential consideration in the academy.

Both the extreme Right and the extreme Left hold the same destructive view. Both Mark Rudd of Columbia and Governor Wallace of Alabama stand in the schoolroom door and, seen from the vantage point of the academy, hold the same low view of reasoned discourse. They believe that force ought to be substituted for sweet reason, that power ought to replace persuasion, and that only "socially approved" voices and views should be heard. They believe that toleration is a weakness, rather than a strength, in intellectual enquiry, and they are in the deepest sense of the word anti-intellectual. They aim at nothing less than the destruction of the life of reason. The university and the parent society have no alternative to repression. These groups cannot be permitted to disrupt and destroy the institutions they so obviously do not understand. They constitute a small minority and it is possible that, had university administrations not been long accustomed by their faculties to suffering fools gladly, these groups would already have disappeared from the campus scene. Their disappearance, however, will not restore the authority of the university.

If the institutional aspirations of education are once more to become credible, universities must regain a sense of modesty and selectivity in the formulation of their objectives. They cannot be all things to all men. The notion of the "multiversity" is rejected with justice by students and by perceptive faculty. They reject it not simply because it is impossible to administer but because it is an institution without goals. It does not know its own mind. The able administrator in the setting of the multiversity is not a man characterized by unusual educational vision but someone whose social acoustical equipment is highly refined and who acutely senses all the many needs of his society. He is committed to servicing those needs and adjusting and compromising between these many conflicting interests. Little wonder that in such circumstances the teacher feels he is an unwanted encumbrance and the student senses that he is forgotten. To compound the problem now by expecting the university to become a court of last resort for the solution of the major social problems of our time will only deepen the crisis which the university faces.

Until there is a restoration of genuine educational purpose there will be no restoration of confidence by society in its institutions of higher education. Higher education has as its chief goals the education of young men and women in such a way as to make them capable participants in our complicated technological civilization, sophisticated and creative members of our common culture, and active and concerned citizens.

In order to ensure circumstances in which teaching rather than research or community service is the primary objective of the university, government at all levels must forgo the temptation of easy recourse to the enormous resources of the university. Recently, there has been a great deal of debate concerning the use of the talent and facilities available in the university for defense research. It is not inconsistent to argue that under very exceptional circumstances the university ought freely to use its talent in the defense of society, and still maintain that both the government and the university would be better served under most circumstances were both basic and applied research in the national defense area done in autonomous research institutes. The same case can be made against the use of the facilities of the university for the solution of social problems. Finally, business and industry should look to sources other than the university for their pure and applied research.

Much of the debate concerning university research at the present time misses the point. War research is no more illicit or licit than peace research. The only sound test is whether or not research enhances or diminishes the primary teaching function of the university. And it must be confessed that in spite of the brave talk to the contrary and considerable administrative legerdemain, research has become the tail that in many instances wags the dog. Faculty members on fractional appointments who spend the greater part of their time in other than teaching activities distort and confuse the educational purpose of the university. Foundation grants for centers and programs that are often inconsistent with the needs and basic educational directions of the institution are as dangerous to the university as government, civic, and business research for which there is no clear-cut teaching mandate.

"Where there is no vision the people perish" is an observation as true of institutions as it is of nations. In education, however, our pressing need is not for a single and unitary vision but rather the opposite. Education cannot be genuinely relevant to our society and its needs unless that education is diverse both in objective and technique. The possibility for educational diversity in America is immense, but in reality American education is homogeneous and uniform. The privately endowed colleges do poorly what the state universities do only a little better, and a handful of determinative major universities, as alike as peas in a pod, set the tone and direction for the whole educational enterprise. American education has become a single mechanism, its professors and students interchangeable parts. Under these circumstances, even student riots are monotonously, repellently alike.

Among the most important functions of education are those of widening the options available to men in the solution of their problems and in the improvement of the quality of their lives, yet our universities steadily diminish and dilute the differences between themselves. Students are still able to choose the quality of their educations; they are unable, however, to do much through their own choice about the kind of education they receive. It is important that we reestablish a free market in education. It is important that the church-related school survive, not as a secularized ghost of its former self, but as a school with a genuinely religious vision of the world, a school in which men learn to serve God and their fellow men rather than themselves. It is important that private humanistic colleges, with their commitment to civilization and decorum and their quiet emphasis on freedom, remain an important constituent of our educational system. It is essential that we have genuine experimentation in curriculum and method and not the pseudoexperiments hatched by administrators and departmental chairmen who need an excuse for hitting the foundations or the legislators once again for funds.

We cannot have this diversity, however, until the federal and state governments drastically alter the roles they play in financing higher education. American education will become diverse and relevant to the needs of both the student and the nation when, and only when, the student is forced to pay a very substantial portion of the total cost of his education. Privilege without responsibility is a very dangerous condition; privilege without either responsibility or choice generates unbearable tensions in the society that makes such privilege possible. State schools, which compete unfairly with private schools through discriminatory tuition rates, have been the chief force in leveling and homogenizing American education. If we genuinely desire diversity we will do all in our power to encourage students to pay for their educations through a tax on future earnings. If we genuinely wish diversity, we will insist that such educational grants as are made by the federal government will be made directly to the student rather than to institutions of higher education.

Only when there is a free market in education, with the student and his parents able to choose from among schools diverse in kind and quality, will we be able to say honestly to students: "We do not pretend to supply the sort of education you wish or need. If you really want a totally unstructured, ungraded course of study, segregated, revolutionary, and socially relevant, you can get it at, let us say, Columbia or Brandeis or Rutgers, but you can't get it here." The growing sense of alienation among students arises in substantial measure from their inability to choose the quality and kind of education they believe relevant to their lives.

Not only should there more diversity in the kind of college and university training available, but this diversity should bring into existence a wide range of educational alternatives. Apprenticeship programs, proprietary schools, technical institutes operated by industry for the training of specifically needed talents, a strengthening and broadening of the junior and community college programs are all of considerable importance in the problem of making education relevant to the needs of the student and the needs of society. The American public must be disabused of the notion that the bachelor's degree holds some sort of magic. For some time it has not been a mark of status and certainly it is not a guaranteed pass to higher income.

The right of entry into a craft union is often more difficult to achieve than entry into the most exclusive college. It strikes me as odd that the New Left, which has been so concerned with the indiscriminate admission of all minority-group students into our colleges irrespective of their qualifications, has had little or nothing to say of the restrictive practices that deny the right of entry of many of these same minority groups into those favored unions which possess monopoly advantages in our economy and society. Someone should say clearly that the way to status and achievement in our society is not through learning Swahili but through learning English. Someone needs to say clearly that the way to affluence does not lie through a bachelor's degree, granted by yesterday's second-rate normal college, but a marketable skill which will secure for its holder and his family the dignity of achievement.

Nearly every professor has in the past several years encountered, in what he thought a rather sober discussion of an academic question, a sudden denunciation by a student member of his audience. The student does not challenge the professor's method or even question his data but simply rejects his position as immoral, as fascist or racist, or as simply irrelevant. There is no debate or discussion, no attempt to identify the question or purposefully expose the issue. It is assumed that absolute right prevails on one side and that moral obtuseness, Marxian false consciousness, or plain wrongdoing characterizes the other side. The issue is not joined; it is not even discussed. Question periods at lectures are not occasions for refining the position of the lecturer but are seen as opportunities to present long, rambling denunciations and counter-lectures. The student usually ends his harangue with a plea for relevance and the lecturer, if he is smart enough, gathers that the young man or young lady (it is sometimes difficult to tell just which it is) is alienated.

L ast fall the *London Times* reported an international meeting of philosophers in Vienna in the following words:

> While their elders and betters solemnly discuss the epistemological significance of the phrases "Johnny has lost his pen. I have found a pen. I know Johnny lost it," the students are racing through the corridors, shouting "What about the Soviet invasion [of Czechoslovakia]," burning Russian and American flags, and wrestling with their professors for microphones during debates. It is disgusting, say the students, that three thousand of the wisest men from every country of the world should have gathered together in the largest philosophical talk-in in history and have nothing forceful to say about the Russian tanks on the Czech border less than fifty miles away. If philosophy has any real function it should be performing it now.

Clearly, what the student seeks is a relevant orthodoxy rather than an agonizing enquiry. Faced with some of the toughest choices in history, and living in a period when traditional certainties and traditional values have been challenged and opposed by alternatives, the student is really calling upon his professor for a clear and definitive answer, one preferably couched in a currently fashionable vocabulary and bearing the marks of current social concerns. To the student, education is irrelevant if it cannot provide a solution—preferably, of course, a solution that costs the student nothing and whose weight is borne by the nonstudent sectors of society. The student wants to know what to think rather than how to think.

And the student has far too many professors who are willing to tell him what to think rather than to attempt to teach him how to think for himself. The student has learned his lessons only too well. His professors, especially in the humanities and the social sciences, have all too often been exponents of an established orthodoxy rather than masters in the art of reasoned enquiry.

The situation is not to be mended by diversifying orthodoxies. That is the student's solution. He wishes to replace the liberal orthodoxy with a New Left orthodoxy, a WASP orthodoxy with a black orthodoxy, a permissive and tolerant orthodoxy with a repressive orthodoxy. What the student wishes is a substitution of orthodoxies rather than an end to all closed systems. His efforts will only compound the problem, for the liberal ascendancy in today's colleges and universities is like the pre-1918 Austrian empire—"an autocracy ameliorated by inefficiency"—while the student Maoist dictatorships would end altogether the life of reason.

The professor, if he is to reestablish the authority of reason must not only admit of the possibility of his being wrong but must have the openness of mind necessary to, as Lord Acton said, "make out the best possible case for error." He must actively court diversity and contradiction rather than seek a world of like-minded men. He must continuously engage in a great debate not only with his students and his colleagues, but above all with himself, and as President Truman said, "If he can't stand the heat, he should get out of the kitchen."

The ideological and cultural uniformity of higher education in America is a disgrace. Why is it that our colleges and universities have conformed themselves over the past two decades to the orthodoxy of secular liberalism? Why has the atmosphere been so increasingly hostile to open debate? Why does it take the crisis of the exclusion of the Negro from the university to make us see that not only people but also ideas have been excluded by higher education?

The authority and the relevance of the university lie in its ability as an institution to explore systematically and rationally the problems men face. Its success is not dependent on current fashions in ideas or current solutions to particular problems. Its success derives from its ability to take the long view and ask the hard questions, and the hardest of these is the question the professor asks of himself, of his colleagues, and of his society, about the possibility of being wrong.

25

The Second Spring of American Conservatism

When George Nash's *The Conservative Intellectual Movement in America* appeared last year, it ushered in a widespread discussion concerning the present condition and the future prospects of American conservatism. Hegel observed in his *Philosophy of History* that "the owl of Minerva takes its flight at twilight." Now that a scholarly book has been written about the conservative movement—now that the owl of Minerva in the very un-owl-like guise of Mr. Nash has taken its flight—is it all over for the conservative movement except, I suppose, for a decent burial at which Clare Boothe Luce and John Kenneth Galbraith would be the chief mourners?

That particular possibility, it seems to me, is very unlikely; and so it seems to a great many observers, even those not especially friendly to America's conservatives. One of these, Jeane Kirkpatrick, concludes in the February 1977 issue of *Commentary*:

> To read such analyses today is to be reminded that the New Right is not really new at all, but represents a strain of nativist populism whose roots are deep in American history and which has already played a highly important role in American politics, especially in the South and Southwest. As such it is no more likely to disappear from the contemporary political scene than it is to become the center of a new majority party. It will fail in its current version because of its hostility to another deeply rooted aspect of contemporary politics—the welfare state, whose benefits no majority in any democratic society has yet forsworn. Nevertheless, in one form or another, it will remain with us for a very long time to come.

And if the tone and some of the content of Miss Kirkpatrick's article lead us to suspect the soundness of her final judgment, we have only to glance at the election returns from the Western world. They reveal a profound unease with social-democratic and liberal explanations and solutions. On questions such as crime, education, and the intrusiveness of big government, the new political climate is deeply conservative— even though during this hesitant interregnum the people continue to vote for conservative fellow-travelers who call themselves "progressives." (Chancellor Helmut Schmidt's economic policies, for example, are somewhat to the right of those advocated by Paul McCracken when he was chairman of the Council of Economic Advisors.) The fuzzy center is dissolving, and both conservatives and Communists are registering marked gains.

In a sense, both social democracy and communism are profoundly reactionary movements. They represent outworn social classes and modes of production. They are the political expression of those groups—both in the Western world and in the developing countries—who have been left behind by the revolutionary changes that have occurred in post-industrial society. It is possible that these groups may impede and in some cases disrupt the development of postindustrial society; they cannot provide leadership for it. The Left today represents an international society of losers. A social-democratic mandate no longer exists, and the persistent problems that confront the world are not soluble through applications of Left-liberal rhetoric and doses of Marxist Geritol for the relief of political tired blood. It is, of course, debatable whether the future belongs to conservatism; it is quite certain that it does not belong to social democracy.

No one can predict the future, and historians, more than most observers, are acutely aware of the folly of attempting to anticipate the developmental processes of history. Indeed, our essential concern in politics is not with the future but with the present. Our question, then, is not about the role of conservatism in the future but about the present condition and prospects of the conservative movement.

Because of the doctrinaire nature of ideology, the parties of the Right and the Left are each committed to a corpus of irreformable dogma, which must be imposed upon a recalcitrant social and political reality. As Edmund Burke might put it, "The theoretical perfection of these dogmas is their practical defect." The reason for their rigidity is easily understandable. Ideologies are born in the political agonies of a particular era; they bear the historical stamp of their origins. They are chained by time to a moment in the past; and, because they embody irreformable doctrine and are thus essentially unalterable, they cannot respond adequately either to changes in the mode of production or to a transformed social and cultural reality.

It strikes one as odd indeed that Marxism, which originally posited the importance of changes in the mode of production for the total political and cultural configuration, should be so incapable of accommodating itself to the historical processes of change. When Marxists view the development of capitalism they rightly identify important changes that have taken place. We may quarrel with their designations of "early," "high," and "late" capitalism. We certainly do not disagree with their thesis that capitalism has had a developmental history and that the present-day society it has produced is vastly different from the seventeenth-century society characteristic of incipient capitalism. If indeed there is such change in the developmental history of capitalism, one might expect equally important change in the developmental history of socialism. If there is such a thing as late capitalism, there must be, one might suppose, something to be described as "late socialism." If Marxists persist in describing imperialism as "the last and highest stage of capitalism," ought they not to be equally willing to describe Stalinism and Maoism as "the last and highest stage of socialism"?

I suggest that they should, for the very good reason that the revolutionary transformation in the mode of production that has characterized the development of postindustrial society has made the varieties of Marxism obsolete in any but hopelessly backward societies. The base of Marxism, that conglomerate class entity Marxists call the proletariat, has been in steady decline in the industrialized world since the middle of the nineteenth century. And this process has been accelerating. Peter Drucker, among others, has called attention to it; Daniel Bell argues its implications elaborately in *The Coming of Post-Industrial Society* (1973). He gives us the gist of his argument in a short statement in the February 1977 *Encounter*:

> Today, in every advanced industrial country, the industrial working class is shrinking relative to the rising new classes in society, particularly the professional and technical classes. In the United States today, one out of every four persons in the labor force is professional and technical and managerial. Probably fewer than 20 per cent of the labor force is engaged directly in industrial production. Yet the translation of these *tendencies* into political groups, and the creation of more appropriate political nomenclatures than those of the present—assuming with "impervious simples" that economic and occupational interests have some overt political counterpart—is a long-term historical process that will take decades to complete.

The evolution of a new class—those who invent, control, command, and enlarge the scientific, educational, and technical apparatus of the new society—is politically and socially an event of the greatest importance.

The dynamics and energies of this social transformation cannot be contained within the rigidities of Marxist ideology. To employ the language of Marxist social analysis, the contradictions and the irrationalities are simply too great. This does not mean that Marxism is going to be swept away in some sudden apocalyptic series of events. Only Marxists believe that these great social disruptions constitute the ordinary process of social change. It is more likely that the Communist states, like a fox caught in a trap, will gnaw off a leg. They will survive for a considerable while, limping into a vicious and degraded decrepitude. So much for the "last and highest stage of socialism."

This transformation of society in the post-industrial era has as many implications for conservatism as it has for Marxism. Some important aspects of it seem, at first sight, to be especially favorable to a continued and even greater conservative influence in our society. There are other factors, however, that may mitigate and might even negate this influence.

Although postindustrial society has been developing for a rather long time, the period of most rapid transformation has been the three decades since World War II. You will recall that the full title of Mr. Nash's book is *The Conservative Intellectual Movement in America since 1945*. The date in the title is of some importance, for it suggests what I believe to be the case: that contemporary conservatism in its broad outlines crystallized in the late Fifties and early Sixties.

Its three major components—the fear of statism and a commitment to market economics; the effort to mobilize against totalitarianism, especially in its Soviet form; and, finally, a growing concern with values, community, and the conditions necessary to a humane society—had been articulated philosophically and had achieved a rather stable balance by the early Sixties. Most of the major creative figures in the movement had developed their positions and achieved eminence in the course of the previous quarter-century. While I do not wish to suggest that those great intellectual heroes of the movement have less or little more to say to our contemporary world than they had to say to the world of 1960, I do want to suggest that meanwhile the world has changed a great deal, and that neither the theoretical formulations nor the practical applications of conservative theory have kept pace with those changes.

A substantial number of major conservative figures have died recently, and it must strike every observer that in terms of intellectual creativity we are an aging movement. No doubt we have established important bridgeheads into the oncoming generation. But this new generation, one suspects, in spite of its energy and its sophistication, is following Galton's law of filial regression, which states that children of distinguished parents are apt to be rather less distinguished.

Let me discuss this second generation of conservative intellectuals at greater length. I believe that they have been powerfully inhibited in the renewal of conservative theorization by the political activism that has marked the Sixties and Seventies. I note with disappointment the number—and among them some of those with the best minds and potentially the most creative abilities—who have turned away from the academy and the intellectual life to what they feel to be a more direct exercise of power in political activism and governmental service.

It is true that, as someone remarked in connection with St. Elizabeth Seton, "The paradox of detachment and involvement is completely resolved only in the saints." It is also true that in the past some major conservative intellectuals have taken an active political role: Burke's name leaps to mind immediately. Even so, political passion and political involvement, I am convinced, have been destructive forces in the second generation of conservative intellectuals—the generation, incidentally, to which I belong.

Intellectuals have a very special and privileged role in society. We have, as Jesus said of that other Mary in the New Testament, "chosen the better part." It cannot be taken from us and we ought not to surrender it voluntarily.

A second and more important factor in what I believe to be the decline in the level and energy of intellectual theorizing is the impact of what has generally been called "libertarianism" on the quality and range of conservative concerns. Here I am discussing not the body of economic theory known as "libertarianism" but the total *Weltanschauung*. "Libertarianism" as a *Weltanschauung* positively prevents thought by reducing the range of options for dealing with postindustrial society to a few threadbare platitudes, which libertarian intellectuals recite superstitiously on every conceivable occasion. Today it is as important to understand the limits and the limitations of liberty as it is to affirm its indispensability to a humane and moral life. It is the failure to discuss liberty in the context of community that gives "libertarianism" its utopian character.

Since 1945, the most impressive influences upon the polity from the side of conservatism have come from economic theory. The impact of the economists has been decisive and overwhelming. But even were their victory complete, the task of conservatism would be only just beginning. As Warren Nutter and many others have remarked, there are no economic solutions to the most important problems in our society.

During the next two decades we will find political and cultural issues, rather than narrowly economic issues, to be of primary concern. This is at least in part due to the fact that our society has moved from scarcity to superfluity. It is, for example, not *need,* but our concern with the amenities of a pollution-free environment—and with the political considerations of the Arab-Israeli conflict—which created the so-called "energy crisis." I do not mean that economics will be unimportant but only that economics will be less important than culture and politics. Similarly, because of the importance of education, research, and professional expertise in the post-industrial era, the role of government in education and research will become an increasingly important question, as will the role of government in culture and the larger issue of the relationship of politics to values. Daniel Bell remarks in *The Coming of Post-Industrial Society:* "The politics of the next decade is more likely to concern itself, on the national level, with such public-interest issues as health, education, and the environment, and, on the local level, crime, municipal services, and costs. These are communal issues. . . ."

And that final remark is just the point. These *are* all communal issues. The atomism inherent in economic calculation must yield to the collective concerns of community. If during the past thirty years economics has dominated the conservative movement, conservatives during the next twenty years will have to engage themselves more completely with the realms of education and science, of community and value. The transition will not be altogether easy, even though a considerable block of conservative intellectuals have from the outset concerned themselves with these questions.

I quote once more and finally from Daniel Bell, this time from *The Cultural Contradictions of Capitalism* (1976):

> Crises of belief are recurrent in human history, which does not make them less significant even if the topic risks becoming banal. The invitation to despair arises because the consequences are real if not always immediate, and yet no one can do very much about them. Gadgets can be engineered, programs can be designed, institutions can be built, but belief has an organic quality and it cannot be called into being by fiat. . . . The major consequence of this crisis—I leave aside its cultural dilemmas— is the loss of *civitas,* that spontaneous willingness to obey the law, to respect the rights of others, to forgo the temptations of private enrichment at the expense of the public weal—in short, to honor the "city" of which one is a member. Instead, each man goes his own way, pursuing his private vices, which can be indulged only at the expense of public benefits.
>
> The foundation of any liberal society is the willingness of

all groups to compromise private ends for the public interest. The loss of *civitas* means either that interests become so polarized, and passions so inflamed, that terrorism and group fighting ensure, and political *anomie* prevails: or that every public exchange becomes a cynical deal in which the most powerful segments benefit at the expense of the weak. Yet even where a sense of *civitas* remains, as in England, the ruts into the future may have been cut so deep from the past—the constraints may be so large, the freedom to maneuver and change so narrow, the institutions, particularly the economic ones, so encrusted—that no regime can substantially stop the slide, and a sense of weariness and despair takes over. These are the greys on grey, the crises of the political order of the next twenty-five years.

The basis of *civitas* is a commonly held set of values and beliefs: it is consensus. "We hold these truths," and unless we do there can be no *civitas*. There is no possible way of deriving *civitas* from a libertarian worldview, and should libertarianism become a determining aspect of conservatism we shall have forfeited both our right and our ability to speak to our society. There must be agreement that such a thing as the "commonweal" exists, and we must explore the nature of the consensus which makes it possible. This I believe to be the chief task of conservatives now and in the years ahead.

It will not do to think of this restoration of common belief as nothing more than the reaffirmation of traditional values. This I call the "pressed-flower school" of conservatism, a kind of Williamsburg restoration nostalgia which from time to time trots out a past that never was for the irrelevant admiration of the present. Institutions and forms of all sorts—the nature of community itself—will have to be sifted and rethought if we are to preserve what we believe to be necessary and perennial values in a world of rapid change. It may be that some of those things which we hold to be essential are in fact only adventitious. The difference between a traditionalist and a conservative is that the conservative is prepared to abandon the historically contingent, no matter how comfortable or beautiful it is, in the pursuit of *perennial* values.

Traditional forms and attitudes are the special mark of the populist element in American society. This faction is, in effect, stuck in the past, seizing upon the form rather than the spirit of old values and institutions. In the recent past, a number of conservatives have argued for an alliance with populism—have argued that there is room for the hardhats and the rednecks under the big tent of a broadly defined conservatism. I understand the temptation, for these groups are of great political importance. I do not believe, however—in spite of the advice of Kevin Phillips—that such an alliance can be formed. And the fact of its impossibility will save conservatism from the temptation of a politics that is reactionary rather than progressive. The conservative intellectual is not going to spend his time constructing defenses for decadent forms.

Conservative intellectuals are particularly well placed to exert their influence in the search for order and community. They are virtually the only political theorists of any importance today. Increasingly, they are playing an important role in the fields of sociology and law. In theology there has been a swing away from the pop theology and the social gospelism of the Sixties to a concentration on traditional questions pursued by conventional methods. In the natural sciences, ethology and sociobiology have opened up important new areas of knowledge which are of the utmost importance to conservative social theory.

The most important single development in the conservative intellectual movement at present is the political and social realignment of America's Jewish intellectuals. Even though a number of Europe's great conservatives—Julius Stahl and Benjamin Disraeli among them—were Jewish, American Judaism has traditionally had a close association with liberalism and the Left. But while American Catholic intellectuals moved steadily to the left, Jewish intellectuals moved to the right. The process of this realignment has been complex and complicated, and surely one of the decisive events of the decade. Mr. Nash alludes to it, but so briefly that it almost escapes one's attention. Were one to read only *Commentary*, one might assume that America's Jews were a bit more conservative than Gerald Ford. For both Judaism and the American polity the importance of this development cannot be overestimated.

In the 1830s and '40s, the Catholic Church in England was finally emerging from the persecution and obscurity that had resulted from the Reformation. On the Continent, Catholic theologians and philosophers had sparked one of the greatest religious revivals in the long history of Christianity, and Catholics in England were quick to appropriate their thought. Neither the ancient recusant families, who had kept their faith intact in spite of segregation and active persecution, nor the Irish Catholic immigrants who poured into the English cities in such large numbers to work in the mills and the factories, were able to provide the intellectual leadership that the growing Catholic population of England was searching for. When that intellectual leadership did appear, it came from a surprising source. The great English Catholic intellectuals of the Victorian era were, for the most part, converts from Anglicanism—Cardinal Newman, Archbishop

Manning, William George Ward, and Frederick Faber, to name only a few. More important still, many who remained in the Anglican Church—men such as Pusey, Gladstone, and Dean Church—were so strongly influenced by Catholic ideas that Anglicanism assumed a wholly new and Catholic character. For a while, Catholic enthusiasts were able to talk of the possible conversion of all Anglicans. Newman in a famous sermon spoke of "the second spring" that the Catholic Church in England was enjoying, and he knew well enough how great a role Anglican converts played in that "second spring."

I have permitted myself this excursion into an obscure corner of ecclesiastical history because I believe that conservatism in America is on the verge of a "second spring." And I believe that the intellectual leadership which will manifest itself in that "second spring" will come from the liberal camp. Even ten years ago one could not have made this bold assertion. Today, conservatism's Oxford converts are pouring in, and, even more importantly, many who do not acknowledge themselves to be conservatives are busy recasting America's culture and politics in a conservative image; the Jewish intellectuals are the visible tip of a very large iceberg. In the Fifties and Sixties liberals and leftists still set the terms and provided the vocabulary for the political and social debate which was reawakening in America. Today, to use a Leninist phrase, conservatives hold "the commanding heights."

It is not important that the Establishment is still largely in place. What is important is that a new generation of intellectuals, men who have passed through the conversion experience, men whose contact with the social and cultural reality of 1977 is quite complete and secure, are forging a new body of conservative social theory and practical application. They indeed represent the second generation and they will produce the second spring. I believe that a new conservative consensus will emerge in American society, that the center of American politics has moved away from the Left. I believe that there is in process a restoration of liberty, order, community, and value in American society. It is an achievement in which we conservatives have participated and of which we can all be proud. It is an achievement we owe most especially to that great first generation of scholars and theorists who did not overestimate the importance of politics and power but who quietly and often at great personal sacrifice wrestled with the intellectual problems of their time.

26

Why I Too Am Not a Neoconservative

I feel somewhat like Mr. Creedy in the Midas Muffler television ad. The engine of the old model of conservatism that I drive is still running well, and, as I believe that "if it ain't broke don't fix it," I have come to view conservatism as a perennial political philosophy that does not admit of neos or "Saturn" models.

I became a Conservative in 1954. Rather, I should say that I discovered that I was a Conservative in 1954. The event was not a conversion experience, but a moment of self-revelation. My experience was not unlike that of a Catholic acquaintance of mine who, one day, as he entered a Catholic church, dipped his hand in the holy-water fount and said with sudden clarity, "My God! What am I doing here?" He left the church, never to return. I dipped my hand in the holy-water fount of Russell Kirk and said, "Home at last!"

Whether or not one is a neoconservative is not simply a generational matter. It is not that I am an "old party comrade" and knew the Twelve Apostles, while those "neos" who came after us belong to a new and different age. After all, Irving Kristol must be nearly as old as I am. No, there are still young big-C Conservatives who enter the movement every day and are as far from neo-dom as I am.

Nor is the great divide a consequence of changing times and altered political and economic circumstances. It is not that most neoconservatives think that Barry Goldwater is "cute" and ought to be honored and revered and humored now and then, but that he belongs to the paleolithic age of the Conservative movement. If that indeed is the case, then I too am a paleoconservative.

It can't simply be that neoconservatives read and often write for *Commentary* magazine. I read *Commentary* and have done so for years. I find myself often in agreement, always stimulated, and now and then put off by *Commentary*. However, I don't think *Commentary* is a reliable test. It often publishes writers I consider big-C Conservatives.

Age, changed circumstances, and an identifiable literary connection have little or nothing to do with the ideological identity of those on the Right. (There, I have uttered that awful word, usually prefaced by "far," as in farsighted.) These differences that separate neoconservatives from Conservatives are differences that have for nearly a hundred years divided the Right.

I have made these personal references because I believe that the way in which I became a Conservative, and my starting point, were very different from the way in which one becomes a neoconservative, and the neoconservatives' starting point. One's starting point and the way in which one achieves an identity have very important implications for what one becomes.

These differences among Conservatives are grounded in the relationship of conservatism to modernity. Increasingly, our culture is becoming aware that it is no longer "modern," though it is totally uncertain just what it is. This cultural break with "modernity" presents us with the preconditions for an accurate assessment of our relationship to it.

By "modernity," I mean that revolutionary movement in culture which derived from a belief in man's radical alienation, in God's unknowability or nonexistence, and in man's capacity to transform or remake the conditions of his existence. The thoroughgoing secularism, the attack upon the past, religious and social, aristocratic or bourgeois, the utopian dream of alienation overcome and innocence restored are all linked together in the modernist sensibility. To be "up-to-date" was, for a hundred years, to be an alienated person. The world was viewed as anarchic chaos upon which man-become-God imposed his own particular dream of order. Often as not, that order was an inverted order, against the grain, against nature. Prometheanism and satanism were one and the same order of man's invention. The Romantic satanic hero is the same man as the Prometheus of Shelley and Marx, the Zarathustra of Nietzsche.

To pretend that the Right, that Conservatives, have been immune to modernity is self-delusion. On the whole, the Right has been much more modernist than the Left because the Right has dared to think consequentially, because the Right knows that he who says A must also say B. It is for this reason that the modernists of the Right have been, almost without exception, fascists and totalitarians, for they know that when things fall apart and the center does not hold, the only recourse is to an invented and imposed order.

Now that we are able to gain some perspective on this past century, we recognize that the social and political consequence of modernity is totalitarianism. We can see that the denial of the existence of order as the ground of being, and the rejection of the transcendent, is a one-way street to Dachau.

If everything is permitted and the will-to-power the only reality, then the Gulag is as logical as a Euler diagram. Those who do not refuse to think the unthinkable have known this for a long while. Hitler did not need to give a specific command for the "final solution." Himmler and the members of the SS Einsatzgruppen knew the "final solution" was implicit in their conception of reality. It is on the ground of modernity that Right and Left are merged and the differences between them are only differences of style and slogans. The Right born of modernity is a radical, a revolutionary Right, which cannot in any important degree be distinguished from the revolutionary Left.

Now it is a matter of fact that most of those who describe themselves as neoconservatives are or have been cultural modernists. They have been, to use Peter Berger's telling phrase, baptized in the "fiery brook." (He was making an elegant pun on the name of Ludwig Feuerbach, the Left Hegelian inspiration of Marx and the church father of alienation theory.) We Conservatives have been baptized in the Jordan, and there is a vast difference between the Jordan and the fiery brook.

It has always struck me as odd, even perverse, that former Marxists have been permitted, yes invited, to play such a leading role in the Conservative movement of the twentieth century. It is splendid when the town whore gets religion and joins the church. Now and then she makes a good choir director, but when she begins to tell the minister what he ought to say in his Sunday sermons, matters have been carried too far. I once remarked to Glenn Campbell of the Hoover Institution that had Stalin spared Leon Trotsky and not had him murdered in Mexico, he would no doubt have spent his declining days in an office in Hoover Library writing his memoirs and contributing articles of a faintly neoconservative flavor to *Encounter* and *Commentary*.

Is it ungracious of me to suggest that political and even religious conversion does not often improve the mind's capacity for sound judgment? Whittaker Chambers, one of the most beguiling intellectuals of the twentieth century, had flawed judgment as a Marxist and said some very silly things on the subject of conservatism once he had become a convert.

All of which is not to say that the rejection of Marxism is unimportant and that the piecemeal rejection of various articles of faith shared with Left-liberal modernists is unimportant. Nor do I wish to imply that the assistance of neoconservatives is unwelcome in the work of dismantling the failed political structures erected by modernity. Conservatives have made common cause with classical liberals, and there is no reason why they should not make common cause with neoconservatives. When the wagon train is attacked, we arm the women and children even though they may in their ineptitude occasionally mistake a friend for a foe.

Still, halfway from modernity is not far enough. Politics has always been inseparable from culture, and both derive ultimately from religion. It is absurd to believe that one can remain a modernist in culture and reject the implications of modernism in politics. Unbelief is incompatible with conservatism. Conserve what? And to what end? Werner Dannhauser, writing in the December 1985 *Commentary*, tells us: "Too many conservatives have failed to come to terms with Nietzsche's thought, dismissing it as an embarrassing attempt to outflank them on the Right. But the challenge he represents will not go away." Dannhauser continues:

> Nietzsche went far beyond Burke, who held out the hope of a time when atheism might cease to be fashionable. Nietzsche postulated an irreversible loss of naïveté in Western civilization. To put the matter crudely, he argued that the cat of atheism was out of the bag. The meanest capacities could now learn that religion was a myth, and when a myth is exposed for what it is, it can no longer serve to provide a unified horizon.
>
> Too many conservatives whose own belief is weak or nonexistent, who will privately admit that religion is "for the troops," continue to try to teach the catechism to those troops, forgetting that the latter have by now been thoroughly exposed to the Enlightenment and its lessons.

There you have it: The dividing line between conservatives is the line separating Burke from Nietzsche. Let me say parenthetically that I could never understand the reasoning processes of Jews who are Nietzscheans. Walter Kaufmann was quite unable to discern that while Nietzsche was not a biological racist he was a philosophical anti-Semite. If Nietzsche's anti-Semitism was less vulgar than that of Julius Streicher or of Nietzsche's friend Richard Wagner, it was no less deadly.

One is struck again by the true and forceful portrait Thomas Mann gives us of the Nietzschean modernist in the person of Adrian Leverkuhn in *Dr. Faustus*. Adrian's music is modernist music not only as a style but in terms of the metaphysical conception out of which it is constructed. It is also demonic. It can only come into existence through the ruin of a soul, the destruction of a mind—and as the work of the composer reaches fruition, Germany is destroyed philosophically and sinks into ruin beneath the rain of Allied bombs. Mann, who made the character of Adrian Leverkuhn out of a composite of Nietzsche and Arnold Schönberg, intended in this, the greatest novel of the twentieth century, to tell us something about the cultural reality of our age. The narrator, Serenus Zeitblom, is a religious and pious Conservative—one, I take it, who had missed the Enlightenment.

I sometimes imagine myself and my fellow Conservatives to be of the type of Serenus Zeitblom. They have a loving regard for their age and their fellow men, and they realize that they must often forgo intervention and permit the tragic drama to play itself out. Because Leverkuhn could not accept an order that, modernist that he was, he felt to be meaningless, he imposed a new order, rational and cleanly articulated as the music of Bach but lacking Bach's attachment to the divine and reconciliation to the human. Leverkuhn's achievement was a great technical triumph, but only a triumph of technique. It is fitting funeral music for a culture that died of pride.

Rational technique in the pursuit of irrational ends: that suggests the modernist condition. That is why neoconservatives are so inventive and often correct in dealing with the realm of technique. But when push comes to shove, ends are of ultimate importance and will finally determine the appropriate technique. What the neoconservatives have done is to divorce techniques from ends in an effort to maintain their cultural modernism while rejecting its social and political implications. This, I say, is quite impossible, and in the long run dangerous. It is easy to see that the utopian social and political programs of the last hundred years have failed. It is not the cat of atheism that has been let out of the bag but the failure of the Enlightenment in all its forms. Neoconservatives are, as Irving Kristol remarked, "liberals who have been mugged by reality," but while they have been detached from their social and political myths, they have not located themselves in a body of principle that makes life worth living, or that one would die defending.

It is important, also, to realize that the phrase "liberals mugged by reality" is only a part of the truth about neoconservatism. Neoconservatism is above all a transmogrification of "the New York intellectuals," in Alexander Bloom's phrase, who, in turn, reflected the instantiation of modernity among secularized Jewish intellectuals. Neoconservatism is culturally unthinkable aside from the history of the Jewish intellectual in the twentieth century. When the New York intellectuals turned from the beguilements of left-wing revolutionary utopianism, they did not in fact become Conservatives but attached themselves to positions that were neoliberal, in the sense that Mises and Hayek were neoliberals; and just as Mises and Hayek are philosophical and cultural modernists, so too New York intellectuals who now call themselves neoconservatives are modernists.

Conservatism has its roots in a much older tradition. Its worldview is Roman or Anglo-Catholic; its political philosophy, Aristotelian and Thomist; its concerns, moral and ethical; its culture, that of Christian humanism.

Most old-fashioned Conservatives are free of metaphysical anxiety and as happy as clams in a world that bears the unmistakable imprint of God's ordering hand. They are free of alienation, and they have absolutely no hopes of a utopian political order. They live with sin and tragedy, not as a consequence of inadequate social engineering, but as a consequence of man's sin and disorder. They believe that human institutions and human culture are subject to the judgment of God, and they hold that the most effective political instrument is prayer and a commitment to try to understand and do the will of God.

If neoconservatives wish us to take their conservatism seriously, they must return to the religious roots, beliefs, and values of our common heritage. They cannot dither in the halfway house of modernity and offer us technical solutions that touch the symptoms but never deal with the causes of contemporary disorder.

Part Eight: Tributes

In this section Tonsor reflects on the men who played a crucial role in shaping his scholarly and academic career. His long friendship with Henry Regnery is epitomized by a truly important correspondence contained in both the Tonsor and Regnery papers at the Hoover Institution. Tonsor here also pays tribute to Joseph Ward Swain and Russell Kirk, who, along with Regnery, helped provide him with the intellectual education that led him to formulate his own unique conception of conservatism.

27

Joseph Ward Swain

He was an unprepossessing man. He looked, indeed, as though he were a near relative of the Sitwells, and he gave one the impression of an absent presence. One, on first meeting him, did not suspect that he was a great lecturer and an acute observer of present and past. His judgment of Ernest Renan was as knowledgeable and as unfavorable as Albert Schweitzer's derogatory picture of Renan. However, one felt that he might have said, as he no doubt reported Renan as saying, "Do not think that you are listening to me. You are hearing history speaking." He would, of course, never have applied Renan's words to himself, both because he was too modest and because he was less certain about the course and meaning of the past than was Renan.

Still, his lecture courses on Greek and Roman history and "The History of History" were crowded. His students were not only the future historians and intellectuals but also the more ordinary Illinois farm-boy and farm-girl types, even though they might be urban dwellers one generation distant from the farm. Veterans, just returned from World War II, gave the audience a certain earnestness, though the "jocks" lightened the atmosphere with their *sotto voce* remarks. Seminars were relatively small in the late 1940s and early 1950s, though most of those who worked in Professor Joseph Ward Swain's seminar went on to finish doctoral dissertations under his direction.

Swain lectured from a carefully prepared set of notes, each topic contained in a manila folder. One day, he appeared in class with a folder from one of his other courses and proceeded to lecture us on a topic unrelated to the course we were studying. No one dared call the mistake to his attention—nor did anyone snicker, not even the "jocks." At last it dawned on him that something was wrong and he beat a flustered retreat.

He was attentive to different styles in lecturing. Of his contemporary at Columbia University, Preston Slosson, who made a great reputation for himself as a lecturer at the University of Michigan and ran for Congress on the Democratic ticket, Swain observed derisively, "He has fathomed the freshman mind." Of one of his masters at Columbia University, the great Carlton J. H. Hayes, later ambassador to Franco Spain, Swain told how Hayes kept his lecture notes on blue and white cards, seven white cards to one blue. The blue cards contained supposed jokes and students prepared themselves for the advent of the blue card by laughing in advance.

At Columbia, Swain had been a contemporary of the "failed priest" and, later, popular historian Will Durant. They were students together in a course on the Enlightenment taught by John Dewey. Dewey for some time discussed *The Encyclopedia*. Finally Durant summoned his courage and raised his hand. "Professor Dewey," he said, "you have mentioned 'the encyclopedia' a number of times. Just which encyclopedia do you mean?" In outrage Dewey replied, "Why! *The Encyclopedia, The Encyclopedia!*"

Swain was born in 1891 and the cast of his mind was essentially Edwardian. The authors he read were the great Edwardians and their contemporaries on the Continent. He shared their mood of elegant existential anxiety. Still, the note of hope rather than despair was dominant in his thought. He was fond of quoting G. K. Chesterton's "Ballad of Suicide":

> The gallows in my garden, people say,
> Is new and neat and adequately tall. . . .
> . . . The strangest whim has seized me. . . .
> After all
> I think I will not hang myself today.

To the Edwardian religious and political crisis, the mood that culminated in World War I, he found a parallel in the religious and political crisis of the ancient world at the moment when Christianity was born and the *ecumene* was subsumed into the Roman empire. For Swain, the time of the breaking of nations and the birth of Christian universalism, so like the historical situation of his own day, bore out the words of the poet Virgil, *sunt lacrimae rerum* ("things have tears in them"), a line of poetry he often quoted.

The religious crisis of the Edwardian era was one in which Swain participated. As an undergraduate at Beloit College he had studied with James Arnold Blaisdell, professor of biblical literature, whom he called "my first and best teacher of ancient history." At Columbia, where he took his PhD in 1912, his professors Hayes and Moon had become converts to Catholicism. And in 1913, when he went to Paris for study at the Ecole Pratique des Hautes Etudes, his roommate was Randolph Bourne, who was later to become a Catholic convert. Swain's doctoral dissertation, "The Greek Origins of Christian Asceticism," underlined his religious preoccupations. When he arrived in Paris the Catholic Modernist controversy was at its peak, and his interest in Alfred Loisy and George Tyrell continued throughout his life. In 1915 Swain published his translation of Emile Durkheim's *Elementary Forms of the Religious Life*. The translation, the first of Durkheim's works to appear in English, had little initial success in the English-speaking world. Its importance was recognized by American sociologists only after World War II, in spite of Merton's work. Old and New Testament criticism was a major focus of his interests. This interest was that of an expert rather than a dilettante, as is demonstrated by his pathbreaking article on the Book of Daniel, "The Theory of the Four Monarchies: Opposition History under the Roman Empire."[1]

It is interesting to speculate that he heard John N. Figgis lecturing or was acquainted with his publications. Figgis had been Lord Acton's only student, and Swain was a devotee of Lord Acton. Of course, Swain studied the Cambridge writers of Acton's day carefully: William Robertson Smith and Sir James G. Frazer. Few Americans knew the works of Cardinal Newman as well as Swain knew them. (After Swain's death his wife sent me, carrying out instructions in a note Swain had left, the Charles Frederick Harold edition of Newman's works.) And Swain had more than an acquaintance with the thought of the Baron von Hügel.

One might suppose, on the basis of these intellectual affinities, that Swain, like so many of his generation, was edging toward Rome. That supposition would neglect the other Swain, the learned skeptic, and it would neglect the religious history of his family. Swain outlined that history in a long note appended to the chapter on "Imperial Idealism and Early Christianity" in *The Ancient World* (vol. II).

> . . . I have been told that, soon after the English translation of Renan's book [*The Life of Jesus*] appeared in this country, my grandfather—a Congregational minister in a New England city—procured a copy. His father, then an elderly man, picked up the volume, glanced over the first few pages, was so horrified that in that book he read no more. My grandfather persevered to the end, commented that "M. Renan forgets that Christianity rests not on the Sermon on the Mount but upon Calvary," and consoled himself with the reflection that "America is still too profoundly Christian a nation to be disturbed by one more infidel book." Several years later my father read the book and was converted by it. I first read the *Vie de Jésus* in my student days. I

admired its beautiful French prose but I could not understand
the commotion it caused.

Swain, the learned skeptic, was in his attitudes not unlike another of his
great enthusiasms, Edward Gibbon. Throughout his lifetime Swain read
and studied Gibbon for pleasure. Swain's great Gibbon book was never
written. Along the way he published a fragment of what might have been.

He described himself as an Episcopalian. However, one day when we
were discussing the Unitarian religiosity of Albert Schweitzer, a man and
an intellectual Swain much admired, he said, "I should probably be a Unitarian but those Unitarians are such queer fellows."

He knew that the place of the intellectual was in the academy and not
in the political lists. Still, he was an acute observer of the political and
social agonies of his own time. I never discussed politics with him but I
would describe his values as those of an aristocratic, conservative anti-
democrat. Democracy was, in his eyes, exemplified in Cleon, the hot-dog
salesman and mini-tyrant of the Athens of the Peloponnesian War. The
Athenian declension from Pericles to Cleon seemed to Swain to have been
what one ought to have expected. Of the Greek dramatists, Swain most
admired Aristophanes and Euripides. The classical historians he most admired were Thucydides and Tacitus.

No doubt these tastes were conditioned by his hostility to militarism
and war. He had served briefly in the United States Army in World War I.
Like the majority of the intellectuals of his day he viewed American intervention in that war as a disaster. He laughed at one of his colleagues, a very
sedentary man, who had exercised violently in order to get his weight down
so that he could volunteer for service only to discover after the war that
American intervention had been a mistake. In his attitude to war Swain had
the experience of Greece and Rome constantly in his mind.

As the 1930s drew to a close the hope for peace in Europe dimmed.
Swain set to work to explore the intellectual and political roots of the twentieth century. His book *Beginning the Twentieth Century* was widely acclaimed,
though its influence diminished as World War II began to eat up the intellectual energies of the Western world. As that war approached Swain found
himself in the "isolationist" camp. The history department at the University of Illinois, where Swain was a senior professor, was badly divided between isolationists and interventionists. (The history of this conflict would
be an interesting study for some future historian.) It should be clear, however, that Swain and his fellow anti-interventionists were not partisans of
fascism. On the contrary, they saw the war as destructive of the freedom
and values that they believed to be distinctively American.

The essential function of the teacher is the transmission of tradition.

The values which he or she conveys to the next generation are values of content and method. In the case of the historian, the transmission of the knowledge of the past, those human experiences which are the ground of present-day existence, is the content of the historian's science (ordered enquiry). But this past is never the dead past. It lives on into the present and manifests itself, for good or ill, in contemporary life. Moreover, the great historians know that past better and more fully than those contemporary with the events which constitute the past knew it. This is the great and enduring meaning of John Henry Newman's *Essay on the Development of Christian Doctrine*—that the past in its fullness can be known only in future time.

The transmission of tradition is not simply the transmission of content; it is also the transmission of the method by which that content can be known and understood. It was for this reason that Swain's course on "The History of History" was so important to me and to his other students. It was for this reason that the seminars in which he taught the methods of both negative and positive (*Schöpferisch*) historical criticism were essential to our historical understanding.

Swain was the heir of the great revolution in historical studies that developed out of the seventeenth-century French savant's invention of the tools, the ancillary sciences of historical analysis, and the distinctive historical consciousness that resulted from German historicism. For Swain, these two traditions were most manifest in ancient history and more particularly in the higher criticism of biblical studies. He knew, above all, that these were not exact sciences and that the historian had constantly to be on guard against his own tendencies to error. These tendencies to error were checked, in a measure, by the community of scholarship. Albert Schweitzer's critique of New Testament scholarship, *In Quest of the Historical Jesus,* demonstrated how wrong historians might be. It was imperative, Swain believed, for historians to take the chance, to read the documents in a sense in which they had not been previously read. No doubt Swain was sometimes mistaken, and no doubt he was sometimes overly bold. Even as a graduate student I recognized this to be the case, but I recognized too that there was greatness in his daring. He taught us sympathetic identification (*Einfühlung*) with the past and a critical methodology by which the past could be known.

But, of course, without kindness and generosity of spirit these intellectual virtues would have been empty and meaningless. The next generation was very important to Swain. He bore out the fact that the identification and nurturing of talent is the mark of a great teacher.

As an undergraduate I majored in philosophy, although I took an equal number of hours in history. As I finished my undergraduate work Swain one day spoke with me. "I have been discussing your work with Professor

Charles Odegaard [chairman of the fellowship committee], and if you decide to do graduate work in history the department will award you a fellowship." I was enormously flattered. I did not financially need the fellowship and I was a bit embarrassed at the thought of being bought, so I declined the fellowship but became a graduate student in history.

This was the first of many kindnesses my wife and I were to receive from the hands of Swain and his remarkable and gracious wife, Margaret Hatfield Swain. He set me on the road to study abroad. He advised me and in his awkward way guided me. He and his wife were happy at the birth of our children. He drove me to Chicago and introduced me to the academic world of history at the meeting of the American Historical Association. It was he and his friend, Charles Odegaard, then dean of the Literary College at the University of Michigan, who secured for me my first appointment.

Above all, he shaped my mind with the books he urged me to read and later discussed with me. Lord Acton and Jacob Burckhardt stood at the center of that world. As a consequence, I wrote a doctoral dissertation on the subject of Acton's mentor, Ignaz von Döllinger.

During the last three summers of my graduate work, my wife and I were employed as lookouts by the Forest Service in the Sawtooth Mountains of central Idaho. Our lookout was atop a ten-thousand-foot peak. One evening I hiked four thousand feet down the trail to the road in order to pick up the mail and a sack of flour. In the mail was a fat envelope containing articles from various sources and reviews Swain had clipped from the *New York Times*. Among those reviews was the laudatory review of Russell Kirk's *Conservative Mind* (1953). Swain had no idea how revolutionary that book would become nor any idea of its influence on me. It is one of the mysteries associated with the great teacher that he is usually unaware of the movements of the Spirit he excites in his students.

28

Russell Kirk

New eras, whether in religion, science, or politics, usually begin with a book. When *The Conservative Mind* was published by Regnery in the spring of 1953, few suspected the book was the harbinger of the most important political changes of the twentieth century. Its author, Russell Kirk, was an unknown assistant professor at a Midwestern cow college whose president had been a professor of poultry husbandry. Providence has a strong sense of irony.

During the previous summer Henry Regnery, while on vacation with his family at a farm he owned in West Virginia, read the impeccably prepared manuscript. Regnery knew immediately "that this was an important and perhaps a great book. . . ." The manuscript had been found—perhaps discovered is the better word—by Sidney Gair, who had been an old-fashioned bookman with a large eastern publisher. It is a matter of interest that it is unlikely today that any bookman, hawking texts from campus to campus, would be able to distinguish Edmund Burke from Karl Marx.

The book appeared at an opportune, a providential moment. The crack in the picture window of modern liberalism had been steadily widening. Shortly after the publication of *The Conservative Mind* Dwight Macdonald could still speak contemptuously of "scrambled eggheads on the Right." Only ten years before the publication of *The Conservative Mind* the *Thesaurus of Epigrams* listed twelve epigrams under the heading "Conservative," one more mindlessly derogatory than the other. The prevailing academic wisdom in the faculties of history, politics, literature, and economics was that the American nation was the fulfillment of liberal utopianism. Little wonder that Kirk suggested as a title for his book "The Conservative Rout." As an alternative, Sidney Gair suggested "The Long Retreat." Neither title displayed much optimism as to the future of conservatism.

Still, there were numerous evidences of a growing dissatisfaction with the world liberalism and the ideologies with which it was associated had made. Halfway through the war against statism in its ultimate totalitarian form Friedrich von Hayek's *Road to Serfdom* appeared and enjoyed an enormous success. The epigraph that introduced Hayek's book was from Lord Acton, and in Europe and America in the years following World War II a revival of interest in Lord Acton was underway. The publication of a translation of Jacob Burckhardt's *Reflections on History* and an abridgment of his letters, both commanding a wide reading audience, deepened the mood of pessimism in thoughtful people as they regarded the growth of statism.

The revival of interest in Alexis de Tocqueville underlined and strengthened the observations of Acton and Burckhardt. Then came the publication of William Buckley's *God and Man at Yale* in 1951, though it is well to remember, as Regnery has pointed out, that the word conservative "is hardly used: Buckley then described his position as 'individualist.'" Russell Kirk's book had the effect of a seed dropped into a supersaturated solution. Conservatism crystallized out around it. Kirk provided a distinguished pedigree for American conservatism and demonstrated that, far from being a minor and subordinate tradition in the American past, it was the perennial character of the American experience.

The overwhelming success of the book surprised everyone. In the days when *Time* magazine spoke with authority, Whittaker Chambers called *The Conservative Mind* to the attention of Roy Alexander, editor of *Time*. The entire book section of the July 4, 1953, number of the magazine was devoted to it. A highly favorable review by Gordon Keith Chalmers, president of Kenyon College, appeared in the May 17 *New York Times Book Review*. Other national newspapers and scholarly journals were equally appreciative of the book's qualities. Conservatism as a cultural and political movement had been launched. Interest in Edmund Burke had throughout the 1940s been steadily increasing. Kirk made Burke the model conservative and did much to stimulate the flood of Burke scholarship that followed the publication of *The Conservative Mind*.

Russell Kirk was not an academician. Although he held a doctorate from the University of St. Andrews in Scotland, he did not much value the safety and ingrownness of the university campus. It is not surprising that he abandoned teaching at Michigan State and, through writing and lecturing, devoted himself to a national classroom. He thought of his mission much as Emerson thought of his public obligation. Kirk estimated that he had lectured on five hundred campuses. He was, in the formative years of the movement, the voice of conservatism. And he wrote: scholarly books and articles, columns for newspapers and journals, fantasy and gothic novels. Whether his topic was politics, culture, education, or entertainment, his purpose was undeviating. His goal was to reform and transform America.

For many years he worked without research or secretarial assistance and to the end of his life he typed his letters. Few men have worked harder or have been more dedicated to what they believed to be their civic responsibilities.

In the summer of 1957 Russell Kirk brought out the first number of *Modern Age.* It was a journal whose purpose was the provision of an intellectual base for the conservative movement. To its pages Russell Kirk attracted the finest and keenest minds on the Right. One marvels at Kirk's ability to add the heavy duties of journal editorship to all his other activities.

Amid this flood of print, Kirk's *Randolph of Roanoke,* published by the University of Chicago Press in 1951 and hence antedating *The Conservative Mind,* and *Eliot and His Age: T. S. Eliot's Moral Imagination in the Twentieth Century* (1971) will endure not only as important scholarship but also as indexes of the mind that created them.

Russell Kirk was a shy and thoughtful man. His conversation was not the dazzling conversation of a Dr. Samuel Johnson. His métier was the written word. Sidney Gair wrote Henry Regnery describing Russell as "the son of a locomotive engineer, but a formidable intelligence—a biological accident. He doesn't say much, about as communicative as a turtle, but when he gets behind a typewriter, the results are *most* impressive." Russell would refer to himself, from time to time, at dinner parties as a "turtle." However taciturn, he was a good listener.

Gair's characterization hardly got at the man. It neglected to say that he was a person of absolute integrity, generous to a fault, charitable even when charity was a mistake, hospitable, and lovable. Few public figures have made so few enemies, and those few enemies, for the most part, were men who misunderstood him.

Russell Kirk was fond of describing himself as a "bohemian Tory." That he was a bohemian was a conceit which ranks with the fantasy stories he produced. There is no doubt, however, about his being a "Tory," though just what "Tory" means in the context of Mecosta, Michigan, might be difficult to explain. My colleagues in the political science department, half in derision and half in envy, called him "the Duke of Mecosta." It is true that he became a justice of the peace and took as much pride in the fact as Gibbon took in being a member of the Hampshire militia.

His politics were statist in the Burkean sense. He believed that the state was instituted to make men more virtuous than they naturally are and to do those things necessary to the good life which men, acting as individuals, cannot achieve. As a consequence of this belief, he was opposed to individualism, libertarianism, and any excessive role or scope for the market economy. Half of the contemporary conservative movement was *terra incognita* to him, a land filled with wild beasts and monsters. He was a conservative, a traditionalist, but not a "man of the Right," as Whittaker Chambers described himself.

In Chalmers's review of *The Conservative Mind,* the *New York Times* set off in a little box, as it often does, a lengthy quote from Kirk's book, a quotation that gets at the essential message of the book. Kirk wrote: "Conservatives must prepare society for Providential change, guiding the life that is taking form into the ancient shelter of Western and Christian civilization." To which most conservatives can shout "Amen!" However, the task of translating the "permanent things" into forms that could accommodate the world of change, the world of history, eluded Russell Kirk.

This was ironically clear at the celebration at the Dearborn Inn of the fortieth anniversary of the publication of *The Conservative Mind* and Russell Kirk's seventy-fifth birthday. The Dearborn Inn, standing in the vicinity of Greenfield Village, had been built by Henry Ford. Russell, in his after-dinner talk, mentioned how, as a young man, he had worked as a guide to the museum and the historic houses of Greenfield Village. Perhaps no man so transformed our world in a sense repugnant to Russell Kirk as did Henry Ford. With his usual charity, Russell said it was "alright," since Ford in the museum and the historic houses of Greenfield Village had tried to save the best of that past. However, the "permanent things" cannot be saved by moving them to the historical museum of Greenfield Village. To endure they must be recast in contemporary forms and idioms.

The vision from Mount Nebo is always a partial one and we ought not to ask more from one who has done so much. Let us praise a great man whose vision enables us to take up the task of recasting "the permanent things" into the living reality of the present.

29

Henry Regnery

Every college and university in the United States has a vice president for development. This (usually undistinguished) bureaucrat has as his most important duty the job of, as one of them once said, "nicing" prospective donors. This afternoon I do not propose to "nice" Henry Regnery, but rather to pay a debt of honor owed him by the republic, by the conservative movement, by the many communities to which he has belonged and which he has helped to put in place and shape, and by our common culture, and most especially to pay the personal debt I owe Henry after many years of friendship.

Shall I bring attention first of all to the debt the republic owes Henry? Lesser men have been awarded the Presidential Medal for their civic and political efforts. It was, however, never Henry's style to press himself forward, to call on presidents, to seek the political limelight, to issue and sign manifestos, to be a political and cultural toady. He saw his role as that of quiet initiation, of support for and encouragement of ideas and policies that would benefit and protect the civic and cultural life of the republic. He was quite content to live in an active and productive obscurity, serving on committees, boards of directors, groups of patrons, and above all publishing the books and pamphlets that reshaped the history and helped reconfigure the culture of the United States.

Sometimes the ideas which he presented, midwifed, and propagated were not well received by the public. Half a Quaker and half a Midwestern isolationist, and always wholly himself, he hated the moral and physical consequences of war and was active in indicting and accusing those who involved the United States in wars and foreign adventures past and present. His views might be contested. They could not be ignored, nor could they be ascribed to any self-seeking or aggrandizing motive. He was a son of the Middle West and "almost" a Quaker. Of course, such *unzeitgemaesse Betrachtungen,* such observations out of season, are not apt to be wildly popular. In politics, economics, and culture, Henry's views were apt to be alternatives to the large loose thoughts of Washington and New York.

Before conservatism had a name, let alone a coherent body of theory, Henry was a conservative. In the dark days immediately after the Second World War, when the forces of collectivism and centralization of power seemed everywhere triumphant, Henry was one of the founding fathers of what came to be called conservatism. In early 1944 Henry, Frank C. Hanighen, and Felix Morley pooled their talents and resources and founded *Human Events*. From this action grew a series of pamphlets which for distinction in authorship, cogency in reasoning, and importance in analysis were unequaled in America in the mid 1940s. Out of *Human Events* and these pamphlets developed the Henry Regnery Company, which we can now see was one of the most influential and innovative presses in the post–World War II period and which today continues its distinguished record. To put it bluntly and without exaggeration, there would have been no conservative movement in America without Regnery's press. It was Henry who published Bill Buckley's *God and Man at Yale*, Russell Kirk's *Conservative Mind*, Frank Meyer's *In Defense of Freedom*, and Willmoore Kendall's *Conservative Affirmation*. To list these books is only to skim the surface, for every major conservative figure of the movement was published by Henry Regnery.

And, of course, he did not make any money; quite to the contrary. It is a truism that in public life only the man who has everything to lose and nothing to gain is to be trusted. Watch out for the man who has nothing to lose and everything to gain. Such a man who has not even honor to lose may even become president of the United States. As the poet Goethe observed, "*Fuerchferlich ist einer, der nichts zu verlieren hat*" ("That man is terrible who has nothing to lose"). I have quoted Goethe deliberately because Goethe has served as Henry's mentor and model. That surely can be said of few Americans.

However, the interests of Henry Regnery are not narrowly political. It is not an accident that *Poetry* magazine was published—and is still published—in Chicago and that many of the roots of American literary modernism are Midwestern. It is a fond conceit of the New York intellectuals and some neoconservatives that they brought the graces of literary modernism to conservatism via the lectures of Lionel Trilling. Surely that is mistaken, for Henry Regnery was personally acquainted with and published the major modernists while *Partisan Review* was struggling with the impossible intellectual task of how to be both a Marxist and a modernist. I might remind you that the modernists, European and American, were conservatives, men of the Right, and reactionaries, and they were not apt to be found in the lecture halls of Columbia University.

Immediately after World War II, Henry began his effort to rescue the German people from the consequences of National Socialist rule and the devastation of total war. To understand this, it helps to be, at least in spirit, half a Quaker, and to have one's roots in the cultural achievement of that other Germany. Henry was certain that Germany had to be brought back from the National Socialist abyss and enabled to become once more an important member of the European Community of nations. This seems self-evident now, but in 1944 the Morgenthau Plan called for the total destruction of Germany, its reduction by starvation and dismantling. One of the first books published by Regnery's press was Hans Rothfels's *The German Opposition to Hitler.* It was important for the world to know that not every German wore a brown or a black shirt. Rothfels's book was only one of many books the Regnery press published that sought to bring the postwar German political, social, and cultural reality to the attention of the English-speaking world. The effort was not always marked with success. Hans Sedlmayr's *Art in Crisis,* one of the postwar era's most important art-historical discussions and criticisms of artistic modernism, sold, I believe, about two hundred and fifty copies in the United States.

Again, it was the Regnery press that published Wilhelm Röpke's *Economics of the Free Society* (*Die Lehre von der Wirtschaft*), which described the economic order that became the basis of the German *Wirtschaftswunder.* Röpke introduced the concept of the "social market economy," a free economy, market oriented, that was socially responsible. It has recently been argued by some self-designated "neoconservatives" that it was they, with their liberal backgrounds, who brought a sense of social responsibility to the economic and social theory of conservatism. Regnery's early-1960s publication of the translation of Röpke's book demonstrates clearly that such a view is ahistorical nonsense.

There is a sad note to my discussion of Henry Regnery's German connection. Henry's major contribution to the creation and acceptance of the new Germany was never acknowledged or honored. Lesser men who had done far less for Germany were awarded *Pour le Merit.* This behavior is in keeping with the German penchant for rewarding one's enemies and ignoring and neglecting one's friends. History, however, keeps better books than the ignorant present.

The publication history of Regnery Company—more recently, Regnery Gateway—is but the shadow of a man. Not many publishers can say that. Henry's father once observed that if he made any money he would probably be publishing the wrong kind of books. Animating that unusual man was a capacity for friendship and a passion for community. To perceive this is to see Henry at the local level, but that, of course, is where all conservatism begins.

Henry was never any place long before he had established a network of personal relationships, formed a committee, organized a string quartet, joined a club, or treated the neighborhood to a concert. His ideal of community was the string quartet, in which the individual voice and ego were subordinated to the common effort. Of course, this being earth and not high heaven, the communities with which Henry was involved did not always, shall we say, play in harmony. Henry grew up in Hinsdale, Illinois, and his model of community was the unconscious memory of what that pre–World War I village was like. Those of you who have not been blessed by the experience of small-town life in America before World War II will never know what you have missed, Edgar Lee Masters, Sherwood Anderson, and Sinclair Lewis to the contrary notwithstanding. Even then, however, Hinsdale was an annex to Chicago, and it was Chicago that Henry eventually took as his community. Henry was well acquainted with the failed efforts and aborted hopes of those who attempted to make the "hog-butcher for the world" into a community characterized by high culture. These efforts he studied and chronicled in his book *Creative Chicago: From the Chap-Book to the University*. That his effort fell on deaf ears is exemplified by the fact that the *Chicago Tribune* did not have the good grace to give it a review. The failing causes of Chicago culture were institutions Henry heavily underwrote. The collapse and disappearance of the Chicago Conservatory of Music and the expropriation of the penthouse quarters of Cliff-Dwellers by a misguided Chicago Symphony grieved him deeply. He had written and privately published a history of the Cliff-Dwellers, Chicago's most important club. Long after retirement Henry continued to interest himself in matters literary and historical, and these late reflections are shortly to be published under the title *A Few Reasonable Words*.

Perhaps no Chicago institution seemed to Henry to hold greater promise than the University of Chicago. His association with the university and its far too young and inexperienced president, Robert Maynard Hutchins, was intimate. Henry was one of the managing editors of *Measure*, the dazzling journal of University of Chicago intellectuals. The Regnery Company published the "Great Books" for Hutchins's Great Books Foundation until the compulsions of knee-jerk liberalism, exemplified by Mortimer Adler, led the foundation to break its contract with Regnery.

It was in the context of the University of Chicago that Henry was to meet so many of the Central European intellectuals who were to play such a large role in his thinking and in his personal life. His relationship to Hutchins was gradually eclipsed by Hutchins's growing incapacity for serious thought.

Politics, community, and personal life: these were the three areas in which Henry's conservatism was most manifest. Of these perhaps his personal life was the most important and exemplary for the conservative movement. To put it boldly, Henry taught us how to behave as conservatives. He was devoted to his family, as a series of privately published family memoirs attests. The greatest of these acts of filial piety was the publication of the massive T. P. Cope diary, the diary of his wife Eleanor Scattergood Regnery's distinguished ancestor. Parenting, as those fortunate enough to be parents know, is filled with both joy and grief. The joys Henry proudly acclaimed and the sorrows he quietly and stoically bore.

The Regnery Company was a partnership—and what a partnership! Without Eleanor, loving, quietly judgmental, generous, and practical, Henry would have been half a man. She is one of the original beautiful people before that designation was tarnished by what forty years ago was called "Cafe Society."

It would have been easy for Henry to be, like so many of his Chicago contemporaries of similar status and position, a "hollow man." Henry's lifestyle and ideal was that of the service aristocracy. Henry and I often discussed the Adams family, and although Chicago is a long way from Boston, the resemblance between Henry and the Adamses of Quincy and Washington was striking.

His capacity for friendship was complemented by a wide and generous charity. Those who were wrong or who had wronged him were rarely confronted. Henry preferred what seemed to me rather tortuous explanations and exculpations of their offensive behavior.

His life has been one of great simplicity. He has a positive aversion for what has been called the fetishism of the material object. To be in beautiful surroundings was important to him, but the beauty was not the beauty of "things" but the quality of natural harmony, interesting and rational conversation, music and literature, and above all, selfless and noble actions. His life has been characterized by *"edele Einfalt und stille groesse"* (Winckelmann), "noble simplicity and quiet greatness."

Notes

Introduction

1. Letter from Stephen Tonsor to Henry Regnery, June 25, 1977, Box 131 (Tonsor Corr.), Henry Regnery Papers, Hoover Institution, Stanford, CA.
2. For a lovely testimonial to this fact, see Joseph A. Amato, *Bypass: A Memoir* (West Lafayette, IN: Purdue University Press, 2000), 115–21. Amato was an undergraduate at Michigan and is a professor of history at Southwest State University in Minnesota.
3. He described himself as a reactionary in a letter to Henry Regnery, Box 7, Correspondence (1980–81), Stephen J. Tonsor Papers, Hoover Institution, Stanford University.
4. There are twelve chapters of the manuscript, all handwritten, in Box 21 of the Tonsor Papers, Hoover Institution.
5. *New York Times,* April 28, 1969, 1.
6. Letter from Tonsor to Frank Meyer, July 10, 1970, Box 2 (Correspondence, 1970–71), Tonsor Mss.
7. Stephen Tonsor, "The Foundation and the Academy," *National Review* (May 14, 1982), 538, from Lee Edwards, *The Conservative Revolution: The Movement that Remade America* (New York: The Free Press, 1999), 140.
8. Stephen Tonsor Papers, Box 8 (Corr. 1971), Hoover Institution.
9. Stephen Tonsor, "Campus Turmoil—Who Is Really at Fault?" *Detroit News,* May 31, 1970, 1E, 12E.
10. Letter from Tonsor to Regnery, April 1, 1991, Box 121 (Tonsor Corr.), Regnery Mss.
11. Letter from Tonsor to Regnery, June 17, 1991, Box 121 (Tonsor Corr.), Regnery Mss.
12. Stephen J. Tonsor, "The Conservative Search for Identity," in *What Is Conservatism?* Frank Meyer, ed. (New York: Holt, Rinehart and Winston, 1964), 134.

13. Letter from Tonsor to Henry Regnery, December 28, 1978, Box 131 (Tonsor Corr.), Regnery Mss.

14. Stephen J. Tonsor, "The Second Spring of American Conservatism," *National Review* (September 30, 1977), 1106.

15. "Elites, Community and the Truth: A Little Story," *Modern Age* (Summer 2000), 313–16.

16. Stephen J. Tonsor, "A Few Paleo-Reflections in Time's Mirror," paper presented at the Philadelphia Society annual meeting, May 1, 2004, available at http://www.townhall.com/phillysoc/tonsorchicago.htm

17. Stephen J. Tonsor, "The Second Spring of American Conservatism," *National Review* (September 30, 1977), 1107.

18. See Paul Gottfried and Thomas Fleming, *The Conservative Movement* (Boston: Twayne Publishers, 1988), 71–72.

19. "Why I Too Am Not a Neoconservative," *National Review* 38 (June 20, 1986), 54; see also Jeffrey Hart, "Gang Warfare in Chicago," *National Review* 38 (June 6, 1986), 32–33.

20. Ibid.

21. Hart, "Gang Warfare in Chicago," 33.

22. Tonsor, "A Few Paleo-Reflections in Time's Mirror."

23. Ibid.

24. Tonsor, "Elites, Community and the Truth: A Little Story." For the uninitiated, Mecosta was the home of Russell Kirk, Woodstock of Frank Meyer, and Three Oaks of Henry Regnery.

2. Decadence and the Machine

1. Adam Smith, *An Enquiry into the Nature and Causes of the Wealth of Nations,* E. Cannan, ed., (New York: Random House, 1937), 734–736.

2. See "Technology and Degeneration: The Sublime Machine," by William Leiss, in *Degeneration, The Dark Side of Progress,* edited by J. Edward Chamberlin and Sander L. Gilman (New York: Columbia University Press, 1985).

3. *Grüne Zwerge, Ein Erinnerungsbuch* (Stuttgart: Klett-Colta, 1978),

4. Herbert L. Sussman, *Victorians and the Machine: The Literary Response to Technology* (Cambridge, MA: Harvard University Press, 1968).

5. Lovat Dickson, *H. G. Wells. His Turbulent Life and Times* (New York: Atheneum, 1971).

6. Ibid., 73.

7. Ibid, 76.

8. E. M. Forster, "The Machine Stops."

9. Ibid.

10. Translated by Mirra Ginsburg, (New York: Viking, 1972).

11. Lotte H. Eisner, *Fritz Lang* (New York: Oxford University Press, 1977), translated by Gertrud Mander and edited by David Robinson.

12. Giovannia Pastrone was a great early-twentieth-century filmmaker whose masterpiece was *Cabiri* (1914), a historical melodrama of the Punic Wars. Freder is

the protagonist in the novel *Metropolis* and in Fritz Lang's film adaptation. *(ed.)*
13. Eisner, *Fritz Lang,* 84–85.

3. The Perception of Decadence

1. Rainer Maria Rilke, *Sämtliche Werke: Erster Band* (Frankfurt am Main: Insel Verlag, 1955), 398

2. Nora Wydenbruck von Purtscher, *Rilke: Man and Poet* (London: John Lehmann, 1949).

3. Rilke, *Sämtliche Werke,* 400; the translation is by M. D. Herter Norton, *Translations from the Poetry of Rainer Maria Rilke* (New York: W. W. Norton, 1938), 74–75.

4. Oron J. Hale, *The Great Illusion 1900–1914* (New York: Harper and Row, 1971), xiv. Hale writes:

> The posturing of the 'decadents' at the turn of the century should not be given undue weight, for the real mood was broadly optimistic and anticipatory. Some pessimists envisioned a 'shipwrecked Europe,' but most observers were convinced that they lived in an age of peace and progress and that there would be more prosperity to come. The 'road to disaster' theme, so often applied to these years, is a highly retrospective construction. No one, including this author, whose youthful years fell before 1914, really anticipated the approaching chaos of our times. I have therefore tried to avoid mistaking the natural optimism of youth and the contrasting sadness of later years for a cosmic transformation.

5. Rilke, *Sämtliche Werke,* 704–05. The translation is from *Duino Elegies,* translated by J. B. Leishman and Stephen Spender (New York: W. W. Norton, 1939), 53.

6. Mircea Eliade, *Myths, Dreams and Mysteries: The Encounter between Contemporary Faiths and Archaic Realities,* translated by Philip Mairet (New York: Harper and Row, 1960), 42.

7. *New York Times,* July 16, 1971.

8. Andrew Hacker, "The McCarthy Candicacy," in *Commentary,* February 1968.

9. Andrew Hacker. *The End of the American Era* (New York: Atheneum, 1970), 229.

10. Koenraad Swart, *The Sense of Decadence in Nineteenth-Century France* (The Hague: Martinus Nijhoff, 1964).

11. Peter Drucker, *The Age of Discontinuity* (New York: Harper and Row, 1969).

12. Zbigniew Brzezinski, *Between Two Ages: America's Role in the Technetronic Era* (New York: Viking Press, 1970), 28.

13. J. J. Servan-Schreiber, *The American Challenge,* translated by Ronald Steel (New York: Atheneum, 1968).

14. Jean-François Revel, *Without Marx or Jesus: The New American Revolution Has Begun* (New York: Doubleday, 1970), 266, 123.

15. Jose Ortega y Gasset, *The Revolt of the Masses* (New York: W. W. Norton, 1957), 31.

16. Edward Gibbon, *The History of the Decline and Fall of the Roman Empire,* edited by J. B. Bury (London: Methuen and Co., 1898), 57.

17. Henry Vyverberg, *Historical Pessimism in the French Enlightenment* (Cambridge, MA: Harvard University Press, 1958).

18. Eliade, *Myths, Dreams and Mysteries,* 234–35.

19. Jerome Hamilton Buckley, *The Triumph of Time: A Study of the Victorian Concepts of Time, History, Progress and Decadence* (Cambridge, MA: Harvard University Press, 1966), 22.

20. Hans Joachim Schoeps, *Vorläufer Spenglers: Studien zum Geschichtspessimismus im 19. Jahrhundert, 2. erweiterte Auflage* (Leiden: E. J. Brill, 1955) and Stephen Tonsor, "The Historical Morphologie of Ernst von Lasaulx," *Journal of the History of Ideas* 25 (September 1964), 374–92.

21. Friedrich Nietzsche, "The Use and Abuse of History," translated by Adrian Collins, in *Thoughts out of Season: The Complete Works of Friedrich Nietzsche,* edited by Oscar Levy, vol. 5 (London: T. N. Foulis, 1910).

22. Ibid., 7.

23. Ibid., 65–66.

24. Ibid., 66.

25. Ibid., 71.

26. Ibid., 71–72.

27. One need only consider the continued triumph of Marxism and Hegelianism in order to evaluate this assertion. Consider too the enthusiasm that greeted Edward Hallett Carr's *What Is History?* (New York: Alfred Knopf, 1962).

28. Ibid., 89.

29. Ibid., 94–95.

30. Mircea Eliade, *The Myth of the Eternal Return, or Cosmos and History,* translated by W. R. Trask (Princeton, NJ: Princeton University Press, 1971).

31. Henri Focillon, *The Year 1000* (New York: Frederick Ungar Publishing., 1969).

32. Mircea Eliade, *The Two and the One,* translated by J. M. Cohen (New York: Harper and Row, 1965), 155–59.

33. Eliade, *The Myth of the Eternal Return,* 117–18.

34. Ibid., 68–69.

35. Herbert Marcuse, *One-Dimensional Man: Studies in the Ideology of Advanced Industrial Society* (Boston, Beacon Press, 1964).

36. Michael Harrington, *The Accidental Century* (New York: Macmillan, 1966).

37. Otto Ernest Schüddekopf, *Linke Leute von Rechts: Nationalbolschewismus in Deutschland von 1918 bia 1933* (Stuttgart: Kohlhammer, 1960).

38. Henry Winthrop, "Variety of Meaning in the Concept of Decadence" in *Philosophy and Phenomenological Research* 31 (June 1971), 510–26.

39. Georg Lichtheim, *Europe in the Twentieth Century* (New York: Praeger, 1972), 88.

40. Robert A. Kann, *The Problem of Restoration: A Study in Comparative Political History* (Berkeley, CA: University of California Press, 1968).

41. Sir Herbert Read, *Art and Alienation: The Role of the Artist in Society* (New York: Viking Press, 1969), 13.

42. Wyndham Lewis, *Time and Western Man* (New York: Harcourt, Brace and Company, 1928).

43. Otto Friedrich, *Before the Deluge: A Portrait of Berlin in the 1920s* (New York: Harper and Row, 1972), 322.

44. Lewis, *Time and Western Man*, 223–24.

45. Lewis, *Time and Western Man*, 8.

46. Graham Hough, *The Last Romantics* (New York: Barnes and Noble, 1961), 146.

47. Joachim Fest, "The Romantic Counter-Revolution of Our Time" in *Encounter* 36 (June 1971), 58–61.

48. Johan Huizinga, *The Waning of the Middle Ages: A Study of the Forms of Life, Thought and Art in France and the Netherlands in the Fourteenth and Fifteenth Centuries* (London: Edward Arnold and Co., 1937), 69.

49. Ronald Berman, *America in the Sixties: An Intellectual History* (New York: Harper and Row, 1970), 8.

50. Lewis, *Time and Western Man*, 16.

51. Jakob Taubes, *Abendlandische Eschatologie* (Bern: A. Francke Verlag, 1947). More especially, see "The Modern Apocalypse," in Frank Kermode, *The Sense of an Ending: Studies in the Theory of Fiction* (New York: Oxford University Press, 1967), 93–124.

52. R. G. Collingwood, *The Idea of History* (Oxford: Oxford University Press, 1946).

4. A Few Unequal and Preliminary Thoughts

1. Sanford A. Lakoff's *Equality in Political Philosophy* (Cambridge, MA: Harvard University Press, 1964), though an excellent and discriminating work, cannot be called a history of the idea of equality.

2. Christopher Jencks et al., *Inequality: A Reassessment of the Effect of Family and Schooling in America* (New York: Basic Books, 1972), 3.

3. John Rees, *Equality* (New York: Praeger Publishers, 1971), 28.

4. Talcott Parsons, "A Revised Analytical Approach to the Theory of Social Stratification," in Reinhard Bendix and Seymour Martin Lipset, *Class, Status and Power: A Reader in Social Stratification* (Glencoe, IL: Free Press, 1953), 92–128.

5. Werner Jaeger, *Paideia: The Ideals of Greek Culture,* translated from the second German edition by Gilbert Highet, vol. 1 (New York: Oxford University Press, 1974), 4.

6. *The Sociobiology Debate: Readings on Ethical and Scientific Issues,* edited by Arthur L. Caplan (New York: Harper and Row, 1978).

7. Alexis de Tocqueville, *Democracy in America,* edited by Phillips Bradley (New York: Alfred A. Knopf, 1966), vol. 1, 4.

8. Ibid., 5.

9. Ibid., 6.

10. George Orwell, *Animal Farm* (New York: Harcourt, Brace and Company, 1946).

5. Equality in the New Testament

1. Rudolf Bultmann, *Primitive Christianity in Its Contemporary Setting* (New York: Meridian Books, 1956), 69.
2. Geza Mermes, *The Dead Sea Scrolls in English* (Harmondsworth, UK: Penguin Books, 1962).
3. Ernst Troeltsch, *The Social Teaching of the Christian Churches,* vol. 1, translated by Olive Wyon (New York: Harper Brothers, 1960), 40.
4. Oscar Cullmann, *Jesus and the Revolutionaries,* translated by Gareth Putnam (New York: Harper and Row, 1970).
5. H. Richard Niebuhr, *Christ and Culture* (New York: Harper and Row, 1951), 15–19.
6. C. H. Dodd, *The Apostolic Preaching and Its Developments* (New York: Harper and Brothers, 1962).
7. Dodd, *The Apostolic Preaching and Its Developments,* 64.
8. Jaroslav Pelikan, *The Christian Tradition. A History of the Development of Doctrine* vol. 1, "The Emergence of the Catholic Tradition" (Chicago: University of Chicago Press, 1971), 131.
9. Troeltsch, *The Social Teachings of the Christian Churches,* vol. 1, 64–69.
10. Niebuhr, *Christ and Culture,* 165.
11. Troeltsch, *The Social Teachings of the Christian Churches;* vol. 1., 72–77.
12. Troeltsch, *The Social Teachings of the Christian Churches,* vol. 1., 74.
13. Werner Jaeger, *Early Christianity and Greek Paideia* (Cambridge, MA: Harvard University Press, 1961), 14.
14. Pelikan, *The Christian Tradition,* vol. 1., 160–61.

6. The New Natural Law and the Problem of Equality

1. Hugh Honor, *The New Golden Land: European Images of America from the Discoveries to the Present Time* (New York: Pantheon Books, 1975). Robert F. Berkhofer Jr., *The White Man's Indian: Images of the American Indian from Columbus to the Present* (New York: Alfred A. Knopf, 1978).
2. Donald Symons, *The Evolution of Human Sexuality* (New York: Oxford University Press, 1979), v.
3. Charles Darwin, *The Descent of Man and Selection in Relation to Sex* (New York, Heritage Press, 1972), xvi.
4. Ashley Montagu, preface to Darwin, *The Descent of Man,* viii.
5. Ibid.
6. Ibid., 117.
7. Charles Darwin, *On the Origin of Species by Means of Natural Selection of the Preservation of Favored Races in the Struggle for Life* (New York: Heritage Press, 1963), 236.
8. Darwin, *The Descent of Man,* 114.
9. Edward O. Wilson, *Sociobiology: The New Synthesis* (Cambridge, MA: Harvard University Press, 1975), 4.

10. Richard D. Alexander, "The Evolution of Social Behavior," in *Annual Review of Ecology and Systematics* 6 (1974), and W. D. Hamilton, "The Genetical Evolution of Social Behavior," in *The Journal of Theoretical Biology* 7 (1964), reprinted in Arthur L. Caplan, ed., *The Sociobiology Debate: Readings on Ethical and Scientific Issues* (New York: Harper and Row, 1978), 191–209.
11. Lionel Tiger and Robin Fox, *The Imperial Animal* (New York: Dell Publishing, 1974), 39.
12. Carleton S. Coon, *The Hunting Peoples* (Boston: Atlantic Monthly Press, 1971).
13. Wilson, *Sociobiology*, 11.
14. Niko Tinbergen, *Social Behaviour in Animals, with Special Reference to Vertebrates* (London: Methuen and Co., 1953), 71.
15. Konrad Lorenz, *On Aggression* (New York: Harcourt, Brace and World, 1966).
16. Tiger and Fox, *The Imperial Animal*, 44–45.
17. Wilson, *Sociobiology*, 291–95.
18. Symons, *The Evolution of Human Sexuality*, 191.
19. Tinbergen, *Social Behavior in Animals*, 71.
20. George Maclay and Humphry Knipe, *The Dominant Man: The Pecking Order in Human Society* (New York: Dell Publishing, 1974).
21. Desmond Morris, *Man-Watching: A Field Guide to Human Behavior* (New York: Abrams Publishers, 1977), 121.
22. Symons, *The Evolution of Human Sexuality*.
23. Tiger and Fox, *The Imperial Animal*, 63.
24. Ibid.

7. Liberty and Equality as Absolutes

1. David M. Potter, *People of Plenty: Economic Abundance and the American Character* (Chicago: University of Chicago Press, 1954).
2. Ibid., 118–21.
3. For two treatments of dominance systems in human society and their implications, see George Maclay and Humphry Knipe, *The Dominant Man: The Pecking Order in Human Society* (New York: Dell Publishing, 1974), and Lionel Tiger and Robin Fox, *The Imperial Animal* (New York: Dell Publishing, 1974).
4. Arthur M. Okun, *Equality and Efficiency* (London: Allen and Unwin, 1976).
5. Alexis de Tocqueville, *Democracy in America*, edited by Phillips Bradley (New York: Alfred A. Knopf, 1966), vol. 1, 6.
6. Ibid., vol. 2, 318–19.
7. David M. Potter, *Freedom and Its Limitations in American Life*, edited by Don E. Fehrenbacher (Stanford, CA: Stanford University Press, 1976).
8. Ibid., 25.
9. Ibid., 34.

8. History: A Revolutionary or Conservative Discipline?

1. Carl Bridenbaugh, "The Great Mutation," *The American Historical Review* 68 (January 1963), 315–31.
2. Erich Kahler, *The Meaning of History* (New York: George Braziller, 1964), 15.
3. John Higham, with Leonard Krieger and Felix Gilbert, *History* (Englewood Cliffs, NJ: Prentice-Hall, 1965).
4. Thomas D. Clark, David D. Van Tassel, Hayden V. White, John Higham, Felix Gilbert, Leonard Krieger, "Higham with Krieger and Gilbert: *History,*" *AHA Newsletter* 3 (June 1965), 6.
5. Ibid., 5.
6. Oswald Spengler, *The Decline of the West*, abridged by Helmut Werner, English abridged edition prepared by Arthur Helps from the translation by Charles Francis Atkinson (New York: Modern Library, 1965), 5.
7. New Haven, CT: Yale University Press, 1932.
8. *The Struggle of the Modern* (London: Hamish Hamilton, 1963), 72.
9. Higham, Krieger and Gilbert, *History*, 171–72.
10. Alfred North Whitehead, *Science and the Modern World* (London: Macmillan, 1925).
11. Stephen Spender, *The Struggle of the Modern*, 191.
12. Cambridge Library MS. Add. 4906.

9. A Fresh Start: American History and Political Order

1. Stephen Vincent Benet, *Western Star* (New York: Farrar and Rinehart, 1943), 3.
2. George W. Pierson, "The M-Factor in American History," *American Quarterly,* 14 (Summer 1962), 275–89; George W. Pierson. "A Restless Temper . . ." *American Historical Review* 69 (July 1964), 969–89; Daniel J. Boorstin, *The Americans: The National Experience* (New York: Alfred A. Knopf, 1965), especially "The Transients," 49–57.
3. Henry David Thoreau, *Walden, or Life in the Woods: The Annotated Walden*, edited by Philip Van Doren Stern (New York: Clarkson N. Potter), 199–202.
4. Richard Weaver, "Two Types of American Individualism," in *Life without Prejudice and other Essays,* edited by Harvey Plotnick (Chicago: Henry Regnery, 1965).
5. Leo Marx, *The Machine in the Garden: Technology and the Pastoral Ideal in America* (New York: Oxford University Press, 1964), 55.
6. David W. Noble, *Historians against History: The Frontier Thesis and the National Covenant in American Historical Writing since 1830* (Minneapolis: University of Minnesota Press, 1965); *The Eternal Adam and the New World Garden: The Central Myth in the American Novel since 1830* (New York: George Braziller, 1968); *The Paradox of Progressive Thought* (Minneapolis: University of Minnesota Press, 1958).
7. Noble, *Historians Against History,* 4.
8. Stephen Spender, *The Struggle of the Modern* (London: Hamish Hamilton, 1963), 191.
9. Dorothy L. Sayers, *The Comedy of Dante Alighieri the Florentine,* vol. 1

(Harmondsworth, UK: Penguin Books, 1949), 256.

10. Peter L. Berger and Thomas Luckmann, *The Social Construction of Reality: A Treatise in the Sociology of Knowledge* (New York: Doubleday, 1966).

11. Peter L. Berger, *The Sacred Canopy: Elements of a Sociological Theory of Religion* (New York: Doubleday, 1967).

12. Sir Lewis B. Namier, "History," in *Avenues of History* (London: Hamish Hamilton, 1952), 5.

10. Freedom and the Crisis in Historiography

1. Edward Hallett Carr, *What Is History?* (New York: Knopf, 1962).

2. Karl Löwith, *Meaning in History* (Chicago: University of Chicago Press, 1949).

3. Carr, *What Is History?* 176.

4. Abraham Tertz, *On Socialist Realism* (New York: Pantheon Books, 1962).

5. Ibid., 33.

6. Ibid., 93.

7. Ernst Troeltsch, *Christian Thought: Its History and Application,* translated under the direction of Baron von Hügel (New York: Meridian Books, 1957).

8. Jakob Burckhardt, *Force and Freedom,* edited by James Hastings Nichols (New York: Meridian Books, 1955), 132.

9. J. B. Bury, *The Idea of Progress: An Inquiry into its Origin and Growth* (London: Macmillan, 1932).

10. Burckhardt, *Force and Freedom,* 320.

11. John C. Greene, *Darwin and the Modern World View* (New York: Mentor Books, 1963).

12. Henry Vyverberg, *Historical Pessimism in the French Enlightenment* (Cambridge, MA: Harvard University Press, 1958).

13. Ernst von Lasaulx, *Neuer Versuch Einer Alten Auf Die Wahrheit Der Tatsachen Gegrundeten Philosophie Der Geschichte,* edited by Eugene Thurnher (Munich: Oldenbourg, 1952).

14. Oswald Spengler, *Man and Technics: A Contribution to a Philosophy of Life* (New York: Knopf, 1932), 104.

15. Erich Heller, *The Disinherited Mind* (New York: Meridian Books, 1959), 195–96.

16. Carl Breidenbaugh, "The Great Mutation," in *American Historical Review* 68 (January 1963), 362.

17. Isaiah Berlin, *Historical Inevitability* (Oxford: Oxford University Press, 1954).

18. Henry Adams, *The Education of Henry Adams* (New York: Random House, 1931), 451.

19. Friedrich Meinecke, *Die Entstehung des Historismus,* 2nd ed., (Munich: Oldenbourg, 1946), 2.

20. Ibid., 1.

21. Karl R. Popper, *The Open Society and its Enemies,* rev. ed. (Princeton, NJ: Princeton University Press, 1950).

22. Karl R. Popper, *The Poverty of Historicism* (London: Routledge and Paul, 1957).

23. Dwight E. Lee and Robert N. Beck, "The Meaning of Historicism," in *American Historical Review* 59, no. 3, 568–77.

24. Popper, *The Open Society,* 454.

25. Ibid.

26. Friedrich Meinecke, "Irrwege in Unserer Geschichte?" in *Vom Geschlichtlichen Sinn Und Vom Sinn Der Geschichte,* 5th rev. ed. (Stuttgart: Koehler Verlag, 1951), 123–32.

27. Troeltsch, *Christian Thought: Its History and Application,* 24.

28. Burckhardt, *Force and Freedom,* 327.

29. Cambridge University Library Add. Mss. 5014.

30. John Higham, "Beyond Consensus: The Historian as Moral Critic," in *American Historical Review* 67 (April 1962), 609–25.

31. H. Stuart Hughes, *Consciousness and Society: The Reconstruction of European Social Thought, 1890–1930* (New York: Random House, 1961), 229–48.

32. Walter Hofer, *Geschichtsschreibung und Weltanschauung* (Munich: Coldenbourg Verlag, 1950).

33. Friedrich Meinecke, "Kausalitaten und Werte in der Geschichte," in *Historische Zeitschrift,* Band 137, Heft I (Munich, 1927), 4. English translation: "Values and Causalities in History," translated by Julian H. Franklin, in Fritz Stern, *The Varieties of History* (New York: Meridian Books, 1956), 268–88. I employ this translation in my quotations from this essay.

34. Ibid., 8.

35. Friedrich Meinecke, *Vom Geschichtlichen Sinn,* 19.

36. Meinecke, "Kausalitaten und Werte in der Geschichte," 19.

37. Berlin, *Historical Inevitability.*

38. Meinecke, *Vom Geschichtlichen Sinn,* 12.

39. Ibid., 19.

40. Ibid., 21–22.

41. Friedrich Meinecke, *The German Catastrophe, Reflections and Recollections,* translated by Sidney B. Fay (Cambridge, MA: Harvard University Press, 1950), 107.

42. Richard W. Sterling, *Ethics in a World of Power: The Political Ideas of Friedrich Meinecke* (Princeton, NJ: Princeton University Press, 1958).

13. The Use and Abuse of Myth

1. D. E. O. James, *The Beginnings of Religion* (London: Hutchinsons University Library, n.d.)

2. Mircea Eliade, *Myths, Dreams and Mysteries: The Encounter between Contemporary Faiths and Archaic Realities* (New York: Harper and Row, 1960), 17–18.

3. Mircea Eliade, "Myths and Mythical Thought," in Alexander Eliot, *Myths* (New York: McGraw-Hill, 1976), 17–18.

4. Christopher Dawson, *Religion and Culture* (New York: Meridian Books, 1958), 49–50.

5. For a discussion of this very important subject, see Gerardus van der Leeuw, *Sacred and Profane Beauty: The Holy in Art,* translated by David E. Green (New

York: Holt, Rinehart and Winston, 1963).

6. These translations of Goethe's *Faust*, part 2, are by Philip Wayne (Harmondsworth, UK: Penguin Classics, 1959).

7. Mircea Eliade, *The Forge and the Crucible: The Origins and Structures of Alchemy*, translated by Stephen Corrin (New York: Harper and Row, 1971).

8. Ibid., 101–02.

9. Ibid., 172–73.

14. Modernity, Science, and Rationality

1. Richard Weaver, "The Importance of Cultural Freedom," in *Life without Prejudice and other Essays* (Chicago: Henry Regnery Company, 1965), 36.

2. Jacob Bronowski, *The Face of Violence* (Cleveland: Meridian Books, 1967), 5.

3. Peter L. Berger and Thomas Luckmann, *The Social Construction of Reality: A Treatise in the Sociology of Knowledge* (New York: Doubleday, 1966).

4. Sir Charles P. Snow, *The Two Cultures: And a Second Look* (New York: New American Library, 1964), 30.

5. Peter F. Drucker, *The Age of Discontinuity: Guidelines to our Changing Society* (New York: Harper and Row, 1969), 71.

6. Daniel Bell, "The Cultural Contradictions of Capitalism," in *Public Interest*, no. 21 (Fall 1970), 16–43.

7. Herman Kahn and Anthony J. Weiner, *The Year 2000* (New York: MacMillan, 1967); Victor C. Ferkiss, *Technological Man: The Myth and the Reality* (New York: New American Library, 1970). Drucker, *The Age of Discontinuity*.

8. Max Weber, *The Protestant Ethic and the Spirit of Capitalism* (New York: Scribner's, 1958), 15.

9. Ibid., 182.

22. Gnostics, Romantics, and Conservatives

1. Daniel Moynihan, "Nirvana Now," *American Scholar* 36 (Autumn 1967), 539–48.

2. Friedrich Heer, *The Intellectual History of Europe*, translated by Jonathan Steinberg, (Garden City, NY: Doubleday, 1968).

3. Eric Voegelin, *Science, Politics and Gnosticism: Two Essays* (Chicago: Henry Regnery Company, 1968).

4. Karl Mannheim, *Ideology and Utopia: An Introduction to the Sociology of Knowledge* (New York: Harcourt, Brace and Company, 1936).

5. David Kettler, "Sociology of Knowledge and Moral Philosophy: The Place of Traditional Problems in the Formation of Mannheim's Thought," *Political Science Quarterly* 92 (September 1967), 399–426.

6. Peter P. Witonski, "Report on the Periodicals," *National Review*, 20 (April 9, 1968), 355–57.

7. Klaus Epstein, *The Genesis of German Conservatism*, (Princeton, NJ: Princeton University Press, 1966).

8. Mannheim, *Ideology and Utopia,* 107.

9. Heer, *The Intellectual History of Europe.* Of the nineteenth century Heer writes: "We ourselves still belong to it, at least those of us who were born around the time of the First World War. Our revolutions, reactions and conservatisms, the way we talk, write and see are still linked to this century in which Europe ceased to be an island and during which an archaic society many thousands of years old and an aristocratic view of the cosmos of almost equal antiquity collapsed together" (vol. 2, 281).

10. Mannheim, *Ideology and Utopia,* 8.

11. Robert A. Nisbet, "Conservatism and Sociology," *American Journal of Sociology* 58 (September 1952), 167–75.

12. See also Robert A. Nisbet, *The Quest for Community: A Study in the Ethics of Order and Freedom* (New York: Oxford University Press, 1953).

13. Eric Voegelin, *Order and History,* vol. 2: "The World of the Polis" (Baton Rouge, LA: Louisiana State University Press, 1957), 1–24.

14. Peter L. Berger, *The Sacred Canopy: Elements of a Sociological Theory of Religion* (Garden City, NY: Doubleday, 1967), 22, and Peter L. Berger and Thomas Luckmann, *The Social Construction of Reality: A Treatise in the Sociology of Knowledge* (Garden City, NY: Doubleday, 1966).

15. Christopher Dawson, *Religion and Culture* (New York: Meridian Books, 1958), 214–15, and Christopher Dawson, *The Movement of World Revolution* (New York: Sheed and Ward, 1959).

16. Though widely discussed, the perception of decadence in Western civilization has not been systematically treated. See Koenraad W. Swart, *The Sense of Decadence in Nineteenth-Century France* (The Hauge: Martinus Nijhoff, 1964), and Hans Joachim Schoeps, *Vorläufer Spenglers: Studien zum Geschichtspessismus im 19. Jahrhundert* (Leiden: E. J. Brill, 1953).

17. Kettler, "Sociology of Knowledge and Moral Philosophy," 408–12.

18. Voegelin, *Science, Politics and Gnosticism,* 86–88.

19. Kettler, "Sociology of Knowledge and Moral Philosophy," 416.

20. Voegelin, *Science, Politics and Gnosticism,* 109.

21. Robert K. Merton, *Social Theory and Social Structure,* rev. ed. (Glencoe IL: Free Press, 1963), 456.

22. This is no place for a lengthy assessment of Mannheim's sociology of knowledge. For that the reader should see Merton, *Social Theory and Social Structure,* 456–508. George Lichtheim correctly notes in *The Concept of Ideology and Other Essays* (New York: Random House, 1967), 34, that Karl R. Popper's *The Poverty of Historicism* (London: Routledge and Paul, 1957), is "virtually a critique of Mannheim." It is an attack not only on Mannheim's loosely constructed "sociology of knowledge" but also on its irrational eschatological content. Especially clear in analysis and critique of Mannheim is Raymond Aron's *La sociologie allemande contemporaine* (Paris: F. Alcan, 1935).

23. Karl Mannheim, "Conservative Thought," in *Essays on Sociology and Social Psychology,* edited by Paul Kecskemeti (New York: Oxford University Press, 1953), 110.

24. Mannheim, "The History of the Concept of the State as an Organism," in *Essays on Sociology and Social Psychology*, 181.

25. Mannheim, "Conservative Thought," *Essays*, 84.

26. Mannheim, "Conservative Thought," *Essays*, 101.

27. Mannheim, *Ideology and Utopia*, 144.

28. Ibid., 22–23.

29. Ibid., 78.

30. Mannheim, "Conservative Thought," *Essays*, 79.

31. Ibid., 98–99.

32. Samuel P. Huntington, "Conservatism as an Ideology," *American Political Science Review* 51 (1967), 454.

33. Mannheim, "Conservative Thought," *Essays*, 101.

34. Louis Hartz, *The Liberal Tradition in America* (New York: Harcourt, Brace, and Company, 1955). The impact of this argument in discussions of American conservatism may be clearly seen in Allen Guttmann, *The Conservative Tradition in America* (New York: Oxford University Press, 1967).

35. Epstein, *The Genesis of German Conservatism*, 6.

36. Peter Viereck, "The Philosophical New Conservatism," in *The Radical Right*, edited by Daniel Bell (Garden City, NY: Doubleday, 1964), 189.

37. Huntington, "Conservatism as an Ideology," 455.

38. Ibid., 460.

39. Robert A. Kann, *The Problem of Restoration: A Study in Comparative Political History* (Berkeley, CA: University of California Press, 1968).

40. Robert W. Lougee, "German Romanticism and Political Thought," *Review of Politics* 21 (October 1959), 631–45.

41. Heer, *The Intellectual History of Europe*, vol. 2, 285.

42. Mannheim, "Conservative Thought," *Essays*, 89.

43. Ibid.

23. Elites, Community, and the Truth: A Little Story

1. This was the original name of the Intercollegiate Studies Institute, the publisher of this book. *(ed.)*

27. Joseph Ward Swain

1. *Classical Philology* 35 (1944), 73–94.

Sources

Prologue

"Hope and History," was first published as "Hope and History" in the *Intercollegiate Review*, 2, no. 1 (September 1965): 90–94.

Part One: Decadence

"Decadence, Past and Present" is taken from Box 37, Stephen Tonsor Papers, Hoover Institution, Stanford University. It is reprinted here by permission of the Hoover Institution.

"Decadence and the Machine" is taken from Box 30, Stephen Tonsor Papers, Hoover Institution, Stanford University. It is reprinted here by permission of the Hoover Institution.

"The Perception of Decadence" is taken from Box 30, Stephen Tonsor Papers, Hoover Institution, Stanford University. It is reprinted here by permission of the Hoover Institution.

Part Two: Equality

"A Few Unequal and Preliminary Thoughts" is taken from Box 21, Stephen Tonsor Papers, Hoover Institution, Stanford University. It is reprinted here by permission of the Hoover Institution.

"Equality in the New Testament" was first published in *Modern Age* 24, no. 4 (fall 1980): 345–54.

"The New Natural Law and the Problem of Equality" was first published in *Modern Age* 24, no. 3 (summer 1980): 238–47.

"Liberty and Equality as Absolutes" was first published in *Modern Age* 23, no. 1 (winter 1979): 2–9.

Part Three: Historiography

"History: A Revolutionary or Conservative Discipline" was first published in the *Intercollegiate Review* 2, no. 4 (January-February 1966): 235–43.

"A Fresh Start: American History and Political Order" was first published in *Modern Age* 16, no. 1 (winter 1972): 2–8.

"Freedom and the Crisis in Historiography" was first published in *Modern Age* 8, no. 1 (winter 1963–64): 25–37.

"The United States as a 'Revolutionary Society' was first published in *Modern Age* 19, no. 2 (spring 1975): 136–45.

Part Four: Ideas and History

"Socialism" is taken from Box 35, Stephen Tonsor Papers, Hoover Institution, Stanford University. It is reprinted here by permission of the Hoover Institution.

"The Use and Abuse of Myth" was first published in the *Intercollegiate Review* 15, no. 2 (spring 1980): 67–75.

"Modernity, Science, and Rationality" was first published in *Modern Age* 16, no. 2 (spring 1972): 161–66.

"The Inevitability of Tradition" was first published in *Modern Age* 36, no. 3 (spring 1994): 229–32.

"Marxism and Modernity" was first published in *Modern Age* 34, no. 1 (fall 1991): 6–11.

Part Five: Politics

"Political Idealism and Political Reality" was first published in *Modern Age* 18, no. 4 (fall 1974): 338–44.

"What Is the Purpose of Politics?" was first published in *Modern Age* 18, no. 2 (spring 1974): 114–20.

"Why I Am a Republican and a Conservative" is taken from Box 8, Stephen Tonsor Papers, Hoover Institution, Stanford University. It is reprinted here by permission of the Hoover Institution.

Part Six: Conservatism

"How Does the Past Become the Future?" was first published in *Modern Age* 42, no. 1 (winter 2000): 8–13.

"The Conservative Search for Identity" was first published in *What Is Conservatism?* edited by Frank Meyer (New York: Holt, Rinehart and Winston, 1964).

"Gnostics, Romantics, and Conservatives" was first published in *Social Research* 35, no. 4 (winter 1968): 616–34. It is reprinted here by permission of the New School of Social Research.

"Elites, Community and the Truth: A Little Story" was first published in *Modern Age* 42, no. 3 (summer 2000): 313–16.

Part Seven: Polemics

"Alienation and Relevance" was first published in *National Review,* July 1, 1969: 636–38, 661.

"The Second Spring of American Conservatism" was first published in *National Review,* September 30, 1977: 1103–07.

"Why I Too Am Not a Neoconservative" was first published in *National Review,* June 20, 1986: 54–56.

Part Eight: Tributes

"Joseph Ward Swain" was first published as "The Man Who Was in Love with the Past" in *Modern Age* 37, no. 4 (summer 1995): 374–78.

"Russell Kirk" was first published in *Modern Age* 37, no. 2 (winter 1995): 99–101.

"Henry Regnery" was delivered as a tribute to Henry Regnery on April 27, 1996, at a meeting of the Philadelphia Society.

Index

About the Author and Editor

Stephen J. Tonsor taught history at the University of Michigan from 1955 to 1991. Born on a farm outside Jerseyville, Illinois, in 1923, Tonsor attended Blackburn College before matriculating at the University of Illinois. From 1942 to 1946 he served in the U.S. Army Signal Corps, seeing combat in the Pacific theater. He received his PhD in European intellectual history from the University of Illinois in 1952. Tonsor lives in Ann Arbor, Michigan, with his wife, Caroline.

Gregory L. Schneider is Associate Professor of History at Emporia State University. He is the author of *Cadres for Conservatism: Young Americans for Freedom and the Rise of the Contemporary Right* and editor of *Conservatism in America since 1930: A Reader.* He lives in Topeka, Kansas, with his wife and two children.